**A Gestalt Institute
of Cleveland Publication**

On Intimate Ground

On Intimate Ground

A Gestalt Approach
to Working with Couples

Gordon Wheeler
Stephanie Backman
Editors

Jossey-Bass Publishers • San Francisco

Chapter Five is adapted from P. Papernow, "La thérapie gestaltiste avec
des familles reconstituées," which is an article that appeared in the journal
Gestalt ("Familles en Gestalt-thérapie," issue no. 5, 1993), a publication of
the Société Française de Gestalt.

   A Gestalt Institute of Cleveland publication

For international orders, please contact your local Paramoun Publishing
International office.

Library of Congress Cataloging-in-Publication Data

On intimate ground : a Gestalt approach to working with couples /
   Gordon Wheeler, Stephanie Backman, editors. — 1st ed.
         p.   cm.   —   (The Jossey-Bass social and behavioral science
   series)
   Includes bibliographical references and index.
   ISBN 0-7879-0039-7
   1. Marital psychotherapy.   2. Gestalt therapy.   I. Wheeler,
   Gordon.   II. Backman, Stephanie   III. Series.
RC488.5.0527   1994   94-17754
616.89'156—dc20   CIP

FIRST EDITION
HB Printing   10 9 8 7 6 5 4 3 2 1   *Code 94122*

Contents

Preface

The Gestalt Model
in Context

The reader who knows the Gestalt model only in its late Perlsian workshop version of psychodramas and empty chairs is in for a surprise—we believe a very pleasurable and instructive one—with the present volume. In place of the confrontation, hyperindividualism, and percussive rhythms of the Perlsian model we have here a very different Gestalt perspective, one that derives from the lineage of Kurt Lewin, Kurt Goldstein, Laura Perls, Fritz Perls (especially the earlier work), Paul Goodman, Isadore From, and many Gestalt writers of the past twenty years—the Nevises and Polsters, Yontef, Zinker, and others. Many of these were our teachers, and all in their various ways emphasize themes of contact and context, dialogue, growth in relationship, the phenomenological perspective, and a constructivist view of the self as the "organizer of the field" and the artist of life.

Because this approach is so different from some common preconceptions, it seems worthwhile to consider briefly what this Gestalt model is and how it fits into the wider context of psychological and psychotherapy models. The discussion will be brief because the entire history of psychology as a science, after all, and of psychotherapy as a discipline and a practice within that science, goes back only about a hundred years—long enough to give some perspective, but still perhaps short enough to allow a summary of a few dominant streams.

The Gestalt Model in the Context of Other Models

A full century has now passed since the earliest beginnings of the Gestalt perceptual model, which completely revolutionized our understanding of human cognition and human experience. With the passage of time we can now understand perhaps better than the early framers of the model some of the implications of the perspective for behavior, affect, cognition, and meaning—which are the components of experience itself. Some of these implications are:

- We perceive in wholes, not in bits and pieces or individual "stimuli" that are somehow added up, as the old associationist and behavioral models would have it; we resolve the whole field at once, or try to, and the parts take on meaning in relation to this context of understanding.
- What we experience is this whole-field resolution; our experience of any given event doesn't lie in the event itself, but in the meaning we attach to it. Psychotherapy, no matter the terminology of the particular school, has to involve the exploration of this *constructed meaning*.
- This means that there is no seeing without interpreting, and no perceiving that does not include feeling and evaluating. There is no such thing as experience that is prior to meaning: both arise in the same act and process of taking in the world. This is a point borne out by contemporary brain research, which more and more shows the involvement of the whole brain in the organization of perception and cognition, and the mediation of perception and memory by affect.
- Our behavior is never the simple product of internal "drives" and "schedules of reinforcement," as the classical Freudian and behaviorist models maintained. Appetites, drives, and conditioning may all be important at various times, but our actual behavior is always mediated and organized in terms of our "map" or resolution of the whole field, the whole context of perceived risks and resources, in relation to our own felt needs and goals.
- In a systemic perspective, the same thing applies. Systems

models sometimes speak as if "systemic forces," "homeosta-sis" and the like were real "things," not just patterns or de-scriptors. In the Gestalt view, systemic conditions are very much part of the field, but again what matters is the person's own subjective, constructed understanding of what those sys-temic conditions are, which then shapes and mediates the person's response. In other words, it's not our view of the "couple system" so much as the couple members' own view that matters, and that needs to be explored.

- This in turn means that we don't act or react in response to events per se, but to our own perception of *patterns* of events and their meaning "in the field," which serves to orient us to changing circumstances. If you think about it, we have to be "wired" this way: after all, it's not what just happened that has predictive or survival value, but what we think will happen next, which is a function of our understanding of the field.

- These patterns and understandings are meaningful subjec-tive constructions, assumptions, and expectations that may be shared and supported by a couple, family, or wider social group or that may involve conflict between one person or couple/family member and another or conflict between one group and another. For therapy, again under any school, it is crucial to bring to the surface or "deconstruct" these expectations, which may be out of awareness until we start talking about them.

- When we are dealing with other people, our actions and re-actions are based not on their behavior per se, but on our own projective understanding of the motives and feelings behind that behavior *in them*. This insight is the whole basis of attribution theory in social psychology, largely deriving from Kurt Lewin's work. Clinically and developmentally, this means that the Gestalt model is intersubjective at its core, in a way that is not always or easily the case with psychody-namic, behavioral, and systemic models.

- Our experiential reality, again, is always a subjective con-struction, made up of some integration of what we see as "out there" right now ("figure" in Gestalt terminology) with the perceived assumptions and expectations we bring to the

moment ("ground" in Gestalt terms; "transference" in psychoanalytic language).

- For behavior to change in any lasting way, there has to be a
change in this subjective reality, this constructed "map" or
ground of past perceptions, expectations, and beliefs, which
are the present dynamic "cause" of the behavior (in the
sense of "controlling conditions," and in interaction with the
press of what's "out there").

- When we say *learning* we mean a change of this kind in our
"map," our constructed meaning, so that a new understanding of the world shapes our behavior differently in the future. Again, this has to be true in any model of learning. In
the Gestalt view, perceiving, listening, learning, and the re-
organizing of behavior are all basically the same process:
they all test a new "figure of attention" against a ground of
prior understanding, and vice versa.

- You can't see meaning, or feeling, or experience. If you want
to know how the subject is constructing or experiencing the
field, you have to inquire about it, or test it with an intervention and then inquire about that. This testing is Lewin's
"action research" methodology in clinical application. If you
want to know the invisible rules and structures of a system
(the "ground"), present a new "figure" (an intervention or
experiment) and see how the system deals with it. The reaction of the person or couple or family then becomes the subject for dialogue.

- The conditions of this dialogue are crucial if new understanding and learning, which mean a change in ground
structure, are to take place. This is the phenomenological
perspective of the model, which simply means its commitment to understanding how the world looks, how meaning
is organized and constructed from the patient or client's
point of view—all things the person may not know in words
but articulates in part for the first time in this dialogue. Thus
the Gestalt model takes the phenomenological tradition
from philosophy and grounds it in the empirical and intersubjective world of the lab and of clinical practice.

- Knowing a person, for the therapist or for the couple members themselves, has to mean knowing this constructive activity for that person from her or his point of view, both in process and in content. This is what intimacy means—knowing a person's inner world or "ground," and making your own inner world known. This makes intimacy and intimate process qualitatively different from other kinds of interpersonal process.

- The view depends on the point of view. Multiple realities—in the couple, the family, the group, and the social system—are not only inevitable: they are the very stuff of contact, dialogue, and exchange, as well as of conflict, "resistance," and for that matter creativity. As with many or all of the points above, the implications for therapy, and especially for couples therapy, are direct and important.

- And finally, to influence another person, beyond giving the momentary prods of reward and pain, means "getting inside" their world in this way, at least to some extent, so as to raise the possibility at least of organizing that inner world somehow differently, with consequences for future behavior and experience. Even in the design of effective behavioral schedules and reinforcers, we have to know a good deal about how the world looks to the person we want to influence, what he or she cares about, wants, expects, or fears, or else the reinforcers we offer will be off the mark. Again, the differences this view makes for individual, couple, and family therapy are provocative and profound.

The Gestalt model, then, is fundamentally constructivist and "deconstructivist," intersubjective, dialogic, and phenomenological in its basic insights and at its theoretical and methodological core. In other words, it is based on perspectives that a number of other models are struggling to incorporate today, especially as they attempt the shift from a "self-in-isolation" stance toward a theory that is better adapted for dealing with experience in the couple or family context. (The work of the Stone Center, with its "self-in-relation" model based on a feminist developmental perspective, is a highly fruitful case in point). By *phenomenological*, we simply mean trying to understand the structure and dynamics of the construction of experience itself. In the Gestalt model, we see this phenomenological perspective not only as a clinical or ethical commitment to the integrity of the patient's own experience, but also as the key to behavioral change, for the reasons outlined briefly above and elaborated more in the chapters to follow. At the same time, we would argue that this "phenomenological constructivism" is the most promising route toward the long-sought and ever-receding goal of a unified field theory of human behavior and experience, which would unite or at least contextualize the various applications and territories of the enormously diverse field that is psychology itself, from neuropsychology to subjectivism, and from individual clinical work on up through the various "levels of system" of applied work—the couple, the family, the group, the organization, and society at large. To the couples and family therapist in particular, working as we do at the live cusp of the intrapsychic and the interpersonal, it would be a great boon to have a single language for talking about individual, relational, and systemic dynamics, rather than having to switch gears constantly, as we do now, when we move from one level to another. Without claiming that the Gestalt model in its present state is anywhere near that larger, overarching goal, we do want to note (and hope to demonstrate in the following chapters) that one of the great strengths of the model for the couples therapist is its flexibility in moving among these various levels of attention and intervention—something which has always been a sticking point in the psychodynamic, systemic, and behavioral approaches that Gestalt in part derives from, and attempts to integrate. Any model is of course a map or an analogy, something that relates the unfamiliar to the familiar by selecting and concentrating on a few central themes. A good way of characterizing any model—and of assessing its "fit" with our own particular style and values—is to examine the central metaphors by which it reduces the infinite particularity of the field into simpler organized wholes. The central metaphors of the Gestalt model are drawn from the contextual and holistic perspectives of evolution and ecology, relativity and indeterminacy. Thus the model speaks of organism and development, organization and contact, self as subject, boundary, energy, and field. This contrasts sharply with the classical Freudian and behaviorist models, which draw their analogies from an older scientific vocabulary of Newtonian forces and action at a distance, linear causation, objects rather than subjects, and nineteenth-century imagery of telegraph codes, hydraulics, and the steam locomotive with its pressure valves and fixed trajectories. Likewise, the older systemic models were based on mechanistic imagery, though to be sure all of these three great clinical traditions—the psychodynamic, the behaviorist, and the systemic—have evolved considerably down through the century, and all of them (we would argue) in a "whole-field" or Gestalt direction.

Again, this "field model" orientation makes the Gestalt perspective particularly well adapted for talking about the intersubjective social field of the couple, family, workplace, or group, or, as we would say in Gestalt terms, the intersubjective internal world of the individual her/himself. How this plays out for the couples therapist in particular, in theory and in clinical application, is the substance of the chapters ahead. These chapters are presented under three headings—"Theory," "Applications," and "Perspectives"—but it should be clear that these are intended as groupings or emphases, not as divisions. Following Lewin's famous dictum that there is nothing so practical as a good theory, our intent as editors has been to support the presentation of both theory and application (and perspective) in every chapter throughout the book. We have also worked to avoid the use of Gestalt or other "jargon," and where particular terms from the Gestalt model have seemed to clarify matters, we have encouraged authors to supply a synonym or paraphrase with nearly every use of any technical term, as befits an approach that prides itself on its "experience-near" quality. In this way we hope to offer a volume that the reader can pick up at any chapter, according to her/his clinical or personal interest, and read without having to rely on a separate "theory" presentation that has to be toiled through before the other chapters make sense.

The chapters themselves are very diverse, ranging from the consideration of particular themes or topics, such as intimacy, language, and power (with clinical application and example), to particular applications and client populations, such as abuse survivors, gay couples, and remarriages (with theoretical reflection and perspective). At the same time, they are unified by certain recurring Gestalt themes and implications, many of which are the points outlined briefly in this Preface.

These same points, in a more directly practical format, are developed further in the Introduction. In place of a comprehensive theoretical presentation of Gestalt theory itself, which is readily available elsewhere, this section seeks to introduce the model and orient the reader by presenting a series of issues or dimensions of couple and therapeutic process that are clarified by the use of a Gestalt lens. These issues are grouped under the headings of phenomenology and resistance, boundaries and energy, support and shame, the experimental stance, satisfaction, and the contextualization of models. With each heading the focus is a dual one: what the particular Gestalt perspective is on this aspect or issue of couple process, and then how this different perspective clarifies the work, how we can use it directly and practically to orient ourselves to the couple dynamics, and the couple to the developmental tasks before them.

These tasks are then taken up more directly in Chapter One, where the particular nature of intimacy and intimate process, in a Gestalt phenomenological perspective, is explored with emphasis on what this means for actual process skills and interventions, both for the therapist and for the couple members. Intimacy, in the argument of this chapter, far from being something added on or even counter to individual development, is essential to the process of individual development itself. This perspective then changes our idea of what the work is about, what the couple's and therapist's tasks are, and how to go about them.

With Chapter Two, Judith Hemming, a distinctive and deeply compassionate Gestalt voice from Britain, shows the power of the Gestalt approach for grounding the client's deepest and most elusive longings and fears in the clarifying terminology of theory and clinical experiment. This chapter could have been placed in any of the three sections. We have chosen to place it among the theory chapters, because of its creative integration of theory and application, so that each informs and enriches the other.

In Chapter Three, Hunter Beaumont, an American Gestalt therapist living and writing in Germany, addresses those very challenging couples whose relational process threatens rather than supports the self-cohesion of one or both couple members. These are the patients who are labeled "narcissistic" or "borderline" in conventional diagnosis, the same ones whose self-stability and engagement are often threatened by the intimacy of the therapeutic process itself. Along with his discussion of self and self-process in these difficult clinical cases, Beaumont also provides a new framing and theoretical grounding of the nature and process of *dialogue*, a term that is often heard nowadays in couples and family work and often urged on us as a good thing, but seldom defined or located in theoretical terms. Beaumont shows how dialogue, much like intimacy itself in the argument of Chapter One, is a necessity and a consequence of a phenomenological, self-organizational perspective. A version of this chapter originally appeared as an article in the *British Gestalt Journal,* and was awarded the Nevis Prize for Outstanding Contribution in the Field of Gestalt for 1993. It is with great pride and satisfaction that we present it again here, in somewhat different form, to readers on this side of the Atlantic.

Netta and Marvin Kaplan, writing from Canada and Israel, have presented widely, as lecturers and in print, on self-organization theory and its affinities with the Gestalt model. Here they turn their attention to these same issues as they arise clinically for couples and families. Again, the terms *self-organization* and *self-organizing systems* are suddenly everywhere in couples and family therapy discourse, often without a clear relation to subjective processes of individual affect and experience. And again the Gestalt model, with its capacity for flexible movement among intrapsychic, interpersonal, and systemic levels in the same clinical language, clarifies that relation and grounds it in clinical application.

Part Two, "Applications," forms the largest section of the book, as befits a model which is experientially and experimentally focused. Part Two opens with a contribution by Patricia

Papernow, a nationally known authority on remarriage and
stepfamily process. Papernow uses the Gestalt model to organize an approach to the remarried couple that is developmental, experiential, and richly illustrated with clinical anecdote.
Her recent book, *Becoming a Stepfamily* (1993), was likewise a
1993 Nevis Prize winner for a book-length work. Here she gives
us the application of her approach to the couple relationship,
per se, on which the success and health of the blended family
depend. With remarried couples and blended families fast becoming the statistical norm in our society, it behooves every
therapist, whether identified as a couples therapist or not, to become familiar with the particular dynamics and issues of this
widespread and challenging couples form.

In Chapter Eight, Isabel Fredericson and Joseph Handlon, themselves a remarried couple, take these same issues in a
somewhat different direction with their treatment of the
ground of remarried life. As with the other chapters dealing
with particular populations in therapy, the focus of this article is
necessarily a double one: to inform the couples therapist about
the issues she or he needs to be aware of in working with this
particular population, and to illustrate the application of the
Gestalt model in this particular kind of case. The two authors
here, with their many years' background in teaching as well as
in clinical work, are well equipped to make this presentation,
which will be thought-provoking even (or especially!) to therapists and others who have themselves experienced remarriage.

In Chapter Six, Allan Singer directs our attention to the
issues of gay male couples in therapy: how they are like heterosexually identified couples, and the important ways in which
they are different. In Gestalt theory, a different ground necessarily changes the meaning of the figure; and if for gay couples
the figure of intimate contact and desire for the intimate other
is a universal one, certainly the ground of the gay couple's life
in society is quite different from that of the different-sex couple.
Singer has an eloquent gift for describing these differences
without losing sight of the context of universality, and for
demonstrating the use of the Gestalt model in orienting the
work and in grounding this richly complex perspective.

Fraelean Curtis takes a parallel approach in her chapter on lesbian couples and "the lesbian experience," though as she and the other authors of Part Two make clear, there is no single "lesbian experience," but rather as many lesbian experiences as there are lesbian-identified individuals and couples—and the same is the case for remarried couples, abuse survivors, and so on. Again, we believe it is a particular strength of the Gestalt model to be able to do justice to the rich particularity of individual experience and an individual couple's experience without losing sight of the commonalities of particular group identifications and experiences or the universality of all these issues at the most basic level.

From Sweden, Barbro and Mikael Curman report in Chapter Nine on their experiences with the Gestalt couples group. The group, as the Curmans maintain and show, is a particularly well adapted format for the exploration of couples' issues—with certain caveats, which are laid out in their chapter. The Curmans, who are centrally involved in the Gestalt Academy of Scandinavia, are part of the large and productive community of Gestalt therapists and related professionals in Europe, where the Gestalt model and training institutes are steadily gaining official recognition in country after country, on a par with psychodynamic and behavioral approaches, as a certified training method for licensed psychotherapists under the national health systems of the various countries. Moreover, as with three other chapters in the book, this article on couples process and couples therapy is itself authored by a couple. In our view as editors, this brings an added richness to the book, very much in the spirit of Gestalt theory, which would argue (in Paul Goodman's phrase) that distinctions like "therapy" and "real life," "personal" and "professional," while useful at times, are "false dichotomies" and represent poles or aspects, not separate categories, of the unified experiential field.

Completing this "Applications" section is Pamela Geib's and Stuart Simon's work on couples therapy where one partner is a survivor of severe early trauma and abuse. Perhaps unavoidably as we grapple with issues that can be horrifying and challenging for therapist and clients alike to process, work in this area in the past has sometimes had the unintended effect of subtly recapitulating the abuse dynamic, albeit certainly in much milder form, by casting the survivor of past abuse, who after all really was a victim in childhood, in a parallel victim role in the current relationship, even when no current abuse is occurring. This happens when the long and harrowing struggle for recovery by a past abuse victim is taken as somehow more valid, more experientially real, *in the present relationship* than the current experience of the other partner. Here the whole-field and phenomenological bases of the Gestalt model support and clarify the crucial issue of equal weight for each partner's own experience and point of view *in the present,* and the necessity and real possibility of doing this without in any way dishonoring the stark reality and destructiveness of the abuse itself.

Part Three, "Perspectives," opens with a stunning contribution to Gestalt theory, shame theory, and couples therapy by Robert Lee, an author deeply steeped in the literature and dynamics of shame in therapeutic process. Again, this is a chapter we could well have placed in any of the three sections of the book. We have chosen to place it here because of this triple perspective, each supporting and supported by the other two. The recent focus on shame growing out of self psychology in the psychodynamic literature, we believe, is particularly important not only for its clinical and experiential centrality but for the way it tends to take the psychodynamic model away from its self-in-isolation heritage and toward a social field perspective that moves beyond the rich insights but somewhat limiting language of "object" relations. The Gestalt view on these issues, we would argue, takes this movement to its logical conclusions in a model that derives individuality from its intersubjective experiential base, rather than trying to "add on" the relational to a theoretical language that is more at home with objects than subjects.

Joseph Melnick and Sonia March Nevis, who have a long and fruitful history of collaboration on Gestalt topics, here bring their many years of wise reflection to bear on the dynamically interrelated topics of intimacy and power. In the process, they clarify the fundamentally inseparable nature of these two concepts in a process view, in a way that will enrich the work of every therapist, in and out of the couples therapy setting.

The topic of language has long fascinated the Gestalt author Cynthia Oudejans Harris, whose most recent book, a translation from the German, deals with the polar complement to language, which is silence itself—in this case the silence in families in postwar Germany about the horrors of the Nazi era (*The Collective Silence*, 1993), and the effects of that silence on the development and identity of the next generations. Here she examines the implications of the kinds of language we use, in therapy and in the couple's context, for the ways we frame experience and relationship. Her argument grounds the familiar Gestalt emphasis on speaking in the present and "speaking to" (as opposed to "speaking at" or "speaking about") in the theory of linguistics and emotionality, and in clinical practice.

The relational perspective, which is a part of what makes the Gestalt approach so well suited for couples work, is taken into a new dimension in Chapter Fourteen, Richard and Antra Kalnins Borofsky's model of giving and receiving, as a structuring and diagnostic instrument in couples therapy. Again, what is strikingly new here is the way the authors ground a familiar topic in a true whole-field perspective, giving us a tool that every therapist will find herself or himself thinking about, at important process junctures, with a great range of clients, couple or otherwise.

The final chapter of the book, appropriately enough, is by Joseph Zinker and Sonia March Nevis, who are certainly the pioneers and the deans of the Gestalt approach to working with couples. Along with Erving and Miriam Polster, Zinker is without a doubt the best known of current Gestalt writers to the wider clinical audience. His new book on this subject, *In Search of Good Form: Gestalt Therapy with Couples and Families* (1994), like this chapter, grows out of a collaboration with Nevis going back over ten years now on the articulation and application of the Gestalt model to work with "intimate systems." Together they have been running the Center for the Study of Intimate Systems at the Gestalt Institute of Cleveland for many years, and through the newsletters of this center their approach to the couple has become familiar to Gestalt and other therapists around the world. Here they bring their unique blend of personal warmth, wisdom, and theoretical depth to the actual experience of the couples therapist—again with insights and perspective that every therapist can use with every patient, and indeed in every aspect of relational life.

The last section, the Epilogue, is the contribution of my coeditor, Stephanie Backman, whose sure grace and delicacy of touch as a therapist and as a person shine through every page of this article—as they have touched and enhanced every page of this book, as well as the process of writing and editing it. Backman's perspective on the "aesthetic lens" in therapy is a vivid demonstration of the integration of the personal and professional and of the disciplined use of self-experience, which is the hallmark of Gestalt work at its very best. In the Gestalt view it is always a mistake, and potentially a destructive one, to deny the centrality of subjective experience, in any professional discipline, in favor of a mythical "objectivity" that can serve more to protect the therapist or researcher than to promote the interests of the client. Here Backman shows how subjectivity need not form another "false dichotomy" with professional expertise, but rather can ground and orient that knowledge and expertise in a way that focuses the therapist's attention and that models the use of self-experience for the clients. Once again, this is a stance and a perspective that can enrich all of our work, Gestalt oriented or otherwise, with couples, individuals, or families, as well as in other contexts and settings.

This then is the book, a rich and nourishing menu indeed. For the reader, our hope and belief is that whatever your received tradition and personal synthesis of therapeutic experience and methods, the ideas and perspectives in these chapters will serve to stimulate your thinking, support the ongoing reorganization of the field, which is growth itself, and freshen your energy and enthusiasm for the work—as they have done for us. In addition to our teachers at the Gestalt Institute of Cleveland, to whom this book is lovingly dedicated, we also wish to extend deep appreciation to our editor Becky McGovern and her colleagues at Jossey-Bass, especially Mary White, for their unfailing support of the project, and to Tom Backman, for holding the fort so graciously while we were out toiling.

Cambridge, Massachusetts   Gordon Wheeler
August 1994

To our teachers and mentors,
the founders of the Gestalt Institute of Cleveland

Marjorie Creelman
Cynthia Oudejans Harris
Elaine Kepner
Ed Nevis
Sonia March Nevis
Joseph Zinker
and the late Rennie Fantz
and Bill Warner

from all of whom we continue to learn so much
with great affection, gratitude, and respect

—Stephanie Backman and Gordon Wheeler

The Editors

Gordon Wheeler, Ph.D., is a psychologist working with children and adults in private practice and therapeutic school settings. He is a member of the teaching faculty of the Gestalt Institute of Cleveland, and editor in chief of GIC Press, publishing jointly with Jossey-Bass, Inc. His recent books include *Gestalt Reconsidered: A New Approach to Contact and Resistance* (1991) and *The Collective Silence* (1993, cotranslated from the German with Cynthia Oudejans Harris). He is currently at work on a book dealing with images of manhood in Homer's *Iliad*.

Stephanie Backman, MSSA, BCD, is in private practice in Portland, Maine, and Wellfleet, Massachusetts. She is a member of the teaching faculty of the Gestalt Institute of Cleveland, an AAMFT-approved supervisor, and a member of the American Family Therapy Academy.

The Contributors

Hunter Beaumont, Ph.D., is a clinical psychologist with a private psychotherapy practice in Munich, Germany. Dr. Beaumont trained at the Gestalt Institute of Los Angeles, where he was also a member of the training staff before moving to Germany in 1980. He has written and published extensively in German on the topics of self and character disorders from a Gestalt perspective.

Antra Kalnins Borofsky, Ed.M., has been in private practice as a Gestalt therapist and marriage and family therapist working with individuals, couples, and groups for nineteen years. Along with her husband, she is the cofounder and codirector of the Center for the Study of Relationship at the Boston Gestalt Institute. She lives in Cambridge, Massachusetts.

Richard Borofsky, Ed.D., is a clinical psychologist in private practice in Cambridge, Massachusetts. For the past twenty-three years he has been codirector of the Boston Gestalt Institute and has taught Gestalt therapy in both the United States and Europe. Together with his wife, he is cofounder and codirector of the Center for the Study of Relationship. He is an instructor at the Harvard Medical School.

Barbro Curman is trained as a clinical child psychologist. She is one of the founders of the Gestalt Academy of Scandanavia, where she serves as director of the four-year Therapist Training Program. She maintains a private practice in both psychotherapy and organizational consulting in Sweden.

Mikael Curman originally trained as an economist and worked for many years as an organizational consultant in corporate settings in Sweden. Since 1985 he has also maintained a private practice in psychotherapy with individuals, couples, and groups.

Fraelean Curtis, LICSW, BCD, is a clinician with nineteen years' experience. She is adjunct visiting instructor at Salem State College School of Social Work in Salem, Massachusetts, and maintains a private practice in Boston. She offers supervision, consultation, and training workshops on working with lesbian and gay male clients.

Isabel Fredericson, Ph.D., has been practicing Gestalt therapy with individuals, couples, groups, and small organizations since 1968. She has taught at several colleges and universities, and remains a senior faculty member of the Gestalt Institute of Cleveland. With her husband Joseph Handlon, she is cofounder of the Santa Barbara Gestalt Training Center.

Pamela Geib, Ed.D., is a lecturer in psychiatry at Harvard Medical School and a faculty member of the Couples and Family Therapy Program at Cambridge Hospital. She maintains a private practice in Cambridge and Newton, Massachusetts, with particular interest in couples and adolescents.

Joseph H. Handlon, Ph.D., is program director emeritus and former chair of the Psychology Program of the Fielding Institute. He has taught at Princeton University and the medical schools of Stanford and Case Western Reserve Universities. With his wife Isabel Fredericson, he is cofounder of the Santa Barbara Gestalt Training Center.

Cynthia Oudejans Harris, M.D., was one of the founders of the Gestalt Institute of Cleveland, where she continues to serve on the faculty. In private practice of psychiatry she has worked with individuals, couples, and families. Her recent works include a translation of *The Collective Silence: German Identity and the Legacy of Shame* (with Gordon Wheeler).

Judith Hemming, M.A., is an associate teaching and supervising member of the Gestalt Psychotherapy Training Institute of Britain, and associate editor of the *British Gestalt Journal*. She has a background in education, and works as a psychotherapist, trainer, and consultant in London and abroad.

Marvin L. Kaplan, Ph.D., was for many years professor of

clinical psychology at the University of Windsor, where he taught Gestalt group and family therapy. With Netta Kaplan he conducts training workshops in several countries emphasizing the self-organization of experience, a theoretical basis for Gestalt work that the Kaplans have written about extensively. Since 1990 the Kaplans have made their home in Israel.

Netta R. Kaplan, Ph.D., is in private practice in Israel, where she uses the self-organization of experience approach in her work with individuals, couples, families, and groups. In addition to maintaining her private practice, Dr. Kaplan concentrates on training programs and consulting in both Israel and Ireland.

Robert Lee, Ph.D. cand., is a licensed marriage and family therapist and received Gestalt training at the Gestalt Institute of Cleveland. He has written extensively on the topic of shame and is currently editing a book on the Gestalt approach to shame dynamics. He maintains a private psychotherapy practice in Cambridge and Newton, Massachusetts, with special focus on couples.

Joseph Melnick, Ph.D., is a clinical psychologist who received his Gestalt training at the Gestalt Institute of Cleveland. Formerly assistant professor of psychology at the University of Kentucky, he currently maintains a private practice in psychotherapy and organizational consulting in Portland, Maine. Dr. Melnick has published widely on a wide range of therapeutic topics, and is now the editor in chief of the *International Gestalt Review*. He is at work on a book dealing with the process of transition.

Sonia March Nevis, Ph.D., has been a member of the teaching faculty of the Gestalt Institute of Cleveland for over thirty years. She is director of the Center for the Study of Intimate Systems and former director of professional training at the institute. She has taught the Gestalt model widely around the world and is currently in private practice in psychotherapy, specializing in work with couples and families. She is also active as a supervisor of mature therapists.

Patricia Papernow, Ed.D., is a nationally recognized expert in stepfamily development and process. Her recent book, *Becoming a Stepfamily* (1993), describing normal stages of development in remarried couples and families, was winner of the Nevis Award for outstanding contribution to the Gestalt field. She is frequently interviewed and cited in national print and television media on stepfamily topics. Dr. Papernow maintains a private psychotherapy practice in Cambridge and Newton, Massachusetts.

Stuart Simon, LICSW, BCD, trained in social work at Boston University. He is a graduate of the Intensive Postgraduate Training Program at the Gestalt Institute of Cleveland. His private practice in Boston focuses on couples, groups, and adult survivors of childhood trauma.

Allan Singer, LICSW, BCD, is a psychotherapist in private practice in Boston, Massachusetts. His Gestalt training was at the Gestalt Institute of New England and the Gestalt Institute of Cleveland. He is a frequent lecturer on gay, lesbian, and bisexual clinical issues in various college and clinic settings.

Joseph Zinker, Ph.D., is a longtime member of the teaching faculty at the Gestalt Institute of Cleveland, where he has also served as head of the postgraduate faculty and as a member of the Center for the Study of Intimate Systems. His 1977 book, *Creative Process in Gestalt Therapy,* was named Book of the Year by *Psychology Today,* and remains a classic and a best-seller today. His new book is *In Search of Good Form: Gestalt Therapy with Couples and Families* (1994). One of the best-known Gestalt writers, teachers, and trainers in the world, Dr. Zinker lectures and gives workshops widely in the United States, Canada, Europe, South America, and Asia.

Introduction:
Why Gestalt?

Gordon Wheeler

What is the Gestalt model, and why should we give our attention to it, as overbusy clinicians and others interested in the lives and problems of couples? What does it have to say to us that other models, other voices, have not already said? Probably most of us who work with couples and families are the products and the authors of some uneasy union of psychodynamic and systemic approaches and methods, which we have synthesized over time into a flexible frame to support and orient our work. To this we have likely added the insights and techniques of a variety of other perspectives, as they seemed promising to us or as we reached the limits of our inherited traditions and methods. Cognitive and behavioral and cognitive-behavioral, structural and strategic, Eriksonian, neurolinguistic, dependency and codependency models, abuse and recovery, systemic self-regulation and autopoiesis—all of these models and more have enriched our competency in this difficult field, even as they have sometimes left us feeling less grounded and more uncertain. Why add another voice to this confusing and sometimes cacophonous medley? To put the question in the plaincst possible terms: what will the Gestalt model do for us, and what can we do with it, that we cannot do as well with what we've already got? Will the new perspective compete with the old ones? Replace them? Or, as we will be ar-

1

guing below, will the Gestalt model fulfill its implicit holistic promise by *contextualizing* the other models so that our menu of technical options becomes an organized experience of meaningful choice? Any method, any school of therapy, after all, comes down to a particular intervention made with a particular couple at a particular time, with particular data and goals in mind. The point of a model is to organize this sometimes bewildering material, thus giving us a particular focus, a *way of seeing*, so that particular choices are supported and brought into relief. But how are we to organize the models? The Gestalt perspective, with its theoretical and phenomenological attention to how experience itself is organized, offers help here in ways that we will take up below.

The Gestalt Model

The roots of the Gestalt model go back a century and more to the pioneering perceptual work of Exner and Ehrenfels, Wertheimer, Koffka, and Köhler (though interest in the *organization of experience* goes back to the Greeks at least, and had been much taken up again by the Continental philosophers of the eighteenth and nineteenth centuries, especially Kant, who in turn was a major influence on Paul Goodman). This early work on perceptual process was then extended into clinical and social domains by Goldstein, among others, and most particularly by Kurt Lewin, principal progenitor of the fields of social psychology, group dynamics, and organizational studies. With Lewin's work, the Gestalt perceptual model came out of the lab and into the "lifespace" of goals, choices, conflicts, exchange, and other "real-life" processes and problems. The term *Gestalt therapy* then did not come into use until 1951, with the publication of Paul Goodman's ground-breaking theoretical presentation, *Gestalt Therapy/Excitement and Growth in Human Personality*, itself an outgrowth of an earlier, apparently now-lost monograph by Fritz Perls.

Building on the pioneering Gestalt work of an earlier generation on the "rules" of perception and cognition, and much influenced by Rank's views of the self as artist, Goodman's particular achievement was the articulation of a new view of self as the *integrator of the field*—the "organ" or function of relationship between the private, seemingly separate world of "inner" life (the "individual," as generally conceived in the Western tradition) and the "outer" world of other people, who are of course engaged in the same field-integrating process. This relationship Goodman called "contact." The process of constructing it, of resolving the "inner" and "outer" worlds into coherent action, he called the self. Thus we can see that the Gestalt model was relational from the start, and at its core—"intersubjective," we would say today—in happy contrast to many other clinical models, including of course the psychodynamic and its derivatives, which still today struggle with how to *add on* relational needs to a view of human nature that was originally conceived individualistically. For our purposes here, of exploring couple dynamics and couples therapy, it would seem promising, to say the least, to begin with a model which affirms the reality of both these primary poles of experience and life, the individual *and* the relationship, rather than one which denies that second pole in its basic assumptions about human nature and the self, only to turn around and try to work on relational problems in therapy.

Since Goodman's and Perls's time the Gestalt model has received a number of critically comprehensive and useful treatments and extensions in print, beginning with the classic work of Polster and Polster (1973) and Zinker (1977) and including a developmental and revisionist critique by this author (Wheeler, 1991) and an excellent and accessible overview by Latner (1992). All of these works and a number of others are in print and readily available. Rather than try to recreate them here, we will turn directly to something that is at once more urgent and more directly practical, to all of us as practitioners and others concerned with the lives and challenges of couples: namely, what can the model *do for us*, and why should we invest the energy and time to learn about it? Our answers to these questions will be organized under six headings, the six "lenses" or new *ways of seeing* we can expect to get and apply directly to problems and choices in our thinking and our work from spending time with the Gestalt approach: (1) the phenomenological perspective: experience, process, resistance; (2) boundaries (and the concept of "energy"); (3) support (and its inverse, shame); (4) experiment and the experimental stance; (5) satisfaction; and (6) contextualization. Each of these represents a theme or cluster of themes addressed by other models; each is clarified and brought into direct practical application by the use of a Gestalt perspective.

The Phenomenological Perspective: Experience, Process, Resistance

What do we mean here by the somewhat daunting word *phenomenology?* Simply put, phenomenology is the study of the organization of experience. When we use it here, we mean how a person's living is organized, *from her or his point of view, as he or she understands it and makes sense of it.* To take up a phenomenological perspective means to try to get inside another person's experience, to understand the person's world and his or her behavior in it as she or he experiences it, and not from some external, preconceived point of view. Put in this way, it sounds quite simple and even self-evident, but it is worth pointing out that this is not the perspective taken up by most schools of psychotherapy and personality theory.

Most explanatory systems of human behavior and experience, after all, are organized *retrospectively* (present behavior is somehow "caused" by the past), "*objectively*" (that is, by looking at the person from the outside), or both. Retrospective systems, such as the classical psychodynamic and most behavioral models, see behavior as caused by some event or pattern of events in the past. "Drive" models, such as the Freudian, look for a configuration of events in the past where an internal drive or energy was released in a certain way, and then that way becomes the template for release of the same energy drive in the future, more or less along the lines of a sexual fetish, say, or some other compulsion. The person is not considered capable of making any choice about this pattern, or even to be aware of it (at least not before she or he is enlightened by the therapist in the form of an interpretation).

Classical learning theory and behavioral models, when you think about it, take essentially the same position on behavior as their longtime Freudian rivals. Again, present behavior is seen as directly caused by some past event or "schedule of reinforcement," which somehow laid down the pattern that is inexorably repeated now. And again, the person herself or himself is essentially out of it: that is, the person is the actor of the behavior, the carrier of it, but not the agent in the real sense of being the source or creator of anything new. In both of these models the *meaning* of the behavior is established from the outside by the therapist or researcher, who uncovers the past cause. The meaning lies in the past cause, which is to be revealed and then altered by therapy (and by the therapist). Meaning and past cause are the same: there is no other meaning. Naturally, in this kind of model the person himself or herself is taken to be the very last one in a position to have any useful opinion about the significance of his or her own behavior, which lies hidden until revealed by application of an outside perspective. If we ask the person anything about his or her own experience at all in this system, it is only to gather more historical data to flesh out our own construction, as outside observers, of what this cause and meaning may be.

Of course, all this is very far from our own experience of our own lives. As we live and experience our own lives, we organize not retrospectively at all, but *prospectively*: that is, as we live we are always and necessarily engaged in organizing to get somewhere, achieve something, avoid something else, and secure, approach, attain, manage, and prevent some other things, and at the same time (and most crucially) we organize all of these goals in terms of each other, in relation to each other. This is what living is; plainly, we wouldn't make it very long or far, as individuals or as species, if we weren't "wired" to organize ourselves and our world in this way. Most of my living—at least the "doing" part of my living—is the vast and interwoven fabric of all these goals pursued (large and small), risks managed, dangers (hopefully) averted, plans and hopes and fears close and distant, and all the myriad interrelations of trade-off and compromise, attending to one thing and deferring another, all of it put together as best as conditions seem to permit at the time.

   Thus if you ask me *why* I do a given thing, my answer will likely lie not in some past event, but in *some present issue or future condition*, some goal or risk that seems to me, in my own best subjective estimation, to move closer or more distant relative to me, be held on to or kept at bay or otherwise managed by my behavior *in the present field as I see it.* In other words, to me as actor and reactor, my present behavior has a *present* cause in the present world as I understand and imagine it. To put this in the words of Kurt Lewin, *we look for the cause of a present behavior in some present dynamic in the field* (see discussion in Marrow, 1964). That is, my experience, if you ask me about it (and I feel you really want to know), is not just my behavior, not even just my thoughts and feelings, but all of this colored by and in relation to my goals, in the present field as I perceive it. Experience, in other words, far from being "driven" in some simple sense by the past, is *always present and future oriented.* Ask me why I do a certain thing, and (again, assuming I believe you really want to know) I generally expect to be able to give you some coherent account in terms of this kind.

   Now certainly it is true that some of my behavior may be puzzling at times even to myself. I may even be disconcerted or embarrassed if you ask me "what I think I'm doing" in some areas, either because I don't care to say or because I suddenly feel I don't have any good answer to your question. But this very embarrassment is the sign that ordinarily I do expect to be able to offer some sensible account of what I'm doing and what it's supposed to serve. And certainly nothing is more common, in life or in therapy, than for me to *find out* what my own reasons are in the course of conversation with an understanding friend, couple partner, therapist, or at times even a stranger. In a phenomenological view none of this means that I am in the grips of an unknown drive or mystical force from the past, but rather that I may not have much experience in that kind of discourse, with myself or another person. I may not have a ready *language of feeling* or the habit of reflecting on my own behavior and experience (and note here that a language of feeling and habit of reflection in this sense are not just "luxury items," available to a few people through therapy, but are themselves natural and essential developmental achievements that are directly related to the quality of a person's life in the real world, to that person's more-or-less successful organization for coherent and satisfying living).

In this case we would say developmentally that I almost certainly missed some of that "empathic mirroring" that supports the acquisition of this language and that habit. But—and this is the crucial point, for therapy as for couple relationships—*the presence of that empathy and that listening and mirroring now will foster the development of those capacities now,* and quickly or slowly I will discover those present reasons that are the basis of how I am organizing myself and my world "here and now." In the process, at a metalearning level I will also be discovering *how to discover* things of this kind about myself and about the other person. Again, the implications for couples' lives and couples therapy are direct and crucial.

Not that the past doesn't enter into my behavior and experience, in this view. It does, in the powerfully indirect sense that past experience has shaped my *expectations and beliefs* in the present, about the present—and it is these expectations and beliefs, along with my desires and current perceptions about myself and the world in the present, that will serve to fuel and shape and check my behavior and experience, *in the present.* For the couples therapist this means a subtle but crucial shift of emphasis and direction: from "What happened to you? How were you treated in the past?" to "What do you expect from your partner *now?* What are your hopes and fears right here? How do you expect to be treated now, by this person, in this relationship?" And then as a corollary, "What do you want to do about it, now? Do you want to violate that expectation, negotiate it, stay with it, test it out in some way?" Both kinds of questions, certainly—the past focused and the present focused—have a place in most couples therapy systems, and both have a place here; the crucial shift is in emphasis, which in turn reflects a shift in the theater of action from the remote to the immediate, from the past world of the couple's separate history to the present world of their living relationship now and what they want to do about it. All this is the experimental stance, which follows from the phenomenological shift from past to present and which will be discussed at some length below.

By the same token, this shift of focus to the phenomenological perspective means a new understanding of another crucial concept in couples therapy, which is the term *process,* another much-used but largely undefined label whose referent is
generally left unspecified. Clearly, by *process* (in any system) we
cannot just mean "everything that happens." That would be a
completely overwhelming and meaningless jumble of data—
not even *data,* really, since even that term implies some selection
and organization of the "booming buzzing confusion" of sensory input into categories and items. Rather, in this view, when
we say "process" we mean events and behavior (including "internal" events and behavior, thoughts and feelings and beliefs)
in relation to what it is the person or persons are trying to do, in the moment and in life: not "everything that happens," but those hap-
penings that are related to the direction in which each person
is trying to go, the meaning she or he is giving to the present
field as she or he sees it, and the organization of all this according to her or his subjective perceptions and goals.

Right away, this distinction has implications for therapy
and for development in general. What if the person doesn't have
any clear idea what he or she is trying to get to or get away from,
doesn't even have the habit of feeling any relationship between
behavior and purpose, actions and consequences? From a Gestalt perspective, perhaps the first thing to point out is that *all of
us, clinicians and nonclinicians alike, immediately recognize this kind
of picture as pathological.* If we are clinicians, we start to think
in terms like "impulse ridden," "sociopathic," "conduct disor-
dered," even "organically damaged" or "delayed." Developmentally, we begin to look for severe disturbance in early bonding,
injuries prior even to the "narcissistic" period (since the "narcissistic" person, or narcissistically organized, as we would prefer to
say, does show coherent organization around the protection of a
sensitive or fragile self-process). But all of this supports our
Gestalt perspective from a phenomenological and "experience-
near" point of view: that is, as the Gestalt model insists, what is
distinctively human and inherently healthy *is the organization of
self and behavior around things we care about,* in the sense developed
here (and thus our assumption of early bonding disturbance,

since it is that basic link between self and caring, behavior and goal, that seems missing or impoverished). This is and has to be how we are "wired," and in a very real sense what living means, as a coherent "self" and in couples and other relationships.

In less severe cases, again, we expect and find that that link, that organized connection, can be brought out and clarified in the dialogue with an intimate other person (here the couple partner, with the support of the therapist). And again, the result of this process, this dialogue, is not just a clarification of a current conflict or dissatisfaction, but an enhanced process of knowing self and other in the future, and an improved quality of living. But even in cases of greater damage, it is still our Gestalt conviction (and our empirically supported assumption) that that organization, those connections, are there at least potentially, and that the person is inherently predisposed or "wired" to "connect up" and organize the self in this way.

This perspective completely changes our notion of "resistance"—what it is and what it serves. From my point of view as the patient or couple partner struggling to be understood, my "resistance" simply means that I don't think you've got it yet. Underneath, to a greater or lesser degree, is surely always some element of protest (or resignation or despair, or all three) about whether you or anybody ever can "get me," whether I can explain myself with any hope (which amounts to the same thing) of ever really being understood. Here too, it is important to remember that these beliefs, this hope or resignation or despair, are operating right here in the present, and can and must be taken up for dialogue, discovery, and experiment—put *into play* in the context of therapy and in the life of the couple.

Resistance, in other words, is information, nothing less than the crucial feedback loop in the dialogic system and in life. As therapists know from experience, the most intractable problems come not from resistance, but from resignation and depression, the loss of hope that even resistance itself can make a productive difference in the field. In that case, the first therapeutic work has to go into supporting the energy of resistance itself, lifting despair to the level of protest, honoring the muted voice, inviting the articulation of everything that hurts, which means sincerely wanting to learn what is not right for the patient or couple partner right here, right now—without the frame of clinical/judgmental categories like "overentitled," "immature," or even "borderline" and "narcissistic." "Borderline," after all, just means a person who is unbearably injured by me in some way at this moment, right here as we speak, to the point of feeling some kind of impending self-disintegration. When this is happening, it is hardly useful to tax the person with how easily he or she is thrown into that state. (In the words of one of my own mentors, the Gestaltist Edwin Nevis, it's not a "teachable moment"; besides, the person already knows how sensitive she or he is all too well.) Rather, hypersensitive or otherwise, the task of living and therapy is to negotiate that moment and that injury in dialogue (or between the couple partners, with you as teacher and guide for that process). In the process, with this phenomenological perspective, the honoring of the validity of the person's own best construction of experience and meaning, inevitably we do find the place and the way, large or small, where we have injured or failed the other person. At which point our own "self-system," our own cohesion and boundaries, are at issue, as we make our own living choice between listening and explaining, defense of the self or openness to the other, which is another polar dynamic of couple relationship and life.

Boundaries and "Energy"

Nearly every school of couples and family therapy makes some use of the term *boundary*, generally without attempting a process definition or drawing clear implications for therapy. A boundary, in Gestalt terms, is simply any "difference in the field." Since we perceive by registering differences, in process terms boundary and perception or awareness are the same thing. And since our "field" is our phenomenological field by definition, our own view of the *world as we see it*, boundary means some difference "out there" *that makes a difference to me* (again, the appreciation in the Gestalt model for how we organize around what *matters* to us, in interaction with what we see as available). And like perception, in the Gestalt model a boundary is not just a mark, a passively registered difference, but is *always organized into some coherent whole*; this is the whole meaning of the Gestalt revolution in cognitive psychology, dating from a century ago. That is, there is no perception, no registering of a difference or boundary, without *meaning*, a resolution or "bounding off" of the perception itself, the "thing we're looking at," in terms of its place and value in the whole field or "lifespace" (to use Lewin's familiar term again). Boundary making and meaning making, again in process terms, are the same constructivist act, the process that it is our human nature to do ("human nature" meaning that which we *cannot not engage in*).

But then what are the "differences that matter," to a couple member or any other patient or person, at a given time? The answer given by Gestalt psychologist Kurt Lewin to this question is, *the need organizes the field.* It is what you are "after" at the moment (or in life) that gives value, positive or negative, to different features of the world as you perceive them (and again we see the identity in the Gestalt model between seeing and valuing). This of course is just another way of saying everything we were developing in the previous section: we organize the "field"—pay attention to it, select out parts, evaluate them and relate them to some whole of organization, some goal state—in terms of something we *care about.* If we don't do this, then our behavior is random, or rigidly repetitive, which amounts to the same thing; in either case, we recognize the pattern or lack of pattern as pathological, possibly at a deep level.

At the less extreme level of most troubled couples and other patients, what we find is that unclear boundaries—around the self, around feeling states, around who is who and who wants what—yield unclear and unsatisfying processes of living. In a way this has to be true, given the picture of life and process that we are building up here. If we do not clearly experience the boundary or coherent difference between you and me, for instance—say, I don't have a clear sense of which one of us wants a certain thing, likes or dislikes some other thing, is having a certain feeling or reaction, like anger, sadness, sexual excitement, and so on—then the energy I invest in those feelings and those actions is necessarily going to be confused, hesitant or jerky, ex- aggerated or diminished. And then the resultant process be- tween us will be confused and unsatisfying, to the same degree. Likewise, if I have no clearly articulated boundaries within my own experience—a cohesive sense of difference, say, between what I want and what I don't want, or what I think about a given thing and what I feel about it (which after all may run in differ- ent or opposite directions)— then again my investment of en- ergy and availability for work, for organizing toward some par- ticular goal, will necessarily be confused or handicaped in some way. Again, this is all very commonsensical or "experience-near" when you think about it: if the need organizes the field, and I can't get a clearly bounded, organized sense of what it is I need, or want, or who it is that wants or needs it, then my prospects for satisfaction obviously start to go down.

Already we are talking about boundaries in terms of *en- ergy*, which means that again we are into the territory of one of those common psychological terms that are everywhere relied on and nowhere defined. By *energy* here we simply mean the *ca- pacity to do work*, to organize and move toward some desired thing or goal (or away from some undesired thing or outcome, as best as we can judge). But then that process is by no means so simple! Just to canvass quickly, we have to be in a position to know what it is we want and feel (or be able to discover these things in dialogue, in the way discussed above), to focus atten- tion on that thing, to see and undertake all the subsidiary steps (since most things we want importantly are not simple or im- mediate), to mobilize *support* (including importantly from our partner or other people), to manage competing "figures of need" and other distractions, to move (literally or figuratively, in our "lifespace")—and all the while relate and integrate this goal, this activity, to the countless other aims and problems large and small that make up the complexity of living (since life doesn't wait for us to pursue things separately, one at a time). This is what living is, and this is why it is all so richly complex and so potentially problematic. Small wonder if part of our deepest yearning is for a friend or couple partner who can *see us in the full complexity of this construction and this experience*—and by that seeing, in that dialogue, support us to discover ourselves, so as to support this process of differentiating and integrating, of bounding off and investing in, in the interest of better living. This is what an intimate couple is, and why intimacy is so necessary to life and growth.

We can cast this same discussion into directly usable clinical terms by saying that the *amount and availability of energy to do work, in the couple or in any life situation, is directly dependent on the condition of the boundaries in the system.* What this means in practice becomes clear if we think in terms of the dimension of *time.* Movement toward a goal (or away from a danger) necessarily implies movement through time, not just through space (indeed, the term *lifespace* includes a notion of time). But this means that the problem of mobilizing and getting anywhere, reaching or gaining anything, alone or with another person, has to involve containing and sustaining a level and direction of energy, over time. Without that effort of sustaining a momentum and a direction, the whole activity fizzles, wanders, gets distracted into all the other demands of life, slows to a stop, or stumbles into some other problem or conflict—in the way of the discourse of many troubled couples. The *boundary* here represents the ongoing choice to continue mobilizing coherently around the chosen goal, which means the ongoing evaluation and choosing of actions and sequences that either belong within the boundary of that activity and contribute to it, or else don't belong and take away from it. This is what *boundary* means, in real life through time. Metaphorically we can think of it as a bowl or a vessel that "contains" the energy, the push and direction of work. If the boundaries "leak" (boundaries of what I know, feel, want, or the interpersonal boundaries of who is who and who gives what direction, what meaning to the field), then the energy to get anywhere likewise "leaks" away. The result is disorganization and dissatisfaction, with more or less confusion about what happened, where it all went wrong.

In Gestalt work, at the most practical level, when we find confusion and dissatisfaction in the couple or other clients, we back up and invite them to explore the condition of the boundaries in the system—boundaries between people, and boundaries in the clarity and articulation of experience. We do this for all the reasons outlined above, which are that doing the work of living together takes organization of energy in a focused direction over time, and that that "bounding" process is key in building the interactions of living toward a satisfying outcome—whether that outcome is a job done, a child raised, a sexual or other nourishing encounter, or the process of dialogue itself, where the couple members themselves become the "bounding agent" or organizing mirror and container for each other's unfolding experience and for the ongoing evolution of self.

Support and Shame

As always in Gestalt, we prefer to start with phenomenological, "experience-near" terms. Support in this sense is simply what I need in order to get where I'm going, beginning with the support I need in order to know where I want and need to go. In other words, to know what is supportive to me you will have to know what I'm trying to manage and do, how my world looks from my point of view—again, the phenomenological perspective. If I don't yet know very clearly where I need to go at the moment—what I feel and want, where my desires and commitments are pulling me—then the support I need is the *intimate dialogue itself* (with the therapist, and/or with an intimate partner) in order to find that out. The dialogue is a process of active listening (including challenge, boundary, the experience of difference), the empathic or intersubjective exploration that validates the person's inner world. This dialogue may well lead to the negotiation of some more material kind of help, as, for example, when I need my partner's support with the kids and the budget, say, in order to be able to go back to school, change jobs, or redirect my life in some way. (I also need support in the sense of understanding why I need to do that in the first place, again in my world: not agreement necessarily, which is another thing, but seeing the thing, and me, from my perspective.) Either way, it is support, beginning with the sharing and clarification of my experiential world, that moves the problem back inside the boundary of the attainable, the realm of things that can be done without superhuman or self-destructive strain. And in this perspective, in therapy and in couple life, that sharing and that clarification are really the same process, the same thing.

The absence of support means a field characterized by stress and resistance. This after all is what stress means, phenomenologically: *challenge without support*, something *with which I am too alone*. Here too, once I know where it is I need to head, it may then be in the task itself that I need the support (as when there is too much work for the energy of one person); or it may be in my own process of bounding and directing my energy, in all the senses developed above; or it may be that I can handle the work, but I am too alone in the *experience*. Once more, the implications for couples therapy are direct and practical. We use the couple members' resistance (to us, or to each other) as the essential feedback loop, the sign that support is too low in the experiential field, by definition. Then rather than interpreting or correcting the patient's construction of the field, we move to provide the support, or support the patient to seek the kind of support she or he needs from us or from her or his partner. And again, the first and most essential support is the knowing and validating of the person's own experiential world.

To the question *What do you need right now* to be able to make the move, deal with the problem, or undertake the change under discussion? the couple partner may react initially with surprise and puzzlement, which just as often gives way to a second level of dawning surprise, as the person realizes that she or he actually knows perfectly well what support would make the step or stance manageable, reduce the stress, reduce and maybe eliminate the resistance, if only that support were available in the field, and *if only he or she were able to ask for it and take it in.* For many patients (and many therapists) this new habit or stance, of framing a problem always in terms of *missing supports*, flies in the face of a lifetime of personal and cultural conditioning that identifies support with weakness, and interdependency with a threat to the self. Thus it may not be at all easy to acquire. Indeed, the deconstruction of the old, culturally syntonic cluster of autonomy, "will," and shame amounts to a paradigm shift from the way most of us were raised, and is one of the most profound implications and effects of the use of a Gestalt lens in working with people. This shift may come especially hard for some male clients, but the couples therapist will do well to assume that no patient is completely comfortable or skilled ("supported," we might say) in this area. If anything, we would expect that those people who are, who organize their own field and their own lives around the building and use of support—for themselves as well as for others—may have much less need for the supportive context and metalearning of formal therapy in the first place. By the same token, when the patient or couple can do this for themselves—can organize and use a supportive field for the ongoing exploration and articulation of their own experience and their own goals, and for marshaling resources and people to move toward those goals together—then the work of therapy is largely over, and they can get on with their own lives, for themselves and with other people.

Resistance, again, is a kind of converse to support, the sign that support is missing in the field. Thus if you move to *support my resistance*, in the way discussed above, you are straightaway providing the first kind of support I need, which is for you to see my world as I see it. Even if what you want to tell me (and what I need to hear) is that I am seeing it "wrongly" (in the way of cognitive-behavioral therapy, pushing me to surface my unexamined belief system), I still need you to see what I see for your feedback to be useful and persuasive.

Once that kind of support is provided, it may often turn out that that is all I need. This is a common experience in couples work. We may often hear one partner say to the other, "I just want you to *hear* me, for once," or "I only need to feel like you *see* the stress I'm under (with the job, the money, the kids, your kids, your/my parents, etc.), so I can know you appreciate it." The therapeutic task then is to help the couple negotiate that seeing and that hearing, both for the sake of learning how to do this for the future, and as an experiment now, since movement to meet that felt need may serve to surface other, more hidden feelings and agenda (such as what you don't feel appreciated about on your side of things, or your difficulty in seeing and bearing problems or strong feelings without "fixing" them—

"being" without "doing"—or even why you are too mad or sad or hurt or scared to give me that seeing, and then what we're going to do about that). If resistance is the converse of support, in the sense of a conversion from one into the other, then the inverse of support is surely shame. Ultimately, support means your *reception* of my internal world, a kind of joining me at the boundary (again, with or without agreement, which is a different dimension entirely) as a construction with its own integrity and validity, worthy of being seen and heard and developed together. Other, more "concrete" support gestures may then grow out of this understanding, but all of us know, as therapists and as intimate partners ourselves, that this reception itself is uniquely necessary, and uniquely valuable, for our own self-stability and growth.

If we are not met, received, or validated in this way, then the result is shame. Shame, in Gestalt terms, is a state of collapse, or threatened collapse, at the boundary *that both joins us with other people and also differentiates us from them.* The insistence in the Gestalt model on the *unity of the field* means recognizing the necessity of contact and connection, not just in infancy and childhood but all through life. This is the essential relational emphasis of the model discussed at the outset of this chapter. Shame, phenomenologically, is the threat of removal of that contact, that context of the self. We're conditioned in our society to think that we can do without that connectedness to others, at least after the "dependency" of childhood is over—even to try to believe that a kind of psychic isolation is a hallmark of health, as in the classical Freudian view. Our experiential reality is otherwise. Even in adulthood, the removal of support, in the sense here of a community of reference who receive and validate us, is a kind of psychic death that results in either disintegration or rigidification of the self. Indeed, much rage and destructiveness in couples is baffling and largely untreatable until we reframe the behavior in a context of the dynamics and management of deep internalized shame (see Robert Lee's chapter in this volume for direct application of this kind of thinking to couples work). Thus shame and support are inversely proportional in some sense, and thus again our great hunger, especially in these times of community fragmentation, for an intimate other who will see us and know us, beyond the level of negotiating and doing, problem solving and planning. Not just the pleasures of intimacy are at stake here, but the actual integrity and robustness of the self. If the pressures all this places on the couple relationship are often intense, the opportunities for growth in the couple and in couples therapy are likewise profound.

Experiment and the Experimental Stance

Even clinicians and others who know little else about the Gestalt model usually have the idea that it has something to do with experiment, with trying out—some would say "acting out"—new behavior. What does this mean, and what does it offer us, in clinical practice with couples and other settings?

To begin with, by this point the reader has probably already gathered that action for its own sake has little place in the Gestalt model. Rather, the emphasis is laid on change in *awareness*—the organization of perception, feeling, and meaning—for the simple reason that the dynamics of perception and meaning are understood as the relevant present determinants of behavior. The experiment, then—the proposal to try out some new behavior—is first and always an experiment in some new organization of awareness, a kind of "playing around" with the couple member's or other patient's *view of the world,* and the possibilities for him or her in it. This may take the form of a formal proposal to try out a particular new action in the session or somewhere outside it, in the way of much clinical writing and description in the Gestalt field (the powerful work of Joseph Zinker comes to mind, some of which is reported in this volume). Or the form of the experiment may be more direct and naturalistic, as in "Try saying that directly to your partner right now," or "What would each of you be doing, if you weren't doing what you're doing right now (arguing, or being stonily silent, or any other familiar sequence)?" In both these simple cases, the experiment is not just the new action itself, but the new thoughts and feelings, the new awareness that is bound to surface if the couple members deconstruct their usual sequences of exchange (their habitual "defenses," in psychodynamic language). When this happens, all those feelings and fears that were deflected or contained in the old, unsatisfying sequence (because they felt unbearable or unresolvable) will emerge as direct demanding issues—"figures of concern," in the Gestalt language. At that point the issue again becomes one of providing and negotiating *support*—directly between the couple members, where possible—so that the real, underlying issues and feelings can stay in awareness, remain "in play," and thus be available for some new resolution, a new way of being organized in the new field. ("Transference," after all, is in this view playing out some issue or dynamic in the present field as if it were in a past field, with past limitations and constraints on action, reception, and support: in other words, a problem in the *organization of awareness*, the *meaning* given to the present field.)

Again in psychodynamic language, we are talking about the old issue of "secondary gains." There was some dynamic reason, some present felt need, for the couple's doing business in the old way, which is by definition unsatisfying, or presumably they wouldn't be in couples therapy. Nothing is more familiar to the couple or family therapist, after all, than to start in (reasonably enough) with some negotiation or agreement or contract to change or end some problematic behavior, only to find that after an initial period of rapid "improvement," they go right back to the same pattern, or some new version of it that presumably serves the same dynamic ends ("symptom substitution," to continue with psychodynamic language). The encopretic child is symptom free for the first time in years, in a single week, just on the promise of an hour's game time every night with his father, whereupon the father stops spending time with him! Or the couple member ends a painful and destructive affair, at which point the problems in the marriage, instead of improving, get much worse. This of course is the razor's edge of therapy, and of life: we want quick improvement and fast relief of painful relational problems, naturally; but we are suspicious of the quick behavioral solution because of our Lewinian understanding that the behavior itself was or is supported by a real and active present dynamic in the field. If it weren't, then it could have been changed by a simple decision in the first place, and the couple never would have come into therapy. And changing that dynamic, again, means *entering the patient's world*, understanding what and where the perceived dangers and pitfalls are, and in the process teaching the couple partners how to engage in this kind of intimate knowledge and supported change, for themselves and for each other. Without this exploration, which is itself the support the couple member needs for a new organization of awareness, *a new evaluation of risks and possibilities in the field*, we are "working uphill," trying to induce a behavioral change that may go against the grain of the client's own best judgment about safety and likely satisfaction in the world. Again, if these points seem obvious, it is equally evident that many schools of psychotherapy do advocate "working uphill" in just this sense, without respect and support for the client's own constructive process, the strength of which is surely related to health itself. And if studies show repeatedly that much of psychotherapy is relatively ineffective, surely that is at least partly because so much work in psychotherapy is of this type, which is to say nonphenomenological, working against the energy and organization of our own best equipment for survival and satisfaction in the world.

By this point the reader may have noticed that when we talk about experiment in this sense, what we are talking about is Lewin's familiar "action research" mode of intervention, transferred to a therapeutic setting. If the best way to learn about the hidden structure of an organization or system is to make a systemic intervention on it, then the analogue is that the way to know the structure of experience, the organization of awareness (a patient's, a partner's, or our own) is to make an experiment in this sense, in action or in thought, and see what comes up. "Try saying to me now the thing that would be difficult to say (to your spouse, your boss, your parent), so we can see how it goes" (to which the answer may be, "Well, if you're you, it's no problem, because I think you'll understand. But if you were really my boss, I'd feel..."). Or we might be more direct: "What is it that is hard to say to me, right here, about me and this process? Try telling me that now." Or, if that is still too difficult, "What is it that makes that hard to do right now? How am I making it harder? What bad thing might happen?" And then of course the same questions all apply between the couple members themselves.

The converse holds as well: if changing something is a good way of studying it, it is just as true that studying it is a sure way to change it. In our application to couples and other therapy patients, this is just another way of saying that the intimate phenomenological *reception* of the other person's world *is itself a powerful intervention for change.* Viewed in this way, the intimate dialogue *is* the experiment, and is the therapeutic intervention, both by the therapist with the patients and between the couple members themselves.

What we are talking about here, with the behavioral and structural, the manifest and the hidden, is the Gestalt distinction in experience between *figure* and *ground. Figure* is the focus of interest at the moment: what we see, what we want, what we are trying to do, the problem to be solved or the goal to be reached. *Ground* is the underlying structure of experience, the fabric of learning, belief, expectation, subjective knowledge, and habitual association—aware and otherwise—that go into how we organize that experience and ourselves, and how we approach that new "figure of interest" now. Learning, by any definition, has to do not with changing the figure but with a change in ground. We don't speak of learning every time there's a new behavior, but only when there is a change of some kind in (presumed, potential) *future behavior* (a change in "behavioral probabilities," as the learning theorists like to say, to try to get around the methodological problem of measuring the future).

Likewise, the Gestalt experiment, as a kind of learning tool, is not really concerned with the figure of behavior per se at all, but with the *ground of belief and expectation,* hope and fear and other related feelings and beliefs. And as a phenomenological learning tool, this means not the change that the therapist or couple partner had in mind, necessarily, but the *reorganization of the ground of awareness as it is constructed by the person himself or herself.* As a therapist and as intimate partner we participate in deconstructing the given ground (by receiving, validating, reflecting, challenging) and then in cocreating that new organization of awareness in dialogue; but ultimately the construction of a person's experience and world of meaning is the creation of that person herself or himself. This is what self and being a person mean, just as that ground of intimate dialogue, in the sense developed here, is what relationship means, and why intimate relationship is so essential in the process and unfolding of life.

Finally, this discussion of figure and ground leads us to the deeper sense in which the Gestalt model is experimental by nature, in its core premises and understandings. "Figures," after all, are not just given; they are constructed by the person, selected and made up out of some mixture of what is "out there," and what I already know and expect to find. I see what's there to see, and I see what I expect to see—both, in some creative synthesis of the two, present field and past experience. In this sense all perception, all new experience, is "transference," in the sense of being conditioned by my memories and expectations, but it is also new in the sense of potentially violating or transforming those expectations. The question is not which one of these two poles but how much of each, and in what kind of admixture, with what kind of mutual influence. If you are my therapist or couple partner, I may expect you to treat me well, or abuse me, or disappoint me, or understand me, or not—*and* you may or may not do all these things, on your own (and in interaction with the field conditions I partly set up, for good or ill, in line with my own expectations). This is what psychodynamicists mean when they speak of the "transference experiment." It is the "test" I am running in my own mind, as patient or partner, of whether you will live up or down to my old expectations or else violate them (hopefully in some positive way).

But then every experience, every "figure," is a test or experiment in this sense: a test of *known ground against the (possible) novelty of current figure,* current interchange. We constantly check or test our prior beliefs against our new experience, and our new experience against our beliefs in this way, in the ongoing process of correcting our orientation in the world and toward the future. If a new experience seems to violate our expectation, and especially if this keeps happening, then we are moved to make sense of this anomaly, to "make a coherent whole of meaning," by reassessing the belief. On the other hand, if the experience falls too far outside the structure of our ground of experience, then we may likely explain it away (it was "just an exception"), ignore it, reinterpret it (there was "something behind it," it wasn't what it seemed), or discount our own perception (it "couldn't have happened," "I must have dreamed it"). *Ground tests figure, and figure tests ground,* in the ongoing experiment of living. Again, this has to be the case, or we could never make the ongoing adjustment to changing present conditions that life keeps requiring.

Here we have the elements of a Gestalt process definition of health, for the individual and for the couple. Health and healthy process must surely lie somewhere in this flexible interchange between the novelty of the figure, the moment, the new, and the ground of established structure and past learning. If every new figure results in a complete reassessment and reorganization of the ground of expectation and belief, the result is chaos and randomness, instant gratification without commitment, coherence, and meaning—in therapy and in life. At the other extreme, if the new figure doesn't influence and deconstruct the received structures of ground at all, then we are left with rigidity, "transference" in the old sense, and ultimately isolation and psychic death. Somewhere in between must lie a supple process of honoring the tension between the poles of the old and the new, the ground and the figure, and the lifting and holding of both, so that each can influence the other in a mutually energizing, life-enhancing way. This is what Winnicott refers to, in other language, as the "ongoingness" of the self. And this is finally what therapy and the intimate dialogue—between us and our patients, or within the intimate couple—are all about.

Finally, interpretation, in terms of the argument developed above, is a *prestructured organization of awareness,* a prefabricated structure of ground. Plainly this poses some problems in a phenomenological, constructivist model, and Gestalt therapists have traditionally eschewed interpretation, in theory if not in practice. The trouble with this, as Bruner pointed out long ago in his work on discovery learning, is that, while discovery (or subjective construction) is an essential tool for powerful and lasting learning (lasting, in this view, because a "discovery" in this sense is by definition integrated into a coherent view of things), at the same time it can be a painfully slow method of finding out the possibilities of the world and of the self. Indeed, if we are "wired" by nature for some particular kind or style of learning, then that preponderant natural style is surely *imitation* (or what in Gestalt is called "introjection") and not critical analysis at all, which only emerges as an essential corrective to the dominant mode; thus the essential role of "testing," an experimental stance in the sense outlined above.

The answer for therapy is that interpretation has an important role to play, *if it is experimental as opposed to authoritarian in nature.* The interpretation, after all, is our construction (or often the couple partner's reading), our hypothesis about the relationship and meaning of various elements of the patient's life and experience. But then why not own it for what it is, a *trial* organization of meaning, a possible way of deconstructing and reconstructing the patient's or partner's experience, offered not as "the truth," but as an experimental figure of interest for him or her to consider? Couples themselves are naturally full of interpretations about each other, and the source of the other's problems. We are all of us naturally equipped and intrinsically motivated to make meaning, to give some coherent structure to the world we see, so as to be able to deal with it. (My predictions about what you may do in the future, after all, are based not on what you are doing right now, which I may understand as purely situational, so much as on my interpretation, my *attributions,* about why you are doing it; the entire field of attribution theory in social psychology is based on this insight.) The issue for couples therapy is not to get the partners to stop doing (or pretend to stop doing) this natural constructive process. Again, this would be to work against the grain of our whole nature and orientation in the world. Rather, the issues are to know *when* you are doing it (as the therapist or as the intimate partner), to own it as your own construction, your own trial hypothesis, and then finally to put the hypothesis or interpretation *into play* in the discourse and dialogue of therapy, and most importantly between the partners themselves. First we might say to the interpreting partner, "What we know so far is that this is the meaning, one possible meaning, that you are putting on what he or she is doing right now." Then to the other partner, "So what do you think of that? Is she or he right? What part of that fits and what misses? *What do you need her or him to know, about you and your world, that is left out of that picture?*" In this way the interpretation itself is in play, available for influence and deconstruction, including objection and argument and new information, and ultimately subject to the creative judgment of the person most involved. At the same time, the concerned partner can't challenge the other's interpretation without doing the very thing that is needed for the intimate dialogue to arise and thrive, which is to say exploring and sharing her or his own subjective world, making it known, and thus rendering it available for influence, support, and greater satisfaction in living.

Satisfaction

With the notion of *satisfaction*, in contrast to most of the terms and concepts we've talked about so far, we come to a central idea in the Gestalt model that we hardly ever encounter at all in nonphenomenological models, other than perhaps in discussions of sex therapy and sexuality. Not that some criterion of quality of living and well-being is not somehow implicit in every model; it's just that in the absence of a truly phenomenological discourse and perspective, it becomes difficult or impossible to bring this crucial dimension of living, the experience that is the very source of our ongoing orientation and evaluation in life, into any kind of useful focus.

Again, let us begin with the experiential: satisfaction is that sense of rightness or good fit between my inner and outer worlds, my own desires, needs, and feelings "in here" and the whole realm of possibilities for meeting and managing them "out there" in the world of other people. In satisfaction—from the Latin "to make enough"—this is my world, and I have a liveable place in it. The opposite pole of satisfaction in the moment is frustration, an increase of energy; but if the frustration is chronic, then one polar counterpart to satisfaction in life is the experience we call shame. Shame after all is that feeling that this is *not* my world, and there is *not* a liveable place in it for me, my own experience, my own hopes and fears and desires.

The experiential hallmark of satisfaction is a state of relaxation and a reduction of focused energy, the withdrawal of focus on the "figure of desire." The sexual analogue is evident, but all of us know the experience, or at least the hope, in every area of life. If my "organization of the field," my way of focusing and mobilizing, is naturally and necessarily around felt needs and other urgencies, then it is just as natural (and necessary) for me to relax that focus once the problem or goal has been managed or achieved (or even temporarily shelved), so as to rest and reintegrate and deal with other things. Along with dealing with things, I also have a need to exhaust a particular kind of response, a particular mobilization, again to be able to turn to other things. Appetites and regulatory activities like sleep, sex, and exercise are like this, and so are many kinds of life problems and tasks that I never really "finish" but need to come back to again and again over time, each time until the energy mobilized has been spent, for now. Once more, if this weren't our natural predisposition, if we weren't "wired" for this kind of sequence and process, we wouldn't get far in life, individually or as a species.

This is by no means to say that people generally know how to identify satisfaction, or what to do with it when they've got it. On the contrary, nothing is more common for partners in couples therapy than for them to rush over, ignore, or even undo those moments when they are actually getting what they have always longed for, at last. The reasons for this go beyond the familiar invocations of "habit" or "systemic homeostasis" (which is itself more a tautology than an explanation). When couple partners are supported to make the experiment of staying with satisfaction—especially the intimate satisfaction of being heard, seen and understood at last—they may very well experience a variety of deep feelings that are troubling and hard to bear, from rage (at caretakers or other life figures of the past) to shame (that they need this so much, and find it so hard to get) to deep sadness or even despair (at the pain and loneliness of parts of their lives). At moments of this kind the notion of satisfaction is particularly clarifying and useful. For anger and the grief that generally lies beneath anger have their own cycle of mobilization and satisfaction, the focusing and expressing and releasing of energy. The trouble with old griefs, old losses, is generally that I have never had enough *support* to stay with them long enough, for that point of "enoughness" or exhaustion of the built-up energy to take place, which is the kind of satisfaction that would enable me to "finish" the grieving, for now at least, and thus to turn to the other business of living with more available attention and energy. This is the theme of "unfinished business" in Gestalt, with its emphasis on closure and a return to the "predifferentiated" perceptual field. In particular, what we should add here is that the important "unfinished business" of couples and other patients always carries a dimension of *necessary grieving* in this sense, and that the intimate couple, with the support and guidance of the therapist, provides the setting for seeing and holding and supporting that process for each other, in the course of therapy and then ongoingly throughout their lives.

Contextualization and Conclusions

We've come a journey, in just a few pages, since our introductory remarks about the Gestalt model and its promise of a new way of seeing our couple clients, their problems, and their potential for growth and healing together. In the process, the reader who begin this essay hoping for some "new tricks" to use with troubled couples, in the way of some Gestalt writing of the past, has no doubt come away disappointed. Rather, what we have tried to do here is to talk about how Gestalt can offer us a new lens, or set of lenses, for understanding and intervening in couples' lives. Along the way we have focused on what we get out of viewing our couple patients in terms of self-constructivism (phenomenology), boundaries, energy, support, experiment, and satisfaction—and how those perspectives, those lenses, change our understanding of the clients' process, resistance, orientation and feeling, satisfaction and shame. At each stage of the discussion we have seen that what the Gestalt model offers is not so much a new set of techniques and interventions (though naturally different interventions do follow from a different perspective and goals), but rather a different way of seeing, a different way of framing the work. Gestalt is not really a matter of particular techniques at all, but of organizing the therapist's experiential field for the therapist's own orientation and choice.

When we use and understand the model in this way, we find that we are focusing on a level of "organized field awareness" that underlies and organizes the perspectives of most other models. We have already seen how the Gestalt view holds and contextualizes transference dynamics and phenomena, and how it can relate the behavioral (schedules and contracts) to the cognitive (underlying beliefs and mapping) and to the dynamic (secondary gains, which are another way of saying systemic homeostasis and self- regulation, on the couple level). The same applies to "structural" and "strategic" kinds of couple and family models, which are understood in Gestalt in terms of experiment and the use of novel figure to test ground, but with the distinctive Gestalt emphasis on the clients' own construction of meaning as the dynamic key to generalization and durability of learning. And indeed, if the Gestalt perspective is useful and valid, then this contextualizing capacity has to follow: that is, if experience is naturally and necessarily organized and understood along the lines we have been sketching here—if these general lines and organizing principles are what experience *is*, how we are "wired"—then it follows naturally (and necessarily) that any model, any approach to working with couples and other clients, can be viewed and contextualized in this way, in relation to other models and ways of working as well as in relation to the Gestalt model itself.

Here we are a far cry indeed from some of the showier early work of Fritz Perls, with its hot seats and empty chairs, though perhaps not so far from the formulations of Paul Goodman about the field of contact, the processes of self, and the crucial organizing function of desire. Certainly the capacity to generate new elaborations and implications of its own basic premises is a test of the usefulness and the universality of any theory. And certainly the Gestalt model, with its holistic and field-unifying claims, should be capable of extensions and applications in any direction of human behavior and experience, at any level of system complexity (see Wheeler, 1991, for a discussion of the Gestalt model as a unifying focus for treating intrapsychic, interpersonal, and organizational and systemic problems from the same perspective).

Today we are seeing a vast deconstruction and realignment in psychology and psychotherapy, with the received models giving way in every field to new perspectives under a generally constructivist umbrella. Constructivism itself, narration, autopoiesis, deconstruction, self-construction and systemic self-regulation theory—all of these and more point toward a new recognition of the century-old Gestalt insights, that process and experience themselves are constructed, not given "in the environment," and that the processes and pathways of this construction are themselves encoded, in a deep way, in our biological substrate and then in our social interaction and discourse. And yet, in couples and systemic therapy as in "individual" psychology, there is every possibility that this revolution of consciousness, this paradigm shift away from positivism, may be accomplished without touching that ideology of *individualism* that is at once the most culture bound and the most arbitrary, the most limiting and potentially destructive feature of that old construction in Western-world culture today.

The Gestalt model, with its emphasis on field unity, its insistence that "self" is not prior to "other," but that both arise phenomenologically in the same experiential act of feeling and constructing the "self boundary," holds out the promise that we may yet unify psychology and psychotherapy in a different direction: the direction of holism, humanism in the communitarian sense, and a true ecology of the mind and spirit. In this volume the work begins with that most intimate and intersubjective setting, the couple; but it does not end there. The perspectives and lenses of the Gestalt model, and the insights and methods that are laid out throughout this volume, have application to relational settings in all our therapeutic work with patients and other clients, and in our own lives.

References

Latner, J. (1992). The theory of Gestalt therapy. In E. Nevis, (ed.), *Gestalt therapy: Perspectives and applications.* New York: Gardner Press.

Lewin, K. (1936). *Principles of topological psychology.* New York: McGraw-Hill.

Marrow, A. (1969). *The practical theorist: The life and work of Kurt Lewin.* New York: Basic Books.

Perls, F., Hefferline, R., & Goodmand, P. (1951). *Gestalt therapy: Excitement and growth in the human personality.* New York: Julian Press.

Polster, F., & Polster, M. (1973). *Gestalt therapy integrated.* New York: Brunner/Mazel.

Wheeler, G. (1991). *Gestalt Reconsidered.* New York: Gardner Press.

Zinker, J. (1977). *Creative process in Gestalt therapy.* New York: Brunner/Mazel.

Zinker, J. (1994). *In search of good form: Gestalt therapy with couples and families.* San Francisco: Jossey-Bass.

1

The Tasks of Intimacy: Reflections on a Gestalt Approach to Working with Couples

Gordon Wheeler

What is intimacy: Is it a luxury? A necessity? A kind of tyranny, as some authors have maintained? A sort of opposite pole to "self-realization" (see discussion in Miller, in press)? Or is it, as we will be arguing here, rather an essential component and condition of the growth and expansion of the self? In this essay we will attempt to offer a phenomenological, process definition of intimacy, distinguishing those processes and the tasks that go with them from some other, related tasks and activities of couples and other intimate pairings. From there we will move to a consideration of the Gestalt model of self and self-process, and develop the argument that intimate process is an essential component of self-development. Our thesis throughout will be that the Gestalt model itself, unlike other dynamic models, is inherently and necessarily relational in its theory and methodology and in its view of the self and human nature. In making this argument we will be consciously and intentionally dissenting from some Gestalt writing, which (like its psychoanalytic forerunners) has been implicitly or explicitly based on an "autonomy" or "separate self" model of

self and development. Finally, with our revised view of the nature and tasks of intimacy in hand, and with this clarification of
the implications of the Gestalt contextual approach, we will consider the tasks themselves of intimate process, and what some of
the differences are in couples therapy when we work out of this
enlarged Gestalt model of self and development.

Exploring Ground: The Couple

The couple gestalt is clearly one of the archetypal human relational patterns. As far as we know, there has never been a human
society not predominantly marked by long- term primary adult
pair-bonding of some kind. Yet the maintenance of a healthy
couple bond over time is plainly one of the most challenging relational tasks we face in human development. By the same
token, studying, facilitating, and intervening in this relationship
and its problems must be among the most challenging tasks for
therapists, and one that is much less addressed and written
about than are individual work and family therapy, within which
couples therapy is often subsumed (see, for example, Weingarten, 1991). As for the study of intimate relationships outside
the couple per se, in psychotherapeutic literature this is so rare
as to be a curiosity. People having difficulties with intimate
friendships are commonly counseled to go into individual therapy, or possibly group therapy, to explore what ails them. The
idea of seeking therapy or consultation with the "intimate
other" (yet not couple-bonded) person they are having difficulties with seldom occurs to us, despite the fact that close, nurturing friendships are known to be predictors of practically all
the other good things of life, from career success to successful
marriage to physical health itself (see, for example, Miller, 1983;
also Zinker & Nevis, 1981a and b; and other publications of the
Center for the Study of Intimate Systems, Gestalt Institute of
Cleveland, for attention to these and related issues).

Here we will focus largely on the intimate couple, while
referring from time to time to other important intimate relationships (as well as to the nonintimate couple). For that reason
it is important to point out at the beginning that establishing or
living in a primary intimate couple relationship, which will be

defined below, is in no sense whatever a prerequisite for a full, healthy, productive, satisfying life; and that if intimacy and intimate exchange are necessary for full human development (as we will be arguing that they are), then that intimacy and that intimate exchange can be found and nurtured in many other places besides a primary couple relationship. And finally, "long-term" does not necessarily imply "lifetime," particularly in these times of longer and longer adult life spans, independent careers and incomes, and more and more attention and opportunity in our society for ongoing adult development and change.

Some Definition of Terms

With this much said, a few definitions are in order. What do we mean by "healthy," and what do we mean by "couple"? A healthy life is one characterized by a sense of satisfaction, by growth of the individual, and by *generativity*, a productive connectedness in which the person is part of and enhances a larger social whole. The healthy person, then, has the sense of achieving significant personal goals, of continuing to generate new goals that are meaningfully larger, and of contributing something important to a community beyond the individual in a way that harmonizes with some larger whole of meaning (whether spiritually, politically, or otherwise conceived). At least these three elements, we would argue, are essential to a definition of health (and particularly to a Gestalt definition): take away any one of them, and we begin to think of unhealth (meaning not whole) or dysfunction, not just a problem in life but a second-order problem of some block or distortion in the processes of life and growth themselves.

By the same token, a healthy couple relationship is one that promotes those processes of health in both partners. The key word here is *promotes*. To promote is to support, nurture, and enhance, something more than just leave each member free to live on his or her own while allowing for the pursuit of some goals in common (like business, child-rearing, or some other career or similar partnership goals). By this we do not mean to say that a relationship that merely allows separate growth or "space," without intimacy in the sense to be developed below, is an unhealthy one; perhaps *ahealthy* or *health neutral* would be better terms. Nor have we yet spoken of intimacy: a healthy or a "health-neutral" couple relationship may be intimate or nonintimate, though it is very doubtful that a fully intimate relationship, in the sense to be developed below, can be other than healthy. Why we want to insist on all these distinctions, and their relationship to the Gestalt model, will be explored below.

Couple is trickier, though perhaps we can say with Wittgenstein that no one except a sociologist or a philosopher would have any difficulty knowing a couple when she sees one. It is common to use the social-psychological definition, which rests on the way a couple present themselves socially and are recognized by the community as in some important senses a single social unit: that is, to deal with one member, at least in some significant areas, is to deal with the other; to harm or benefit one is to harm or benefit the other. In Gestalt terms, we would say that this definition locates the couple in terms of their external boundary with the world and suggests some of the phenomenological consequences of that boundary. This last helps us to get at the internal experiential hallmark of couples that set them apart from some other kinds of adult dyads and partnerships. This is the sense of *identification* between the members: to enhance (or diminish) my couple partner's welfare, across a broad spectrum and in a personal sense (not just financially, say), is to enhance or diminish my own welfare. If we come across a social pair who present themselves and are treated in some important ways as a bounded pair unit and yet do not exhibit signs of this identification, then we say things like "Well, they're married (or dating, or living together, or whatever), but they don't seem like a couple," or other words to that effect. Something essential to our notion of couple is missing. Again, why this sense of identification, this internal or phenomenological hallmark, is central and crucial in our view is something we will try to clarify below.

The Nature of Intimacy

Now, what about the trickiest term of all: *intimacy*? Melnick and Nevis (1993, also in this volume), in their extremely fertile series of meditations and discussions on the interwoven topics of intimacy, power, and abuse, have this to say toward defining intimacy: "The experience of intimacy involves being in synchronicity with another person of equal power over a period of time—whether a split second or a lifetime" (1993, p. 18). The emphasis here is on mutuality, but the authors build on this to make some penetrating and often-neglected distinctions between and among intimate moments, pseudo intimacy, one- way intimacy, and intimate relationships themselves, which they would insist are extended-term, at least. By *synchronicity*, I understand them to mean, as their examples suggest, shared "figural process," in the Gestalt sense of a mutually negotiated and agreed-upon direction or undertaking: that is, that process and capacity for wanting the same thing, or sufficiently overlapping things, importantly and repeatedly over time, as well as the ability to move together toward accomplishing and realizing those shared goals in some way that results in satisfaction for each. This is the Interactive Cycle of Experience model developed and taught widely by Zinker and Nevis (1981a and b; see also Zinker, 77, Melnick & Nevis, 1991), among others, which relates a Gestalt "experience cycle" model of healthy needs satisfaction to our real lives in relationships, and begins at least to talk about what healthy relational process looks like in Gestalt terms. The "intimate experience," the authors write, "can only occur when one is in rhythm with another in terms of placement within the cycle."

While this is no doubt true, and all these terms and distinctions are highly useful, I believe that something is left out here, and that something is of the essence of what we mean and experience as intimacy. In their emphasis on understanding intimacy in terms of shared goals, common figure, and a Gestalt model of interactive needs satisfaction, I believe these authors have given us tools for understanding any working dyad, but not necessarily for distinguishing the intimate relationship and the particular processes and tasks of intimacy from other productive dyadic relationships and their working tasks and processes. Specifically, I want to argue that intimacy has more to do with intentionality[1] and state of mind ("ground," in Gestalt terms) than with "figural" process at all, in the usual sense of action, plan, and accomplishment, mutual or otherwise. I also want to argue that the tasks of intimacy per se are different in nature from the other life tasks and decisions these authors and others often use as examples in illustrating their view. This is not to say that there are no "figural" actions or tasks at all in intimate process: there are, and we are laying the groundwork for discussion of those particular tasks and processes below, along with their implications for couples therapy under this approach. And certainly these tasks and processes, like any patterns of behavior, can be analyzed and influenced through the use of a needs-satisfaction rubric such as the Gestalt Interactive Cycle Model— but always with the caveat in mind that the goal of the activity of intimacy is awareness itself, and not some other more "manifest" action. Again, why we want to insist on this point will be developed at more length below, once we have taken a look at the Gestalt model of self and its implications for relationship. Meanwhile, an example may serve to clarify some of these distinctions.

Suppose that I work, as I do, in a clinic with other clinicians, in a shared enterprise with some shared goals having to do with providing mental health services to a client population. Now clearly, in the course of working together, in dyads and other configurations, we do have to use and nurture processes that permit and support "shared figure" and mutual needs satisfaction in this sense—negotiation, articulation of shared or overlapping goals, energetization, accomplishment, and so forth—as we try to realize individual and team tasks of designing treatment interventions, mounting a training program, dealing (unfortunately) with a larger health care system that is generally adversarial, managing our own boundary and exchange with clinic administration, other departments, and so on. And clearly, to do all that we have to do all the things that Zinker and Nevis, and Melnick and Nevis (1993), describe so usefully and clearly. We operate together over long periods of time with fairly equal power and a fair degree of synchronicity and satisfaction, at least much of the time. These things are all characteristic of any working dyad or functioning team, and certainly they have to characterize the lives of couples, or else the rent won't get paid, the children won't get raised, even (or especially) sexual joining in the couple won't happen, or won't happen with satisfaction (though, as we know, sex itself can be a subtle and effective defense against intimacy). All of this can happen, and must happen, and does happen, but it isn't yet intimacy.

In the course of this work I may come to know some or more of my colleagues more "intimately"—in the everyday sense of moving beyond knowing, say, what this particular colleague wants to include in the training program, to knowing something more of why she or he wants this, where she or he is "coming from" (and note here the everyday use of the familiar Gestalt distinction between "figure" and "background"). In the same way, I may come to know that this one, let's say, has just had a death in the family and won't be pulling his or her weight for a while; that that one needs to be handled with flattery and reassurance; that the other one is not going to do well with alcoholic men, say, because they remind him of his father; and so on. If some of these colleagues are superiors, I may well feel I need to know them a good deal better in these ways than they bother to know me (and here we see the usefulness of Melnick and Nevis's clarifications about the relationship of intimacy and power: the slave knows the master intimately; the converse is not generally true). If some of them are dysfunctional superiors, it may well behoove me to know them a lot better than they know me; this gets right to the heart of what we mean by the popular term *co-dependent*, which is a kind of one-way intimacy, taken on as a character style.

In all of this, the intimate knowledge that I begin to develop about my colleagues (and they about me)—even need to develop to guide and facilitate the shared figural work process—is largely instrumental to the accomplishment of those shared "figures" (or the furthering of my own agenda). The work goes better, as we know, if we're comfortable with each other, not living in fear of nasty surprises, and generally able to accommodate regularly to each other's strengths, quirks, and rhythms in reaching satisfaction (here again, the sexual metaphor suggests itself, but any shared goal will do), where there is enough overlap of goals in the first place to make the interactive cycle possible and worthwhile all around (what

Zinker & Nevis, 1981b), have written of as "middle ground," the nonconflictual arena of shared figures and processes).

But then something else may happen. In the course of learning things about other people instrumentally, as a ground for the work, I may well (indeed, inevitably will) come to know other things about them, their wishes and feelings and fears behind the acts, or "figures," they offer publicly, and they about me. This "getting to know each other" may then start to take on a life of its own beyond anything instrumental for the work— though of course supporting the work, unless and until we run into a painful intimate difference. We may get to be friends— "work friends," or "tennis friends," meaning still that our knowing each other has to do with things we want to do together— or, not contradicting this, but moving beyond it, "real friends"—the difference between "I knew him or her pretty well at work" and "We were or are good friends," even "I know her or him intimately."

This leads to the first hallmark of what we mean by *intimacy*: intimacy is a kind of knowing of another person, and being known by that person, in a way and to a degree that is for its own sake, not instrumental to any other goal. To the extent that the knowing is in the service of some other goal, then we add qualifiers to the word, as in Melnick and Nevis's "pseudo intimacy" or "task intimacy" or (as they are right to emphasize) "one-way intimacy." (Note that such one-way intimacy may be perfectly appropriate and healthy, as between parent and child, where in the healthy condition the parent knows the child much more intimately than the child knows the parent; too intimate a knowledge of the parent's inner life would burden and distort the child's development, for reasons we will say more about below.) Intimacy, in this view, is not just a means to accomplish "figural" goals, shared or otherwise, nor is it only a sort of side effect of repeated "interactive figure formation," though it may be all of those things. Rather, intimacy is a primary need, like growth itself, which may at times serve many other needs but cannot be reduced to them. Why and how this should be so are questions the Gestalt model, with its analysis of phenomenological reality, can answer perhaps better than any other. To begin to sketch those answers, let us turn to the Gestalt model of the self and development, and some of its implications for relationship, growth, and intimate process.

The Gestalt Phenomenological Self Model

I live, experientially, in two worlds. This duality, this sense of a boundary bifurcating my own experience, is at the innermost heart of experience itself, so phenomenologically basic that we don't often think about this awareness condition, for the very reason that it is the condition of awareness itself: it is what we mean by experience, or subjectivity, or consciousness, or self. The one realm is private, known to me but not directly to others (though others may make useful guesses about features of that private world, inferentially, which were unknown to me— this happens all the time in psychotherapy, for example, where this kind of guess is called an interpretation). This is the world we usually call "inner" (though the distinction is imperfect), and includes all my memories, impressions, sense and interpretive data about myself and also about the "outer" world and its conditions, and thus includes my "map" or table of perceived possibilities for action and satisfaction, for me, in that outer world. In a certain sense this is a world of more power than satisfaction. I can imagine what I like, but making it happen is another matter, though the power has limits, and certainly the satisfactions of thought and imagination can be real enough.

The other world is the shared world, the world that is negotiated with others (and perceptually negotiated with others as well, in the coconstruction of a consensually valid perceptual reality). This is the world of action, of materials needs and physical realities—a world, we might say, of limited power but potentially high satisfaction, as well as a quality of necessity: if I don't reach at least some minimal level of satisfaction in that world, I will literally die. Above all, this is the world of other people, which then means other subjectivities, other experiential processes like my own, with all the same exigencies and opportunities, satisfactions or otherwise. We don't know exactly when or how the existence of the internal subjective world of the other person emerges as part of our own awareness, but developmental research keeps pushing the point back earlier and earlier, certainly into the first year of life. Just as the self of the infant, in Winnicott's memorable image, resides first in the caretaker's eye, so the infant's perception of the subjectivity of the caretaker may be thought of as being located first in the infant's own cry. For why cry—and most importantly, why continue crying and even modulate crying—unless there is an influenceable other in the field? This might be understood in purely behavioral terms, but then consider how a well-bonded[2] infant of under a year old will take her caretaker's head in her hand and turn it in the direction the infant wants him to look, with all the implications this kind of action carries for a developing sense that the other person is a source of experience, in the same sense as the infant is beginning to feel and understand herself. Indeed, it is clear in this light that the developing understanding of self in this sense goes hand in hand, for the child, with the developing sense of the other person in the same intersubjective way—neither one makes any sense without the other.

The integration or resolution of this "inner" world of needs, desires, wishes, fantasies, appetites, perceptions and fears with the "outer" world of resources, obstacles, stimuli, opportunities, and other experiencing subjects (not just "objects") is then understood as the fundamental ongoing problem of living, or as living itself. It is also what the Gestalt model calls "contact." The integrated relationship of these two realms over time is also what we call the "self." (Thus Goodman says that the self is "given in contact;" it is also the "system of contacts;" Perls, Hefferline, & Goodman, 1951.) This contact, or contextual model of self, is very much Paul Goodman's contribution and constitutes (along with his radical revisioning of the nature of desire and its role in health and growth) a large part of his particular legacy to psychology and psychotherapy. What this involves is a redefinition or relocation of the notion and processes of self in such a way that self is no longer inherently, definitionally, opposed to other, in the polar way of the Freudian model and of the Western tradition of individualism in general. Nor is individual particularness lost sight of, as in some Eastern traditions, in which Goodman was also versed (see Stoehr, in press). Rather, self and other both remain meaningful terms but join Goodman's list of "false dichotomies" (Perls et al., 1951) like poetry and prose, mature and childish, mind and body, individual and social, and so on. Here self is regarded as a process, and that process is found "at the boundary," in the integration of the two phenomenological worlds. This model is, I believe, much truer to our actual experience once we get used to thinking this way, and once we find a new term for that "internal" world that in the West at least has generally been treated as coterminous with "self." In fact, self—your self, my self—although certainly individually particular and different for each person, is by no means really wholly private; and if we are in the habit of thinking of and referring to our "innermost self," we should remember to think of our "outermost self" as well.

It follows that the development and articulation of self—"self-actualization"—involves and requires both exploration and experiment in the "outer" world and in the "inner" realm as well.[3] But this is by no means a simple or straightforward business. Often in Gestalt, as in the psychodynamic and some other models, we have spoken and written as if the internal world were really a very simple place of a few plain feelings—body urges, really—the knowing of which was just a matter of unblocking, undoing prohibitions (which become inhibitions), relabeling these simple physically based states, and then "organismic self-regulation" would do the rest (see Perls et al., 1951; for example, p. 219ff). This has made it very difficult, in our model as in others, to talk about important constructions of experience like courage, moral dilemmas, values, choices, disappointment, trade-offs and regret, long-range planning, spiritual feeling, compromise, relationship, commitment, nurturance, loyalty, politics—no doubt you can think of many others. Certainly the body is an essential source of possibly "authentic" data about our own nature, appetites, desires, and other needs; and certainly that essential information has often been neglected or devalued, and we have to learn or relearn how to attend to it and make use of it. But our desires, choices, and values—our structured personal "ground"—cannot be reduced to body truths, even if those truths were always univocal and not socially mediated or constructed themselves, which is far from the case.

A kind of self-process that takes no account of the outer world, the world of consensual validation and coconstruction, but focuses only internally, we would properly call schizo-phrenic ("split mind," meaning the absence of just that inte-grative function of self, that ability to achieve some satisfying in-tegration and resolution of the internal and external worlds in terms of each other). One that focuses only externally would be close to Winnicott's "false self," where the needs and desires of others (originally important caretakers) are felt as more real and urgent than any that are internal to the person (again, as a character style this is close to the current popular term *codepen-dent*). Now Goodman, writing at about the same time as Winni-cott, eschews the terminology of false and real selves on exis-tentialist grounds: that is, the self that *is* the self process that actually exists; it may be constricted but cannot be "false." How-ever, since he speaks of "authentic" and inauthentic self-process, I think this comes to the same thing.

To return to the discussion of intimacy, the model makes clear that each of these realms, "inner" and "outer," serves as ground for the figural display and exploration of the other; that is, my expression and choice of means and goals in the "outer" world are very much informed and constrained (and sup-ported) by my internal "ground" of memories, permissions, hopes and fears, values, expectations of good and bad out-comes, resources past and present, and so forth—all of which is organized and dynamically structured in ways that we are only now struggling to describe in an adequate language. A con-stricted or impoverished world of inner experience means a constricted and impoverished range of activity and choice in the "real" world, without the flexible support of a well-organized, well-articulated experiential ground or the indispensable com-pass of a nuanced language of affect and value (and here again we see the inadequacy of a language dependent on a sharp dis-tinction between "inner" and "outer" experience, since the "real" world, the world that is perceptually or phenomenologically real to me, is very much a coconstruction based on past experience and future expectation).

But how then do we know, how articulate, that "inner ground"? The answer is, we are not born knowing ourselves or even knowing how to know ourselves, in the usual sense of the words—how to explore and create and articulate inner experience. It is rather that knowing and those processes of knowing are themselves acquired developmentally and that process of acquisition is a lifelong intersubjective process. To be sure, we are born "wired" to perceive differences, as Aristotle pointed out long ago and as Goodman was fond of quoting (see, for example, Goodman, 1994). But we aren't born knowing how to organize and make use of internal differences and connections, how to be productively interested in and curious about ourselves. All this we have to learn, and we learn it from and with another person who takes an interest in our internal world. This much-neglected point cannot be stressed too strongly: it is the crux of an intersubjective developmentalism, of the kind contained by necessary implication, at least, in the Gestalt model. The "inner" world, our private personal ground that shapes and supports our "outer" figures of action, is not "discovered" by merely "looking within" or "getting in touch with our feelings" (though certainly these are essential aspects of that knowing) so much as it is constructed, elaborated, and articulated in the company of a bonded other person and by virtue of that person's interest— which is to say, intimately coconstructed[4]. That is, the inner reality is "given in contact," to use Goodman's phrase, in just the same sense he uses to describe "reality" itself (which he certainly does not mean to locate only externally to "ourselves;" rather, it is coterminous with ourselves). This is the full meaning of Kohut's "emphatic mirroring," which he rightly sees as essential to the development of self (self in his system meaning a set of system-stabilizing processes, the property of the system that enables it to go on, to continue in time; see, for example, 1977). We would define self more comprehensively in the Gestalt model, but still in basic agreement with Kohut (and Winnicott) on the point that the self is "that which goes on" about a person (see Gustavson, 1986).

Again, this knowing, this exploration and coconstruction of an increasingly articulated, ever more richly structured inner world, is a lifelong developmental task. Once started, once well grounded in the experience of empathic attention and resonance, certainly the process and the person can carry on "by it/her/himself"—that is, if you look at the phrase literally, under conditions of being next to oneself, being one's own other. But, thinking again of Goodman and Aristotle's observation about the dependence of perception on differences in the field, the process of self-exploration purely in private, over time, will be necessarily impoverished compared to the potential growth from the same process lived out in intimate dialogue. It is in this sense that intimacy—as intimate dialogue, intimate witness and exchange—remains a lifelong requirement of our nature, a primary ongoing support for health and growth (which in the Gestalt model are inseparable), and thus a primary life need in its own right.

The Intimate Relationship: Tasks of Intimacy

At this point we can offer the following definition of intimacy based on the phenomenological self model developed above: intimacy is a mutual process of knowing and cocreating another's personal ground and of making one's own ground available and known. The process of exploring and articulating my own inner world in the illuminating light of the interest of the intimate other then likewise invites that intimate other person to join in the ongoing creation of my inner world, the ongoing cocreation of my self. Building on Goodman, we can say that self is process, and that process is intersubjective at its core, not merely intrasubjective, both in early development and ongoingly throughout life. The nature of intimacy, and its goal, is that ongoing cocreation of the self and the other, each of which gives rise to the other, builds on and off the other in her or his experiential field, and continues to unfold in intimate exchange. And again, this process of growth and articulation of self, which is our very nature, that which we cannot not do, remains impoverished if pursued largely or only alone.

Clearly, there may be partial or instrumental or one-way versions of these processes; but they are not full intimacy, though they may be developmental precursors of it (as in the parent-child relationship discussed above, or the one between therapist and patient). This kind of distinction then sheds some light on the much-debated questions of use of self and self-revelation by the therapist in therapy. If the therapist is an "intimate presence" and the session is a "real encounter," then in what sense and under what conditions can or should the therapist "share herself" with the client(s)? (See Zinker, 1977; also Speier, 1993.) The answer is well conveyed in Gestalt language: the therapist may share "figure," as in "I feel moved/saddened/impatient/outraged by what you are telling me now." She may even share "ground" to some degree: "I know something of what you're feeling, because I also lost a parent at a young age," or "I've struggled with that all my life, and I don't have the answer." But the therapist does not (appropriately, productively) *explore* her personal ground with the patient, as she might with her own therapist, friend, or any intimate other person. After all, this is a large part of what the payment of a fee is all about: the payee suspends ("retroflects," in the terminology of the Gestalt contact model) her natural drive for intimate self-exploration to leave a clearer space for the payer to engage in that exploration. Many patients feel this imbalance acutely—not just early on in therapy, when the issues may be power and vulnerability, safety and orientation and exposure or shame, but also toward the end of therapy, when the patient begins to become aware of a new and unused "muscle," the nascent capacity to join in the mutual process of self-exploration as the active other, and not only as the subject of exploration and cocreation. In individual therapy, renewed curiosity and the need to know more about the therapist personally may be a sign that the patient is ready to move on to termination, or possibly to work in a group setting. In couples therapy, where this capacity and these tasks have been the focus from the beginning, this new energy and the growing intimate skills of the partners can of course be turned toward each other. How we support that as therapists, and what those tasks and skills are, will be the subject of the next section. But first an additional word about intimacy and power (and abuse).

Melnick and Nevis, again, insist on a condition of "equal power" in order for intimate process to take place. Lee (in this volume), viewing the process more phenomenologically, likewise insists on "emotional safety" as the condition of intimate exploration for the couple, whether in the therapy office or at home. The converse must be true as well. Just as some feeling of sufficient power and safety with the other person is necessary before intimate self-exploration can start, so by the same token the experience of intimacy—of mutual exploration and self-revelation—may well tend to subvert objective power differentials. This is one reason behind attempts to prohibit sexual activity in hierarchical settings such as the military or the workplace: sexual activity itself is very likely at least to be accompanied by some experience of unguarded self-process and self-revelation, which is intimacy; and that experience of intimacy in turn is likely to lead to some greater equality of real power between the two people, which may contradict their positional power relationship in the organizational structure. (Of course, there is also the issue of protecting the low-power party from possible abuse, but the organization may well be more worried about the freedom of action of the more powerful partner than the boundaries and welfare of the less powerful one.)

Because intimacy is never without consequences, there are good reasons in all kinds of settings for not wanting to "be intimate," not wanting to know "too much" about the other person. "Don't tell me your personal problems," the boss says to her subordinate, because then she would have to take them into account! Likewise between couples: if I actually stop and find out what your statement, feeling, or position means to you, where you are "coming from" with it, then I may well find myself accommodating you more than I do if we just continue to battle about who's right and who's wrong, and whose turn it is to get his or her own way. You, for example, may want to change careers, but I don't want any diminishment to our income. But if I really let you tell me, and let myself find out, what your hopes and dreams really are and how unhappy you are, then I will have to face some hard choices in a new and more responsive way. What all this means for the couple and some of the implications for couples therapy will be taken up in the next section.

Tasks of Intimacy

It follows that the processes of intimacy—the attitudes, aims, and activities involved in intimate dialogue and exchange—will be somewhat different under this model from the way they are conceived under some other models. In Lewin's memorable phrase (1926), the need organizes the field, which is to say, the activities and processes we consider to be essential to intimacy will follow from what we understand the goals of intimacy to be. To put the argument developed above into slightly more comprehensive words now, we think of the goal of intimacy as being the cocreation and coarticulation of the subjective field, the "inner" and the "outer" worlds and their resolution into meaning and satisfaction, which is the operation of the self. This collaborative, intersubjective process supports and yields a distinct self and self-process for each person. But those selves are not "inner" and private only: they are informed and cocreated by the reception and reflection, the resonance and the differences, of the intimate other.

This informing and cocreation has both a proactive and a receptive dimension. On the proactive side, there is my own exploration and articulation of my own subjectivity, my "inner" and "outer" perceptions, which I come to know for myself in telling them to the interested, intimate other. Nothing is more common, after all, than the sensation that I know very well what I think, want, feel, or am upset about, only to discover in the telling that what I "really" want—what would really satisfy me— is importantly different in some way from what I started out thinking. And this is discovered, articulated, and constructed not only in hard battle for the position I already think I know— and not even in friendly negotiation for what I already "know" I want—but rather in the process of telling it to an intimate, actively receptive listener. The subtle but crucial shift is from wanting to feeling: from the goal I think I know, to why I want it, what it means to me. It is a shift from seeking to get what I want, with all the skills of negotiation, prioritizing, compromise, and so on that are involved, to seeking rather to *explore* what I want or feel or fear—to know it, and myself, and to construct that knowing, and my self, in and through the intimate receptive company of another person.

This in turn means a shift in process skills, or perhaps better, a shift in emphasis on particular skills over others. Whereas in negotiation work—work on the "figure" of what I want and how I can have it, with and from you—the important skills have to do with evaluation, presentation, accommodation, choice, and the like, here the relevant processes have more to do with identifying, sharing, and clarifying the subjective meaning of those feelings and desires: attending to receptive sensation (of my own discomforts, pleasures, feeling states); developing a nuanced language of feeling and desire for conveying these states (to another and to myself); exploring the interior relationship between the figure of my current feelings and the ground of my past experience; and, most crucially, building the capacity for trust that is both a consequence and a necessary precondition of all these processes.

We are calling these skills proactive, but clearly they each have their receptive side as well. Not only are the activities of inner exploration and self-reception closely intertwined, but the business of sharing my inner states and processes is itself a back-and-forth process, between telling and checking, exteriorizing what is private and then taking in the reaction or validation or question of the other person, letting myself be impacted and influenced, and then continuing the process from that progressively different place.

On the other side, there are the skills and processes of active listening, again with the dual poles of proactivity and receptivity, each intimately bound up with the other. To begin with, in order to hear you actively, fully, with satisfaction, and the possibility that we both will be changed, I have to want to know you. This may seem obvious, but even in couples— perhaps particularly in couples—there are costs and consequences, considerations and reasons, why I may not want to know in this sense, or may feel ambivalence about knowing, in general or at a particular moment. At this point my own skills in naming and knowing this feeling (which by implication in this model are very nearly the same thing), as well as yours in receiving, exploring, and constructing it with me, come crucially into play. Here we are already in potential difficulties in this far-from-simple matter of intimate exchange: after all, my ambivalence about knowing you deeply may itself be deeply wounding to you, and all the more so if it recapitulates the reluctance or incapacity of other important people in your life on this same dimension. Thus knowing and being known require support. This again is another aspect of the dimension that Lee (in this volume) and others discuss under the heading of "emotional safety," which becomes more and more obviously crucial as we explore the processes and stakes involved. Some of the conditions and implications of this safety dimension will be spelled out more below as we turn to direct discussion of issues for therapy itself under this model.

Therapeutic Tasks in Couples Work

Intimacy, to repeat, is never without costs and consequences. To ignore this is to miss the crucial dimension of *dynamic phenomenology*, which is at the heart of all Gestalt work. By this we simply mean that whatever I do, I do it for some reasons that seem cogent and even urgent to me at the time. Certainly I may be unaware of some or many of those "reasons." I may have "unexamined beliefs" or "basic assumptions," in the terminology of some other schools; and certainly much of therapy and intimacy itself has to do with exploring, articulating, informing, and sharing those "ground" beliefs and patterns in an interpersonal, intersubjective setting. If intimate process, as we've tried to demonstrate here, is necessary for health and self-development, and if I do not or cannot carry on this process with some measure of grace and satisfaction, then that must be for one or more reasons: (1) I do not know myself well enough to know how to start sharing my world and finding out about yours (because of developmental deficits in my own intersubjective history);

and/or (2) I do not want to have to deal with the consequences of knowing you in that way, in the sense discussed above; and/or (3) some of the material I might come upon and share—hopes, fears, fantasies, feelings, desires—has been so shamed, in my own history, that I don't want it to be seen and known to another person; and/or (4) current conditions are just not safe enough, in my estimation, for me to embark on the whole uncertain journey that intimacy implies. Let us look at the therapist's tasks, in each of these issues.

First is the familiar case, to all of us, that the initial block to the couple's deepening intimacy is the limited capacity, of one or both, to know herself or himself well enough to speak or listen deeply (note that our capacity to listen and hear is also limited by our capacity to know ourselves, since in this perspective we view active listening as empathic intersubjective exchange, and not just a passively receptive process). It is in this area that couples therapy and individual therapy blur and become indistinguishable, with only the difference that as long as you remain in the couples therapy setting, the "real-life" application and laboratory for the expansion of this capacity for inner knowing is immediately present, with all the advantages and disadvantages of the additional duress that that implies. Certainly there are times when the client has to have the quieter and less pressured field of individual therapy to begin that self-exploration, but there is no reason in principle why the same process and the same individual growth cannot take place in the context of couples (or group) therapy. Indeed, in this perspective a gain in individual growth and self-knowledge is exactly what does happen in successful couples therapy, and is what intimacy is all about.

In the couples therapy setting the therapist and the therapeutic process have the additional support (and pressure) of the intimate partner's real need to know the inner world and experience of the other, for urgent personal reasons. Moreover, by definition, to work in this way on the personal issue of one partner is to work on the complementary issue of the other partner. Thus an intervention addressed to one, such as "Are you finding out all you need to know about what this means to him or her?" necessarily calls into play both the expressive skills and capacity of the one partner and the capacity for inquiry, reception, and resonance of the other. At the same time, interventions of this type, which are intended to support the process of mutual creation and understanding of meaning (which is the process of intimacy), also serve to reframe the couple's task from problem solving, negotiation, and decision making per se to the larger and underlying goal of greater knowing of the self and other (which will serve to inform and clarify, at least, problem solving and decision making as they come up in life together).

Of course, in couples therapy just as in an individual setting, a person's limitations in her or his capacity for self-knowing are never just a matter of skills learning; rather, those limits are dynamically held in place. There is a felt reason for not pushing in that direction— perceived dangers, prohibitions and shame, anxious feelings, and other bad anticipations. To address and explore the person's reasons is more than just "working with resistance," though it is certainly that: it is the very process of intimate self-exploration, sharing, and cocreation of meaning that the therapy, and the couple, seek and at some level yearn for. Thus in the Gestalt model, process and content are always one and the same; and thus the Gestalt dictum that the figure of the moment (in this case the "resistance," or fear and reluctance to engage in intimate self-exploration) carries all the meaning and dynamics of the person's self-organization under the conditions at hand, which is the theoretical rationale for work in the "here and now," by now widely adopted by other schools and methods as well.

The same holds true for the second reason: the fear of the consequences, in terms of diminished personal freedom, of knowing you too well. *Tout comprendre*, as the saying goes, *c'est tout pardonner*—to know all is to forgive all, to lose the fine edge of my outrage, and perhaps to become caught up in actions and decisions that you need but that I am not ready to face and deal with. And what if my outrage serves other dynamic purposes in my own world—helps me manage my own shame, for example, or in some other way sustains my fragile self-organization? Again we see, in common with other schools, how quickly a couples issue can "collapse" to a personal issue (and vice versa). Again, the therapeutic task is the joint exploration of this constellation of dynamics so that the fears, shames, apprehensions, and longings that are darkly coloring my availability for intimacy can become the subject of intimate exploration. To weep together— the couple themselves, or the three of you—over the weight of fear or shame or apprehension one partner is carrying all the time under the surface can be one of the most transformational, deshaming experiences therapy has to offer.

At this point we are already discussing the third "resistance" outlined previously, the habitual fear that the very contents of my internal world are shameful and not to be exposed. The role and dynamics of shame in therapy, in development, and in life are only beginning, since the pioneering work of Kohut, to be articulated and explored (see Morrison, 1989; also Lee, in this volume, for discussion of this topic in a couples context). Here, we can also point out that shame, if not dealt with, is very nearly an absolute block to intimacy in the sense developed through this argument, *and that intimacy, when mutually achieved, is inherently deshaming.* Under the Gestalt model we understand shame to be not merely an affect, but a state or condition in which self-organization and self-process break down, or threaten to break down. The Gestalt contextual view insists, with Lewin (1935) and Goldstein (1939), that "I" or "we" come into existence in contact, in the act of organizing the contextual field, and that that contact, that organizing process (which is the self), gives rise to "me" and "not me" simultaneously. Shame is the environmental threat of withdrawal of the field from the "boundary" of the person, a boundary that identifies me as an entity (to me and to others) and joins me to the context (and then of course that external threat can become internalized, meaning that I experience it without the presence of the original shamers). Thus shame, in the extreme, is an experience of life-threatening panic, a kind of psychic death, just as to the infant the same menace carries the threat of physical death (see also discussion in MacLeod, 1993). Under the classical psychodynamic model, which was individualistic to the point of solipsism, it was largely impossible to construct a useful understanding of shame dynamics, which are relational and contextual. The revisions of Kohut (1977) and others, which have amounted to a complete reconstruction of the psychodynamic model along lines much closer to Gestalt, have opened the way to a very productive discourse on shame dynamics and shame effects. This discourse is further clarified and somewhat reframed by using a Gestalt perspective, which enables us to see phenomenologically what shame is, and why, in the extreme form (like depression, rage, or mania), it is not properly classed among the affects, which are orienting and valuing processes ("boundary processes," in Gestalt terminology), but is rather a self-state (in this case, a self-state of breakdown: as we would say in Gestalt, the breakdown of the boundary process itself).

This perspective helps us see why intimacy, when achieved, is inherently deshaming. The shamed self is the self that knows that important parts of the inner world of the person cannot be used in the organization of the field. Thoughts, feelings, desires, and inner voices that cannot be received by some important other person in development become split off, buried, coded with shame, and shrouded with anxiety. Thus the "authentic self," in Goodman's terms (Perls et al., 1951), becomes separated from the "false self," to use Winnicott's phrase—the public, presentable self-facade, behind which lies an inchoate, unarticulated world known neither to other people nor (very well) to the person himself or herself. The reception, then, of this hitherto unreceived "inner self" holds enormous potential for healing and the resumption of self-development on a new, more solid, and expansive footing. But this "reception" is not for the most part the simple imparting of something already formed and whole, a sort of secret that can now be told. Rather, the shamed self does not know itself, has been arrested in its own development, and now must be revivified, reassured, supported, and intimately cocreated through an active process of intersubjective reception. The delicacy of this process, the reliving of the old injuries that were contained and managed by the old "defenses," and the inevitability of new wounds and failures along the way, all combine to make this the most challenging of therapeutic tasks, as well as the most rewarding.

Every couple carries inner shame, to a greater or lesser degree, depending on the degree of abuse, neglect, and active shaming in the course of development of each partner. To the extent that these wounds and this damage have not been dealt with in therapy, not merely has the "content" of self-knowledge suffered, but the person is impaired in the very process of self-knowing and does not know how to go about knowing himself/herself better, with all the required intersubjective skill and presence and support. And even when these deficits have been dealt with in individual therapy (where, after all, one person is being paid to pay close intersubjective attention to the other, with relatively minimal risk of new wounding from the intrusion of the therapist's own shame and other issues)—even then, the same issues may well come up again in couples therapy, to be re-worked in the more demanding live theater of a "real" relation-ship, of a less protected kind. By the same token, if the couple can learn these skills and this process, if they can be supported to find the way to hold and support these most excruciating parts of themselves and each other, then they will have suc-ceeded in coconstructing a "beneficent circle" of success breed-ing success, support building on support, which is the ground for a new flowering of the self. This is the very goal and nature of intimacy itself, and is no doubt why we all need intimacy throughout life, yearn for it when we are without it, and seek it when we can.

And finally, there is the question of current safety for the exploration of the underdeveloped (inner) self, both in the couple and in the therapy setting itself. Here again, in Gestalt we bear down on the importance and the usefulness of validat-ing the current felt reality and beginning with what is, in the cur-rent and present field. Thus to continue with the example of shame, felt or anticipated: at some early point we need always to address the question "What am I (the therapist) currently doing, here and now, to make this problem worse?" If the an-swer (from the patient) is nothing, or I don't know, then we can ask, "What might I do?"—and then look for where I've proba-bly already done it. In a couples setting, the same question needs to be explored in all directions between the couple partners. We insist on this because of our understanding of perception and meaning making themselves: that is, we understand the "figure" of current attention, whatever it is at a given moment, as a coconstruction of felt inner reality and perceived outer reality, in the way of the self-process model described all through this chapter. In other words, to continue with Gestalt language, the manifest figure implicates and illuminates the hidden ground. This is again Lewin's principle of "action research," on an intrapsychic, intersubjective level: if you want to understand a structure, intervene on it and then study the effects (see discussion in Marrow, 1969). Again, this is why we are able to use the current figure of real concern as a representation of underlying or "historical" issues, without the costs of abstraction and indirection involved in just talking "about" the problem: we can live the problem, in the urgencies of the here and now, and experience all the same dynamics we would otherwise look for only indirectly (in "transference," which after all is really the same concept, that current figures of perception and feeling are informed, at least, by past felt realities). The additional gain of this approach is that we may avoid recapitulating the original injury (and/or supporting the couple to reinjure one another), which is the inevitable result of denying the validity of the patient's own felt reality.

If you are concerned about shame (or loss, or loneliness, or anger, or any feeling or condition) here and at this moment, then one part of that concern is something that is happening or threatens to happen, in your estimation, here and at this moment—something being done, here and now, by your couple partner or by me the therapist, or both. Our choices at that point are to interpret and correct your experience by pointing out how blameless I or we are in your feeling, thus deblaming and deshaming ourselves, at your expense, in the way of many troubled couples and all too much therapy under various models, or we can seek to explore your experience with you intersubjectively, so as to construct together an understanding or understandings of your own world and how it makes sense to you. (But watch out, because inevitably the therapist will discover that she *has* done something shaming, or hurtful, punitive, abandoning, and so on, and must be well-enough supported herself to hear and bear that.)

To put this choice another way, we can, as therapists or as intimate partners, leave the person *alone* with his or her experience, with all the implications that may carry for impaired self-process and inhibited self-development, or we can *join* the person in the cocreation of that experience, with our receptivity, our interest, our differences, and our active listening. This listening may then unblock the development of the self, which was to some degree arrested at that point because of this failure in receptivity somewhere in development. These are the choices, personally and clinically; and certainly to analyze the person's experience "objectively" from the outside in the light of our preconceived system of what her or his experience must "mean" represents the former choice at best, and at worst recreates the injury or shame that inhibited development in the first place.

Aloneness and shame are, after all, very close developmentally: there is an existential and individualist sense in which this condition is an irreducible truth of conscious life and cannot be solved, but still may be borne together. And there is another existential and spiritual sense in which our solitude is not ultimate at all, but is only the far pole of our oneness. To give up on intimacy in the sense developed here, as many popular voices and not a few therapeutic models do, out of a philosophical or personal despair born of our habitual clinging to the individualistic pole of this complex field of truth, is to resign ourselves unnecessarily to an impoverished self-development, and ultimately an impoverished community and world.

Conclusions

Intimacy, in the full sense developed here, is a difficult and challenging business, perhaps the most difficult and ultimately the most essential of all the tasks of human development. Separateness and union, after all, are the most fundamental poles of our experience, from earliest development through to death, and perhaps beyond. Intimate process does not negate that polarity or the fact of our individuality: it transcends and transforms it through the free and creative operation of the self. The couples therapist, after attending to issues of immediate crisis and safety, urgent negotiation and compromise, problem solving and decision making of every kind, ultimately must address the couple's *way of being together*, that intimate reception and participation in meaning making that all of us long for—and the absence of which accounts for so much pain and conflict between couples, whatever the manifest issue may seem to be. The Gestalt perspective, with its basis in phenomenology, the construction and understanding of experience itself, supports and informs that task, which is nothing less than the fundamental task of life itself: to receive and belong to you, without losing myself, and to enact and develop myself, without losing you and that larger belonging. For each of these tasks, my need for you, and yours for me, are irreducible. This is the meaning of self-process in the Gestalt model. In the familiar words of Hillel: "If I am not for myself, who will be? If I am for myself alone, what am I? If not now, when?"

Notes

1. I am indebted to Hunter Beaumont for use of the clarifying term *intentionality* in this context; see discussion in this volume.
2. The term *well-bonded* is crucial here, because in this perspective we understand *bonded* as equivalent to *treated intersubjectively*, as an experiencing being. This sense of the word is implicit but not well enough articulated in much of the literature on attachment and bonding (see, for example, Ainsworth, 1979, or Bowlby, 1969).
3. The very use of the terms *inner* and *outer* is an artifact of the old individualistic paradigm, shaping and informing our categories of language and experience so that it is difficult even to imagine another way of seeing (of course, this is what *paradigm* means). Certainly the development of a new, phenomenologically truer terminology that conveys the interpenetrating and mutually structuring nature of these two realms will go a long way toward reframing the current cri-

sis of world community and ecology. This reframing is now
the most urgent task of phenomenology, in both philosophy and psychology.
4. For further discussion of this and related points, see
    Wheeler, in press.

References

Ainsworth, M. (1979). Attachment as related to mother-infant
    interaction: A theoretical review of the infant-mother rela-
    tionship. In J. Rosenblatt et al. (Eds.), *Advances in the study of
    behavior.* New York: Academic Press.

Bowlby, J. (1969). *Attachment and loss: Vol. 2. Attachment.* New
    York: Basic Books.

Goldstein, K. (1939). *The organism.* Boston: American Book
    Company.

Goodman, P. (1994). *Crazy Hope and Finite Experience.* San Fran-
    cisco: Jossey- Bass.

Gustavson, J. (1986). *The complex secret of brief psychotherapy.* New
    York: W. W. Norton.

Kohut, H. (1977). *The restoration of the self.* New York: Interna-
    tional Universities Press.

Lewin, K. (1926). Vorsatz, Wille, und Bedürfnis. *Psychologische
    Forschung, 7,* 330–385.

Lewin, K. (1935). *A dynamic theory of personality.* New York:
    McGraw-Hill.

Marrow, A. (1969). *The practical theorist: The life and work of Kurt
    Lewin.* New York: Basic Books.

McLeod, L. (1993). The Self in Gestalt Therapy. *British Gestalt
    Journal, 2,* 25–40.

Melnick, J. & Nevis, S. (1993). *Intimacy, nurturance, power and
    abuse.* Unpublished monograph.

Miller, M. (in press). *Intimate terrorism.* New York: W. W. Norton
    & Co.

Miller, S. (1983). *Men and friendship.* San Leandro, CA: Gateway
    Books.

Morrison, A. (1989). *Shame: The underside of narcissism.* Hillsdale,
    NJ: Analytic Press.

Perls, F., Hefferline, R., & Goodman, P. (1951). *Gestalt therapy: Excitement and growth in the human personality.* New York: Julian Press.

Speier, S. (1993). The psychoanalyst without a face: Psychoanalysis without a history. In B. Heimannsberg & C. Schmidt (Eds.), *The collective silence* (Cynthia Oudejans Harris & Gordon Wheeler, Trans.). San Francisco: Jossey-Bass.

Stoehr, T. (in press). *Here now next: Paul Goodman and the origins of Gestalt therapy.* San Francisco: Jossey-Bass.

Weingarten, K. (1991). The discourses of intimacy: Adding a social constructionist and feminist view. *Family Process, 30,* 285–306.

Wheeler, G. (1991). *Gestalt reconsidered.* New York: Gardner Press.

Wheeler, G. (in press). *Compulsion and curiosity: A Gestalt approach to OCD. British Gestalt Journal, 3*(1).

Zinker, J. (1977). *Creative process in Gestalt therapy.* New York: Brunner/Mazel.

Zinker, J., & Nevis, S. (1981a). *The Gestalt theory of couple and family interactions.* Cleveland: Gestalt Institute of Cleveland.

Zinker, J., & Nevis, S. (1981b). *Complementarity and the middle ground.* Cleveland: Gestalt Institute of Cleveland.

2

Contact and Choice:
Gestalt Work with Couples

Judith Hemming

This chapter illustrates some aspects of my perspective on the theory and practice of Gestalt therapy with couples. It is easier for the reader to see a theory lived out in practice; in any case, Gestalt theory emphasizes the concrete over the abstract. So I will describe some of my time with a couple I call Martin and Janet and use it to illuminate some of my guiding maps and principles.

I imagine some couples therapists may recognize the following description with a little sigh. I could have been a therapeutic sorceress when I first met these two and still have made little impact. Like many couples who must reach the level of desperation to come into therapy, they had closed up their boundaries, both in relation to each other and in relation to the environment that included me. A couple system that is open can convert energy from the environment to replenish itself and grow; the two can enter into dialogue, dare to be curious; they can evolve their problems. But at this time Martin and Janet felt too besieged. Their mode of operation had become almost entirely polemical, with tactics designed to win rather than find mutual solutions. Not yet having sufficient skill to relate as differentiated beings, they had chosen a relationship of mutual isolation rather than the greater terrors of confluence. Their attention was not on me at all but on their own intractable positions. Locked in mutual meanness toward the other, their catalogue of complaints interminable, they seemed more like bickering siblings than adults in their late thirties. Their notion of therapy when they arrived in my room was as a place to get the other put right rather than as a place to change or grow. We had no shared or manageable agenda.

They lived apart and wanted to see if they could live together, but only if she would dislodge the lodgers in her home to make some privacy for him and their little son. She would not give in to any of his demands until he "shaped up" financially and domestically, and he threatened to leave unless she was willing to be sexual with him and less critical and controlling. They met two or three times a week, and occasionally she allowed him to spend the night in their house in the spare room. They could not work out how to live together or apart. Neither dared open himself or herself to the other; like old boxers, both had withdrawn to their separate corners bruised and resentful. They had eroded an alarming amount of what common ground they once had, alternately fearing engulfment or abandonment. If it hadn't been for their hopes and vision for their beloved little son, they would probably have shut the door on each other already. This stalemate position, of "I will if you will," is a familiar one, creating a deadlock of demands and consequent lack of free energy. Both demands and energy needed attention and their meanings explored.

A key concept in Gestalt is that of figure and ground, and of how meaning is made from the relationship between the two. The meaning of their difficulties would therefore be found by considering not only what they did and how they were as I met them in the present, the demands and issues that were figural for them, but by helping them relate those demands to their whole being, their history and context. Change is only possible because the relationship between figure and ground is not fixed; our awareness of either can shift or deepen, and any shift makes another gestalt out of how we see or configure the world. Meaning changes as often as do our changing states. When we allow ourselves to be aware, we discover we are always in flux; we recreate our autobiographies every time we tell them according to our present context. It is not only a couple's history as such that matters but their responses to it, the decisions they have made about themselves in relation to it. The gathering of case history, the making of meaning, is a totally unfixed and subjective affair. Nevertheless, facts are important. Once somewhat neglected in favor of an emphasis on the present moment (or what is figural to the therapist or client), the gathering of a case history information is an essential part of establishing a meaningful and useful relationship with any couple or individual. I was therefore interested in how Martin and Janet described themselves and what they thought to tell me of their lives.

Janet's childhood had clearly been traumatically insecure, but she made it clear straightaway that she was firmly against delving into it; she barely even saw it as a factor in her present life. Her clearly stated view was "I am free: the past is over." This past included the fact that her father had been an institutionalized schizophrenic during most of her childhood and her mother had given her at an early age into the care of relatives. Martin, on the other hand, believed himself trapped by his history, apparently the opposite view but equal in its potential for crippling his capacity for change. He was extremely critical of his family, seeing his mother as having been controlling and his father, especially after becoming unemployed, a pathetic and henpecked husband. He felt victimized now as well as in the past, at work and especially by Janet.

Both initially saw my role as judge, demanding that I be on their side and get the other to change. Left to themselves in those early sessions, she would attack him with great energy and he would withhold spitefully. They clung tenaciously to their stories, yet when I asked them what they most wanted, their hopes coincided beautifully: that they could become a happy family unit with their son. During the time I met with them this single vision opened up into the articulation of many other passionately felt needs, for wholeness and safety in loving, a shorthand for everything they felt they had lacked and longed for and had not yet created. I recognized and was touched by the poignancy of their longings. All people develop ways of being in the world that have structural and functional unity, a sort of integrity. Their symptoms and complaints make sense. Neither had come to see me to change them but rather to have them seen and validated. So it was important for me to respect that integrity with all its characteristics while also investigating whether they were interested in any new perspectives. Were there any parts of their relationship that they would be willing to experiment with? They hadn't chosen to do individual therapy; what they presented was their relationship, so that was my client.

And what did they think a relationship was? We all develop models based on ones we have somehow come to know, whether from memory or from fantasy. The models of relationships they had inherited were superficially poles apart, yet they had contained some fascinating similarities. It is a commonplace view in marital literature that this will be the case. Briefly, the argument goes that we all have a compelling need to choose people like our parents; when we meet someone who has (or is perceived to have) key similarities to both their positive and negative qualities, they are the ones we fall in love with. Initially we can experience wholeness, since the person will manifest those parts of our being that we were cut off from in childhood. We maintain this illusion through projection, denial of evidence and transference of parental longing, putting responsibility for core aspects of our survival onto our partners. Eventually through these same similarities we are likely to reopen our own and each other's childhood wounds in our search for that wholeness. It is usually those original but restimulated wounds that a couple bring into therapy.

It is always fascinating to me to explore the extent to which another *can* learn to meet some of these core transferential needs. Believing so deeply that our source of salvation is external, most of us are unwilling to relinquish such longings or learn to be our own salvation. So it is a key question what a couple need to learn so that both can experience some healing or at least be relieved of some of their suffering. What mixture of insight, experience, or behavioral work will raise their level of consciousness and help create enough safety and support for a more unconditional love to flourish? Gestalt therapy, because it strongly emphasizes both self-responsibility and experiment, offers much to those struggling with this perennial dilemma. It exemplifies both perspectives: both the opportunity to relinquish or transform archaic dependencies and projections as well as the opportunity to learn to meet each other's needs in ways that are health promoting for both. This is a fascinating and delicate balance faced by all couples, between changing the other and changing oneself.

So, back to Martin and Janet and their similarities. In essence, both had grown up in situations that had exemplified a highly discounted view of men and a belief in the controlling power of women. This they still lived out and in their deepest wisdom sought to change. They both had strong beliefs that their source of salvation depended on the other, a kind of fusion that would save them. Yet neither believed it was safe to let much in; they had not experienced the true separation from their families that would allow for individuation and bonding with each other. Martin's boundary seemed to depend on saying "no" to anything Janet really wanted, and hers depended on the wall of her house. Until their son was born they had been able to be hesitantly romantic, maintaining their hopes for contact, since her front door and his withholding were not struggling with the demands of becoming a family unit. Janet saw in Martin's everyday practical incompetence, idealism and commitment an opportunity to work with someone to whom she had something to offer, someone who would improve under her care. Wanting to have a child fueled her romantic vision of him too. Martin admired her clarity of purpose, her sociability, and her capacity to express her feelings directly. He also felt compassion for her difficulties at work, where she was talented yet easily snubbed. Neither of them had any experience of previous satisfying intimacy; they had been amazed and grateful that each had found someone who desired the other at all.

So there was a basis for enjoying a middle ground: romantic idealism, a similar educational and political level of sophistication, a love for their child, a potentially supportive attitude to each other's difficulties, and common assumptions and introjects about the roles of men and women. Negatively construed, this amounted to a low opinion of both men and women. More positively (and traditionally) it might mean that men needed women's competent care domestically whereas women needed the financial and worldly protection and status of men. When they first came to see me, these assumptions were extreme in their negativity; both were withholding what the other wanted and struggling for specific affirmations from the other, with the result that neither dared open themselves to the other. The boundaries were seemingly impenetrable. Janet spoke of all the men she knew as having been either absent or unstable like her father or financially solid but emotionally unavailable like her male relatives. That was "how they were": a sort of lit-eralness of vision, in contrast to Martin's passionate view that all should be different from how it had been. He was still angry with his parents, unaware how his strategies in life rested on his childhood skill of thwarting—evading, taking power negatively, withholding, and refusing responsibility. When he spoke of these strategies he sparkled, the fighting spirit in him still alive. After they had told me their histories, I began by admiring both their stances, reframing his withholding and her ability to be stoically accepting as heroic rather than merely recalcitrant or insensitive. This surprised them; it was new to be recognized and validated in this way. It also introduced them to the idea that they might still see and create a world through those prisms they had forged when growing up. In the terminology of Gestalt therapy, such prisms are defined as fixed gestalts likely to interrupt the possibility of fresh contact and needing completion.

It was an interestingly propitious moment to start therapy, to find an ally for the best in each of them, to see in their de-spair the hopes for growth that lay buried. They were getting on so badly they had little to lose. I often marvel at the mysterious preciousness of the crises that can bring a couple into therapy and the importance for me to find a way to be "with" their predicament and to understand its structure so that the inte-grative processes can begin, wherever they may lead. It is im-portant for a therapist not to be invested in wanting to change the couple in a preordained direction. My impartiality and lack of investment in a particular outcome was crucial, since the way they had arranged matters would mean that any change was likely to be seen as unfair by one of them. Partners need to be accepted, mirrored, and understood more than advised. A central tenet of Gestalt theory is the phenomenological approach: the process of the therapist being fully present and describing what is seen and heard and experienced rather than interpreting its meaning. Janet and Martin, like many other couples, found this experience as novel as any kind of explicit experiment we engaged in. Heightening awareness in itself can help free up stuck patterns of relating as long as the energy, once freed, can be used for real contact. Their energy was so stuck in anger toward the other that it was not contactful; in fact, it increasingly damaged their hopes and capacity to respect or understand the other. What I thought it had led to was a form of insecurity; they were so deeply enmeshed in their furious demands and counterdemands that they paradoxically could now risk finding some autonomy. In practice, even more paradoxically, they lived very independent lives; this arrangement could give them some scope to begin experimenting with little moments of intimacy. But I had no idea whether they would ever be willing to let go of where they were or tolerate the anxiety of either greater intimacy or separateness. In any case, I told myself, change might be very slow. They had so many developmental lacunae, were inexperienced and unsupported in so many areas of their life. It was important for me to settle back into a patient frame of mind, counterbalancing my (and their) anxious suspicion that they needed everything simultaneously—skills to communicate, unfinished business to complete, understanding of themselves and each other, and time and opportunities to grow a sense of themselves both together and apart. Gestalt therapy is an active and an educative process, a chance to build new lenses through which to see the world—not by taking ideas on trust or by understanding alone but by experiencing in a new way. This novelty is likely to involve the destructuring of self-image and the relinquishing of old cherished lenses; it can feel painful. A few couples come knowing that they risk such pain, and it is gratifying to work with them; they can show us the power of the approach or the therapist at their best. Most clients, like Martin and Janet, require careful support to orient themselves to these ideas.

It is worth stressing that there is nothing objective or fixed in the ideas that a Gestalt therapist works with. Clients are invited to share in the particular learning edge and values of the therapist. The fields of therapist and clients are intrinsically linked. When a couple are in the consulting room, they seem to be the ones that are suffering or benefiting; but as a therapist I cannot take a couple further than I know myself. My toleration of anxiety or excitement affects theirs; their predicaments will evoke mine. I will be confluent with their conservatism if I am timid in those same areas in my life. Insofar as I am committed to a particular understanding of relationship and contact, I will inevitably foster it over other views. Even if I bracket and take care of my concerns with the utmost responsibility, even if I am deeply respectful and centered, there is still no such thing as a value-free intervention or detached position. Far from being a problem to be eradicated, this is a central truth of field theory and Gestalt therapy, and the therapist therefore requires of herself a high level of self-development and self-awareness as well as a willingness to share and make explicit these concerns and values. So I have to take account of the impact of my own framing in an active way. When I saw the "child" in Martin, but without cocreating myself as parent, for example, I often felt compassion. But when I felt myself slip into a less than adult way of construing the world in relation to him, I discovered I could see Martin much as his mother had done—I had moments of exasperation, a desire to control, even to coerce him. I felt highly critical in a generalized way or I wanted him to acknowledge me, a kind of "look what I'm doing for you" position. It was not easy to catch what he had said or done that invited me into this. Obviously these were my feelings and not his mother's, but Martin's familiarity with being experienced in this light set up conditions favorable to my finding that way of configuring myself; it was not how I felt with other clients. I sometimes felt judgmental about Janet too, was frustrated by her implacable self-righteousness, wanted to give up on her, did not experience her as the sacred or vulnerable person she often was. I would muse on how her parents and caretakers may have felt, or find myself suddenly aligned with Martin. I could enrich myself with these speculations and discoveries as long as I saw them as working hypotheses and interpretations open to greater elaboration through phenomenological inquiry. I did not want to add to their sense of injury by further repetition of these powerful self-other configurations.

Another central aspect of Gestalt theory is the notion of polarity, which emphasizes the importance of reenergizing ourselves by attending to what is missing in the field at any particular time, on the principle that whatever we are not aware of does not cease to exist but will inevitably crop up in covert form. Polarities can be seen as a way of simplifying complex field phenomena; by labeling opposing forces experienced within or between people we can make some kind of pattern out of the complexity of the forces in the field. This opens up the possibility of dialogue and play and integration. Since everything in the field is important, playing its part in the particular configuration of the whole, the therapist must pay attention to both sides of any polarity. The function of the therapist is therefore to "hold the whole" while the protagonists hang on to the parts. This way of thinking is central to all our work and directly fuels many of our interventions.

In the first meetings with Martin and Janet what was most urgently missing in their field was any appreciation for how well they were doing. They had no idea of their own virtues and even less of each other's. So I supported and appreciated their energy and passion even though they were hardly enjoying its fruits. I admired their courage in coming and his generosity in paying for her share, highlighted their capacity for hope, congratulated them when they were willing to take any kind of risk or experiment with a new perspective. Even the fact that they were deeply and repetitively stuck I reframed as supportive: how well they protected each other from other more difficult agendas. Given how unspecial they felt in their lives, I did little things to indicate their entitlement to special status—brought them coffee, made flexible arrangements over starting or ending at times that helped them. I modeled in little ways the missing dimension of generosity. Whatever seemed to be most missing at a particular time I gave myself the task to restore to awareness. Thus, when they arrived and were so urgently seeking change, I moved to slow them down, bringing back the missing dimension of measured patience, framing their task in years rather than weeks. As they recounted stories in matter-of-fact tones about deprivations and traumas in their childhoods, I was openly outraged on their behalf. They had very little interest in me; I insisted that we attend to building a relationship. Giving attention to another missing dimension, that of there being more to life than problematic relationships, we took "time off" to talk about politics and the wider world, and to gossip about our lives as parents or workers. I often sat just wondering at them, taking them in, as they rehearsed their arguments to each other. Just occasionally they could take me in too, and this seemed to soften them, like a little sunshine lighting their landscape. I became the first real witness to their relationship, someone who pointed out its durability when they focused on its fragility, and to their vulnerabilities as they hurled boulders of attack at each other.

Holding the wider gestalt involves the therapist in constant reframing. She also needs to notice how a couple give negative or positive loading to their particularly favored polarities; a couple may benefit from fresh perspectives on these same energies or qualities. For instance, Martin came labeling Janet's attitude to money as rigid, constipated, and mean, but he felt differently when he saw those same qualities as orderly and farsighted. She could see his behavior as spontaneous, which she liked, or as irresponsible, which she disapproved of. The lens determines what is seen, and a reframe, which alters the lens, can therefore permit new behavior. Thinking in terms of the multiple polarities that energize the couple will help the therapist, ideally, to be free to move around the entire territory, the life spaces of the couple, between levels and ages: past, present and future, parts of the body, and regions of the field. Depending on what perspective she views as potentially engaging, using a kind of inner map of the whole context of the relationship, she can set up appropriate experiments to heighten awareness and thereby invite new behavior or understanding.

The above describes an aspect of field theory which is intrinsic to Gestalt therapy. Field theory reminds us that everything is potentially relevant and interconnected and that the meaning that we give to events and qualities will always be context dependent; the total field will stretch not only over our whole lives but also over generations past and future. And since a couple have come to see a therapist, the development and profile of marital therapy is also part of their field, as is the complex and changing culture of marriage and divorce. For example, neither Martin nor Janet were contending with the massive disapproval that being unmarried would bring to many couples from other cultural communities. But they were contending with the more pervasive norms about the importance of parents cohabiting. Both felt somehow "wrong" that they were not a geographical unit, though how they related to this norm was unique to them.

Field theory also allows us to adjust the level of magnification of our perceptual lenses. We can move from the wide canvas to the fine detail. On the one hand, there are situations when a couple are well aware of their larger patterns and are better served by completing the issue in hand. But a couple like Martin and Janet who come weighed down by a plethora of seemingly intractable difficulties were helpfully stopped in their tracks by considering what they might be facing if they "solved" all their problems. At one time I asked them to fantasize this. Janet spoke of yawning terror of being a nobody with nothing to cling to. Martin spoke sadly of having to "grow up" and be a man. This question enabled them to move to another perspective; it uncluttered their field of vision in one fell swoop.

I want to outline some of the other core dimensions or polarities that guide my thinking in practice and that were also relevant to my work with Janet and Martin.

Psychopathology versus Sociopathology

Sometimes I have found it helpful to look at the odds stacked against a couple by virtue of societal forces, the parts they are not personally responsible for, almost to deepen their sense of being a statistic. Examples might be the forces of the recession causing undeserved unemployment; the culture of a workplace that demands absurdly long hours or levels of commitment, or a powerful "macho" culture; the lack of institutional support for a single parent or handicapped child; or even the crime level in the neighborhood. These are all examples of pressures that may call for a collective and not only an individual response. The culture's definitions of marriage, the expectations generated about what a marriage is supposed to deliver, are also sociopathic. Looked at in this light, it is society that is sick; a couple may be managing heroically, just as their parents had probably done. An example: the economic recession that hit the region in which Martin's family grew up destroyed the stability of whole communities who depended on a strong male/female divide with men's world being outside the home. Janet's mother had chosen between the extreme poverty of what welfare had to offer after the war and giving away her child once it was clear that her husband would never recover. In later meetings we were able to reach a point where we could celebrate their family's heroism in the face of odds stacked against them, feeling compassion for their parents' predicaments, recognizing that they might not have done any better themselves in those circumstances. It was good to get occasionally to that place, rather than feeling resentment or idealization. Such moments felt almost miraculously peaceful.

But before getting there, we focused for a long time on how they were contributing to staying victimized: how, for instance, Martin had chosen work that demanded such long hours that he wasn't ever available when his little son was awake, and how he discounted other work options; how he kept his home in such a state of shambles that it was not safe to take his son there; how Janet chose to organize her house so that her lodgers shared their living space, and how she had chosen not to do paid work with the result that she was financially dependent on Martin. I was blunt about the fact that these were real choices, asking them to be explicit about what they had discounted. Both Janet and Martin felt uncomfortable experiencing their respective choicefulness, as if they were losing something important in their view of themselves. It was only as they found some meaning and dignity in the tenacity with which both of them had held on to these identities that they began to feel less victimized.

So a couple may be heroic, or they may not have discovered optimal strategies for working the system as best they
can. They may use the truth of societal factors to stay passive.
Our culture, while it stresses individualism and self-reliance,
places very little emphasis on the true self-responsibility and
what it entails. Many couples come wanting to find ways of getting their needs met better by someone else; only a few come
initially willing to undertake the learning and practice necessary
for self-responsibility and personal growth. They are often genuinely ignorant of the very concepts and may need to be taught,
step by step, about the whole notion and language of self-
responsibility. I may make interventions that are therefore
openly directive and educational, teaching clients to make "I"
rather than "you" statements, to say "I feel" rather than "you
make me feel," and to say "I don't want to" rather than "I can't."
This change requires far more than a simple linguistic shift—it
is the manifestation of a radical reorientation in the world.
Learning what we are responsible for and taking ownership of
our feelings and choices is at the heart of Gestalt therapy. This
includes a readiness to relinquish responsibility too, to know
what cannot be changed.

Ideology versus Actuality

Couples I meet always have some kind of set of beliefs. They are
feminists, for example, or left-wing unionists, perhaps orthodox
in their religion, deeply romantic, or committed to a collective
life-style. A few are also full of the ideology of therapy! A shared
ideology is often very supportive of the relationship. It can offer
stability, common goals and reference points, the middle
ground of the relationship that provides a peaceful everyday
space for living. The problem with ideologies is that they also
tend to generate a high level of "oughts" and at times make it
hard for a couple to see what is right under their nose or to
adapt to changing circumstances creatively. At times I want to
challenge these oughts and invite them to unearth the wants
hidden underneath. Couples might benefit from work that
strongly holds their attention on what is rather than what should
be. Perhaps, for example, a woman will then discover she really

prefers to spend more time with her baby uninterrupted by paid work, despite her feminist beliefs that work must not suffer. Or conversely, she may need some kind of paid work to feel content with her role as a mother, even though she believed that babies should never be "abandoned."

At the other end of the polarity I also meet couples who have given very little attention to asking themselves or taking any note of what they really care about and believe in, who have no clear value system to steer by, or who have introjected such laissez-faire attitudes that they get something important from the challenge to come up with some goals that they would like to build on. It is useful for them to ask themselves not only "What am I feeling?" but "Is this what I want in the longer term?" They can take on the challenge to find some integration be-tween immediate and larger needs, and to discover how the truest needs might be satisfied. But it was the former focus that was relevant to Janet and Martin.

Martin was an outspoken socialist and advocate of the growing men's movement in Britain, which supported his long-ings to feel like a "man"—someone strong and respected and fought for, a model for his son. In practice he expected to be served and looked after, and he often felt rejected by, bored, and impatient with a small child's needs. He took no exercise, ate poorly, and looked rather "feminine." His engagement with politics was more at the level of theory than practice. Janet's feminism, strongly articulated, was contradicted by her behav-ior, which showed, for instance, that she felt that only women could really be trusted with children. Despite wanting him to share in child care, she hovered over him if he tried to change a diaper or engage in a game with his son, criticizing every move he made. Janet and Martin became more aware of such contra-dictions that could be highlighted cognitively but not changed by thought alone; they were the reflection of fixed gestalts, stuck energy patterns, rather than of poor thinking. It was only as they slowly shifted away from a vision of themselves as depleted and oppressed toward a vision of fullness and even some surplus that their interpretations of these belief systems shifted too. When Janet felt safer, less "empty" inside, her version of feminism in-cluded his more active involvement in child care. And Martin

actually changed his appearance as he saw himself as less oppressed; he looked more manly and took care of his appearance
better—stopped oppressing himself, in fact.

Systemic versus Individual

Gestalt therapy has traditionally tended to place a strong emphasis on contact between client and therapist. It calls for a different skill to see the couple as a system and to focus on their
contact with each other. One person, for example, is dominant,
but how exactly does the other collude in this state of affairs?
One complains forcefully and the other deflects. All contact is
interaction; both parties are completely implicated. Exploring
how behaviors fit together has the potential for ending the
racket of blaming and taking sides; because the focus is on mutual process rather than content, the therapist is less likely to get
snarled up in the hopelessly subjective problems of who is right
or wrong. If I ever get caught in taking on being judge or jury,
which many couples want, I am in trouble. Paradoxically, when
the focus on content can be shifted onto process, there is sometimes enough freshness of outlook for an individual to see content in a new way, even to be willing to experience remorse. But
content is so seductive; it can lead the therapist to responses that
can only be based on countertransference, however beautifully
dressed up as wisdom. Solutions based on content fail also to
support the couple in any future conflicts because they are not
learning how they manage to get stuck but only that a therapist
can unstick them, an expensive solution. When I first met Martin and Janet, they spent most of their time together blaming
and defending; they were brilliant polemicists and dedicated to
their lists of complaints and specific events in their lives. So, in
keeping with my focus on what was missing, what they were
not attending to, I looked at the energy and engagement they
brought to bear on their quarrels. I looked systematically at the
"how" of their fighting rather than the "why." Awareness building at the level of energy interchange of the couple can be powerful. I would say things like "When either one of you pays the
other a compliment I see the other discount it," or I'd point out

how he disappeared as she attacked. I once likened them to two thermos flasks, alternating between hot and cold. It was a metaphor they liked and developed; it encouraged them to look together at how they kept their insulating process going, but humorously, which usually makes difficult learning more bearable.

Another way of addressing couples systemically is to ask them to undertake a shared task in the room with me, aimed at either helping them discover or restore their fund of their common ground, or to encourage differentiation and spice things up with a little open disagreement. Couples can neither flourish nor separate properly without believing in themselves and having some basic self-respect. Janet and Martin needed more common ground as well as self-respect, since they had eroded so much of what they once had. So I invited them to tell each other in turn something they appreciated rather than criticized about the other. It could be about whatever they chose—each other's parenting skills or appearance, enjoyable kinds of time off together, beliefs they shared, skills, attitudes, capacities they admired. They were encouraged to receive these "gifts" in silence rather than immediately answering each other. It helped them take in what the other said, rather than absorb themselves by rehearsing what they were going to say next. Slowing down habitual responses can provide a "chewing" period that avoids either wholesale interjecting or spitting out. They also practiced the vitally useful skill of reflecting back to one another beliefs, complaints, and desires, getting coaching from each other in seeing each other's point of view. This was laborious but illuminating.

Another important systemic activity focused on exploring and experimenting with their characteristic energetic and physical stances as they argued or discussed. In coping with past and present criticism and abandonment, both Martin and Janet had desensitized themselves to their experiences of hurt, but their bodies still reflected these wounds. His face was often contorted into a grimacing kind of clenched-teeth grin, his voice quiet and sounding ground down, his body curled up as if he was trying to fit into a small but highly charged space. She usually sat up rigid and prim, her voice evenly shrill and emphatic. I sometimes stopped them and invited them to study themselves and each other—to "freeze" a moment and deepen their awareness of their bodies, of what "holding in" they experienced. Just drawing attention to this would subtly shift their energy; they could feel the familiarity of what they did. This would change the dialogue just a little, shift the dynamics. Even more interesting were experiments where they assumed each other's physical positions and explored the unfamiliar but additional perspectives these seemed to provide. Janet tried whining; Martin became schoolmarmishly upright. Their dialogue opened up. I also asked them to tell each other very specific changes they wanted from each other that they believed would build their hopes and trust. When they experienced being given what they said they wanted, we would stop and explore their many negative responses—but reframe them as the fear of anxiety of their self-image shifted. For example, when Martin gave her more money, instead of being pleased Janet focused on it not being enough, or on the awfulness of her financial dependence on him. When she shooed the lodgers out of their living space, Martin complained even more vociferously about being relegated to the box room to sleep. I would explore and make understandable their anxieties about losing their deeply held self-images and would encourage them to continue experimenting. They discovered old family rules and powerful introjects that interfered with their capacity to receive pleasure, ones they themselves were responsible for; they could not continue to blame the other so easily.

But to return to the other side of the polarity: seeing the couple not as a single entity but as two individuals. Set against the important vision of working with the couple systemically, there are strong arguments for doing the opposite at times. It can be invaluable to undertake a major piece of therapeutic work with one person in the presence of the other and to work on separating out their issues, helping them really see each other beyond their usual projections. The witnessing partner may deepen compassion for the one who is willing to explore an important issue with the therapist, maybe entering states of great vulnerability assisted by the therapist's modeling of another response and protected from the immediacy of the partner's habitual one.

I have been inspired in this work by Hunter Beaumont's writing on couples therapy (in this volume), which emphasizes the violation of self-responsibility and betrayal of self that comes from believing that another has the power to deliver or prevent our own wholeness. He speaks of the sacrifice of "I-Thou" in the attempt to get regressive needs met, elaborating this experience as "loss of self," when what couples fight over can feel like life and death issues, when the "I" and the "other" become "locked in a tragic dance of negative mutual creation." His work involves actively entering into the pain of self-loss, phenomenologically, and consists of individual work in the presence of the other. It is another way of relating to the central polarity that all couples face: that between unconditional love and an instrumental view of the other (I-Thou versus I-It); and between fusion with the other versus a separate sense of self. Every couple veers at times between confluence, loyalty, commitment, desire for stability, and familiarity of habits that allow a sufficient middle ground to develop, a "rest from alertness," and the fear of engulfment or abandonment, the need for separateness and individuality, the excitement of the unpredictable, the heightening of the difference, and the desire for strong boundaries. So the therapist, in keeping with her task of holding the widest gestalt, may need to attend not only to developing their awareness of themselves as a couple but equally to their individual needs and processes.

There were some individual explorations with Martin and Janet about key issues that made an impact on the course of our time together. For instance, I spent a long time following through what Martin meant by longing to be a man. He elaborated a vision of having tremendous physical force, of being able to shout; we constructed restorative experiments that led to his remembering being a tiny boy who had longed to be enjoyed as a male by his parents, and having "agreed" to be somehow neuter so as not to frighten them. It was precious for him to be witnessed and recognized in his feelings of rebellion and of placation. Afterwards he recaptured moments when he had felt accepted and what that felt like somatically, how he experienced the world when he was in that state. And with such knowledge notched into his body, supported by a different way of configuring himself, he completed some archaic communications with his parents though not with the elderly couple he sometimes visited. He recognized that the son he had once been was not equipped to protect them from themselves nor could he now get what he wanted from them. After one such event Janet was deeply moved by his vulnerability and suffering; she reached out toward him with great tenderness. It opened the door to her memories of her father and her terror of his occasional rampages before he was finally hospitalized. She understood better her terror of Martin becoming more "manly" if it were to involve chaotic noise and violence and could see that his version of maleness was not the same as her father's. Martin was able to listen momentarily without feeling victimized. I encouraged them to spend a long time talking together about what the episode had been like for each of them, what they had discovered. Telling each other, rather than telling me, intensified the value they could get from the experience and increased their sense of connectedness further. They described feeling an actual bodily shift, no longer so tense and defended.

Janet was much more ambivalent about having the focus on her, though she could report the "magic" of getting attention when she did allow it. Since her key issues related to her home, we undertook a long exploration of what being in charge of her house meant for her, of what it felt like in her body when she faced losing control of "home." She could relate this to childhood feelings, her experience of homelessness. But rather than focus on the past, which she disapproved of, we shifted from the figure of homelessness to what must also be somewhere in the ground, her active fantasy of being safely "at home." Here she could focus on and develop her somatic awareness of this precious experience. Configuring the world in that way, she was able to allow in fantasy some incursions into her fortress from Martin. More respectful of both her terror and her generosity, though no less adamant that he wanted to be seen as safe and let in, Martin increased his financial contribution to her household soon afterwards.

We once explored Martin's no longer so hidden delight

in resistance; he even got playful enough to exaggerate it, find his maverick saboteur. I invited him to expand his saboteur's range, whereupon he found more energy and voice ("When I walk past the unwashed dishes and 'sit it out' until you've done them I feel excited—I've won!") He had a moment of sudden and excruciating sorrow (remorse), immediately sabotaged by Janet's triumphant "I told you so." I used myself as a kind of Geiger counter to track this process—how I'd felt my energy rising, a peak of excitement, and then a rapid shutdown. Martin reported the shutdown as painful, and Janet reported her excitement as unnerving. I followed this by asking if Janet was interested in exploring her postural rigidity as she sat feeling "unnerved." After a long pause she talked about feeling invisible. Would she be willing to become more visible now, rather than audible? They melted into a brief and delicious giggle as she wiggled her body provocatively at Martin. She was taken aback by feeling tearful as she straightened up again into her "prim" invisibility. How old did she feel at the moment? She talked about the taboos on provocativeness in her adopted family. Martin's delight in seeing her playful offered her a powerful counterintrojective force, a moving inroad into their limited repertoire of contact. A little later in the session Martin spoke of being glad she hadn't "wiggled" any longer; he had also felt disquieted by her sexuality. She immediately reassured him by saying she'd only wanted to be noticed, not to "do" anything sexual. He relaxed, visibly. Martin remembered his childhood mother in a new dress, how "hungrily" she had looked to him for affirmation. This was a beautifully helpful reformulation of what he had previously seen as her undifferentiated hostility and disappointment in him, and by extension his father. We were in a slowed-down time frame together, shuttling between past and present configurations of reality, between following their process and interrupting it in a little space we had made where the usual rules of combat were relaxed. I enjoyed this fluidity, admired their receptivity to each other, told them so, no longer needing to be the only one to feel compassion and connectedness. Such work involves inviting clients to work with archaic ways of configuring their reality and to allow in fresh possibilities that may lie unattended to in the field. When they lead to alternating individual work and real dialogue, it allows a welcome move from polemics to contact.

We can see from these examples how Gestalt therapy emphasizes contact in the context of the entire gestalt, honoring what needs to be common ground and shared between the participants. It encourages us to explore how differently a couple will have experienced key issues in such a way that they may genuinely come to understand each other's perspective. To do this may mean ranging deep into their childhood, even those of their parents, exploring their family orientation as well as their national and cultural assumptions. It can take the form of "talking about" something, creating a narrative of the past, and yet it is essential in creating the conditions for healthy immediacy. Our deepest stories are multigenerational, awesomely complex, and always relevant. A commonly understood ground must be the basis for meaningful contact. What is apparently figural is not necessarily helpful. It may be easier to resolve a conflict by accessing some part of the field which at that moment is completely out of their awareness. This was certainly the case in the work just described. Both Martin and Janet remembered and restored valuable states that allowed them fresh ways of connecting. These individually witnessed pieces of work, when they were possible, not only deepened compassion and safety but helped them see how different they were, both from each other and from the children they had been and the parents they had had. They could resource themselves with new knowledge of their present capacities, recognize the archaic nature of some of their longings. My intention was to help them find resources within themselves rather than continue the fruitless battle to be rescued by the other, though paradoxically they had more to offer each other as a result, not least in simple liking and respect.

There is no definitive "outcome" to this or, in my belief, any therapy. Having a third person join the couple for a while is only one of so many other factors in their lives; how can its specific impact be calibrated? After some months I noticed that Martin spoke less often of leaving; he began yoga classes and stood up for himself more at work. He got more support from

Janet, who criticized him less about tired old issues. She said she could no longer imagine pushing him out completely; she took a part-time job and "gave" Martin more time with their son at weekends. They resumed an intermittent sexual relationship. But their overall style was still cantankerous and often bitter and righteous. They still felt frequently at the mercy of what they perceived as the other's shortcomings. They were often wary of "going into all this stuff" that therapy seemed to relentlessly require of them. After a while they had good reason in terms of work schedules to stop coming and they said a (perhaps temporary) good-bye. I count this as a "good enough" experience. They'd had enough—I imagined they would take time to chew on their experience, assimilate its meanings and possibilities, continue to do battle between fixed gestalts and new still alarming but exciting perspectives. Perhaps they were aware they liked what they had a little more, knowing at some level of awareness that despite protestations to the contrary they didn't want further major change—they might take up the adventure later when the field conditions shifted again. Most relationships have this stop-start sort of quality. We stop to build support, regroup, and attend to something else. That is part of the process, congruent with my own personal experience and the observations of others.

Since I have had no follow-up to these sessions with Martin and Janet, I do not know whether they are now more together or more apart, nor do I know what course of action would be most appropriate for them in the long or short run. It may seem obvious to state, but there is no actual "closure," so emphasized in Gestalt theory, to life other than the end of life. So when can participants assess the quality of what they have achieved? I emphasize this quandary because there is a bias that has often crept into the presentation of what is characteristically Gestalt work but that is not actually intrinsic to the theory of Gestalt. This bias has led to an emphasis on excitement, growth, individualism, progress, closure, expression, sensation, and spontaneity. Although these might be valuable emphases in certain circumstances in couples therapy (as in any kind of therapy), a therapist might want to attach importance to the very opposite of these values: the value of communality over individuality, of a long-term value over an immediate desire, the possible value of low energy or even of depression, the recognition that there may be no immediate closure, the importance of letting go, decay as opposed to growth, cyclical change rather than progress, the usefulness of being able to hold back on self-expression, and the value of self-reflection, conscious egotism, and retroflection. This is in keeping with the larger argument of this chapter: that of working with and holding what is missing or being avoided, of seeing beyond all polarities. We all need access to everything, the whole range of ways of being; any reaction will only seem healthy or unhealthy according to circumstances. In truth, neither therapist nor couple can ever know enough about those to determine what is appropriate for themselves or another. However little, it has to be enough to have offered a couple the opportunity to open up their field of vision and increase their range of choice.

3

Self-Organization and Dialogue[1]

Hunter Beaumont

When I think about a Gestalt couples therapy, I think about actual people I've worked with; I see their faces, I hear their voices. For the most part, they are good people, sincere, capable of love and hope, willing to work hard in therapy. They come to therapy because they are caught in a cycle of disappointed hopes, of hurt and anger, and they know that they are destroying their love for one another in spite of their good intentions.

I have been working to understand these people's processes for a long time, first as a bewildered adolescent trying to come to terms with my own life and later as a trainee and therapist. I suspect that the people I will describe, if treated in the context of individual psychoanalytically oriented psychotherapy, would be diagnosed as character disorders, or preferably, as disorders of the self. In Gestalt terms, they are people who may be capable of good contact, but who are vulnerable to sudden and severe breakdown of their contact functions in some situations of intimacy or stress. The combination of their episodes of contact disruption and their intense yearning for something better makes their relationships and their therapy difficult, and both partners and therapists may lose courage.

Rather than analyze single foregrounds of contact, I will argue that successful therapeutic work with these couples requires attention to a specific "sense of self" (Stern, 1985) that gives continuity to experience over time and in a variety of situations. (This is of course consistent with Wheeler's recent [1991] plea for attention to the structured ground.) This specific sense of self may be conceptualized as arising out of a process of holistic and systemic or "organismic" self-organization.[2] Martin Buber's "I-Thou" philosophy offers a beautiful language for understanding the phenomenology of this sense of self. It also lends color and richness to our understanding of the phenomenology of these people; its depth and existential scope are an antidote to the flip deflections of some love-phobic Gestaltists. His focus is not on pathology, but on the universal structures of relationship, the forms that organize the field of "betweenness" separating and connecting humans. Under his gaze, the couples I will describe assume dignity and magnitude; their sometimes trivial bickerings become the sounds of the human soul struggling for its own fulfillment. Although Buber's importance for Gestalt therapy is generally accepted, the *theoretical* relationship between his "I-Thou" and Gestalt concepts such as the fertile void, organismic self-organization, and contact has not yet been completely worked out (see Jacobs, 1989; also Hycner, 1985, 1990, for some initial attempts; I am sure they will both agree that much remains to be done).

In attempting to develop a theoretical understanding of these couples, I have followed Paul Goodman's contextual method (Perls, Hefferline, & Goodman, 1951, p. 243ff), bringing various different views into the field together, enduring the resulting discordance, and trusting that a new and pregnant gestalt will emerge. It's a little like cooking soup; at first, there are just the vegetables and the bits of bird floating around. With skill and good ingredients and enough heat, it can become delicious. Each new ingredient in the pot changes the soup, opens new observations, changes the flavors of old assumptions, changes the way I see and interact with these clients. Because they are "seen" differently, the couples themselves respond differently than they would have had they seen me earlier in my career. Accepting the subjectivity of experience and its enmeshment in the hermeneutic circle of lenses controlling our vision,

I relinquish any claim to objective truth. I do not argue that things are as I describe them, only that they can be seen to be so. It is my hope that the perspective I attempt to describe here will have some usefulness for others struggling with these processes with clients or in their personal lives.

The Phenomenology of These Relationship Systems

Psychotherapeutic phenomenology (Spinelli, 1989), working close to the patient's own experience, is one of the most beautiful aspects of Gestalt therapy, but difficult to master. For one thing, the patients' phenomenology changes from moment to moment as well as during the course of the therapy. For another, the therapist's implicit theoretical assumptions (in the hermeneutic circle) act as a lens actually changing his or her perception of their phenomenology. Viewed through my particular Gestalt therapy lens, three aspects of these couples' phenomenology stand out: Loss of Self, Longing for the Self-Organizing Self, and Betrayal of Self.[3]

Loss of Self

Most of these couples have good times together, periods when they function together as a couple very well. Yet as the therapist listens to their complaints with an ear tuned to process phenomenology, she or he hears them describing periods of extreme contact disruption, times when communication goes wrong and things are said and done that wound and destroy. These are the times of raging or of cold withdrawal. Usually they call these periods "fights." Nathan Schwartz-Salant (1982) calls them "emotional thunderstorms," and Johnson (1984) goes further, coining the term *minipsychosis*. Mostly they just hurt one another, repeating lines that they both know by heart, like two old actors doing a vaudeville routine for the one-thousandth time. The fights bring no new clarification, no new insight, just a familiar destructiveness. During these fights, they do not contact well. One may rage while the other stares helplessly at the floor, silently wondering what to say, wondering how long this must be endured, mouth and mind strangely disconnected. (Tomorrow she or he will think of many excellent things which could have been said.) Or they may shout with a certain fury, saying with conviction things that, in a different mood, they know to be untrue. There are promises and threats too, which in the light of day seem grotesquely exaggerated: promises of revenge, threats of separation and abandonment. And there may be times of violence when control breaks and their frustrations seek physical expression.

Although they have repeated these fights and forgiven one another a hundred times, each time a little something of the relationship dies, and forgiveness gradually becomes cautious, reluctant, tinged with mistrust and fear; the scars thicken, become more visible. Often they have become afraid to talk with one another, afraid that a word or gesture or tone of voice will start one of these episodes, will trigger a fight that is destructive and changes nothing for the better. Often they have withdrawn from one another and from life. Here, many have been additionally hurt by therapists who encouraged "getting the feelings out," falsely believing such feelings to be "truth," or that their expression could start the gestalt cycle moving once again toward resolution.

(From the perspective recommended here, such feelings are the product of a contact disturbance, and therefore, although they are phenomenologically actual for the person involved, they are still not "real" in some absolute sense. Such feelings invariably have to do with unfinished situations from the past and do not belong primarily to the partnership. Thus "getting them out" can bring an emotional catharsis for one of the pair, usually at the expense of the other, but it does not build communication in relationship; often it is abusive, confusing the partner with persons from the past. In contrast to contactful anger, which can bring constructive communication and closure, or the cathartic expression of rage in individual therapy to help people reaccess long-repressed behaviors and finish situations from the past, in couples therapy the expression of these rages damages, wounds, and destroys love. In working with couples I have become so convinced of the destructiveness of contactless emotionality associated with fragile self-organization that I usually intervene to stop it.)

If you have personally experienced one of these episodes or are skilled in listening phenomenologically to your clients' descriptions, you will know how these periods "feel" from the inside. One woman described her experience:

> I feel like I come apart. Something in me closes up, something in my body near my heart or my solar plexus. As soon as that happens, I know that it's all over. I know that I'll never get through to [my husband]. Something happens to my eyes and I can't look at him anymore. I can't think of anything to say. I just want him to go away, I want him to leave me alone until I get right again. Sometimes he just keeps talking at me, boring into me, interrogating me until I explode and say something terrible to get him to stop. I hate him at these times, really hate him. I can't even remember the good times we had.

Her husband spoke of his experience:

> [My wife] is so hard sometimes. I want to be close, maybe to make love and she says something which hurts, or gets interested in something else or she just ignores me. That makes me hurt and angry because I think she is doing it on purpose to hurt me. She can be so caring for other people and for the kids, but when I need something, she pushes me away. I try to tell her what I'm feeling, sometimes I get angry. Sometimes I hurt her feelings and she cries or explodes and breaks things. I feel strange at these times, far away and cold. My feeling dries up and I know how cruel I really can be.

They see these times as episodes in which "I'm not myself anymore." This is the Loss of Self. The "I" of these times is somehow different from the normal "I," and actions that seem perfectly justifiable at such times may be very difficult to live with later. As one man put it, "It's like I'm possessed by a demon who makes me do things I don't like to do. Later, when the storm has passed, I feel ashamed at what I have destroyed, as if I have betrayed myself—like Dr. Jekyll after Mr. Hyde had passed." The following report of the Loss of Self is especially interesting since it came during the first session from a woman without previous therapy experience. As this woman's "I" shifts, her perceived world shifts too, and both she and her husband have difficulty remembering what is good about the other. The Loss of Self is also the loss of "other."

> I can't stand it when [my husband] doesn't trust me. It hurts too much. Something in me dies. I get so threatened, as if I'm fighting for my life. I become a gutter rat, a New York gutter rat, or one of the alligators that the people in New York flush down their toilets and that live in the sewer. I bite and I scratch. I'm a wild animal. But I'm fighting for my life. It hurts my heart so bad when he doesn't trust me.

We see plainly that such shifts of identity are subjectively a matter of life and death. It is a source of great shame for these couples that they are so vulnerable to sudden shifts in the quality of their contact, that very small "triggers" can produce such dramatic changes in their sense of self. A word or a certain look or a tone of voice is often enough to precipitate one of these reactions, reactions of a magnitude far beyond what might be appropriate to the cause.

A therapist skilled in the art of phenomenological tracking or *clean language* (Grove & Panzer, 1991) can help these couples to "stay with" their phenomenology, supporting them to consult deeply the experiences they try so hard to avoid. Very often in the course of therapy, having mastered the technique of middle-mode awareness (that is, of phenomenological tracking), they succeed in entering the experience of Loss of Self. They describe powerful experiences of confusion and inner emptiness, of profound loneliness, of the abyss, of a vast whirlpool or gyre of spinning blackness into which they might fall (Almaas, 1986; Beaumont, 1988a, 1988b). In the existential and phenomenological literature (Spinelli, 1989) this phenomenology has been discussed in terms of fear of death, loneliness, nausea, and existential anxiety. In the language we are using here, it is the Loss of Self. Fritz Perls called it the "fertile void" (Perls, 1973).

Much of the literature of existentialism, which purports to be studies of the phenomenology of this nothingness, is in reality the study of the phenomenology of *refusing to enter* this experience. Time and again, patients who learn to enter their own confusion using middle-mode awareness discover that the phenomenology changes. One example is the experience of a fourteen-year-old patient who had recurring nightmares of being chased by a wolf. One night he thought while dreaming, "I'm dreaming. The wolf is in my dream. In my dream he can't hurt me at all. He can even eat me if he wants to." With this thought, he turned in the dream to face the wolf, which changed to become an inner guide of great value in dealing with problems. This phenomenon will be familiar to many Gestalt therapists.

Long for the Self-Organizing Self

If one major aspect of clients' phenomenology is the Loss of Self, another is an intense Longing for the Self-Organizing Self. At the beginning of therapy, many of them do not have the skill to formulate clear and comprehensive statements of their wants and needs. They say things like "I just want to be happy" or perhaps, "I don't feel understood." Many want their partner to be different, believing that the new and better partner would bring happiness. Some couples describe their wants in terms of material security, or fulfillment of sexual desires, or wishes for family and a feeling of home, for "warmth" or "closeness," "being seen," and paradoxically, "just to be left alone." But even when these particular wants are fulfilled, there remains a quality of something missing. As one woman put it, "If this is all life is, I don't want it."

Their sense of missing something may be almost physical, a pain or pressure in the center of the chest or a gnawing in the stomach. Many have experienced such strong pains in the area of the heart that they went for a medical examination fearing a physical illness. At the beginning of therapy, the discomfort of this phenomenology is so great that few are able to explore their experience carefully. Generally, they just want the negative feelings to go away, and it requires patience and therapeutic skill to help them explore the hope implied in their suffering.

Paradoxically, their frustration and anger confirm their hope. If we listen to their demands and complaints phenomenologically, with a "gestalt ear,"[4] we can hear them describing with some accuracy what they long for, the hope behind the need. As they develop the ability to explore the phenomenology of hope more carefully, they often discover that their awareness of their needs changes. What they believed to be sexual need or desire, professional ambition, love of company, and longing for a relationship were all, at least in part, the "means whereby" to achieve an *experience* of "being really me." They may develop the patience and skill to delay acting out long enough to undertake a thorough phenomenological exploration of their experience. One man, a poet already skilled in observing his inner process, described a condition of Being in which he would feel whole and alive, the "gnawing hunger of his heart would be stilled," and he would feel "complete," "just being me, really me." However awkwardly they may express it, they hope for an inner sense of well-being, a wholeness or solidity that allows them to release joy and their deepest laughter. They talk about subtle, longed-for sensations in the physical or "energetic" body, about a sexual orgasm in which something in them "opens" and the whole body "flows." This is the hope for "me," for the real self (Masterson, 1985). Without this hope, there would be no frustration, anger, or longing. For reasons that I hope will become clear below, I have termed the longed-for experience "Self-Organizing Self."

This point deserves additional clarification. In Gestalt work that is informed by the need- fulfillment model, patients are encouraged to get their needs met, usually through enhancing their aggression. The implication is that what they need is in the environment. In a couple relationship, the assumption is that the partner has what is missing. But if the need is a need for more stable self-organization, this assumption is false. Therapeutic work that aims to help them "get their needs met" paradoxically strengthens the dependency and the contact disturbance of the people we are discussing by confirming the false belief that the missing quality is in the environment and not in the self. They are thus not supported in deepening their understanding of their "needs," but rather in the mistaken fantasy that if their needs were met from the outside, they would not be feeling pain and discomfort. Such needs-oriented Gestalt work is contraindicated for these couples. Rather, the position I am arguing for encourages them to explore the phenomenology of their experience, seeking to deepen awareness before they prematurely try to make the painful experience go away. The "need," according to this perspective, is the need for a better self-organization, which at least at this point in development is a function of the organism itself. At most, the partner can contribute to a supportive environment for the development of this capacity for a self-gestalting self.

Betrayal of Self

As they deepen their awareness of their own phenomenology in the course of the therapy, couples often uncover a profound misunderstanding: the expectation that the partner's love could or should prevent the experience of Loss of Self and restore the Self-Organizing Self without diminishing autonomy. They believe that the environment (their partner) has what they want, and to meet their needs they must get him or her to give it. Their false expectation is based on a misunderstanding of the nature of the phenomenology of the Loss of Self.

One man described how he expected his partner to be the door to paradise, to love him so much that he would be happy, freed from his neurotic compulsions and his inhibitions. He was convinced that his wife could have done that for him if she had wanted to. When she didn't, he was hurt and angry. "If you really loved me, you'd help my hurt." Having neither the ex-

perience of a Self-Organizing Self nor the skill safely to ride out
the emotional storms of Loss of Self, he depended upon his
wife's love to restore him to himself when his sense of self frag-
mented. His dependency upon her was profoundly destructive
to them both, for it rigidly defined their roles and robbed them
of flexibility to respond freely to one another. Depending upon
his wife to prevent the experience of Loss of Self, which he
could not tolerate, he gave her the power of subjective life and
death over him.

Most of these couples have an implicit belief that what
they yearn for can only be given by another person. (It is true
that we may experience these states of well-being in moments
of great intimacy and sexual intensity, but it is not true that
they may only be experienced when our partners treat us as we
demand.) Their false belief violates the Gestalt value of self-
responsibility, insisting that "you must change" so that "I"
have less pain and more satisfaction. They confuse the end
goal (having a sense of being themselves through better self-
organization) with one possible "means whereby" (getting the
partner to give them what they believe they need). In so doing,
they devote their primary efforts to getting the partner to
change. They frequently suspend their attempts to understand
more deeply what is missing, and they suspend their efforts to develop other means to the same end, slowly abandoning their
freedom to develop alternatives, turning their partner into an instrument for avoiding the emotional pain of intentionally entering into and understanding the experience of Loss of Self. In this
misunderstanding there is neither freedom to give (since love is
demanding) nor freedom to receive, for receiving confirms dependency and gives the partner the power of life and death.

Unable to maintain a stable sense of self and to explore
the phenomenology of emptiness, they make their relationship
into a stabilizing instrument. The tragedy of these couples is
that in instrumentalizing their "betweenness" to avoid the terror of Loss of Self, they betray their freedom to participate with
awareness in their own becoming, making the Self-Organizing
Self all but impossible. Their relationships become battlegrounds in which they wrestle with one another, trying to con-

ceal the handicaps of their dependency, trying to get "needs" met without losing too much autonomy. In such a relationship, separation is a terrifying perspective, for when the partner leaves, one of the most important stabilizing elements of the self leaves too. Loss of the partner is subjectively equivalent to death. This dependency has been termed Betrayal of Self.

Of course, the phenomenology of Loss of Self, of Longing for the Self-Organizing Self, and of Betrayal of Self is not a complete phenomenology of such couples. Nevertheless, it seems to me that it is an essential aspect of their relationships and suggests a possible shift for Gestalt therapy theoretical thinking. These three phenomena seem to be asking us to shift our therapeutic attention from the issue of single episodes of contact with the environment toward the larger issue of organization of the self and its accompanying "sense of self." The problem of these couples is not primarily poor contact between organism and environment (they are often capable of excellent contact), but rather that their Self-Organizing-Self system is not stable through time. For them the conceptual model of a phenomenologically given "organism" that regulates itself via contact with its environment is inappropriate. Their "sense of self" is neither stable nor identical with their physical organism.

This argument parallels the divergence between ego-psychology, self-psychology, and object relations on the one side, with classical psychoanalytic drive theory on the other. Freud assumed a well-formed ego in conflict with its environment. The ego-psychologists challenged this assumption, arguing that many disturbances can only be understood by examining deficits in the formation of the ego. Not all people have a well-formed ego that can come in conflict with its environment. It is strange that much Gestalt work tacitly follows the older Freudian model as reflected in the widespread idea in Gestalt that the "organism" contacts its environment in order to fulfill its needs: hence, "organismic self-regulation." Here too, the "organism" is just biologically given; there is no conceptual means of investigating how the organism organizes itself. The idea of a self-organizing organism thus brings the Gestalt model up to date.

It may help us here to examine Martin Buber's description of this phenomenology before considering some of the theoretical implications.

Buber's Dialogic Perspective

Relationship, according to Buber, requires both separation and connection, that is, "betweenness." He speaks of two possibilities in the "betweenness," two "primary sentences" that may be "spoken." The act of speaking either of these phrases "gestalts" or organizes both the "I" that speaks and the "other" to whom it speaks. The two primary sentences are relationships, "I-It" and "I-Thou."

The first of these sentences, the interaction that Buber calls "I-It," is the *common* type of interaction: eating food, moving rocks, splitting wood, selling cars, scolding children, falling in love, talking about problems. All of these have a quality of manipulating objects, of using things, of *commerce*. (Yes, even the beloved is an object in this sense, for she or he is present in our experience as "other" or as "not-I.") Buber speaks of "instrumental" or goal-oriented relationships. Thus to speak the sentence "I-It" is to enter into the world of the many, of separated objects, the world of "using and experiencing." As such, it characterizes the greater part of human interactions and is indispensable to life. However, the "I" of this sentence is an "I" that "uses" and "experiences," and is used and experienced in turn, one object in a world of objects.

The second primary sentence that humans can speak is the sentence "I-Thou." In speaking this sentence, both "I" and "Thou" move into a dimension of meeting where the gap that separates is closed and each is as close to the other as to himself or herself. In a more psychological language, we might speak of a mode of consciousness in which a primary relatedness transcends the usual subject-object separation. For Buber, the speaking of this sentence is the act of love. It also is the act of self-creation. The "I" of this sentence is different from the "I" of the sentence "I-It." The "I" of this second sentence does not experience itself as an "I" that uses and experiences or that is used and experienced, nor does it experience its "Thou" as a thing to be used or experienced. Buber describes the "I-Thou" as being a "participatory relationship" of "I" and "Thou." Participating in the *Being* of another, one cannot instrumentalize the other. Thus "I-Thou" excludes the possibility of approaching the partner expecting a need to be filled. That would be speaking the sentence "I-It," and does not reflect the full human possibility of participatory relationship.

This "I-Thou" moment must be carefully distinguished from transference phenomena and confluence. Not infrequently these couples come into therapy because one or the other has "fallen in love" with someone else. In the state of being in love, they feel confident that their new lover will fill their needs, that they need not experience abandonment, loneliness, or the Loss of Self. One way of distinguishing between a true "I-Thou" moment and confluence or transference is that the "I-Thou" moment *heals*; it comes unexpectedly, goes quickly, leaving behind a particular sense of peace and balance. In contrast to confluence and transference states, there is no sense of wanting or of needing, just the experienced meeting.

Buber, although specifically acknowledging the developmental and pathological possibilities in human relationships, moves the "I-Thou" beyond the limitations of pathology, suggesting that the yearning our couples describe is more than a regressive wish for the mother or merely the yearning for a "mirroring object." For Buber, it is the longing for a human soul, the hope to become a Self-Organizing Self expressing itself in an "I-Thou" relationship. The unborn child

> does not rest only in the womb of the human mother. Yet this connection has such a cosmic quality that the mythical saying of the Jews, "in the mother's body man knows the universe, in birth he forgets it," reads like the imperfect decipherment of an inscription from earliest times. And it remains indeed in man as a secret image of desire. Not as though his yearning meant a longing to return, as those suppose who see in the spirit—confusing it with their intellect—a parasite of nature,

when it is rather nature's best flower. But the yearning is for the cosmic connection, with its true Thou,
of this life that has burst forth into spirit.

Every child that is coming into being rests, like all
life that is coming into being, in the womb of the
great mother, the undivided primal world that
precedes form. From her, too, we are separated,
and enter into personal life, slipping free only in
the dark hours to be close to her again; night by
night this happens to the healthy man. (Buber,
1958, p. 25)

As I understand Buber, the emptiness and the lack of
wholeness of which our couples complain is the result of not
speaking the sentence "I-Thou." Thus their yearning for relationship is not just the longing to get their "needs" for closeness
and warmth *filled*. It is rather the longing to *speak* the sentence
"I-Thou." It is the yearning to achieve full "I" by actively entering into a relationship with "Thou." For Buber, the full human
self exists only in and through the "I-Thou" relationship.
     The shifts of mood and sense of self, the rages and lone-
liness that these couples know so well, may be understood in
terms of loss of the "Thou." Buber has made it clear that the sentence "I-Thou" establishes full humanness, or in psychological
terms, "self." He also writes, "But this is the exalted melancholy
of our fate, that every Thou in our world must become an It. . . .
The It is the eternal chrysalis, the Thou the eternal butterfly"
(Buber, 1958, p. 17). If speaking the sentence "I-Thou" satisfies
the longing for a full sense of self, speaking the sentence "I-It"
breaks it. The "I" of the sentence "I-Thou" shrinks, becoming
the "I" of the sentence "I-It," and enters into the separated world
of object relations. In this movement it dies to one relationship
and is born to another more limited relationship. Sometimes
this movement actually may feel like death, for it is the loss of
the "I" that was created in speaking "I-Thou." Certainly it is the
ground of loneliness and of the void. The "exalted melancholy
of our fate" is that we must suffer this repeated reduction of the
"I" from "I-Thou" to "I-It." It is a basic quality of human exis-

tence that we cannot hold on to the moment of "I-Thou" but must yield before the inevitability of becoming the "I" of the sentence "I-It." It is a great temptation to believe that if "Thou" were different, "I" would not need to endure this loss of larger self.

The dilemma of these couples when viewed from this perspective is twofold. First, they have not yet developed the inner resources to speak the sentence "I-Thou" consistently, and second, they seek to avoid the emotional pain of feeling the loss of "I-Thou," the "exalted melancholy of our fate." They attempt to deny an intrinsic aspect of being human by demanding to hear the sentence "I-Thou" rather than by demanding to speak it.[5] Speaking the sentence "I-Thou" is an act of the highest-order of self- organization. Certainly it is an act of love. It may also be the act of participating in creating a full human being.[6]

Organismic Self-Organization and Contact

A gestalt is a form that organizes our perception of the material world, but it also organizes the thing perceived. For example, the gestalt of "spiral" organizes the vast movements of the galaxies, fluids, and gases (the water in your bathtub, cyclones, the eddies of a babbling brook), the growth of a snail's shell, and many psychological experiences as well (how many patients have dreams or fantasies of floating in a twirl into blackness?). The gestalt "branches-trunk-roots" organizes many life forms (trees, hydras), nerve cells, rivers, certain mathematical functions, blood vessels, and so on. Such gestalts are the universal principles that both give processes form and that presumably also allow the human perception of form.[7]

From this perspective, a person is such a self-organizing system, a gestalt, a whole of mind, body, soul (Portele, 1987, 1989, 1992). So *organism* in Gestalt theory cannot merely mean physiological body, for it refers to both the process of self-organization that "precedes" body and mind and soul, giving them their systemic wholeness, and also to that whole which is the result of the self-organizing processes. Together mind, body, and soul form a dynamically interacting systemic whole that is greater than the sum of its parts.

The "I" that expresses this organismic wholeness is the "I"

of the sentence "I-Thou" and not the "I" of the sentence "I-It."
The "I" of systemic wholeness cannot be achieved or produced
by efforts of one of the smaller "I's" because it transcends them
and integrates them into a new gestalt. Yet the habits of language are like a gravitational field that works against this process
holism, and all Gestalt theorists have struggled to escape its grip.
Simkin, having observed the shifts in self-organization, suggested a metaphor (1976): the personality is like a rubber ball
floating in the water, most of it submerged at any one time, and
the exposed portion changes constantly as the ball rolls. Applying this perspective to our couples, the ball represents the
gestalt of the whole person (potentials, memories, conditioning, feelings, thoughts). The part showing above the water is the
phenomenological "I."

Unfortunately, Simkin's metaphor suggests that the
wholeness of the person has a thinglike quality, a ball, and the
metaphor gains its credibility from this comparison to material
objects. We understand what he means, but we lose a feel for the
process orientation that Goodman, Perls, Goldstein, Lewin, and
the other Gestaltists were striving to establish. What if the personality is not like a ball but like a giant whirlpool, an autopoietic (Maturana & Varela, 1980) self-organizing system that
organizes the flow of personal human Being like a whirlpool organizes the flow of water molecules at certain places in a white-
water canoe river? As the flowing water moves into the realm of
influence of the whirlpool, the molecules move according to
the gestalt of the whirlpool, circling around for a while under
the influence of the gestalt "whirlpool" before they are released
once again to be gestalted by the flowing river.

If some leaves fall from a tree into the whirlpool, they too
whirl around and around under the influence of the whirlpool
system, and for a time at least, hold their positions relative to one
another. If a dragonfly were to flit from one leaf to another, experiencing the world from each different leaf, it might represent
the "I" of the various "I-It" systems. The "I" that names the whole
gestalt—whirlpool and leaves—would be the "I" of wholeness,
what the dragonfly hovering above the whirlpool would see.

To apply this metaphor to our couples, we might imagine

two whirlpools in the same river just next to one another, each with its leaves and its dragonfly. Each dragonfly flies from leaf to leaf in its own whirlpool, calling to the other from its momentary leaf as it whirls past. The two dragonflies relating to one another in this way might represent the "I-It" quality of our couples' relationship. But these two whirlpools, as they move closer to one another, suddenly merge, all their molecules surrendering to the gestalt of one larger whirlpool, forming one complex flowing system, and after a time, move apart again. In a very approximate way this phenomenon from the physical world might represent the "I-Thou" quality of human "betweenness," one large whirlpool as a systemic whole emerging for a while from two separate ones and then returning to separateness.

The systemic view of "organism" as an autopoietic self-organizing system and the phenomenology of shifting "I" raise interesting questions about the Gestalt understanding of "contact." In traditional Gestalt usage, *contact* often refers to the activity of the contact boundary between the organism and its environment, but it may also refer to the interaction of the subject "I" to its object in a more psychological subject-object interaction ("I am in contact with you"). Both usages oversimplify the complexity of the process view. They imply a thing (organism) "in touch with" its (external) environment. Not only Goodman, but also Erik Erickson (1951/1980), had already shown in 1951 that the human environment is not only "outside" of the person, but also "inside".[8] The "environmental field" of human life includes socialization, language, memory, physiological state, culture, family systems, and so on. If "organism" is understood to be a whole of systemic self-organization and is not identical with "thing/body," and if "environment" is not limited to "outside the body," then how are we to understand contact? What can we mean when we speak of contact between the organism and its environment?[9]

The simplistic view of contact ("I am in contact with you"), which implies that you are "out there" ready for me to contact and that "I" am always the same, seems sadly anachronistic and strangely out of sync with the thrust of Gestalt psychology. It assumes a very outmoded psychology of perception and cognition and ignores the role of the perceiver in structuring the field or ground of perception. Contact is clearly a creative process, as Goodman emphasized, "constructivistic" in the contemporary language (Goolishian, 1988; Teschke, 1989). When we contact one another, we gestalt ourselves and also the other. Contact is not passive perception of a fixed objective reality, but rather the creation of a phenomenal experiential reality. It is interactive and creative, truly "creating the meanings by which we live."

According to this view of contact, our couples are not able to gestalt and to maintain the "I" of their wholeness when their partner does not act as they demand, and thus their contact functions are diminished. The concept of the gestalt contact cycle does help us understand any single "self-other" unit (scheme) or episode of contact, but it does not support our understanding of the abrupt and hurtful discontinuities of experience through time that so torment these partnerships. It does little to help us observe and understand the phenomenology of Loss of Self, Longing for the Self-Organizing Self, and Betrayal of Self.

The woman who sometimes feels like a "New York gutter rat" requires the "trust" of her husband in order to feel stable. When he acts contrary to her requirements, he deprives her of support to maintain her "I" and her contact system shifts. Her "I" becomes a gutter rat. Her "other" is the husband who is cruelly boring into her so that she has to fight for her life. Her hurt is more than hurt feelings; it is the pain of the "exalted melancholy of our fate," the dissolving personal reality as her self-other system of contacts shifts. As her self-other system shifts, so too does her husband's. Feeling rejected and hurt by her negative image of him, he in fact becomes much like the person she had feared, thereby confirming her fears.

Similarly, when the man "gets to thinking" he shifts his contact system and changes his personal reality. His wife then may feel abandoned or annihilated since he does not see her wholeness. Unable autonomously to maintain her own whole-person self-organization without his confirmation, she reacts with fury to this subjective abandonment or annihilation, either with withdrawal or with aggression. In either case, the husband notices her shift and both feel confirmed in a vicious circle of distorted contact, "I" and "other" locked together in a tragic dance of mutual negative creation. Each participates in the self-creation of the other in a systemic whole of hurtful experience.

For either to say to the other, "I am angry with you" would be phenomenologically "true" but overlooks the systemic complexity of their interaction. To believe that either is "objectively" perceiving the other during such episodes, that their coldness and anger are objectively "real," denies human freedom. It is true in a sense that they are angry and hurt and perhaps afraid in such moments, but when we remember how they are in other moments, we see that this is a momentary truth, *not* their whole truth, not the truth of their whole Being. They still have other possibilities of being that are momentarily unaccessed, possibilities that are present in the field or background. They *are* then much more than their momentary self-gestalting. To remember this "more" comes close to speaking the sentence "I-Thou" because it addresses an aspect of their Being that is *present* in the field, even when they temporarily have "forgotten" it. The continuing tendency of some Gestalt therapists to understand "contact" in a foreground-bound manner is theoretically and phenomenologically unsound. Goodman's interest in overcoming the false organism-environment split remains essential and sadly neglected. Person and environment together are best conceptualized as a single system. Contact is not the action of one upon the other, but a mutually creative interaction. Each participates in the creation of the other. Partners define one another in their relationship.

Implications for Treatment

Viewing the problems of fragile self-organization from this Gestalt perspective, many of the usual therapeutic assumptions are reversed. It cannot be the primary and immediate goal of the treatment (although of course it is often a long-term result) to reduce or remove neurotic pain and suffering or to get "needs" met. The therapeutic process is to increase *self-organization* and to support the evolutionary becoming which that implies by means of learning to speak the primary sentence "I-Thou." As always in Gestalt therapy, the means for doing this is to increase awareness and acceptance of what IS—foreground and background.

Fate, with its seeming indifference to questions of guilt and merit, has presented these couples with the phenomenology we have been considering. They may not choose to have this phenomenology. Their freedom is limited to what they choose to do with this fate, and in choosing, to determine whether their fate is a blessing or a curse.

Couples who choose the "curse" live according to the principles of hedonism and pleasure characteristic of the "new narcissism," believing that the goal and purpose of relationship is to fulfill "needs." They may change partners in the belief that there is a perfect lover who possesses the qualities they seek. Some of them cling tightly to a victim position. Some may become locked into a program of reforming each other, sucking life from one another until both are psychologically emaciated and bitter. Not a few enter into a twilight grotesque of hate and revenge, seeking therapeutic help only to gain personal advantage. Others are so entangled in their fate and in their fear of the Loss of Self that they cannot defend themselves and reel from one abuse to the next. We all know couples among our friends and clients who have chosen one or more of these alternatives.

Some couples are able to choose the "blessing." They learn to accept their task as being the long and difficult process of cultivating a stable Self-Organizing Self in the context of relationship. Once this decision has been made, the trials of relationship may be welcomed as learning opportunities, and nothing that happens, regardless of its pain, is without some usefulness.

Thus one essential aspect of the work with these couples is the clarification of values (Fuhr, 1992; Zinker, 1987). Another is the therapist's ability to remember and thus to hold the clients' wholeness present in the field (in addition to whatever they may manifest in any given state of self-creation). The therapist working in this way sees more than merely the clients' mo-

mentary foregrounds. Remembering the clients' wholeness, she
or he can remind them that they are more than what they
presently manifest. Therapists who work in this way must bear
in mind that the process of inviting a client to change implicit
thought models and identifications *is* an invitation to surrender an old identity. Thus "resistances" are to be expected—not
resistances to the therapist, but resistances to the subjective experience of the nearness of death contained in the process of
giving up an old identity. As the master of understatement put
it, "To suffer one's own death and to be reborn isn't easy" (Perls,
1969). Shortly before he died, Perls wrote:

> The person who is capable of staying with the ex-
> perience of the fertile void—experiencing his con-
> fusion to the utmost—and who can become aware
> of everything calling for his attention (hallucina-
> tions, broken up sentences, vague feelings, strange
> feelings, peculiar sensations) is in for a big sur-
> prise. He will probably have a sudden "aha" expe-
> rience; suddenly a solution will come forward, an
> insight that has not been there before, a blinding
> flash of realization or understanding.

> What happens in the fertile void is a schizophrenic
> experience in miniature. This, of course, few peo-
> ple can tolerate. But those who do find confidence,
> having successfully cleared away a few areas of con-
> fusion, and having found that they did not fall to
> pieces completely in the process, will acquire the
> courage to go into their junkyards and return more
> sane than when they went in. . . . The aim of con-
> sulting the fertile void is basically to deconfuse. In
> the fertile void, confusion is transformed into clar-
> ity, emergency into continuity, interpreting into ex-
> periencing. The fertile void increases self-support
> by making it apparent to the experimenter that he
> has much more available than he believed he had.
> (Perls, 1973, p. 100ff)

In one sense, this is Fritz Perls's answer to those existential philosophers who saw and so powerfully described the phenomenology of the void. He was one of the first contemporary writers, in spite of his many other shortcomings, who learned how to enter into the "death space" and rediscovered that the great existential "nausea" is the nothingness out of which everything has been created. It seems to be the ground of being. Those couples who learn, like Fritz, to enter into the fertile void return to discover that their partnership has changed. When their fear of the loss of the sense of self (existential loneliness) is overcome by the development of the skills of awareness that allow the free "experimentation" with inner space (especially negative or painful experiences and feelings), then the partnership can be deinstrumentalized and the sentence "I-Thou" may be spoken. It is then no longer necessary that the partner do or be any certain way so that the experience of emptiness may be avoided; betrayal of the self through dependency becomes unnecessary and the "I" of the sentence "I-Thou" becomes an experienced reality that comes and goes according to the "exalted melancholy of our fate." Perhaps it is the case that "I-Thou" may only be spoken within the fertile void and that such "dying" does hold the promise of "rebirth."

Notes

1. This paper, which was previously published in a somewhat different version in the *British Gestalt Journal* (1993, Vol. 2, No. 2), was awarded the Nevis Prize for 1993 for outstanding contribution to the Gestalt field. Parts of the paper are based on an earlier German paper (Beaumont, 1987).
2. The concept of autopoietic self-organizing systems is central to this discussion. I am drawing heavily on Erich Jantsch's excellent introduction to this research in *The Self-Organizing Universe: Scientific and Human Implications of the Emerging Paradigm of Evolution* (1980/1992).
3. The term *self* here is phenomenological. The sentence, "I don't know what came over me, I just wasn't myself" describes an experience recognized by most people. We know

when we are not ourselves. Similarly, many people recognize a desire to be "really me." We seem to have a sense for when we are ourselves and when we are not, even though this sense may not always function well. "Self" is then that which we lose when we are "not ourselves," and that which we long for when we want to "be ourselves." Seen in this way, "self" is an *experienced* reality. (See also Stern, 1985.)

4. Listening and looking for gestalts (as opposed to foregrounds or figures) in therapy is an important technique. It rests on the phenomenon of the Gestalt figure-ground principle. Looking at the vase in the famous Gestalt vase/face profile picture, one can also see exactly the outline of the two faces. Knowing the shape of the vase tells us a great deal (but not all) about the shape of the ground (the two faces). Thus listening to complaints tells us a great deal about wants and hopes, even when clients are not yet able to express their wants clearly. I call this process "triangulation." If we know the patient's foreground and observe his or her actual behavior, we can often "triangulate" what must have been in the background to have produced this gestalt. This process has a different level of abstraction than the usual psychotherapeutic interpretation, and used skillfully, it can be very helpful to the therapist in suggesting *hypotheses* about the wants and needs and hopes of his or her client. It is not, however, totally free from the danger of reading something into the client's experience that is not there.

5. The Yontef/Hycner/Jacobs/Friedman line of Gestalt therapy seems to suggest that the "I-Thou" between therapist and client can become the basis of a therapeutic "dialogue" or dialogic therapy. I agree that "I-Thou" does sometimes occur between therapist and client. In fact, it may be the most important healing agent. But I do not agree that it can ever become the basis of the therapy. The position and situation of the client and the therapist are different; thus "I-Thou" as a *basis* is not possible. The therapist cannot make an "I-Thou" moment happen. To attempt to apply it as a therapeutic technique makes it into an instrument and negates the very nature of the moment. What we can do is

to teach the conditions, skills, and values that are most conducive to the "I-Thou" experience, in this case between *partners*. Nevertheless, when it does happen, it is indeed very healing.

6. "I-Thou" encounters, as acts of self-organization, are not acts of will and cannot be achieved by conscious volition. What does seem possible, again, is for couples to practice the "intention" to meet one another in an "I-Thou" manner, to create the conditions in which this may occur (clean and clear I-messages, sensitive listening to the other, respect, honesty, and so on), and to practice avoiding those behaviors which tend to hinder the "I-Thou" experience (accusations, blaming, projections, and so on).

7. Wheeler's 1991 discussion of the history of the concept of Gestalt itself is interesting here. He reviews the long-standing discussion about the nature of a gestalt. Is the gestalt an order that the mind imposes on experience? Is it rather an order "out there" in the material world that the human mind recognizes? Or is it more of a Platonic/Kantian "idea" or form that organizes (precedes) both the organization of the world and the activity of the human mind? I opt strongly for this last option as being the most satisfying. Why cannot a gestalt (a self-organizing system) organize the flow of thoughts and the flow of electrons equally well? I refer the interested reader to Jantsch (1980/1992) for a more scholarly introduction to this theme.

8. "The traditional psychoanalytic method, on the other hand, cannot quite grasp identity because it has not developed terms to conceptualize the environment. Certain habits of psychoanalytic theorizing, habits of designating the environment as . . . 'object world,' cannot take account of the environment as a pervasive actuality" (Erikson, 1951/1980, p. 24).

9. This is one of the areas where Perls, Hefferline, and Goodman (1951) lack theoretical clarity. Goodman is at pains to refute the "neurotic split" of inside/outside or "organism/environment," clearly pushing for a process orientation. Nevertheless, he succumbs to the pull of language gravity and speaks of the interaction of organism and en-

vironment as if they were two separate things, not quite reaching escape velocity. In spite of this, the work remains prophetic in its struggle to formulate a process-oriented holistic psychotherapy in 1951.

References

Almaas, A. (1986). *The void: Inner spaciousness and ego structure.* Berkeley, CA: Diamond Books.

Beaumont, H. (1987). Prozesse des Selbst in der Paartherapie [Self-process in couples therapy]. *Gestalttherapie, 1*(1).

Beaumont, H. (1988a). Ein Beitrag zur Gestalttherapietheorie und zur Behandlung schizoider Prozesse [A contribution to Gestalt therapy theory and treatment of schizoid processes]. *Gestalttherapie, 2*(2).

Beaumont, H. (1988b). Neurose oder Charakterstoerung: Fehldiagnosen in der Gestalttherapie [Neurosis or character disorder: Misdiagnosis in Gestalt therapy]. In F. Latka, N. Maack, R. Merten, & A. Trischkat (Eds.), *Gestalttherapie und Gestaltpaedagogik zwischen Anpassung und Auflehnung* [Gestalt therapy and Gestalt pedagogy between adjustment and denial]. Munich: Society for the Humanization of Education.

Buber, M. (1958). *I and thou.* New York: Macmillan.

Erikson, E. (1951/1980). *Identity and the life cycle.* New York: W.W. Norton.

Fuhr, R. (1992). Jenseits von Kontaktprozessen [Beyond contract processes]. *Gestalttherapie, 6*(1).

Goolishian, H. (1988). Constructivism, autopoiesis and problem-determined systems. *The Irish Journal of Psychology, 9*(1).

Grove, D., & Panzer, B. (1991). *Resolving traumatic memories: Metaphors and symbols in psychotherapy.* New York: Irvington Publishers.

Hycner, R. (1985). Dialogical Gestalt therapy: An initial proposal. *The Gestalt Journal, 8*(1).

Hycner, R. (1990). The I-thou relationship and Gestalt therapy. *The Gestalt Journal, 13*(1).

Jacobs, L. (1989). Dialogue in Gestalt theory and therapy. *The Gestalt Journal, 12*(2).

Jantsch, E. (1980/1992). *The self-organizing universe.* New York: Pergamon Press.

Johnson, R. (1984). *The psychology of romantic love.* London: Routledge & Kegan Paul.

Masterson, J. (1985). *The real self.* New York: Brunner/Mazel.

Maturana, H., & Varela, F. (1980). *Autopoiesis and cognition: The realization of the living.* London: D. Reidel.

Perls, F. (1969). *Gestalt therapy verbatim.* Lafayette, CA: Real People Press.

Perls, F. (1973). *The Gestalt approach and eyewitness to therapy.* Palo Alto: Science and Behavior Books.

Perls, F., Hefferline, R., & Goodman, P. (1951). *Gestalt therapy: Excitement and growth in the human personality.* New York: Julian Press.

Pörtele, H. (1987). Gestalt-Theorie, Gestalttherapie und Theorien der Selbstorganization. *Gestalttherapie, 1*(1).

Pörtele, H. (1989). Gestalttherapie und Selbstorganization [Gestalt therapy and self-organization]. *Gestalttherapie, 3*(1).

Pörtele, H. (1992). *Der Mensch ist kein Waegelschen* [Man is not a pushcart]. Koeln: Edition Humanistische Psychologie.

Schwartz-Salant, N. (1982). *Narcissism and character transformation.* Toronto: Inner City Books.

Simkin, J. (1976). *Minilectures in Gestalt therapy.* Albany, CA: Wordpress.

Spinelli, E. (1989). *The interpreted world: An introduction to phenomenological psychology.* London: Sage.

Stern, D. (1985). *The interpersonal world of the infant.* New York: Basic Books.

Teschke, D. (1989). Der radikale Konstruktivismus und einige Konsequenzen fuer die therapeutische Praxis [Radical constructivism and some consequences for therapeutic practice]. *Gestalttherapie, 3*(1).

Wheeler, G. (1991). *Gestalt reconsidered: A new approach to contact and resistance.* New York: Gardner Press.

Yontef, G. (1988). Assimilating diagnostic and psychoanalytic perspectives into Gestalt therapy. *The Gestalt Journal, 15*(1).

Zinker, J. (1987). Gestalt values: Maturing of Gestalt therapy. *The Gestalt Journal, 8*(1).

4

Processes of Experiential Organization in Couple and Family Systems

Netta R. Kaplan
and Marvin L. Kaplan

Systems thinking has been widely embraced by couple and family therapy theorists as the most promising means of bringing observations of the functioning of family members into a relational perspective. But efforts to produce a comprehensive theory of family systems have fallen short (Bogdon, 1984; Dell, 1984; Kaplan & Kaplan, 1982; Schwartzman, 1984). These efforts have foundered on the issue of the relationship between observations of couple and family functioning and systems constructs: is the theory to be based on observations of family functioning that are made by researchers and clinicians, or should observations be derived from a theory of how functioning occurs?

At the heart of the matter is the relationship between how systems are presumed to function and the nature of observational data. The kinds of observations that family therapists make have been described as constructions that observers impose on what is observable rather than on what may actually be occurring (Bavelas, 1984; Bogdon, 1984; Doherty, 1986; Kantor & Kupferman, 1985; Keeney, 1979; Schwartzman, 1984). Moreover, in a system perspective, there is a second difficulty: observational methods inevitably reduce continuous processes to discrete "things." Processes are not things or structures but are continuous and continually changing in relationship to their context (Dell, 1984; Kaplan & Kaplan, 1982). The difficulty in relating observational data to what is actually occurring is highlighted in Bateson's (1975) emphasis on the continuity of events: "Is there a place or time where one thing begins and another ends?"

It is, of course, true that couple and family therapists do not restrict themselves to the kinds of behaviors that family members are likely to focus on, but rather attend to what are referred to as processes of relationships among observed events. Nevertheless, to recognize and to identify what is "out there" as an "event" calls for the imposition of some arbitrary structure on functioning that is actually continuous and embedded in context. When segments of functioning are designated as "events," the assumption is made that an event that is identified as occurring at one point in time is equivalent to, or in the same category as, one that occurs at another time (Bavelas, 1984; Bogdon, 1984; Doherty, 1986; Schwartzman, 1984). The patternings derived from such categorizations are then assumed to exist in the form in which they are identified, and they are treated as indicators of how a family system is actually functioning (Doherty, 1986). The same point is made by Keeney (1979) when he says that constructs derived from observations of family functioning are metaphors of processes rather than descriptions of actual processes.

The Problem of Explaining System Self-Maintenance

The difficulties that arise when systems formulations are derived from observations of couple and family functioning are illustrated in the use of the concept of homeostasis. Family systems appear to function as stable organizations despite considerable variations in how they function over time. In fact, the remarkable appearance of stability is the basis for assuming that the variations that are observed represent recurrent, regular, and patterned characteristics of the system (Dell, 1982, 1984). More-

over, families appear to resist change efforts on the part of therapists in ways that suggest that they function in a closed, homeo-
static manner (Dell, 1982, 1984; Ford, 1983). These observations
have led theorists to assume that a family system exists as an enduring "thing" that maintains itself on the basis of a homeosta-
tic property. Dell (1982, 1984), DeShazar and Molnar (1984),
and Bogdon (1984) suggest that what is observed by therapists
and ascribed to homeostasis can be better understood as how
observers are interacting with the system. In this view, observations of "change resistance" reflect how a couple or family is
functioning in relation to therapeutic effort. Dell (1982) notes
that rather than describing a system as "not changing," one may
view it in any situation as tending to "fit" or adapt to its environment. Hoffman (1981) has recognized these limitations and has
attempted to move beyond the concept of homeostasis in explaining how a couple or family system maintains its stability yet
is open to change. She proposes that a system develops in an evolutionary way. At various times random fluctuations occur, and
some in a way that helps the system avoid disorganization and re-
balance itself. Processes that serve in this way are assumed to become integrated so that as a system develops greater complexity
in its range of patterns it becomes organizationally more stable.
This formulation explains how systems can change, but changes
are assumed to produce some kind of patterned entities that in
turn exert a causal influence on events. That is, the assumption
is made that the system functions as it does because some enduring factor makes it do so.

The Nature of Living Systems

Is it possible to develop a way of understanding couple and family system functioning that does not entail ascribing regularities
in functioning that imply the influence of enduring causal factors? This course appears to be unthinkable: how can observers
identify actual processes that are continually active, continually
changing, and embedded in context? Indeed, a number of family therapy theorists who recognize the problems inherent in observational methods suggest that there is no alternative but to
proceed with the inexact observational methods that are avail-

able (Cousins & Power, 1986; Doherty, 1986; Ricci & Selvini-Palazzoli, 1984).

However, another starting place is suggested by Dell (1982, 1984, 1985), who has made use of Maturana's work on the nature of living systems. This approach begins with a formulation of system principles. Dell says that, when the nature of living systems is examined, it appears that there is a fundamental difference between how an organismically based and continually functioning system operates when compared with a system that results from the interaction of other systems. The former, an actual system, is how an organism functions as a continuous, coherence-maintaining organization, whereas the latter describes the kind of coherence that comes about as actual systems interact to produce an interactional system (Dell, 1982, 1985). An individual person exists in the form ascribed to an actual organismic system—that is, as a continuous structured being in space and time. An actual system cannot lapse in its continuous functioning without terminally disorganizing. In contrast, an interactional system can be disrupted in ways that result in discontinuous functioning and discontinuous change, and can be reconstituted (Dell, 1985).

Applied to couple and family functioning, these ideas produce a rather startling conception: individuals function as primary systems in ways that produce the secondary coherence of an interactional couple or family system (Dell, 1982). A couple or family interactional system exists as a function of interactive processes among family members as they are occurring. In Maturana's language, an interactional system is being created as actual systems engage in structural coupling within their media (Dell, 1982).

Maturana's work is important because it deals with how systems appear to exist as enduring and as patterned without assuming enduring properties. Based on his work on the biology of living systems, Maturana says that system functions are "structurally" determined. At any point a living system (or organism) has a structural existence, and this structure determines how it will couple (interact) with its medium (Maturana, 1978; Maturana & Varela, 1980). As used by Maturana, the term *struc-*

ture does not mean that a system is static; rather, it means that at any point in time the organism has an existence in time and space, and what form this takes is how it is functioning at that moment. A system is continually being restructured as ongoing interactions (couplings) are occurring. In fact, the structure of a system is continually evolving by way of restructurings as it is continuously engaging its environment. Thus a system as it exists at any moment is not its history but its current structure as evolved to that point in time. Moreover, a living system appears to be part of or embedded in an interactional system because it has developed its structure through its existence in this medium, and it depends on its medium for its concrete existence (Maturana, 1978).

This abbreviated view of Dell's and Maturana's work suggests a new direction for resolving some of the dilemmas with which systems theorists in the field of family therapy have been struggling. Family therapy theorists have assumed that a system describes how a family functions over time and how the patterns, regularities, oscillations, or cycles of functioning that occur define this system. Maturana's conception says that a system exists as its immediate structure and functioning, and thus the focus shifts from identifying a system to how system processes are occurring in the immediate present. Moreover, family therapy theorists have assumed that a systems perspective could only be introduced at the level of the family as a whole, and that to consider individual functioning would result in explanations based on linear causality. Dell's and Maturana's ideas enable us to appreciate how individual functioning can also be seen as systemic, how the properties of an individual system differ from those of an interactional couple or family system, and how the couple or family exists as a secondary interactional phenomenon.

The Organization of Experience

There is a theory of human functioning that is consistent with these ideas. A conception of the functioning of individual persons as ongoing organizations of processes in relationship to the environment is embodied in Gestalt therapy theory (Kaplan & Kaplan, 1982, 1985). The relevance of the Gestalt therapy position may be surprising to those readers who view it as an experientially oriented therapeutic method rather than as a theory of human functioning. However, the early Gestalt therapy theorists (Goodman and Perls in Perls, Hefferline, & Goodman, 1951; Perls, 1969) described human functioning as an ongoing system of experiential processes. They assumed that the human organism functions holistically: an integral organizational process encompasses how self-maintaining experiential functioning proceeds. In this formulation, the discrimination of various personality functions or "parts" is considered to be an "illusion" of discrete processes that are actually embedded in the whole of an ongoing organizational process.

Although the early Gestaltists were not developmentally oriented, their ideas appear to us to be readily understood within the framework of a developmental progression that emerges as a holistic process of experiential organization. Developmental psychologists have assumed that a person evolves as the differentiation and integration of discrete functions (Flavell, 1984). They have also assumed that these functions interact and become coordinated in a cohesive manner. Among these presumed discrete functions are perceptual organization and perceptual constancy, the ability to focus and maintain a span of attention, motor coordination, conceptual processes including those of relationships and causality, and the differentiation of a self-concept.

A rather different view of development is that these functions appear to be discrete when they are studied under predefined conditions, but functioning actually comes about as a unitary evolutionary process. This process develops around the emergence of cohesive experience. In the process of evolutionary restructuring the individual organismic system emerges along the lines of a developing experiential coherence. What occurs through continual interaction with the environment and continual restructuring is a progressively more complexly organized process that emerges around how the human organism can maintain itself as an experiential whole. In this view, how organismic functioning becomes organized and maintained as an integrated whole is the same process as how the person is able to experience himself or herself as "coherent." The individual organismic system coheres around one's ability to create experiential stability and continuity through processes of experiential organization.

Maturana describes the development of perceptual functioning as a process of differentiation embedded in the ongoing whole of organismic structure (Dell, 1985; Maturana, 1978). The position that is presented here is similar but describes the organization of experience as "taking over" or at least as becoming a central aspect of structure-determining functioning. It does so on the basis of how it serves to create experiential coherence, continuity, and organizational stability.

The Configurational Process

In a Gestalt therapy perspective, experiential organization develops as a progressively more differentiated configurational process: a focal process in relationship to nonfocal experiential activity as background (Kaplan & Kaplan, 1985; Perls et al., 1951). The development of an ability to create experiential organization constitutes the organism's ability to achieve focal attention in relationship to contextual activity that is not focal. Focal attention emerges as the organismic system develops the ability to organize experiential constancy, and as it does so it is able to create objectified experience and thus its own reality. The organism relates to its own construction of objectified (linear) reality as a means of achieving experiential stability and continuity. What people recognize, attend to, and identify as stable (and linear) are their own constructions. These constructions are actually being created nonlinearly as an ongoing organizational process.

The configurational process not only describes how people create their own "objective reality" that serves as an "anchor" for stable experiential functioning, but also explains how they go about identifying experiential phenomena that are actually embedded in a whole configurational process. What people attend to, recognize, and identify constitutes the focal process that is always functioning and is always being modified in relationship to the ongoing functioning of a whole configurational context. For example, in observing a red, wooden cube we may create visual redness as focal. Woodenness and cubeness (and other qualities) are now unrecognized, contextual background modifiers of the experience. If we feel woodenness and cubeness with our eyes closed, redness (and other qualities) remain as background modifiers of the experience. The figural properties that we identify are linear constructions embedded in a context of nonlinear activity, and as we maintain figural organization we maintain experiential stability.

As people are focusing attention they are creating recognitions of discrete components of functioning. These recognitions are linear constructs that do not actually exist in the objective form in which they create them. The distinctions that they create of discrete functions and properties are artificial; there are no such entities as mind or body or discrete functions such as cognition, memory, perception, or emotion. On the other hand, the constructs themselves constitute their recognized experience. How people go about creating and regulating these organizational processes occurs in terms of how they know how to function at the moment of functioning—or, in Maturana's conception, how their current functioning is structurally determined.

As people are creating an objective linear "out there" that exists in relationship to themselves, they are simultaneously creating their experience of themselves. They experience themselves in relationship to what they create as objective reality. For example, as someone recognizes another person as "warm and friendly," the experiencer is creating this experience, and he or she is being the person who is recognizing and relating to warmth and friendliness in another. The objectified recognized experience is embedded in the ongoing whole configurational process, and the organized whole constitutes a person's immediate recognized (as well as unrecognized) self-experience.

It is important to note that what is being described as a focal process in relationship to background represents the whole of a person's experiential functioning. It is not equivalent to cognition in relationship to affect, or mind in relationship to body. These are linear discriminations. Instead, the focal process is how people organize their experiential functioning to create an objectified sense of things and events, but these recognized experiences are actually embedded in a holistic process of ongoing experiential activity. This perspective can be compared with the experientially oriented approaches that are based on linear conceptualization. Johnson and Greenberg (1987) offer a sophisticated model for discriminating critical experiential phenomena that occur in interactional functioning. This conception, however, assumes that discrete feelings, emotions, and cognitions exist as enduring phenomena that require focalization and attention.

In creating a focal process, what is being organized as focal and how this process occurs is how an individual is functioning in an immediate time dimension, and constitutes how he or she is simultaneously experiencing self. As a person is "seeing" and "hearing" a movie, for example, he or she is creating a focal, objectified meaningful organization and simultaneously being the creator and the attender of the organization that is being created. The person can shift focal attention, let us say to bodily discomfort or to one's sense of self as viewer; at this point the "movie" is no longer focal but becomes background. The change in self-experience occurs in terms of how the focus of attention is being directed in a different way, and thus a new focal objectification of experience emerges that constitutes a different experiential configuration. Although the individual has shifted his or her organization of experience, at the same time he or she is maintaining continuity of self-experience by being the director of the shifting. The processes that people engage in as they modify or shift their organizational configuration are actually processes of continuity maintenance.

Mutually Supportive Functioning in Couples and Families

As individual, primary, organismic systems interact, they create interactional couple and family systems. Members of the couple or family can be seen as functioning in relationship as they co-ordinate their functioning so that the "reality" each person is creating is experienced as supported. Observations of regularities and patterns in family functioning that have been attributed to how a family system manifests itself over a span of time can be located in the interaction that people are continually engaged in as a mutual coordination process. In each instance they are creating and maintaining their individual processes of experiential organization as they mutually create familiar and expected mutually supportive processes that fit the immediate situation. These coordinating processes function to maintain the stability and continuity of experiential organization processes within the individual members.

To illustrate this kind of functioning, consider a situation in which a mother is criticizing her teenage daughter for various behaviors with which she finds fault. The daughter is defending herself and criticizing her mother for not respecting her, while the father is acting aloof. A family therapist may recognize this brief description as a pattern that presumably occurs frequently in this family and that can be viewed as an expression of the family system. However, what is being termed a pattern can be seen as a support process that is currently being created among these family members as they recognize and anticipate familiar, expected functioning. In attending to how each person is functioning rather than to the overall pattern, one notices specific features in the functioning of the members. These specific features can reflect cautious and tentative shifts in how the individuals are organizing themselves, maintaining themselves, and giving continuity to their existence in relationship to one another. We notice that at one moment the mother seems to lose forcefulness, hesitates, and looks toward her husband, and as he does not seem to respond or even to notice this action, she turns back to her daughter, sighs, and says, "I don't seem to be able to get anywhere with you. I think you're hopeless." The mother's actions may be understood as a momentary beginning effort to reorganize from an assertive position to one of uncertainty and hesitancy with accompanying feelings of helplessness and wanting help. This perspective can be recognized as a tentative self-organizational shift, a cautious exploration of possible support for change, and in the face of a lack of responsive support, a retreat to more familiar supports.

A family that might be described as enmeshed or "locked in," a designation that implies the existence of a time-enduring system, can be described more accurately as often functioning in what appears to involve highly familiar mutually coordinated ways (Kaplan & Kaplan, 1982). For example, in one family the members are observed to lock in easily on mutually supportive functioning that facilitates each in experiencing himself or herself as vulnerable and as required to stand up to each other's blaming. This interactional process is being created as the members are recognizing highly familiar environmental support for their current organizations of experience. Family members function in anticipation of such processes, and the creation of these processes is readily accomplished and appears to be a reactivation. As family members engage in these processes, they experience difficulty in releasing themselves from familiar support processes, and the family appears to be entrenched and stable in its functioning.

Observing the Organizational Process

While a great deal of functioning is occurring at each moment, each person's organizational process can be seen as embedded in how mutual support processes are being recognized. What may be concretely observed is how organizational regulation is simultaneously evident in the functioning of individuals and in the whole interactional system. The following situations are presented as illustrations of these simultaneous processes, and they show how coordination can proceed in different ways in the family context. The same processes, of course, apply to the two-person interactional system of the couple.

Situation 1. A father is being sharply critical of his teenage son and telling him what he finds irritating in his behavior. After a few minutes the mother interrupts with a statement defending the boy and indirectly implying that the father is unduly harsh. The father reacts by becoming quietly sullen.

Situation 2. In a similar situation, as the father is speaking, the mother is observed to show distress: her face looks troubled and she shifts uncomfortably in her seat before she proceeds to interrupt with her statement of defense of her son and implied criticism of her husband. The father reacts as above.

Situation 3. Again the situation is similar and again the mother appears distressed. In this instance, however, she takes a deep breath, holds her head upright, and speaks in a shaky voice. She tells the other family members that she feels upset and sad about what is happening. The father responds with concern for her feelings.

The first and second situations portray family functioning in ways that therapists are likely to recognize as "maintaining the system." Even though a fluctuation is noticed in Situation 2, it is unacknowledged, and the pattern sequence proceeds. What has been termed a fluctuation can be appreciated as an indication of an exploratory shift in the mother's organizational processes and in how she might use support processes. She may not recognize that she is exploring a different experiential existence or that she is not experiencing support from others for pursuing this change. In the absence of support for change, her fluctuation is passed over, and she and the other members continue to pursue a familiar, expected course as if the fluctuation had not occurred.

The third situation, however, describes the mother as continuing to move into a different experiential organization. In effect she alters how she is regulating herself, and she does so in a manner that provides altered support for others and opens the way for others to express their supports differently. The family members now begin to shift in a direction that supports a change in how they relate to one another and function together.

Qualities of the Mutual Support Process

When a couple or family system is viewed as existing as it functions through the ongoing mutual support processes of participating members, it is possible to discover how a system functions from moment to moment. Rather than identifying regular and patterned events, we may observe an ongoing process. This process manifests itself in how each member is functioning as a change-regulating organizational process in relationship to environmental supports, and how the whole is functioning as a system of corresponding mutual support processes. Three general qualities of support processes can be observed: relative stability of the coordinating process, shifts in the process, and support for modifications in ongoing processes.

1. A mutual support process can be described as having relative stability when family members are experiencing one another in highly familiar and well-coordinated ways that support functioning that they "know well." This kind of functioning is what family therapists frequently recognize as recurrent regularities and patterns. Family members also recognize these forms of functioning, although they do not articulate or explain them in the same terms as therapists. The earlier example of a mother who was criticizing her defensive daughter while the father remained aloof illustrates a "pattern" that the family knows well. When the mother cautiously sought support for an alternative, she quickly abandoned this effort as her cautious move was unrecognized, and the ongoing support process remained stable.
2. A shift in process occurs when one familiar and relatively stable form of support gives way to another. Families may appear to rapidly shift from one well-known "pattern" to another. But rather than postulate some enduring cause for the appearance of a cycle or recursive loop, what is observed can be seen as movement from one form of relative stability that escalates or in some way moves toward destabilization and gives rise to the emergence of another familiar form of mutual support in which restabilization occurs (Kaplan & Kaplan, 1982).
3. Support for modification of experiential organization is the third quality of supportive functioning. This is a support process in which family members are able to release themselves and one another from familiar forms of support, to

allow themselves to explore different or untried organizational processes, and to integrate new experience. This process occurs when family members anticipate support for moving beyond known and safe ways of organizing themselves and open themselves to functioning that can be described as a process of individuation.

Family members attempt to avoid relying on uncertain and unfamiliar support processes as they anticipate danger in loss of support for their ongoing process of experiential organization. They vary not only in how they organize themselves, but also in the kinds of dangers they anticipate if they depart from familiar and predictable safe ways. In some situations people fear losing the experience of being stably organized. Others anticipate falling into organizations of vulnerability, being ashamed, isolated, out of control, and so on. People function in restricted and risk-avoiding ways not only because they dislike or anticipate the hurt or pain that may accompany change, but also because they anticipate "becoming" these experiences.

Therapeutic Method

This discussion of variations in the quality of support processes helps us recognize how a therapist can help a family move to modify support for risking, discovering, and exploring different functioning. The approach corresponds to Gestalt therapy's method of working with here-and-now experiential functioning as well as in facilitating awareness, but as used here the approach is oriented toward influencing the supportive process in which functioning is occurring (Kaplan & Kaplan, 1982). In recognizing how interactional support processes are functioning in the immediate present, therapists can participate in ways that facilitate support for change. They notice how couple or family members are going about coordinating their support processes, but they attend primarily to activity that reflects tentative or cautious or exploratory change efforts. The therapeutic focus is on activity that reflects maintenance or changes processes in the ongoing support system. We will illustrate this process by briefly describing an opening of a family session.

The four family members enter in a light and pleasant manner, but once seated they become serious and appear to wait for someone to start. The father looks at his wife as if expecting something, but she turns away. The therapist says, "Jim, I see you looking at Rose; do you want something from her?" Jim replies, "Well, she said plenty in the car, and I don't know why she is so quiet here." The therapist then says, "So, how is it for you to want her to speak, and she doesn't?" Jim looks uncomfortable and says, "I feel frustrated and I don't understand why she isn't talking." At this point he looks away and appears downcast. The therapist comments on his looking away and asks him about this. He says, "I don't like being critical of Rose—maybe she felt nervous talking here or something." Again he looks at his wife, who at this moment has turned toward him, and he asks her, "Well, what are you feeling?" Rose responds, "You're right, I was nervous. I know I said a lot in the car, but this is different. I guess I do feel better now that you asked me how I felt rather than insisting that I say something." The mother now looks at the other family members, who had been sitting quietly but seemed to be listening attentively. The therapist comments on Rose's looking toward her children, and therapy proceeds as she expresses concerns about how the children felt about what she said in the car, and about how open she can be in therapy.

This brief illustration describes a key aspect of the therapist's efforts to support change in the ongoing mutual support system at critical points of tentative modification. There is an effort to bring into focus the tentative and exploratory functioning of the members as they are organizing themselves in relationship to support processes. In this illustration the focus is not on the father's content issues, nor on how he feels about his wife, but on how he is organizing himself and how he modifies his organizational process in relationship to the supports he experiences as the therapist draws attention to his tentative shifts. In functioning this way, a therapist does not wait for the family members to move into highly stable support processes, but immediately draws focal attention to and encourages support for experimentation in modifying self-organizational processes.

Couple and family therapists who are oriented to how system members function as processes of experiential organization notice the appearance of regularities, patterns, and dominant themes of couple and family functioning, but they conceptualize this kind of functioning as how the members are currently mutually developing and clinging to familiar ways of organizing themselves. What therapists attend to and focus on primarily is how the members are experiencing themselves at the moment, especially how they are experiencing support in relationship to the other members, including the therapist. This functioning is assumed to reflect the actual, ongoing organizational processes that people are creating in relationship to one another. When the therapist attends to and directs attention to what appear to be significant emerging change processes, couple and family members are supported in a very concrete and focused manner. As the members modify their functioning, these modifications in turn affect the way other members experience support in the interactional system. Attention to how individuals are functioning constitutes the same observational focus as attention to the whole system as it is currently functioning.

Therapists who view couple and family functioning in this way recognize that for a person to reorganize his or her self-experience constitutes a risk in venturing beyond recognized, familiar, and safe supports and requires a willingness to explore what is anticipated as relatively unsafe. The therapeutic approach that is derived from this recognition calls for therapists to function in ways that help to create in family members experiences of relative safety, willingness to risk, and anticipation of sustained support. In this orientation, therapists cannot fulfill this function by demonstrations of knowledge and professional skill alone. They must offer a relationship that can be experienced as genuinely supportive.

Summary

In the beginning of this article, we described some of the difficulties that have been recognized in applying systems thinking to couple and family functioning. It seems clear that these difficulties come about as a system is assumed to exist in a time-enduring manner. Couples and families appear to exist as historical entities with highly stable boundaries, but this appearance has misled therapists and theorists. They have assumed that the appearance of recurrences reflects actual, existing patterns of functioning that in turn are assumed to be characteristics of an enduring system. This conceptualization requires constructs that explain recurrence on the basis of enduring causal factors.

There is a similar issue with respect to human experiential functioning. Here, as in couple or family functioning, conventional wisdom as well as our personal sense of ourselves leads us to assume that our psychological functioning exists as an enduring thing. However, in both kinds of contexts—couple and family or individual functioning—explanations of enduring factors that must somehow be the basis of recurrence and stability fall short of what systems principles require.

Dell's and Maturana's work provides a basis for conceptualizing processes as ongoing and changing, and as organized contextually and relationally as an actual system. This is the basis for recognizing individual functioning as a primary or actual system, while interactional couple or family functioning is a secondarily created process; couple or family functioning is the medium of individual systemic functioning. This perspective helps us describe human experiential functioning as being organized in a way that concretely recognizes time: that is, people actually function as ongoing, continually changing, self-organizing, experiential processes. But as they function they are organizing their ongoing experiential process and creating objectified, linear experience. They are "structured" (in Maturana's sense of structure as current existence and functioning) to function in this way because they have developed in the medium of their environment and depend on relationship with that environment for their current existence.

This description of individual and couple or family functioning recognizes how people go about maintaining their ongoing organizational processes in a relational context in terms of a coordinated mutual support process. How couple and family members go about this process is seen as creating the appearance of recurrent, patterned functioning, but the processes are actually being created in a unique form as individuals are functioning in the immediate present. These ongoing mutual support processes *are* the system as it exists and as it functions. Changes in what is occurring are changes in support processes as well as actual changes in how individuals exist and experience. A therapist functioning within this perspective appreciates how risk is involved as changes occur, and how modifications in the coordinated support system and changes in functioning occur together.

Note

A version of this chapter was originally published in *Psychotherapy* (Fall 1987, Vol. 24, No. 15).

References

Bateson, G. (1975). Some components of socialization for trance. *Ethos, 3*, 143–156.
Bavelas, J. (1984). On "naturalistic" family research. *Family Process, 23*, 337–345.
Bogdon, J. (1984). Family organization as an ecology of ideas. *Family Process, 23*, 375–388.
Cousins, P., & Power, T. (1986). Quantifying family process. *Family Process, 25*, 89–106.
Dell, P. (1982). Beyond homeostasis: Toward a concept of coherence. *Family Process, 21*, 21–41.
Dell, P. (1984). Why family therapy should go beyond homeostasis. *Journal of Marital and Family Therapy, 10*, 351–356.
Dell, P. (1985). Understanding Bateson and Maturana: Toward a biological foundation for the social sciences. *Journal of Marital and Family Therapy, 11*(1), 1–20.
DeShazar, S., & Molnar, A. (1984). Changing teams/changing families. *Family Process, 23*, 481–486.
Doherty, W. (1986). Quanta, quarks and families: Implications of quantum physics for family research. *Family Process, 25*, 249–263.
Flavell, J. (1984). Discussion. In R. Sternberg (ed.), *Mechanism of cognitive development.* New York: W.H. Freeman.

Ford, F. (1983). Rules: The invisible family. *Family Process, 22,* 135–145.

Hoffman, L. (1981). Foundations of family therapy. New York: Basic Books.

Johnson, S., & Greenberg, L. (1987). Emotionally focused marital therapy: An overview. *Psychotherapy, 24,* 552–560.

Kantor, D., & Kupferman, W. (1985). The client's interview of the therapist. *Journal of Marital and Family Therapy, 11,* 225–244.

Kaplan, M., & Kaplan, N. (1982). Organization of experience among family members in the immediate present: A Gestalt/systems integration. *Journal of Marital and Family Therapy, 8,* 5–14.

Kaplan, M., & Kaplan, N. (1985). The linearity issue and Gestalt therapy's theory of experiential organization. *Psychotherapy, 22,* 5–15.

Keeney, B. (1979). Ecosystem epistemology: An alternative paradigm for diagnosis. *Family Process, 18,* 117–130.

Maturana, H. (1978). Biology of language. In G. Miller & E. Lenneberg (Eds.), *Language and Thought.* New York: Academic Press.

Maturana, H., & Varela, F. (1980). Autopoieses: The organization of the living. In H. Maturana & F. Varela (Eds.), *Autopoiesis and cognition.* Dordrecht, Holland: D. Reidel.

Perls, F. (1969). *Gestalt therapy verbatim.* Lafayette, CA: Real People Press.

Perls, F., Hefferline, R., & Goodman, P. (1951). *Gestalt therapy.* New York: Julian Press.

Ricci, C., & Selvini-Palazzoli, M. (1984). Interactional complexity and communication. *Family Process, 23,* 169–180.

Schwartzman, J. (1984). Family theory and scientific method. *Family Process, 23,* 223-236.

5

Therapy with Remarried Couples

Patricia Papernow

When we think of "family," most of us picture a mother, a father, and their children. In fact, by the year 2000 stepfamilies where one or both adults bring children from a previous marriage will be the predominant family form in the United States (Glick & Lin, 1986). As the divorce rate approaches one-third in many European countries, the number of stepfamilies is growing there too, since most of these divorces involve children, and most adults remarry. As will be obvious from our second vignette, I am using the term *remarried* loosely to mean recoupled, with or without the benefit of formal marriage vows. The intensity, complexity, and confusion of early stepfamily life bring many of these couples to clinicians who remain sadly unprepared to provide appropriate and effective help.

Vignette 1. A "Single" Stepfamily (a parent-child unit is joined by a stepparent without children)

John and Regina come into couples therapy in the second year of their marriage. This is Regina's first and John's second marriage. John, the father of nine-year-old Tammy, is telling Regina in an irritable and tense tone that she is too withdrawn and unavailable at the family dinner table. Regina is anxiously asking questions: "How do you mean?" "What do you expect me to do?" "You should participate more," says John. "Just join in. You sit there like a lump." Regina is silent, and then says in a small voice, "But your daughter doesn't even acknowledge my existence." "That's ridiculous," John responds. "You're the adult." Regina's shoulders slump and she becomes silent. John folds his arms; his face and his body are full of tension. "I'm so frustrated," he says. "How can we get anywhere with this if you won't even participate in a conversation about it!" Regina becomes a shade paler. The muscles around her mouth appear to tense. John slumps in his chair and the conversation ends in silence.

Vignette 2. A "Double" Stepfamily (two parent-child units come together)

Sheila, the mother of two boys aged thirteen and ten, and Aaron, the father of two girls aged nine and eleven, have just moved in together after a two-year relationship. They had planned to get married in two months. However, after a lively, satisfying courtship, they have come into couples therapy because they are suddenly fighting about "absolutely everything."

Sheila begins the session almost in tears, talking very fast. "What kind of parent are you if you won't even buy my boys their school clothes! My boys will be devastated. You've really let them down . . . ." Aaron shoots back, "I'm not their father. What do you expect! Besides your kids can't even sit down to eat their food. They stand around and eat out of the refrigerator like tramps." Sheila retorts, "Why don't you try cooking after working all day? How come I'm doing all the cooking any-

way?" "Because you criticize everything I make,"
Aaron retorts.

Sitting with remarried couples like John and Regina and
Sheila and Aaron can be anxiety provoking and overwhelming
for even the most experienced therapist. This chapter will draw
upon Gestalt theory and practice to help us organize what we
see, hear, and feel as we sit with stepcouples, and to choose a
point of intervention. In Gestalt language, this chapter will help
organize a ground full of compelling and conflicting possible
figures.

Let us pause to define the critical Gestalt terms *figure* and
ground. Early Gestalt experiments identified and described the
normal perceptual process of being able to allow a particular
thought, image, feeling, or goal to stand out from the background, or become figural. Gestalt theory and practice are
based on this discovery that most of us are wired to do this.
Healthy functioning is dependent on our ability to organize our
experience into figures that are clear enough and accurate
enough so that we can act effectively. Many things may interrupt
or affect this process. A personal history in which normal needs
for attention or affection were not met or shamed may result in
self-blame or numbing of feelings that derails the process of
identifying current needs. Expectations that are not congruent
with reality can distort the process: if I come to a new relationship expecting disapproval, I may notice even the smallest signs
of criticism while missing expressions of support. An extremely
confusing (too much is going on) or treacherous environment
(every move is greeted with criticism) may make figure formation difficult.

A poorly defined figure does not provide a clear enough
focus for action. Too many competing figures produce scat-
tered, ineffective action. Inability to form any figure results in
paralysis. Repetitively forming the same figure whatever the situation results in inappropriate action.

Ground refers simply to the background from which a figure emerges. In my office the ground may consist of all that is
on my desk, as well as the view through my window. The ground

may also include the previous night's dream, the morning's conversation with my daughter, as well as my history as an oldest child who is expected to produce, and my longing for another cup of coffee. The figure I choose is dependent not only on my ability to focus in this confusing array, but also on the content and organization of the array itself. It will be easier to make writing this chapter figural when it is a gray winter day, my desk is neat, I only have one project due next week, and I am in touch with my ability to get things done. It will be harder to focus on a beautiful spring morning when my desk is piled with overdue and incomplete projects, if I had a fight with my daughter before school, and if I were a youngest child consistently outshined by an older sibling.

Although all families have some things in common, the history, structure, and developmental and therapeutic challenges of second-time-around families differ markedly from first-time families. In Gestalt language, the ground from which figure formation must happen differs markedly in stepfamilies. Like so many others like them, the couples in our two vignettes have come to stepfamily life bringing ground that does not support them in organizing their present experience. As a result, normal developmental dilemmas have become painful emergencies. Energy that needs to be organized effectively to meet these normal developmental challenges has become misdirected and turned into blaming. Unfortunately, in their work with remarried families, all too many therapists compound these dilemmas by working with stepfamilies as if they were first-time families. As a consequence, the process of figure formation is irreparably distorted with results that are at best unsatisfying and all too often disastrous.

Our first task, then, is to describe the ways in which remarried couple life differs from what I call "first-time family" life. As we understand more deeply the impact of stepfamily structure on the people who live in it, we can fill in the background from which the dynamics we saw in our opening vignettes emerge. This will enable us to make more sense of what we see, and to help our clients to do the same. We shall then move on to describe four lenses that help to focus the Gestalt therapist's process of figure formation in the face of these dynamics. Our two vignettes will illustrate the discussion.

The Ground: How Stepfamilies Differ
from First-Time Families

If the above two families were to become our neighbors, they would initially look very similar to any other family group consisting of parents and children. A closer look would reveal differences that have enormous implications for both family member and their therapists. To understand the tangles we saw in our vignettes we first need to understand how stepfamilies differ from first-time families.

Stepfamilies begin with one or both adults bringing children from a previous relationship that has ended as a result of separation, divorce, or death. These facts have a profound impact on even the smallest interactions for the couples in our two vignettes.

Parents in a first-time family begin their lives together with time to experience their similarities and explore their differences. When a first child arrives, their connection, whether biological or adoptive, is equal. Together, over time, they work out how "we" handle crying babies, how "we" do the tree at Christmas or the haggadah at Passover. When a second child arrives, much must change, but much has already been established about the texture of the family's life together. Norms and rhythms are built over years of experience together. As in all organizational systems, some of the rules and norms are clearly stated while many of them operate powerfully but out of awareness.

Separation, divorce, or death changes the family constellation dramatically. Children are now members of at least one, and often two, single-parent families. Adult-child boundaries loosen as discipline becomes more difficult to enforce with just one parent. As children cope with multiple losses and changes, significant regression is common. A child who had been toilet-trained returns to using her diaper. A five-year-old who had dressed himself now needs help again. Maintaining rules becomes appropriately less important than providing empathy and comfort.

In the new single-parent family, decisions that had been made (or argued over) by adults are now made by the remaining adult and his or her children: "What movie shall we watch?" "What shall we have for dinner?" Time the adult would have spent with his or her partner is spent with children: Friday night Mom and the kids may curl up in front of the television with dinner. Week-day evenings Dad and the kids may snuggle and read on the big bed. In time single-parent family life develops its own rhythms and rituals.

As a result of these developments, when Mom or Dad recouples, the new stepparent begins in a very different position from the original parent. In a healthy first-time family the "insider" and the "outsider" roles rotate. Sometimes the adults are close, excluding the children. Sometimes one child and a parent team up and the other parent becomes the outsider. Sometimes the second child plays with the parent and the first child is the outsider.

In contrast, throughout the early stages of development in a stepfamily (Papernow, 1993), insider and outsider positions remain stuck. The stepparent begins as an outsider to a biological parent-child unit with a shared rhythm of daily living, with often unaware agreements on everything from how loud a voice is, to whether sugar cereal or nonsugar cereal is "good," to whether it is normal or offensive to leave one's coat on the dining room chair. The biological parent begins as the insider; he or she is closest to everyone concerned—children, stepparent, and ex-spouse. Frozen insider and outsider positions that would be seen as pathological in a first-time family are the normal result in a stepfamily or a family structure in which the parent-child relationships precede the adult couple relationship.

In the first vignette, John and his daughter Tammy form the insider unit. Regina is the stuck outsider. As Tammy turns to her dad at the dinner table, what is a natural father-daughter conversation for them is for Regina exclusive and impossible to join. Meanwhile, John is the stuck insider, with a closer relationship to both Tammy and Regina, who remain relative strangers to each other. From the ground of a first-time family, John is organizing his attention around the question "What's wrong with Regina that she can't participate in the family?" Likewise, an uninformed therapist might be inclined to join John in blaming Regina for her lack of participation. A better understanding of normal stepfamily dynamics would make all more likely to ask, "What support does Regina need as the outsider to this intimate pair?" "What would help John in his role as the go-between?" "What would make it easier for Tammy to deal with a stranger at the table?"

In the second vignette we see what happens when two parent-child teams come together in what researchers call a "complex stepfamily." Often one family unit holds the insider position. In this case it is Sheila's family. Aaron and his children have moved into Sheila's home, making Sheila and her children the experts on everything from where the silverware goes to the "correct" position of the chair in the living room. In addition, Sheila's children reside full-time with the couple, whereas Aaron's visit. In other double families, the noisier, quicker unit may dominate decisions about everything from what television shows will be watched to what food the family eats, leaving a quieter, slower unit dazed and confused.

For children, too, becoming a stepfamily is very different from entering a first-time family. Although a new partner is a gain for the child's parent, the introduction of a strange adult is often yet another in a series of unchosen changes and losses for the child. In separation and divorce children lose the crucible of their identity, their family. By the time children begin a stepfamily the rhythms of their everyday lives have already changed dramatically, often several times, and without their choice. The family doesn't have pancakes as a family on Sunday morning anymore. Familiar furniture may be missing. Daddy doesn't come home for dinner. In the relocation after a family breakup children may have lost friends and neighbors and even their school. For a while Mom is more tired and irritable.

Most single-parent families establish their own new norms and rituals. The old fancy divan is replaced with a used futon couch with a couple of large pillows. Dad and the kids have Chinese food together at a local dive once a week. Mom and the kids make popcorn and watch a video together every Friday night on her big bed.

Whereas remarriage for adults may feel like the end of bad times, for children remarriage may signal the beginning of more hard times. Mommy is spending time with a new boyfriend who doesn't welcome children and popcorn in his bed. Daddy cooks dinner together with his new wife and the children are barred from the kitchen. The pillows on the futon couch, which had just begun to feel comfortable and familiar, are replaced. The new person has a different smell, a different feel, and new disciplinary expectations. Gestalt theory tells us that changes in our field of experience, especially when unchosen, can be disturbing and disorienting to adults. For children, whose identities are even less separate from the systems in which they are embedded, the massive changes of divorce or death followed by remarriage can be overwhelming.

Equally important, and all too often most painful for children, the entry of a stepparent often creates a loyalty bind. "If I love my Dad's new girlfriend I've betrayed my mother." When the adults in their lives are badmouthing each other ("How can he be with that jerk!" "Your father left us and he doesn't love you.") the resulting bind can create unbearable choices: "If I don't say hello to my stepmother, she'll be mad. But if I do, my Mom will be mad."

For the new stepcouple, all of these facts mean that every time a child walks into a room, the biological parent, the stepparent, and the child will have profoundly different experiences. Often the child will look at and talk to his or her parent (after all, that is where the attachment is and the other adult is the interloper). The child naturally directs questions and conversation to the biological parent, treating the (from the child's point of view) intruding stepparent with disinterest or outright hostility. As a result, the biological parent feels pulled, engaged, and concerned. The *same interaction* leaves the stepparent feeling distanced, rejected, and jealous or resentful. Likewise, when a crying child interrupts an adult conversation for the fifth time, the tears are signals of distress for the biological parent. The stepparent is more likely to find the same behavior manipulative and irritating. Behavior that signals a need for attention from the biological parent indicates a need for limits to the stepparent. As a result, in order to talk to each other John and Regina must deal with the fact that they begin with strikingly different figures. As Gestalt therapists we know that two people may organize their experience of the same event very differently. Although theoretically neither experience is right or wrong, "mine" always feels more real and understandable than "yours." Furthermore, although differences are an inescapable fact of all human relationships, stepcouples are confronted immediately with this fact every time they engage over a child, early in their relationship, before they have a strong bond as a couple. Couples who enter with some information about normal stepfamily dynamics at least begin with some understanding of the very different ground from which their partner's different focus emerges. Without that information the gap in understanding between the new couple may widen with terrifying quickness over an apparently small issue.

Heinz Kohut (1977) and other self psychologists have alerted us to a basic human need for "mirroring" (the sense that another person truly understands our internal experience). Kohut reminds us that this need extends into adulthood. When everyday experiences result in constant "breaks" in the mirror, even the healthiest of us gets anxious. To combine Kohut and Gestalt, it is much easier to mirror when two people share the same figure and ground. It is much harder to "mirror" or emphasize across large differences in awareness. Herein lies the primary developmental dilemma for remarried couples—how to bridge fundamental gaps in awareness that occur with relentless and anxiety-provoking frequency well before the couple has built a solid relationship.

The task is made more daunting by the fact that the breaks in the "mirror" extend beyond differing parental attachments. Stepfamilies bring together already established "mini-families" (Keshet, 1980), each with its own culture (Papernow, 1987). What feels natural to one family unit is anathema to the other. In our second vignette, Aaron, who is used to sitting down with his children at each meal, has moved in with a mother and her children used to eating meals standing up in the kitchen raiding the fridge. Regina, in the first vignette, who had always depended on her early morning shower as a special event of the day, finds that her stepdaughter and new husband routinely leave their towels in a wet pile on the bathroom floor. Although these things seem minor, they are the threads out of which the fabric of our existence is woven. They form part of strongly held "fixed gestalts" that simply feel like "reality." Many of them are held unaware until early stepfamily life assaults them.

The response is often first experienced wordlessly as a physical feeling of shock or violation. For some, like Regina in the first vignette, the surprise collapses into depression: "What's wrong with me that I can't adjust to this?" and silence. For others, like Aaron and Sheila in the second vignette, the initial sharp feeling of surprise and helplessness turns to panic and shifts immediately to outrage: "How *could* you eat like this?" "What do you mean," may be the equally shocked answer. "We've always done it that way. Who are you to say it's wrong!" The panic and shock are likely to be particularly intense if the couple comes into remarried life expecting an immediately "blended" family.

None of these responses is conducive to the slow building of awareness and curiosity necessary to explore, understand, and resolve the differences inherent in early stepfamily life. It is the Gestalt therapist's job to help remarried couples accomplish this crucial task. Gestalt therapy's greatest strength lies in teaching us to pay attention to here-and-now process. However, even the most skilled attention to process is not enough in many stepfamily systems. Successful work with the couples we have just met requires knowledge of the content (the ground) of the stepfamily experience and its impact on each individual in the family, including the children, as well as its impact on the couple. For this reason we will begin this chapter with the information needed by both therapists and clients to support the work of becoming a successful and nourishing stepfamily.

Working with remarried couples involves shifting among several lenses: (1) We must deal directly with stepfamily issues.

(2) We must build awareness. That means helping each family member to find language and a voice for his or her own experience, as well as to gain some understanding of each other's experience so that the amount of shared ground increases. (3) We must attend to here-and-now couple dynamics that support or block shared figure formation. (4) We look for unfinished business that may be blocking contact in the present. This chapter will describe each of these lenses, looking at how each changes our focus on the couples in our vignettes, and at the ways in which they interact with each other.

It is worth noting that the principles that inform our work with stepfamilies are not different in kind from those that guide any Gestalt therapist's work. We deal directly with the current issue, we build individual awareness, we look at system dynamics, we attend to unfinished business that may be distorting current figure formation and we explore the interaction of present and past.

The differences lie in the specific phenomena of remarried families, the somewhat different view we get from each of our four lenses, the aesthetics of both separating and weaving together the data from each of these lenses, and the difficulty for both therapists and clients of figure formation amidst the intensity of stimuli created by stepfamily living.

Lens Number 1: Stepfamily Basics

Although our educational role may remain more in the background in other therapeutic work, remarried couples (and their therapists) require sufficient information about normal stepfamily dynamics to have enough ground to support decisions about where to focus attention in a field littered with compelling figures.

Often the first task for the therapist is to provide normalizing information to a distressed remarried couple. We can guess that neither John nor Regina knows that their dinner table dynamic is not a symptom of an inadequacy or lack of caring, but a normal result of their family's history and structure. Likewise in the second vignette, we can guess that Sheila and

Aaron have come to stepfamily life with the very common fantasy (Papernow, 1993) that they could "blend" like a first-time family. As a consequence, each new and unexpected difference is a signal that the family isn't working. For new parents encountering two-year-old temper tantrums a developmental framework provides perspective and guidance about where to mobilize energy (we remove a screaming two-year-old from the supermarket; we do not attempt to reason him out of his tantrum). Likewise, both these couples need some information about normal stepfamily dynamics before they can refocus their energy from blaming each other or themselves and trying to prevent the inevitable, to trying to understand each other and manage the normal developmental process together.[1,2]

Gestalt principles serve us well in our educational role. They remind us to remain ever attentive to the size of our clients' appetites. Two or three items at a time are much more likely to be fully digested than a flood of information. This is particularly true in a family system already flooded with more than the normal human has attention for. Gestalt principles also remind us to respect boundaries, asking for interest before beginning to talk ("Would you like some information?"). The oral imagery of the original Gestalt therapists (Perls, Hefferline, & Goodman, 1951) reminds us that swallowing whole without digesting is not real learning and reminds us to support our clients' process of integrating any new information we offer ("Is this useful to you?" "Can you turn to each other and talk to each other about what fits and what doesn't fit in your experience of your family?")

Conversely, it is entirely unfair to a desperate couple to treat a request for guidance as a sign of "introjection." Providing good help to remarried couples often requires that we extend our educational role to offering specific actions that help the couple to more effectively meet the challenges of living in this kind of family system. A few good pieces of "advice" can help remarried couples withdraw their energy from hopeless pursuits and invest their energy where it can be most useful. All too often, however, therapists make suggestions based on their own faulty combinations of what works in first-time families and the fantasy of the quickly "blended" family (make a tight couple unit quickly, make a single set of rules, treat all children equally, spend time together as a whole family). The results are disastrous. The following action steps, many of which couples cannot invent by themselves, will be more supportive of stepfamily development.

One-to-One Time

The urge to "blend" immediately often leads new stepfamilies to plan most of their activities as a whole family, with unhappy results. In fact, energy spent "blending" would be much better spent "compartmentalizing" (Papernow, 1993, p. 390). Adequate one-to-one time is important in any family and critical in a stepfamily where any time the whole family spends in one room will intensify insider-outsider issues, loyalty binds, and clashing fixed gestalts of how things "should be." The adult couple need time alone without the interruption and divisive pull of differential close relationships with children. The stepparent-child pairs need time alone without the pull of the stronger parent-child relationship. Biological parent-child pairs need time alone without having to accommodate a stranger.

In our vignettes, one-to-one time would provide reliable opportunities for Regina to occupy the insider role with John as well as with Tammy. It would give Tammy, and Sheila and Aaron's children, reliable connection time with their parents, and time with their stepparents where they can get to know them without an intervening parent. Biological parents in both of these families need time alone with their children without worrying about abandoning or offending their new partner, and time alone with their spouses without having to attend to their children's needs. Their ex-spouses need clear time to communicate with each other about children that doesn't interrupt the new couple's time together.

Clashing Cultures

Gestalt principles remind us that good contact requires differentiation. This is counterintuitive to many people's picture of "family" as a place where values and rituals are held in common. It may help remarried couples to be reminded that in first-time families shared norms develop a little at a time over many years. The constant experience of differences in early stepfamily life, although upsetting and frustrating, is part of a normal process of bringing together two different cultures. Asking any part of the family to abandon its identity too quickly invites resistance. The goal is to redirect the couple's energy away from straining to forge a single family culture precipitously and toward getting to know each other.

The work involved can be overwhelming, and couples like Sheila and Aaron often need help allowing a few things to become figural and letting the rest stay in the background until there is sufficient awareness and energy to attend to them. Setting aside regular time to discuss step issues, taking one item at a time, choosing only an initial few areas for change, and allowing many differences to remain in place can make the process more manageable.

Single stepparents like Regina entering an established biological parent-child system can be encouraged to pick two or three things they would most like to see changed to make them more comfortable. More changes are too hard on children. Fewer changes unfairly require the outsider to remain entirely a stranger in foreign territory. When two sets of children are involved, as in Sheila and Aaron's family, the family needs to choose at the most four or five central household rules that everybody follows, leaving other differences in place at least for a while. The shared set of rules will work best if no more than two or three changes are asked of each set of adults and children and if each child (and adult) is asked to adjust equally. Children's difficulties following new rules can often be most accurately attributed to struggles with multiple changes and losses and painful loyalty binds rather than "poor behavior." Sheila and Aaron's children are old enough to participate in the process of establishing those rules. Younger children can be consulted on what is hard and what is easy for them, with decision making left in parents' hands.

In Sheila and Aaron's family, it may be that all children are required to clean up their own dishes, but the family may have some nights where the whole family eats like Sheila's and some when the whole family eats like Aaron's, and a few where each family eats in its own way.

The anxiety-provoking task of confronting differences will proceed more easily if the therapist helps new stepfamilies to make more figural what they *do* have in common. Aaron and Sheila both love to play. Both left marriages in which there was very little fun. They need encouragement to take time apart from children to revel in that easy connection. Regina's step-daughter Tammy wants to learn to swim, and this desire provides an opportunity for Regina, a champion swimmer, to teach her. Particularly in the early stages, experiencing commonalities in steppairs will require one-to-one time without competition from the stronger biological connection. As step relations strengthen, this will become less necessary.

Children

Parenting children in a stepfamily is a complicated task that generates many questions from remarried couples. Couples laboring under the fantasy that a stepparent can move easily into a parental role will find themselves especially frustrated and anxious. "We do know some things about what works here," the therapist can say. "Would you like to hear?"

Until children and stepparents know each other well, discipline is best left in the hands of the biological parent with the stepparent operating as a sounding board, out of children's earshot. The early stepparent role can be framed very much like an aunt or uncle or babysitter. The stepparent is in charge, as any other adult would be, when the biological parent is not present. He or she enforces the rules of the household (which include the two or three new ones brought by the stepparent). As in all new and awkward situations for which there are few guidelines, scripts help. Couples often ask what to say when a child says, "But you're not my mother." The stepparent can reply, "You're right. I'm not. It's a lot of changes for all of us. Your mom will always be your mom. You and I will get to know each other slowly. Maybe we'll come to love each other. Maybe not!

Meanwhile I'm the grown-up in charge tonight and it's your bedtime, the same bedtime you always have."

Research on children's adjustment in divorce and remarriage has very clearly established that those who do the most poorly have parents who remain in conflict with each other (Hobart, 1987; Johnston, Gonzales, & Campbell, 1987; Kline, Johnston, & Tschann, 1991). Whereas adults can and must separate from their ex-spouses, children remain inextricably and forever, biologically and emotionally, tied to the parents who formed them. When one or both members of a remarried couple cannot resist the urge to fight in front of children, or to bad-mouth an ex-spouse or his or her new partner, children deteriorate. The "language of wishing" is again useful: "Of course you wish you could just get rid of your ex-husband." A vivid metaphor helps make the point as strongly as it needs to be made: "The truth is that to ask your children to reject their father is to ask them to reject a piece of themselves. It's like asking them to chop off a piece of their hearts. They can't do it without bleeding to death." Loosening children's loyalty binds extends to resisting the temptation to use children to carry unpleasant messages. "Tell your Daddy he isn't giving us enough money," is *never* a good task for a child. When parents cannot desist, it is a therapeutic issue.

It is worth repeating that we need to resist the urge to offer more information than is digestible in an already overloaded system. Gestalt principles remind us to match information to current felt needs, and to facilitate the couple's integration process: "Will this work for you? Talk together about this." "Can you help each other voice what will work for each one of you, what you can't do?" "Can we look together at what you might be able to do with some support?"

And we need to remember that whereas the fact that stepfamilies cannot function like first-time families may provide relief to some, it will be very disappointing news for others. For some couples normalizing information will provide enough new ground to free the family to function more successfully. For others letting go of the old "gestalt" may prove painful indeed. Gestalt principles of respect for resistance remind us that we cannot immediately disabuse our clients of their longing for what in our culture remains the image of a "real" family. Difficulties with relinquishing these deeply held wishes should be treated not as recalcitrance but as griefwork. We explore what is being lost: "What had you imagined? Do you know when you first thought about that? Can you tell your partner about that?" We support the partner: "Your job is just to listen and be curious, if you can." We create a safe space for expressing the feelings of loss and disappointment that this is not the family either had imagined. And we can stem the embarrassment at having "wrong ideas" by validating for them that many many couples come to remarriage with these kinds of wishes.

Lens Number 2: "I" and "Thou" Awareness

As Gestalt therapists we know that fully developed and shared awareness is the building block for any good relationship. This is especially true in remarried couples, where our Gestalt training guides us to pay particular attention to how the couple builds awareness of each member's very different experience of the same event. It helps to conceptualize this as a dual task: borrowing from the language of Buber, an "I" task and a "Thou" task. The "I" task involves each family member gaining language and a voice for his or her particular stepfamily role. The "Thou" task requires using eyes and ears to see and hear and understand other family member's experience.

In our work with stepfamilies we need to listen for whether the person in each position in the remarried system can describe his or her experience. If not, we will need to provide some support. Stepparents may need help finding language for their outsider position: "I get jealous when every time I talk to you your child can interrupt us." "I can't seem to get a word in edgewise." "No one looks at me or speaks to me when your children are here." Biological parents may need support to describe their dilemmas as the insider: "I feel so torn." "Everybody wants a piece of me." "I can't balance all these needs." Often family members need help telling each other about their losses. For stepparents it may be, "I so wish I could love this child like my own," or, "I thought your kids would welcome me. It's so painful that they don't." For the biological parent it may be, "It's so sad that this family can't be like a first-time family." Children may need help talking about what the divorce and remarriage have been like for them: "I was so surprised." "I miss Daddy when I'm with Mommy and I miss Mommy when I'm with Daddy." Children especially need language for their loyalty binds: "I hate it when Mommy says bad things about Daddy," and for all of the changes in their lives.

When all stepfamily members have language for their experience (even if they are not yet listening to each other) they are to be congratulated on achieving a crucial milestone in becoming a stepfamily—they can talk about what it's like. If not, one of our first tasks is to help this to happen. We approach the task of deepening awareness in stepfamilies with the understanding that many obstacles make this task a difficult one. The feelings to be named and voiced are nobody's favorites (jealousy, disappointment, fear, inadequacy). Acknowledging them may bring on a wave of shame. As we have seen, mirroring and empathy from one's partner ("Oh, I know what that feels like. It's like you're invisible, isn't it!"), which assists in deepening awareness and lifts shame, is especially hard to come by in the stepcouple system. Last, but not least, most couples bring ground full of images and expectations rooted in first-time family life. This puts them in the position of trying to find their way around brand new territory with an outmoded map, with road signs that distort and confuse present experience. The expectation, for instance, that parents should love their children unconditionally makes the stepparent's experience of jealousy, disconnection, and inadequacy feel like a wrong turn rather than a rocky passage on the way to forging a new relationship. Finally, the legacy of loss upon which new couples must build their lives together sharpens the pain of facing the differences that inevitably emerge as awareness deepens. Thus, as in every other therapeutic endeavor, what appears as "resistance" is often pain or shame.

Gestalt principles remind us that good therapy often involves providing appropriate support to promote healthy process. A variety of moves will provide support to stepcouples' individual awareness.

1. Support begins with the therapist's ability to pay full and (unlike the partners) nondefensive *attention*. It is especially hard to find language when the other person's figure competes for attention. In a stepfamily the therapist may be the only person able to pay full attention to each family member's inner sensation long enough to help him or her access often negative and as yet unformed feelings. A stepparent may be able to find language for her experience in response to "What does it feel like, Regina, when Tammy doesn't talk to you?" from an empathic and interested therapist. The same question from her anxiety-ridden husband is more likely to sound like "What in the world is wrong with you?" and is more likely to be silencing rather than supportive.

2. Support for awareness may extend to *offering language* that moves the person from an uncomfortable physical sensation to feelings with words: "I'll bet it's painful that your wife can't connect with your daughter the way you do." "Ever feel torn?" "Ever feel like you're caught in the middle?" "Would the right words be 'left out'?" As Gestalt therapists we do not presume that we know the experience or the "real meaning" of our clients' behavior. We must make informed guesses, but remain respectful of the clients' subjective experience.

3. Like all therapists, we empathize. "That must be painful." "I'm betting that was tough to hear." Our attention and our empathy heighten the feeling, and, like airing the down in a comforter, gives the feeling room to loft.

4. Our Gestalt training guides us to pay attention not just to verbal content but to the *whole physical organism* of our clients. Particularly at moments of step dilemmas, nonverbal cues may lead the way to helping a partner find his or her voice: "I noticed your shoulders just slumped when John said that. I wonder what you were feeling?"

5. *Attend to pain and shame.* The feelings that must be named, voiced, and heard in stepfamilies are often hard to bear and hard to hear. The attendant shame distorts awareness and si-

lences communication. We can guess, for instance, that her response to the negative valence of her feelings underlies Regina's difficulty expressing herself. When she finally managed to say that she felt invisible, we can guess that perhaps John's critical snipe ("That's ridiculous. You're the adult.") might have been preceded by searing disappointment that Regina is not comfortable in the new family. The cycle of shame and pain continued as Regina was further shamed by John's response and so became silent, in turn increasing John's disappointment.

We can begin to interrupt this cycle by turning our full, accepting attention to each partner's internal process. To John we might say, "What happened inside you when Regina said she felt invisible?" "I wonder if you felt sad or disappointed?" To Regina we might say, "What happened inside you when John said, 'You're the adult'?" "Is it embarrassing that you feel so badly? A lot of people in stepfamilies feel this way. Is that surprising to you?" Then we might check for digestion: "Does that help at all?"

6. Implicit in the above exchanges is the truth that when engaged in individual work it is crucial that we *remain systemic*. To blame either partner, or to focus exclusively on one partner, will not serve stepcouple development. This remains as true when working with individual stepcouple members as when working with the couple or family.

It is worth noting that all of these supportive moves—paying full attention, providing language, empathizing, heightening nonverbal experience, watching for pain and shame, and refusing to blame either partner—also provide some of the mirroring that is so often missing in early stepcouple life. Increased mirroring lowers anxiety, which in turn opens the airwaves for both individual and joint awareness.

Whereas the "I" awareness task focuses on each individual's attention to his or her inner process, the "Thou" awareness task depends upon the willingness and ability to pay attention to the *other's* experience. Family members who have mastered this notice each other: "I notice you haven't said much during dinner." They express interest in each other's struggles: "What's happening with you?" They respond to each other with respect and genuine curiosity ("That must be hard. Tell me more.") rather than blame ("What's wrong with you that you're so quiet?") or dismissal ("That's ridiculous, you're the adult.").

In a stepfamily we listen for whether both insiders and outsiders, adults and children, can speak about their experience *and* have begun to understand what it is like for other family members. When stepfamilies do this well, whether consistently or (equally important) intermittently, we need to congratulate them, to highlight and support this crucial developmental achievement for successful stepfamily living.

When they do not, we need to look for moments in which this skill can be taught: "Everyone in this family seems to have a real good voice. You all seem to speak up really well. I'm impressed with that. But things are hard around here, and I think it's partly because what's missing is the listening part. Do you recognize what I'm talking about?" "There, I saw it right there!" We then provide concrete, immediate data ("Sheila said . . . and then Aaron said . . .") that tie our intervention to the couple's actual experience in the session.

In building both individual and joint awareness, Gestalt theory and practice direct us to pay attention to whether each person in the couple is speaking in a way that is most likely to connect with the other person. Direct requests will communicate much more information than indirect accusations: "You never even look at me" provides less information and creates more static than "It would make such a difference to me if you would look me in the eye every now and then while your children are visiting." Building connection may include providing support for "hanging in" to get heard when a partner doesn't get it. To Regina we might say, "Do you feel like he got it? Do you want to ask what he understood?"

Knowledge of stepfamily dynamics, then—insider and outsider roles, sharp differences in experience, differential attachment—guides us in helping couples like John and Regina and Aaron and Sheila to begin connecting more fully with each other. The "I-Thou" perspective and the importance of individual and mutual awareness provide a frame in which we can view the therapeutic process and help couples achieve these crucial developmental tasks.

Lens Number 3: Couple Process

For some remarried couples some good information about step-family dynamics, a little help identifying their own feelings, and some support to hear each other through the pain and anxiety is enough to untangle the knot and facilitate further movement. Work with these couples often focuses primarily on the therapist answering questions and engaging individually in turn with each partner. For many couples the dilemma lies not only in lack of good information, but in *how* they work together to meet the challenges their family structure presents. In more troubled stepcouples we often see a pattern of interaction between the couple that actually intensifies their step issues.

Our vignettes describe two very common couple dynamics, both of which intensify already challenging step dynamics. In the first vignette one person seems to dominate while the other collapses. In the second both members are highly mobilized. In both cases we will need to ask the couple to turn to each other and talk so that we can see the choreography that is getting them into trouble. Often, as we will see, couple work is enhanced by individual awareness work and vice versa.

In the first vignette, John initially appears to have the more powerful voice, while Regina is having difficulty finding her voice and getting heard. We can imagine that this might be true even if John and Regina were a first-time couple. However, the fact that John is the adult in the already more dominant insider team and Regina is the outsider with no other support in the family intensifies the dilemma. I am guessing that neither John nor Regina knows that their dinner table dynamic is a normal one in early stepfamilies. But in this case I choose to begin with the couple process, saving my normalizing information for later. Another therapist may make a different decision. I am assuming that John and Regina's appetites for information about normal stepfamily dynamics and their ability to digest it may be larger after their anxiety has been lowered and they are more tuned in to each other.

I might begin with my appreciation, which might sound like "You have between you two skills every couple needs: talking and listening. John is very good at talking and making statements and requests. Regina is good at listening and asking questions and following up with another question. Have you noticed that?" (I do notice that John's "talking" does not give much information about what he is feeling, but I am willing to let that go for now, to keep the focus on their uneven dynamic. Likewise, I will wait until later to explore with them how their particular choreography parallels and intensifies their stepfamily dynamics.) Both nod vigorously, and I ask them to talk with each other for a bit about what they recognize. Soon John again begins to express his frustration at Regina's "lack of aggressiveness" and Regina again begins asking questions. I stop them and say, "Guess what. It's happening again! Did you notice? John is making statements and Regina is asking questions." They laugh a bit and we talk some more about that. As Gestalt therapists we are interested first in raising awareness—helping the couple to become aware of how they do what they do individually and as a couple.

Once they are more fully focused on their process as a couple and a little more relaxed, I may stop to give them a little bit of information about their "insider" and "outsider" roles. "You know, some of what is happening to you here would happen between you two no matter what kind of family you lived in. You, John, are a person who makes statements and demands when you are upset. You, Regina, are a person who asks questions and holds back when you are upset. But some of what is happening here has to do with the fact that you are living in a *stepfamily*. In this family there are 'insiders' who know each other and have a lot of agreements about how things should go and an 'outsider' who doesn't know the rules of the game or even all the players as well as they know each other. And there is no question that it is easier to find your voice as an insider than it is as an outsider. So you have two layers of things going on here and they both go in the same direction. So that makes it extra hard."

As Gestalt therapists we are interested in giving our clients the tools to do something different in the here and now. Sometimes raised awareness alone is enough to enable a couple or an individual to take more control of their behavior and try something that works better. At the same time, many people need an actual experience of something new in order to change their behavior. We call this new behavior an "experiment." Much has been written about the Gestalt experiment (Zinker, 1977). For this chapter, suffice it to say that the *experiment* is presented with the attitude the word implies—let's try this and see what we can learn. Further, we aim to design an experiment at the right level for the people involved: it can neither be so elementary as to be boring nor so difficult as to be paralyzing.

The combination of complementary and probably lifelong emotional habits, a couple interaction that puts the two together in a polarizing way, and a stepfamily structure that intensifies each side of the interaction makes this a dynamic that is particularly daunting for John and Regina. Now that this stepcouple are fully focused on *how* they interact, they have enough attention and shared energy to try something new, but they do not have the resources to invent it themselves. It's time for a small experiment. "What I've noticed is that you each have *one* of the two skills. Plus the stepfamily structure you're in supports the side you already have. Would you be interested in learning the other?" They nod vigorously.

"How about if John asks questions, and listens? In this experiment John can *say only what he hears or sees or understands about Regina.* He must add nothing new of his own to what Regina says. Regina's task is to *make statements* about what she is thinking or feeling or seeing. She is to ask no questions of John. Would you be willing to try that?" In this experiment we are interested in teaching both John and Regina a "nonintuitive" skill, something they don't bring naturally to this relationship. These skills would be important and desirable for any couple with John and Regina's dynamics. But because they are in a stepfamily it is crucial to this family's development for the outsider stepparent to gain enough voice so that more information enters the already established parent-child system, and for the insider to be able to open his ears and his heart to that information.

As John and Regina attempt the experiment, Regina begins in a halting voice to struggle for words to describe what it is like to sit at the dinner table and watch her husband and his daughter talk to each other. We pause several times as John abandons his mirroring role and attempts to talk Regina out of her "wrong" feelings and Regina collapses and shifts her attention back to him. As we continue working at the level of the couple's interaction, we continue to focus our lens "systemically," looking always to give feedback to both members of the couple rather than blaming one or the other and appreciating fully what the couple are doing well. We marvel with them at how hard this apparently simple experiment is. We notice how very hard they are working to try something new. We also notice that although John says he wants Regina to speak up he "accidentally" makes moves that shut her down. We notice that Regina seems to allow him to do this.

Work at the couple level may move back to the individual level before one or both members have enough internal connection to continue at the couple level. When Regina withdraws in silence for the third time, despite the fact that John is now fully attending to her, I ask, "What happened to you just then?" It is important to remember that for stepparents like Regina, intimate moments with one's new spouse are repeatedly interrupted by a child with whom the partner has a longer and in some ways more intimate connection. Thus attention to Regina's tight mouth and slumped shoulders will likely bring her to feelings like jealousy, loneliness, inadequacy, and resentment. Although these are normal responses to being left out, they are nobody's favorite feelings. For Regina, raised in a family where "selfishness" was a sin, these are likely to be particularly shameful feelings. She will need some support from the therapist to keep expressing them rather than withdrawing in shame. Support may range from education (these feelings are universal responses to this kind of role) to supporting awareness work (helping Regina to describe, or describing for her, the many real things she actually sees and hears that make her feel like an outsider) and, as we will see in the next section, individual work with "unfinished business" (identifying where she learned her definition of "selfish" and sorting out the present from the past).

It is important then to return to the couple: "Can you tell John, 'When you and Tammy talk only to each other and you don't even look at me, I feel...'?" John listens for a while as Regina gains her voice, but then he tenses and begins again trying to tell Regina she shouldn't be feeling that way. Regina becomes silent again. To balance our intervention we now turn to John to deepen his awareness of what happens inside him at those moments, and to provide some support that might help him stay with the "Thou" task of hearing Regina.

Now that Regina has more of the voice John thought he wanted, we can ask him whether he is aware that he blocks her just when he's getting what he thought he wanted. "I'm interested in that. Are you?" The couple work now requires some individual awareness work as we guide John to attend inside himself. I ask him to attend to what happened *just before* he began speaking. He may begin with "tense, frustrated." Again, as Gestalt therapists we remain respectful of our clients' boundaries. Before intervening, it is as if I am interested in having John come to the "door" of his self and decide he wants to let me in rather than barging in with my expertise. If he is not ready, or he says that he is but his body position suggests otherwise, then we turn our attention to the missing supports required for new awareness: "What's stopping you from being interested in this right now? What would you need to be ready to talk about this? What might happen if we did talk about it—how do you think you might feel?"

Combining our knowledge of stepfamilies with what I know about John, we can guess that as the biological parent in this system, John is faced with feelings engendered by his stuck insider position: feeling inadequate, frightened, and responsible that the family "isn't working," feeling torn, and wanting everyone to love each other, desperate that it isn't going to work out. We can also guess that these feelings of helplessness are likely to be especially shameful for a "doer" like John. For John we can guess that the fact that Regina cannot feel or act like an insider in the presence of John's intimate parent-child relationship with Tammy is not easy to sit with. What looks like an attack on Regina every time she opens her mouth may actually be John's attempt to soothe his own pain by fixing something that cannot be fixed at this time in his stepfamily.

As with Regina, we can provide support on a number of

levels. One may be educational: we can tell John how normal his feelings are given his position in the new stepfamily. We can draw his awareness to his wishfulness. For stepfamily members eager to fix what cannot be fixed, the therapist needs to appreciate and respect the urge to action while transforming the energy from hard and forward-pushing action to softer awareness. What I call "the language of wishing" is helpful here: "You so *wish* that Regina could enter this conversation easily." "You so *wish* that Regina could love your daughter as you do." "You are a do-er. It must be so hard for you to sit with . . ." Or we can go back to the past to sort out how John learned the urge to fix, what holds it in place, what his fears were if he didn't fix it, and again, sort present from past. Because this is an ongoing dynamic in Regina and John's relationship, we will have many opportunities to intervene on this issue, and we may choose different places to intervene at different times. And, as the couple are ready, we can continue to provide a few more basic pieces of information about normal insider-outsider dynamics.

Whatever the individual intervention we choose, it is important that the therapist return to the couple. "Can you tell Regina what you understand better about her role and yours?" "Can you tell Regina how much you wish Regina could love your daughter as you do?" "Can you tell Regina what it is like inside of you when she tells you that she feels left out?"

Moving to the couple dynamics in our second vignette, we can see on the positive side that both Sheila and Aaron are lively, highly articulate, passionate people. What is missing is the listening and absorbing end of the continuum. In addition, both partners are more blaming than informative, and both mobilize fully around each item that enters their awareness. As a result, their expressiveness does not result in greater understanding. Nor do they engage over any one highly conflicted item in a way that could resolve it. Rather, each exchange generates more tension and anxiety, heightens the couple's polarization, and adds to the already overwhelming number of lively figures under consideration. In any couple, this is a hard way to live. In a stepfamily, where every moment of contact already offers more engaging, potentially polarizing figures than can be humanly digested, couples like these find themselves completely overwhelmed.

Again we begin with positive, affirming feedback to this distressed couple. "You two have something very important in a healthy couple. You both have full, strong voices. Is this something you're aware of and value about each other?" For Sheila and Aaron this engenders a surprisingly warm and sweet conversation about how they met passing notes in a graduate school class, how both had been married to rather stolid quiet partners, and what fun they had with each other.

Now we can move to "This works great when you're both excited about the same thing. The problem is that when you have a difference, neither of you is listening to the other. Have you noticed this? Does this interest you?" As they explore this they launch into another argument. "You two are *great* at objecting. This makes life really exciting. It worked OK when you weren't living together. Now that you have more to deal with it makes life very rough. Does that ring true for you?" For this couple, who chronically move too fast, taking time for digestion with each new input is especially important.

Now the couple are beginning to slow down and listen—to me at least. "What's missing is any kind of 'joining' or reaching out to each other. I have an idea. Are you interested?" They nod vigorously. I want their full attention before I offer them an experiment. "I think this is going to be a real challenge. Still interested?" They nod again. "Would you like to see what happens if you try finding *one or two things you understand* about what your partner said *before* replying. Understanding is not the same thing as agreeing. You may not agree. But the important part of this exercise is finding something you *understand* before you add anything new. Would you be willing to try that?"

This does indeed prove to be a difficult exercise for Sheila and Aaron. Both need much support and direction to stop and say what they understand before launching. We spend much of the session marveling, and occasionally giggling, over how hard it is. The exercise proves successful, however, providing a structure in which each gives the other a little of the missing mirroring, and small bits of information get heard. As they each feel a little more understood, the tension begins to recede and little moments of genuine understanding of each other take hold. Sheila and Aaron have made a tiny start on the "Thou" task.

For this couple, working slowly continues to require tremendous attention and self-control. Normalizing information about multiple "culture clashes" in a double stepfamily provides considerable relief from the sense of inadequacy. An article about this proves validating to both of them (Papernow, 1987). Having discovered that Sheila and Aaron left first marriages with people who were steady and reliable but proved to be too dull for them, I congratulate them wholeheartedly for having chosen something very different this time. "Now the task is to learn how to manage this much energy in a situation that gives you a lot of things to be excited about. This is hard for most people. It's especially hard for you two!"

On this theme another simple but still quite challenging exercise will be to keep count of the number of issues they are attempting to discuss in any several-minute period. "You know how we've been saying that the beginning of living in a stepfamily is a culture clash. There are lots and lots of differences you didn't expect. When you have two people as lively as you are, it's easy to find yourselves engaged with many issues at once. Can we count the number you've already mentioned?" Again, as their interest mounts I can try an experiment: "Would you be willing to try to take one at a time?" If the experiment proves difficult, they need us to move back to awareness rather than forward to action. "Did you know you just added another issue?" "Let's stop for a moment. Can we just *add up* the number of things you're trying to talk about right now?"

It may be that they cannot do this on their own and will need me to let them know each time a new issue has been added. Because this is such a difficult task for this couple, it may help them to move out of their solely verbal mode. We could get out a piece of newsprint and print the issues as they come up. I could stick a pencil in a soft drink can and rattle it (or have them rattle it) each time one of them adds something new. "It's happening again. Did either of you notice?" Better yet, we could ask a couple like Aaron and Sheila to make a mark each time one of them responds *on the same subject,* much as you would keep track of how many times two children were able to hit a volleyball back and forth.

As Gestalt therapists, our attention to the whole body provides us with many other interventions that support slowing down: "Has either of you noticed how you are breathing? Can you feel the tension in your body? When you feel that way, try sitting back and taking a breath instead of moving forward and holding your breath. Try it right now and see what happens." Again, the task is to build Aaron and Sheila's awareness of *how* they are managing the wealth of step issues facing them, and to give them some behaviors that will help them work better together as a couple.

The Gestalt therapist who watches the remarried couple is looking for the following: How does this couple's choreography support the full development of each person's awareness and good contact across the differences created by their stepfamily structure? How does it interfere? The fear and polarization inherent in remarried life make it especially imperative that the therapist follow the basic guidelines of all systemic work: describe each partner's contribution *equally,* and begin by describing what is working *well.* Then (and only then) can the therapist look for what Sonia Nevis and Joseph Zinker of the Gestalt Institute of Cleveland call "the underbelly," what is not working so well (Zinker & Nevis, this volume).

Lens Number 4: Unfinished Business

In a basically healthy stepfamily, accurate information, attention to the couple's here-and-now process, and a few useful suggestions are enough to resolve most difficulties. As in any therapy, when we experience substantial resistance, it is likely that current step dynamics are evoking painful unfinished situations. For a stepmother who occupied a "left-out" position in her family of origin, information about normal step dynamics will not provide enough support to bear the evocative pain of the constant slights and disconnections of the stepmother role. A man who grew up in a chaotic alcoholic family will find the anxiety of new and imperfect step relations much more anxiety provoking than someone from a family where differences were regularly resolved without someone getting hurt.

An image I call "the bruise theory of feelings" helps clients to understand this concept. When you hit your arm by accident on the table where the flesh is healthy, it hurts. If you are already bruised there, it hurts a whole different way. If the hurt was large, the pain can be almost blinding. Family living is inherently bumpy. Stepfamily living is that much more bumpy, especially in the beginning. If you have old hurts, there are lots of opportunities in a stepfamily to get them banged again!

As we look for unfinished business in stepfamilies, however, we need to remain impeccably attuned to the dangers of pathologizing our clients' behavior. *Early stepfamily life can make the sanest of us crazed.* We begin *always* by first treating even very powerful feelings like disappointment, jealousy, and irritation over differences as *normal responses to remarried family life.* We provide normalizing information, offer a few appropriate action steps, help our clients identify the normal stepfamily events that are evoking their feelings, help them find language that fits their experience, help them talk to each other and listen to each other in a way that builds connection and enhances problem solving. Only when stepfamily members persist in organizing their experience in a way that doesn't fit current reality is it time to look for "unfinished business" that is interfering.

Our second vignette provides an example. Despite normalizing information about stepparent-child relationships and a great deal of work on their couple process, Sheila's disappointment that Aaron cannot fill a father role continues to consistently turn to anger and blame, and Sheila and Aaron continue in cycles of conflict over Aaron's stepfather role. Sheila persists with "But Aaron *should* be the father. He's not being reliable." Meanwhile Aaron seems unable to muster more than a few moments of sympathy for Sheila's difficulty with this. Aaron's lack of support seems to hasten Sheila's flight back to shrill "shoulds," which in turn intensifies Aaron's rigidity. When realistic information makes so little impact, we can guess that current events are hitting old hurts. As long as those old experiences remain "unfinished," they will interfere with Sheila and Aaron's ability to come to terms with the challenges of forging a workable stepfamily. We need to do some individual work with Sheila and with Aaron to explore the old hurts.

My preference is at least to begin this individual work in the couple setting so that each partner gains a fuller understanding of the other's dilemmas, rather than reverting to individual therapy. It is important that individual work be balanced between the partners. This may mean doing a piece of work with each partner in a single session or returning in subsequent sessions to the other partner. Because the goal is a better-functioning couple, it is equally important to return to the present to teach the couple how to work together with awareness of each other's vulnerable spots.

In fact, further exploration reveals painful old bruises for both Aaron and Sheila that their experience of being in a stepfamily is hitting. Until we can attend to the pain from these old hurts, it will distort their current experience. We begin this time with Sheila by asking her to pay attention to what she feels inside her as she says, "Aaron should be the father." "A tremendous pain" is the answer. And then she launches again into "But it shouldn't be this way. Aaron should be the father."

"Can I ask you something?" I say to her. "Can you tell me something about your own family?" It emerges that Sheila's father gambled. She attended seven schools in five years as houses were bought and lost. Her father would promise her a new bicycle, which would appear one day and disappear when it was reclaimed for bad debts a few weeks later. The theme of "unreliability" now makes sense. It begins to become clear to all of us that it is Sheila who was devastated by an unreliable father, not her sons. We acknowledge that Sheila solved this problem in her first marriage by choosing an extremely steady, predictable man. Although this marriage was initially healing and soothing, it proved ultimately dull and passionless. In Aaron Sheila has made a much more challenging choice. He is much warmer and more engaging. However, his very spontaneity also makes him less predictable than Sheila's first husband, and this combined with his step role puts her in much fuller contact with her own loss. Sheila needs help grieving over the original loss of a steady and reliable father. It is to her own father, not to Aaron, that Sheila needs to say, "You should be the father." "Can you imagine your father in your mind?" I ask. He is dead but she can picture him. "I think now that he no longer has to deal with everyday life he could really hear you. Do you think you could talk to him? Do you think you could say to him, 'I needed you to be the father.'?" Sheila now begins to finish some of her "old business" with her father, speaking to him and crying as she is encouraged to tell him what it was like to be a little girl with a daddy who gambled.

Because this is couples work, exploring unfinished individual business includes helping the couple connect with each other. Aaron has clearly been moved watching Sheila work. "Can you tell Sheila what you felt like inside as you watched her do this?" Aaron tells Sheila how painful it must have been for her, how sad he felt, and how mad, for her. "Can you tell Sheila what you understand better about what happens inside her when you say you aren't going to do something fatherly?" "It must really hurt," he says tenderly. Sheila is then asked to tell Aaron how she feels as he is talking to her. "So loved," she says.

As we move back into the present, Sheila also needs help separating her griefwork from her current experience. In fact, Aaron is extremely reliable. He coaches one of her son's soccer team, cooks, makes a decent living, and almost always does what he says he will do. It is likely that Sheila's sons are quite comfortable with his genuine interest in them, and that his unwillingness to step fully into a fathering role spares them a loyalty bind with their own father.

Sheila's disappointment with the limits of the stepfathering role hits so close to her own father's unreliability that she needs help to see the ways she can depend on Aaron through the blinding pain of her old hurts. We help Aaron and Sheila to agree upon some ways in which he can remind her that he is reliable, even when he disappoints her. And we note, as the session is ending, that today was Sheila's turn for some individual attention, and in another time we will explore Aaron's side of the equation.

Sure enough, in a subsequent session Sheila again begins to panic and becomes accusing over a stepfathering issue and

Aaron's rigidity returns. Being careful to balance the work, we are as interested this time in Aaron's lack of empathy and his rigidity as we are in Sheila's pain. "Somehow you've both forgotten that this is a signal that you've hit an old bruise," I say, and to Aaron, "What happens inside you as Sheila panics and begins to push?" "I just shut down," he says. "Can you tell me how you learned to shut down when you feel under pressure?"

Aaron's history reveals that he was an asthmatic child with many restrictions on his play. His father was rather distant and unavailable and his mother was extremely intrusive and demanding. As a child Aaron had little voice for his own needs and no permission to say "no." His repertoire in the face of differences or demands remains extremely limited. He panics, and either attacks or withdraws in silence, which in turn intensifies the pressure from Sheila, which evokes further rigidity from Aaron. "Can you tell Sheila some more about what happened when you and your mother disagreed?" This time we explore the past, not as a piece of an individual piece of work between the therapist and one member of the couple, but in a conversation between the couple. "Can you tell Sheila a story about a time your mother pressured you?" "Sheila, can you tell Aaron what you've learned about him?"

Now it is clearer how Aaron's past organizes his current experience of differing with a lively woman. Like Sheila, Aaron had avoided this problem in his first marriage by choosing a passive, very self-contained woman. Like Sheila, we all note, this was very comforting for a number of years. But as both Aaron and his first wife matured the marriage became confining for both of them.

With Sheila Aaron has an opportunity to learn some new skills, but he needs support to remind him that he does have a voice in this new relationship. We give Aaron a "mantra": "I have a voice in this relationship. Sheila loves me and wants to listen even if she forgets sometimes." We work on helping him tell Sheila he is getting scared before he shuts down, and on helping her lean back and take a breath rather than pushing forward.

We now understand the unfortunate "lock" between Sheila's panic and Aaron's rigidity. Sheila agrees that when Aaron says he needs to stop, she will withdraw, as long as he tells her when she can rely upon him to finish the conversation with her later. At another point we work on helping the couple manage their "trigger points" better, raising their awareness of when they start to tense, helping them each to sit back, take a breath, and slow down, rather than lean forward and speed up.

The chaos and multiple differences and disappointments of combining two lively families would be challenging for anyone. Sheila and Aaron's highly mobilized couple interaction, although it worked well when they were courting, made living as a stepfamily much too charged. And an underlying layer of old individual hurts made step issues like forging a workable stepfathering role much more treacherous. Even if they were not a stepcouple, Sheila and Aaron might have gotten locked as Aaron's spontaneity evoked Sheila's fear of unreliability, and Sheila's habit of accusing and pressuring when she gets frightened triggered Aaron's old rigidity. But, again, issues that might have been challenging in a first-time couple became unbearable and almost unmanageable in the stepfamily setting. In Sheila and Aaron we see the ways in which normal step issues, painful individual issues, and a challenging couple process all intensify each other. Successful work in this couple will continue to move between dealing with current step issues, attending to individual dynamics, and working on their couple process.

Conclusion

Gestalt therapy is an inherently intuitive and multilayered process. Work with stepfamilies is that much more so. I hope that this chapter has contributed to solidifying our own ground and has given us some clues about how as Gestalt therapists we can sort out what we see, feel, and hear as we sit with remarried couples like John and Regina and Sheila and Aaron.

Let us end with the reminder that the skills required to do good work with stepfamilies are not isolated and specialized. Although working well with stepcouples does require knowing something about the special dynamics and developmental tasks of this particular family form, much of what we have discussed here is basic to any good therapy. However, working with step-couples does require the best of us.

It requires, for example, that we remain rigorously systemic, maintaining at all times a wider picture of all the forces at work, refusing to blame any player (including an absent ex-spouse) lest we fracture an already polarized family. It requires balancing a willingness to actively step in and teach while maintaining our full awareness of, and respect for, resistance. It requires validating the power of present stepfamily structure to generate intense feelings while staying tuned to past hurts that will make step dilemmas impossible to resolve by present focus alone. It challenges our abilities to deepen awareness in the face of pain and shame. It stretches our creativity in teaching couples to work together to help each other as their family life awakens old bruises. In many ways, then, couples like John and Regina and Sheila and Aaron provide us with a kind of aerobic training as couples therapists. The concentrated effort, done at one's level of ability, and with appropriate coaching if needed, can be invigorating, strengthening, and even inspiring.

> Several years ago as I neared the end of an airplane trip, my seatmate turned and asked me where I was going. "To a national conference on stepfamilies," I replied. "That sounds boring," he said. "Not a chance," I replied. What is lost in predictability and security is more than gained in an exciting and invigorating family life. It is the very fact that healthy stepfamily living requires full engagement in living well that I find most hopeful, and that makes this work worth it to me. (Papernow, 1993, p. 380)

Notes

1. Any work with stepfamily members should include a referral to the nearest chapter of the Stepfamily Association of America, 212 Lincoln Center, 215 So. Centennial Mall, Lincoln, NE 68508. (402) 477-7837. A list of local chapters is in-

cluded with membership materials, as well as a subscription to the SAA newsletter, which is full of useful articles by both stepfamily members and professionals. Local chapters usually meet monthly, providing educational programs and supportive contact with other stepfamilies. Great Britain also has a very active stepfamily association, and other European countries have recently begun chapters.

2. Many stepcouples appreciate written material they can digest at their own pace and return to repeatedly as needed ("bibliotherapy" one of my clients called it). The publication *Stepfamilies Stepping Ahead* (1989), available from the Stepfamily Association of America as part of the membership fee or at a nominal cost, is an excellent basic primer. Articles and books (see Papernow, 1984, 1987, 1993, *The Stepfamily Bulletin*, and anything on the SAA book list) can also provide much of the mirroring that is missing in early stepfamily life.

References

Glick, P. C., & Lin, S. G. (1986). Recent changes in divorce and remarriage. *Journal of Marriage and the Family, 5*, 7–26.

Hobart, C. (1987). Parent-child relations in remarried families. *Journal of Family Issues, 8*, 259–277.

Johnston, J. R., Gonzales, R., & Campbell, L. E. G. (1987). Ongoing postdivorce conflict and child disturbance. *Journal of Abnormal Child Psychology, 15*, 493–509.

Keshet, J. K. (1980). From separation to stepfamily: A subsystem analysis. *Journal of Family Issues, 1*(4), 517–532.

Kline, M., Johnston, J. R., & Tschann, J. M. (1991). The long shadow of marital conflict: A model of children's postdivorce adjustment. *Journal of Marriage and the Family, 53*, 297–309.

Kohut, H. (1977). *The restoration of the self*. New York: International University Press.

Papernow, P. L. (1984). The stepfamily cycle: An experiential model of stepfamily development. *Family Relations, 33*(3), 355–363. Also available in monograph from the Gestalt Institute of Cleveland, 1588 Hazel Drive, Cleveland, Ohio 44106.

Papernow, P. L. (1987). Thickening the "middle ground": Dilemmas and vulnerabilities for remarried couples. *Psychotherapy, 24*(3S), 630–639.

Papernow, P. L. (1993). *Becoming a stepfamily: Patterns of development in remarried families.* San Francisco: Jossey-Bass.

Perls, F., Hefferline, R., & Goodman, P. (1951). *Gestalt therapy: Excitement and growth in the human personality.* New York: Julian Press.

Stepfamily Association of America. (1989). *Stepfamilies stepping ahead.* Lincoln, NE: Stepfamilies Press.

Zinker, J. C. (1977). *Creative process in Gestalt therapy.* New York: Brunner/Mazel.

6

Gestalt Couples Therapy with Gay Male Couples: Enlarging the Therapeutic Ground of Awareness

Allan Singer

A chapter on Gestalt couples therapy with gay male couples is another sign of the continuing evolution of awareness that same-sex coupling exists and occupies a place in our sociocultural fabric. The inclusion of this chapter in a book on couples therapy expresses an increasing recognition of the reality and importance of gay male coupling among the various forms of intimate possibility. Our culture's awareness of same-sex coupling is emerging very gradually, prompted by the continuing movement toward gay, lesbian, and bisexual rights and the recognition of homosexuality as a legitimate social issue that can no longer be denied. If the world at large is being compelled to become more inclusive of gay male coupling, then the therapeutic community needs to prepare itself to understand as well. In the mental health community, the consideration of gay, lesbian, and bisexual issues in the development of clinical theory and practice both mirrors and informs the larger societal trends. In the past several decades, theoretical models in mental health have shifted from those that pathologize homosexuality to models that increasingly affirm the benign reality of variation in sexual orientation from one individual to another. The clinical shift, in turn, is instrumental in fostering the evolution toward recognition and validation of gay coupling in the culture at large. In adding to the body of literature on intimate relationships and couples therapy within the framework of gay male coupling, I hope that this chapter enlarges our understanding of a Gestalt perspective of the complex textures inherently embroidered within the fabric of any gay male coupling.

The Adventures of Loving: Encountering Common Ground

I'd like to immediately make a disclaimer of sorts. I don't believe that Gestalt couples therapy with a gay (or lesbian or bisexual) couple differs markedly in form from therapy with a heterosexual couple. In some basic sense, a couple is a couple is a couple, regardless of sexual orientation. Each couple, regardless of gender composition, is unique, while also drawing from the common cup of human need for closeness and the desire to belong with another person, deeply. No matter what the sexual and affectional orientations of the pairing, whether same-sex or opposite-sex, coupling endures for many, if not all, as a grand experiment in orbiting two worlds of meaning together, and in defining how two "I's" create a "We," while maintaining their separateness-in-joining. Inevitably, coupling involves a willingness to encounter the mysteries of loving another human being while allowing oneself to be loved.

So, what is this thing called love? And how different, really, is gay love and gay coupling at heart? From a romanticized, poetic frame, love is mysterious, regardless of the genders involved, defying the reductionism of logic: "love is blind." On the other hand, love may involve all degrees of "optical" acuity. Some couples seem to locate each other, and each other's emotional nooks and crannies, like heat-seeking missiles (to use an image that is both phallic and militaristic) or, as a colleague once said, "like bats in the night." Coupling, gay or straight, may occur as an accident of fate, a coincidence of fortune, or an act of longed-for intention. To make an effective coupling, gay or otherwise, I believe that we need to experience a wish to belong in a committed way to another person. In defining a commitment, we typically experience some form of intensified attraction toward another, an attraction toward personal and/or physical characteristics, interests, and/or values. We typically develop beliefs about the other person's wishes, goals, and personal capabilities, which inform our decisions to get closer. Our beliefs about the other may be informed by experiential data, or perhaps may be enlarged projections of our deepest longings and yearnings, applied as a wishful image onto the other. Over time, an increase in realistic understanding and empathy for the other supports a developing sense of caring for the other's well-being. Ultimately, the movement toward coupling, regardless of sexual orientation, is defined by the belief that we have some things to give to the other and want to receive from the other, and that the cycle of giving and receiving enhances our respective lives enough to inform a mutual commitment (as well as to tolerate the price of what doesn't feel good or what's less than ideal in the coupling).

Whether they realize it or not in defining their commitment, any couple enter into the experiment of joining together implicitly entertaining both the expansive sense of promise and hope for their relationship, and the ultimate challenges in encountering differences, which sometimes result in emotional and interpersonal contraction. Likewise, any two people in intimate combination carry their emotional and relational blueprints with them, and throughout their relationship they will experience emotional stirrings emanating from their own regressive grounds of history, their respective riverbeds of early issues. So coupling, regardless of sexual orientation, is a great adventure, sometimes sailing along the high seas of hopeful expectation, sometimes navigating rocky shoals of difference, and sometimes subject to being buffeted, if not beached, along the voyage through charted and uncharted emotional-relational terrain.

Although a couple is a couple in defining the common grounds of loving, on the other hand there are differences implicit in gay coupling, and specific issues that are necessarily unique from heterosexual coupling. What certainly does differentiate any gay, lesbian, or bisexual couple is the sociocultural experience of being part of a marginalized and stigmatized minority. Gestalt therapy emphasizes that the meaning of any figure draws on its relationship to the meaning of its context, its ground. Growing up and ultimately identifying oneself as gay means growing up within a complex field of negating beliefs and attitudes, unavoidably introjected or internalized in the course of development. As therapists, failing to understand this complex field would be a serious error in appreciating the potential tensions and conflicts embodied in the Gestalt notion of "polarities" in a given gay couple. In addition, the claiming of a gay identity, and subsequently an identity as a gay couple, given the existing ground of prejudice, inevitably fosters the employment of certain defenses and resistances to contact as a necessary survival strategy. When individual resistances have been developed in a heightened way, they will manifest in the couple synergistically in an equally heightened way. Later in this chapter, I will discuss these clinical considerations with greater depth. For now, I invite the reader to consider the necessary differences implicit in gay male coupling, along with the similarities to any form of coupling. I believe with conviction that as therapists, Gestalt-trained or otherwise, we hold a much richer experience of what is figural for a given gay couple if we appreciate what exists in the ground of the couple. We then have a more textured ground for our own figures to emerge as well.

A Brief Gestalt Primer

What is Gestalt therapy, and how does it support us in dealing with couples and, specifically, gay male couples? Since readers may approach this chapter with varying degrees of familiarity with the fundamentals of Gestalt theory, I'd like to outline some of the basic precepts that inform a Gestalt therapist's ground for understanding and intervention in any intimate system. Briefly, Gestalt therapy is a systemic therapy with a particular fascination with the quality of contact in the here and now. Making effective contact between self and other requires ongoing movement

from physiological sensation to cognitive and emotional awareness, to excitement and mobilization, and then to effective action, followed by withdrawal from contact in order to digest the
experience and reorient for the next sequence. These sequences are subject to interruption or resistance at any point
along the way. The cycling of awareness and contact for any
given individual is influenced by a multitude of systemic factors
that include the individual's physiology, genetics, personal history, and belief systems: the entirety of bio-psycho-socio-cultural
array of impacts. This context informs each individual's self-
identity; his or her awareness of internal needs, wants, desires,
and drives; and his or her personal construction of meanings
about the world and what's possible to derive from these meanings in interaction with the world.

The human capacity for awareness and the striving for
need satisfaction continually yield "figures of interest" emerging into the field of personal awareness. These figures orient us
to our internal states, to our awareness of the environment, and
to our awareness of what we want now in the present moment.
Our present awareness represents the integration of these internal and external perceptions, an integration which, in the
Gestalt model, is the integration of the self. As Gestalt therapists,
we pay specific attention to our clients' awareness of experience
in the present moment, to how they identify what they want fig-
urally in this moment, and to how they make contact in pur-
poseful efforts to seek satisfaction and resolution. Since a fundamental therapeutic task in Gestalt therapy is to increase
clients' self-awareness in order to support their increased sense
of choice in mobilizing toward effective action, as Gestalt therapists we show significant interest in how, when, and where
clients *interrupt themselves* in their contact.[1]

Now, consider the following Gestalt polarity: coupling is
a mystery; coupling can also be analyzed and understood. As a
Gestalt couples therapist, we utilize the phenomenology of the
couples interaction and presence to inform the figure and
ground of our data, perceptions, and interventions. In the therapy office, when a couple present themselves, typically they're
having difficulty with their contact in some form, resulting in
unsatisfying conflict. Most couples arrive organized around a

problem or a set of symptoms. The problem may be presented as a diffuse couples issue, such as "We're not communicating well"; "We're fighting a lot"; "We're not close." The couple may cite specific concerns or symptoms, such as the absence of satisfaction sexually, or tensions expressed around differing financial capabilities. The symptoms may also be attributed as one partner's responsibility, such as: "He's always so angry and critical of me." Likewise, the matters of distance regulation—how the couple manage their individual needs for distance or closeness in the relationship, boundary maintenance, division of labor (who takes out the garbage), and the negotiation of power and control—are universal couples issues, regardless of sexual preference. Although the content of any given conflict may be figural for the couple, as Gestalt-trained therapists our primary figure of interest is the process of contact between the couple. Our therapeutic tasks in noticing the couple's contact process begin with an appreciation for the evident strengths of their contact, those qualities that support the individuals involved in being fully present and "alive" with each other in their giving and receiving.

We also pay specific attention to how, when, and where contact between the two partners seems to be weak, underdeveloped, or fully interrupted. This intervention, given the couple's sufficient interest and curiosity, forms the basis for the development of therapeutic *experiments*. An experiment may be designed to enlarge a couple's awareness of an existing, unrewarding pattern of contact, or it may create an opportunity to try a new behavior in the interest of enlarging the couple's range of contact.

I've taken this opportunity to describe some common denominators of coupling within a Gestalt theoretical frame of intimate systems, homosexual or heterosexual. I do this out of a profound wish to demarginalize gay coupling. In this view, same-sex coupling takes its place squarely in the midst of the human dance, an important and valued variation on the basic, human theme of the wish to belong intimately with another human being, to see and be seen in the mirror of the other person's eyes, to give and receive with the holding of each other's hearts.

So finally, as this chapter's original figure reemerges,

what are the important, distinguishing aspects of gay male couples? First, some of what I say may apply to gay, lesbian, or bisexual couples. However, for the sake of this chapter, I shall refer only to gay male couples, unless I indicate otherwise. Moreover, some things may apply to some couples and not others. Finally, just as each coupling is unique, so each therapist's perspective is unique. This is mine, and your reading of this chapter is part of the construction of your own perspective, which the perspectives and considerations here are intended to enrich in some way.

Gay Male Coupling Distinctions

Male Gender Training

First, starting with the obvious (always a useful Gestalt prescriptive), these are *two men together*, each of whom has been socialized in a shared gender training with all the values, beliefs, and attitudes that are encouraged by our culture as part of the package of being male. Culturally (in Western culture, at least), males are taught early in development that certain feelings and forms of expression are acceptable, and others are not. Introjects such as "big boys don't cry" and "that's for sissies" are pervasive and insidious, often leading to emotional and expressive numbing or constriction. The "softer" feelings, culturally typed as "feminine," are associated with emotional openness and potential vulnerability, feelings such as sadness, hurt, fear, and disappointment. For many men, including gay or bisexual men, softer feelings are often extinguished in expression or anesthetized in experience and are therefore unavailable to awareness.

There is a certain cultural assumption that gay males have succeeded in "opting out" of this constricting package of gender training. Indeed, some self-identified "straight" men may express envy or resentment of gay men, prompted by a stereotyped notion that gay men are more "like women" in their emotional sensitivities and/or presenting behavior and therefore may have an easier time being closer to men and women alike. Such stereotyped notions of gay male sensitivity certainly apply to some; paradoxically, many gay men have spent long years trying to "fit in" to established cultural norms for boys. Some degree of retroflection and splitting off of emotional self-awareness is an adaptive strategy of boyhood for most males, encouraged on the playground, if not by the families of origin. As boys, we learn that expressing our softer tissue comes only at the risk of being labeled effeminate, "like a girl." Other common denominators of male socialization include internalized messages around being powerful, in control, and self-reliant (otherwise known as counterdependent), and around building self-esteem by competitive one-upmanship, being on top, "king of the mountain." We learn that it's unmanly to recognize or admit to our dependency needs and areas of insecurity. A wide range of feelings may get funneled into more socially approved forms of masculinity, such as getting angry. In turn, the male kingdom emphasizes its approval for quick movement into action; what gets encouraged on the football field often translates directly into other relational arenas. Characteristic values involving being aggressive, taking charge, fixing problems, and moving on are introjected (swallowed without reflection), rather than values that encourage reflection, or toleration of ambiguity, ambivalence, and, hence, anxiety.

Traditionally male-stereotyped traits, of course, may be sources of potential strength as well as potential limitation. Likewise, the latter applies to female-identified traits, such as empathy, listening, and sensitivity to others' feelings. When gender-typed traits are introjected in rigid and polarized ways, they risk becoming stifling to the individual(s), reducing the possibilities for creative expression and problem solving for the couple. Hence, when as therapists we sit with a gay male couple, yes, they're gay; *they're also male*, and they may need help in becoming aware of their introjected enculturation as males. In terms of second-order effects, the issue is not just one of having two gender-influenced individuals in a room who may exhibit constricted access to inner experience, but a question of the interaction between them. For instance, if both men feel anxiety or shame about certain types of experience and are constricted in their expression, they may polarize each other further in their interaction. Again, the fact of having an intimate sexual relationship with a person of the same sex does not always liberate a gay couple from all the other aspects of a gender-polarized culture. The movement toward reexamining culturally typed sex roles supports the deconstruction of those roles in couples therapy.

As Gestalt therapists, through the use of guided experiment, we might interest our couples in expanding their range of available role behaviors. We may need to help our gay male couple learn the basics of expressing their needs and wants clearly and in words. We may need to help them become aware of their underlying feelings in the moment of their interaction, helping them to learn the language of expressing feelings, such as "I feel sad and I want you to hold me" or "I feel disappointed when you say that." Whereas gay men, as men, often have developed strengths in expressing their differentiations, their respective positions, we may want to interest our couple in experiencing more empathic styles. For instance, mirroring as an experimental technique, where each partner practices just reflecting what he hears the other saying, provides practice in the skills of listening and demonstrating understanding. Without rushing in quickly to represent one's own position, or to "fix" the problem, or to give unwanted or un-asked-for advice, lovers can experiment with tolerating the experience of having a process that supports listening and understanding versus winning a position. Of course, in contrast, in male couples with a higher degree of confluence, learning to express differentiations and respective positions might be foreground in the experiment.

Differences in Being "Out" in the World

Two gay men in a couple relationship may have different levels of being "out" or publicly identified as gay. Therefore, they may experience differences in their needs for keeping coupling private, or they may have differing levels of comfort in specific behaviors that express the coupling, such as expressing affection publicly. One partner may want to hold hands at the movies, whereas the other may feel too anxious. There may also be differences in how much each partner has disclosed his sexual orientation and coupling to friends, family, or coworkers.

Internalized homophobia and unaware retroflection, or holding in, are typically an ongoing presence to some degree in both partners. Whether to come out, when to come out, and how to come out are persistent questions throughout any gay person's life. The notion that one's sexuality, with its rich brew of attendant feelings, thoughts, attractions, and fantasies, may lead to rejection and social disgrace supports retroflection as a necessary, adaptive defense. The anxieties of self-disclosure, therefore, get restimulated in the couple when they deal with even the most basic decisions: for example, "Do I take my lover to my office party, and if so, how do I refer to him, and how does he feel about it?" "When family members visit with us, do we pretend that we're just "roommates," refrain from expressing affection, or engage in other masking activities such as hiding pictures of the two of us?" With respect to the larger systemic context of social oppression, we can ask ourselves, as therapists, how many relationships can withstand the tensions emanating from the conspiracy of silence and collusion of masking deflections in the face of prospective social and familial derogation.

The Expressions and Validations of Commitment

In heterosexual coupling, when the couple move from dating to defining more of a commitment, typically it's a cause for celebration among family and friends. The engagement pictures or parties, the gifts, the good wishes all support the framework of intensifying bonding. For gay couples who identify their coupling to families of origin, this action represents another level of coming out, one that families often do not embrace each other with unreserved cheer. The reality of a lover/partner/spouse/boyfriend/mate frequently precipitates a breakthrough of the family's denial about a loved one's sexual orientation. It's one thing to know that your son is gay;

it's another thing to see his lover standing beside him, let alone retiring to the bedroom with him.

In addition, Betty Berzon (1990), a clinical psychologist, refers to the expectation of failure in gay and lesbian coupling. Most heterosexual couples enter into their intimate, marital relationships with an expectation that they will endure. For gay men, there's a sense of tradition born of a cultural history that gay relationships are made of transitory, secretive, anonymous contacts, surrounded by a fear of discovery. As Berzon states that, in this tradition, "being in a same-sex relationship [requires] constant vigilance, strategizing, and deception" (p. 10). As Gestalt therapists, we may appreciate how the strategies of introjection, retroflection, deflection, projection, and confluence contribute to a gay couple's experiential voyage in a homophobic world, and even make that voyage possible. In the face of such adversity and even hatred it's actually quite a testimony to the human capacity for emotional and psychic survival, and the deep human desire and need to bond, that long-term gay coupling exists at all.

Since Gestalt therapy supports attention to the clarity of contact boundaries and the delineation of clear figure from ground, as aware therapists it's useful for us to pay attention to how the gay couple have defined their commitment. Do they employ a descriptive, disclosure-oriented boundary, designating themselves as lovers, spouses, partners, significant others, or the equivalent, or do they use a more diluted, ambiguous, masking-oriented description such as "roommates" or "friends"? Also, what markers do they use to identify and celebrate their commitment, whether in symbol, ritual, or statement? Until recently, gay and lesbian couples have not had marker events to define the change in status from a dating or cohabiting couple to that of a committed couple with the same level of commitment as that expected in a marriage. With whatever else they may connote, heterosexual wedding rituals legitimize a couple's boundaries, making a statement of public expectation that the relationship will continue into the future. More recently, some gay couples have created ceremonies of commitment for themselves, sometimes within organized religious contexts. Some couples may ex-

change rings, and some others may define their commitment
and observe an anniversary of the date of moving in together,
renting an apartment, or purchasing a house as the marker
event.

Thematically, I'm discussing validations in various forms.
For instance, how validated is the couple within the context of
their network? How connected or isolated are they? Is there
enough outside support to lend recognition and stability to the
relationship other than what they create for themselves? Do
they have friends as a couple as well as apart from each other?
Couples who are not "out" may often express a greater degree
of confluence in their relationships, and the therapist needs to
be aware that this "fusion" may represent not individual pathology but the condition of the couple's boundary with the larger
world. This interactive relationship of the couple's internal and
external boundaries will be discussed at greater length below.

On the cultural level of validation, there's an absolute
dearth of role modeling for gay coupling. On television, in the
movies, in recordings, and in mainstream literature, not much
evidence of gay coupling exists at all, let alone images of how
gay couples can work through conflicts or differences in the interest of maintaining an enduring relationship. Furthermore,
in gay and lesbian couplings, there's an absence of legal and social supports, which heterosexual couples enjoy through the institution of marriage. Without legal sanctions for gay relationships, couples don't have access to insurance benefits, tax
breaks, spousal discounts, and other practical rewards that reinforce coupling. A heterosexual couple married for one hour
have more rights and privileges than a homosexual couple living together for twenty years. As comprehensively "grounded"
Gestalt therapists, we mustn't assume that the couple have already made arrangements for legal protection. Again, the underlying societal message is that homosexual couplings are considered a lesser form, transitory, not to be taken seriously or
accorded the same respect. Therapeutic interventions, therefore, may need to address whether the couple have considered
mutual needs for legal and financial protection. We might ask:
Have they enacted living wills, ensuring the right to act on one

another's behalf if illness strikes? Have they executed estate planning to ensure that each spouse is protected, particularly when the family of origin may claim otherwise?

Learning to Dance Their Dance: Together and Apart

As I mentioned earlier, the dance of negotiating closeness and distance in the relationship is an ongoing dance enjoyed by all couples, regardless of sexual orientation. Sometimes that dance may appear like a well-orchestrated, mutually executed waltz, with a minimum of stepping on each other's toes; sometimes the couple perform their dance like an impassioned tango, with dramatic moves and abruptly changing directions, filled with obvious emotion; or sometimes it's like a wildly energetic, loud-rapping hip-hop, organized around a multitude of platform statements, often barely understandable in the midst of the ca-cophony of sound. Whatever the imagery, distance regulation is a necessary and creatively organic part of coupling. Again, as previously elaborated, two men together have been socialized in a culture that supports "male values" around independence and self-reliance (again translate: counterdependence). Concur-rently, gay men, in the course of their personal histories of hid-ing, masking, suppressing, and sublimating their true desires and wishes, often develop pronounced "object hunger," which may translate into profound yearning for closeness and belong-ing with other men, on both one-to-one and group levels, along with concomitant anxiety about disclosing those wishes for closeness. Therefore, the dance of a gay male couple may in-volve an intensified process around both the wish for meaning-ful and close belonging and the wish for maintaining adequate autonomy and self-definition (which can also translate into fears of engulfment or enmeshment).

Additionally, as Sallyann Roth of the Family Institute of Cambridge has indicated (1989), there's a complex interaction between the position of lesbian (and gay) couples within the context of the surrounding heterosexual community and the boundary-regulating behavior within individual couples. So, ex-trapolating from Roth's discussion of lesbian couples for instance, when the gay couple's attempts to define their bond meet with no response or a response that's invalidating, the partners may overcompensate by rigidifying their couple boundary to ensure their integrity as a couple and thereby develop an increasingly closed couple system. In a closed couple system, individual boundaries are easily blurred (confluence), and this blurring may often call into play some type of distancing strategy to protect against dangers of overcloseness or fusion (such as distancing by one partner, or by both in an alternating sequence; open conflict; or triangling in a third element such as extracurricular romantic involvement or increased work involvement) (Roth, [1989] p. 288). Hence, distance regulation problems, inevitable for any couple, can be exaggerated for the gay or lesbian couple by the bond-invalidating activities of the surrounding heterosexual world. Additionally, in closed or overprivatized coupling, "any excursion outside the couple boundary may seem threatening to the partner" (p. 13). Movement toward developing friendships outside the couple, for instance, particularly same-sex friendships, may inspire suspicion or jealousy.

Once again, using the phenomenology of the couple's interaction in our office, we may encourage their awareness of how they pull toward and/or push away from confluence. We have the opportunity to support our couples in defining their fears of and wishes for separateness. Simple experiments where each person makes "I" versus "we" statements enable the couple to experience differentiation and increased self-definition. Altering the experiment to have one partner state "I want" requests of the other while the other partner's assignment involves practicing saying "yes" or "no" furthers the couple's conscious awareness of their contact boundary. A homework assignment that involves each member's gathering information or making trial visits to gay community resources, groups, social events, and so on may be useful in eliciting interest in an expanded sense of community for the closed-system couple. Ideally, in therapy the couple increase their awareness of how they're "dancing" together, sharpening the boundary of awareness of what does and doesn't satisfy. Each partner, through the therapeutic experiment, can experience the impact of making a change in his steps, learning to negotiate the change in an existing routine with an understanding of the impact on each other.

Sex Roles and Sexuality: Polarities, Projections, and Stereotyping

Even among the most sensitive, sophisticated, and intelligent people, stereotyped notions or projections about gay men and gay male couples can permeate one's thinking. Cultural beliefs based on polarized notions of sex roles and sexuality run deep. For instance, gay men have often been popularly conceived of as "feminine" or effeminate. A visit to a Gay/Lesbian/Bisexual Pride Parade would, of course, dispel such a limited view. The appearance and behavior of gay men reflect the entire spectrum of gender role style, from classically "macho" to stereotyped "feminine" to all variations in between. In addition, some people believe projectively that gay couples necessarily divide themselves into polarized gender-typed roles in order to be a couple. This is not true, necessarily. Stereotyped behavior along male or female role lines may or may not be more prevalent in older gay male couples, considering historic cultural influences. Given the impact of the contemporary feminist movement and the increasing emphasis on personal option in gender role behavior for males and females, flexible role behavior may be more the current relational norm. In other words, couples who present themselves to us may negotiate and renegotiate their roles together over time, in accordance with individual differences, strengths, and curiosity in experimenting with or expanding behavior. Nonetheless, sometimes gay men in couples do express anxiety about whether their role in the couple somehow represents a loss of masculine identification, given (archaic) polarized sex role stereotyping.

I believe that it is essential, as therapists, to pay careful attention to our own introjects or unexamined beliefs and assumptions when considering homosexuality, sex roles, and sexual behavior. Stereotyped projections, after all, interrupt our own "contactfulness" and our ability to see clearly the couple

who are in front of us, and whether or not *they're* experiencing
satisfaction with their behavior together. The Gestalt therapy
model is particularly useful in its support for awareness of such
projections as they exist. When we enable people to see their
projections clearly, we then have an opportunity to interest
them in considering disowned, split-off, or otherwise suppressed aspects of the self, as expressed in the coupling. The
Gestalt premise in reclaiming awareness of our projections is
that the fuller the figure of each self in the couple, the richer
the expression of contact, liveliness, and flexibility for the
couple.

As in all couples, sexuality itself may or may not be an
issue in gay male coupling. Sexuality sometimes serves as a
symptomatic ground for acting out deflected conflicts and
retroflected affects, such as anger. A couple's sexuality may shift
over time in intensity and in frequency, varying in levels of ap-
petite, degrees of excitement, and sense of intimacy. Negotiating a satisfying sexuality for a gay couple, as with a heterosexual
couple, involves (ideally) the willingness to express clearly one's
sensations, feelings, desires and wishes in order to enable the
partner to consider responding in a mutually satisfying way. As
we know, this "ideal" process does not always occur in the course
of a couple's life and may present itself in the therapy office for
discussion and attention. For men, including gay men, raising
sexual concerns or dissatisfactions often raises shame or embarrassment. Polarized male gender notions of being in charge,
in control, and performing upon demand lead to unrealistic expectations of self and other. For some, particular sexual practices may evoke embedded anxiety about whether they're being
"manly."

Sexual practices vary among gay couples in accordance
with individual differences in what the individuals involved experience as pleasurable. Simply stated, what one person enjoys
the other may or may not. Understanding and negotiation
based on understanding, as usual, are the best prescription, and
the couple need to be able to sustain an effective process together in order to accomplish this. The menu of gay male sexuality includes, but is not limited to, kissing, hugging, touching,

rubbing, fellatio, anal intercourse, and mutual masturbation. For one or another of these activities, some people prefer a receptive role (*passive* or *bottom* are commonly used terms as well), others prefer being "active," "dominant," or "top" in the activity,[2] and some enjoy both. Specialized and/or fetishistic "turn-ons" involving activities such as S/M (sadomasochism), B&D (bondage and discipline), or the wearing of specific clothing (leather, "drag") may appeal to some. Heterosexual couples, of course, sample from the same menu, with the addition of vaginal intercourse and cunnilingus.

Why am I detailing these sexual activities? First, since I'm discussing the issue of projections and polarities, I believe that it's essential as therapists for us to be in touch with our own. We cannot presume to know what the gay male couple in front of us find sexually pleasurable without their discussing it, if they want to. In turn, unless the couple express an issue or symptom with their sexuality, we may never witness (or need to know) the details. On the other hand, we need to be aware of and comfortable enough with the *sexual* in *homosexual* to support our couple in discussing their sexual concerns, differences, and inhibitions. In Gestalt language, we pay attention to how the couple's wants and desires get expressed as opposed to retroflected, deflected, or otherwise interrupted. We also note the projections expressed by each partner and whether those projections are grounded by reality testing in contact with each other. Again, it's not necessarily the content per se that fascinates us, but our interest in *how* the couple allow themselves to educate one another in what does and doesn't feel good or enhances arousal.

Additionally, we need to be aware of our assumptions, values, and introjects regarding monogamy and nonmonogamy. We must ask ourselves, "Do I have a bias?" "Can I respect that different gay couples (like different heterosexual, lesbian, or bisexual couples) work out different relational contracts ranging from exclusive monogamy to mutual nonmonogamy to arrangements where one is and one isn't?" Is it hard for us to validate these options or to get interested in how the given arrangement works for the couple? I believe that betrayal through secrecy is often the potentially toxic issue that abrogates basic trust in a relationship. For me again what is figural is *how* the couple communicate about their values regarding monogamy, their mutual sexual expectations, and their related feelings, as opposed to whether they ultimately choose exclusive monogamy. And in an age of HIV/AIDS, open discussion about sexuality in or out of the couple needs to address the issue of safety and mutual protection, without which there can be no foundation for trust. Again, we pay attention to how comfortable the couple are in discussing "safer sex" practices, and how each partner defines safety and acceptable risk for himself.

HIV/AIDS

The reality of HIV and AIDS as a fact of life certainly impacts every gay man, as it does all of us, regardless of sexual orientation. Although this matter deserves a chapter unto itself, at least I would like to refer to it for consideration when working with gay male couples. Being a gay man in the 1990s means, almost certainly, knowing someone who has the HIV infection and/or has died from its progression. In a profound sense, the gay community is a community living currently within a context of grief. Gay couples sometimes face the loss of important friends, who may be regarded as "chosen family" and have served as cherished sources of support for the couple. The couple may be addressing HIV/AIDS most directly as an issue for one or both partners. When they are dealing with HIV in their own coupling, the person(s) may be at various stages of infection—from being symptom-free to having occasional transient symptoms to having acute or chronic opportunistic infections—characteristic of progression to AIDS. The issue of HIV as it affects the couple may be figural, or it may rest in the background as the couple go on about their business of living; as always, this figure/ground is subject to change in the moment for one partner or the other.

When someone is HIV-positive, and depending upon his stage of progression, typically a shift occurs around the sense of immediacy in mortality, the perception of time as precious, lim-

ited, or fleeting, and the reality of living with heightened uncertainty and anxiety. For a gay couple, given the stigma of the
infection, HIV-positivity or AIDS often precipitates a second
coming-out crisis for the individuals involved and their coupling. Whom to tell, fears of rejection, how the family will react;
when to disclose; the restimulation of internalized homophobia
and shame; how to find support in the community—all of these
are necessary and inevitable considerations. For the couple,
these issues, grounded as they are in fear and anxiety and usually the wish for support, may surface symptomatically, such as
with heightened tensions, changes in sexuality, or impulsive decision making.

For example, in one couple I work with, "Steve" and
"Dave," both partners are HIV-positive. Steve, usually conserva-
tive but now more aware of time passing and wanting to achieve
certain goals, wants to spend money on some "extravagances."
Dave, who would otherwise enjoy those extravagances, prefers
to plan more cautiously for future needs. Though both are HIV-
positive, Steve has progressed into AIDS, while Dave remains
symptom-free. Each gets angry with the other for his respective
position on the money issue. And both tend to soften and listen
more clearly when they identify their underlying fears. A larger
ground of understanding enables Steve and Dave to consider
where they might compromise with each other.

In a group I once led consisting of HIV-discordant couples (one partner is HIV-positive, the other HIV-negative), every
couple expressed their experience of great isolation and of relief at coming together as a group. None of them at that point
had come out about their HIV status outside their relationship.
In that particular grouping, each HIV-negative partner expressed guilt for being concerned about his own needs in the
face of his lover's diagnosis. Certainly, HIV-positive couples, discordant or otherwise, need to attend to how they want to include their partners in their respective fears, hopes, angers, sor-
rows, and joys. They each need to identify their respective needs
for support for themselves, and determine if they have each
other's permission to go outside the relationship for that support when necessary. As Gestalt therapists, we recognize organ-

ically that the figure of life does not exist independently of the environment, from which we need to draw and digest life support. This is a particularly poignant consideration when dealing with a couple facing a life-challenging illness such as AIDS.

Addictive Behavior

I want to mention briefly that, as well-grounded therapists, we need to be tuned into the possibility of addictive behavior, such as alcoholism or sexual compulsivity. Some research suggests a higher percentage of chemical abuse and dependence among gay men versus the overall population (Finnegan & McNally, 1987, p. 31). Alcohol has often been used as a means of mediating stressors relating to society's hostility or to one's own internalized homophobia and feelings of low self-worth. Additionally, coming out for many gay men often occurs in the social context of gay bars, where alcohol is freely available to medicate anxiety. Likewise, many gay men, like men in general, learn about sex before they learn about intimacy. Given a personal history of necessary secrecy, coupled with societal disapproval of the overt homosexual relationship, sexual compulsivity in the form of repetitive or unsatisfying one-night stands or anonymous encounters, sometimes in dangerous places, can become an overdetermined defense against a whole range of anxieties. Again, addictive behavior may or may not be present in the coupling, but given the social stigmas and stressors placed upon homosexuality, we need to stay aware and listen carefully.

Seeking Closure

In my desire to be comprehensive about the various differentiations and similarities in working with gay male couples, I've only scratched the surface of all these issues. I haven't mentioned issues for gay male couples who have children, or who desire to have children. I haven't addressed gay coupling in the context of racial, ethnic, religious, or class differences and their potential impacts for the couple. I have tried to impart an understanding of some of the various challenges and attempted resolutions that gay men face in the process of defining their self-identity and that may enter into their couplings. In describing a perspective based on the precepts of Gestalt theory, I've tried to highlight how gay couples necessarily employ resistances to contact as adaptive strategies for surviving in a culture that is only very gradually beginning to reassess its positions on sexual orientation. Again, as Gestalt therapists, we appreciate how the strategies of introjection, retroflection, deflection, projection, and confluence contribute to a gay couple's experiential voyage in a homophobic and heterosexist world.

I have also attempted to convey at least some of the spirit of a Gestalt couples therapy approach and its unique contribution to working with gay male intimate systems. The beauty of Gestalt therapy's focus on phenomenology, on how the partners make contact with each other in their efforts toward intimacy, lies partly in the fact that it provides a gay couple with an experience of heightened attention to their actual process together. This attention, this stance of phenomenological *respect*, is inherently "deshaming" and validating for the gay male couple as they struggle, like every couple and every person, to articulate and construct their own experience, relationship, and lives. The Gestalt therapist witnesses and encourages the couple's efforts, enabling them to see their own process more clearly and offering them opportunities through experiment to expand and develop their skills in giving and receiving. Of course, no school of therapy is "the only way," and Gestalt couples therapy does not guarantee an ultimate outcome. However, for a gay coupling grounded in such a backdrop of sociocultural self-denial, to be seen so carefully in the here and now and potentially with such appreciation for the efforts involved is ultimately an experience of love that cannot be denied.

Notes

1. Interruptions and resistances to contact include projection, introjection, deflection, and confluence. Refer to *Gestalt Therapy Integrated* by Erv and Miriam Polster (1973) or Wheeler (1991) for a more thorough discussion of resistance.

2. This language implicitly contains an enculturated sex role bias.

References

Berzon, B. (1990). *Permanent partners: Building gay and lesbian relationships that last.* New York: Penguin Books.

Finnegan, D., & McNally, E. (1987). *Dual identities: Counseling chemically dependent gay men and lesbians.* Minnesota: Hazelden.

Polster, E., & Polster, M. (1973). *Gestalt therapy integrated.* New York: Brunner/Mazel.

Roth, S. (1989). "Psychotherapy with lesbian couples: Individual issues, female socialization, and the social context. In M. McGoldrick, C. Anderson, & F. Walsh (Eds.), *Women in families: A framework for family therapy.* New York: W.W. Norton.

Wheeler, G. (1991). *Gestalt Reconsidered.* New York: Gardner Press.

7

Gestalt Couples Therapy with Lesbian Couples: Applying Theory and Practice to the Lesbian Experience

Fraelean Curtis

Jill and Mary are a lesbian couple who have been together for two years. This is Jill's first lesbian relationship and it is Mary's third. Mary is thirty-three and she is active in the local lesbian community. Jill is twenty-five and she is in the early stages of coming out. She has told only her sister and a few close friends that she is involved with a woman. Jill is feeling ambivalent about the relationship, whereas Mary feels a growing commitment to it. They agree to go to couples counseling. They live in an area where there are few lesbian therapists and Mary has socialized with most of them. They decide to see a recognized couples therapist who is a heterosexually identified woman.

Jill and Mary arrive at their first session. They enter the room and sit close to each other on the couch across from the therapist's chair. After a brief hello, Mary takes Jill's hand, pushes her lower back into the couch, takes a deep breath, looks at the therapist and says, "I'm feeling awkward here because I know you are heterosexual and I'm not sure I can work with you." She rubs her hand back and forth over her upper leg as if to comfort herself. She takes a deep breath and continues saying, "I'm concerned that you won't understand our relationship." Jill is looking down as Mary speaks. She feels pleased that Mary is being direct and she is afraid to look directly at the therapist. She shifts her feet on the floor and crosses her legs. She clears her throat even though she has no words to say.

The therapist feels the tension in the room and she feels tense herself. She thinks that she wants to reassure this couple and she wants to let them know that she is a competent couples therapist. With feelings of goodwill she makes eye contact with each of them and states that she intends to work with them in the same way she would work with a heterosexual couple. She smiles, believing that she has just supported Jill and Mary by "normalizing" their relationship. She still feels the tension in the room but she continues to speak, hoping her words will make everyone, including herself, more comfortable. She tells the couple that she respects and values them as a couple and she adds that she considers the issues to be the same regardless of the gender configuration of the couple. She knows she has not yet made a connection with either Jill or Mary. She is thinking about what she might say next when Mary interrupts her thoughts saying, "I can't believe you just said that." Mary feels the stiffness in her neck and she thinks that this therapist really doesn't know anything about lesbian life. Jill holds Mary's hand tighter as she feels tears welling up in her eyes. She feels disappointed and hopeless. She wonders how they will find another couples therapist. She wants to leave and she leans toward Mary and quietly tells her so.

Mary nods. She is also ready to leave. She wants to tell the therapist that they are leaving but her head is pounding and her jaw is tight. She hears Jill informing the therapist that they are leaving and she is relieved.

The therapist looks from Jill to Mary and she is aware she feels disappointed. She expresses her confusion at their leaving so abruptly. Jill looks at the door behind the therapist and says that they just have to go. They all stand and the couple leaves.

The therapist sits down, shaking her head and thinking that working with lesbian couples can be very confusing. She reviews in her mind what has just happened but she can't understand why she wasn't able to reassure this couple of her skill and intent.

This therapist has her heart in the right place, and certainly there are many issues that all couples do have in common, regardless of their gender configuration, issues such as problematic communication styles, attachment and autonomy, trauma and scars from their separate pasts, differing abilities within the couple to express affect, differing sexual appetites, alcoholism and addiction, the stress of raising children, and on and on. However, some issues are inherent to lesbian relationships, and it was the therapist's ignorance of these issues that prevented her from connecting with this couple. She was not aware that she voiced her own inexperience in working with lesbian couples, as well as her heterosexual bias, when she told the couple that she would work with them in the same way that she would work with a heterosexual couple. To Jill and Mary, this statement meant that the therapist would use heterosexuality as her point of reference for couples therapy.

The therapist presented here was not working out of a Gestalt model, which might have helped her to validate and remain curious about a lesbian couple's concerns regarding the therapist's heterosexual identity, and to acknowledge, highlight, and address the tension that existed in the room at the moment. This would have joined all three parties, couple and therapist, on the same "figure of awareness," an essential starting point for working in the Gestalt model.

It is always understood in the Gestalt model that ground or background, the information that the therapist holds about the couple, including their culture, socialization, and life experience, codetermines the figure, the material that becomes the focus of attention in the session. An intuitive understanding of this process was what made Jill and Mary unable to work with the well-meaning therapist in the case example above: they believed that the therapist's unexamined heterosexist ground would color and distort the figure picture formed of them as separate persons, and as a couple.

Many heterosexual clinicians do not have any formal training in addressing the needs of their lesbian, gay, and bisexual clients. They may have the best intentions, but they may not have confronted their deeper prejudices, which are unavoidable in our society. The societal message that homosexuality is a perversion is pervasive and powerful. Heterosexual therapists must work as hard as lesbian, gay, or bisexual therapists to undo the negative messages about homosexuality that they have internalized. Without awareness of these internalized messages, the best-intentioned therapist will reflect his or her bias in the therapy with these clients.

Heterosexism

Heterosexism is replacing the term *homophobia*, which was popularized by George Weinberg (1972) in his book *Society and the Healthy Homosexual.* Homophobia originally referred to the intense, irrational fear and dread of homosexuality and homosexuals. Finnegan and McNally (1987) point out that its meanings and connotations have broadened over the years so that it now refers to all prejudicial attitudes or feelings toward homosexuals (p. 32).

The term *heterosexism* describes more precisely what was included in the term *homophobia.* It places the attention on the heterosexist prejudice, not on whether one's fear of homosexuals is irrational or not. Heterosexism is the continued promotion by the major institutions of society of a heterosexual lifestyle while simultaneously subordinating any other life-styles. Heterosexism is based on unfounded prejudices, just as racism, sexism, and so on are based on unfounded prejudices. When our institutions knowingly or unknowingly perpetuate these prejudices and intentionally or unintentionally act on them, heterosexism is at work.

We all live in a heterosexist society that promotes heterosexism. Lesbian, gay, and bisexual therapists usually begin, at least, to undo negative heterosexist messages as they come out and learn to value who they are as sexual human beings. This recovery is probably never complete in a society that so consistently reinforces negative messages about homosexuals and homosexuality.

An awareness of the power of heterosexism and the lesbian life experience, including issues related to the socialization of women, must be present in the mind of any therapist who is working with lesbian couples. It is this ground or background that influences the work with a lesbian couple, making it different from the work with a gay male or a heterosexual couple.

Gestalt Couples Therapy

In a couples session the Gestalt therapist attends to the phenomenology, the immediate organization of experience, that she or he sees—the "here-and-now" information: the eye contact, the tone of voice, the feelings expressed, the behavioral movements, the gestures. All these data are observed until the therapist forms a clear picture, a "figure," of what is happening now in the couple's system, in the present. The therapist may need to observe the couple system for some time before the clear figure forms. After the figure is formed, the therapist describes the data she or he has observed to the couple. The therapist does this to increase the couple's awareness of the dynamics between them. At this point the therapist may suggest an experiment to the couple that will help them appreciate and work with these here-and-now data. The experiment helps the couple become an active agent in studying and modifying their interactive process.

Thus a unique quality of Gestalt therapy is its emphasis on modifying a person's behavior in the therapy situation itself. This systematic behavior modification, when it grows out of the experience of the client, is called an "experiment." The experiment is the cornerstone of experiential learning. It transforms talking into doing, stale reminiscing and theorizing into being fully here with all one's imagination, energy, and excitement (Zinker, 1977, p. 123).

A ground that is rich with the knowledge of the lesbian life experience will allow an enriched range of experiments to occur to the therapist. Gestalt couples therapy with a lesbian couple without this rich background will leave the therapist in an impoverished position without the connected understanding that would support the work.

Differences in lesbian and heterosexual couples' experiences are many. Falco (1991) suggests that these differences can be viewed as arising from two main sources: the lack of support and recognition of the lesbian relationship as a valid relational form (which includes issues arising from living with a stigmatized identity); and the fact that two women make up the couple, and each brings with her (in her own individual way) her particular psychological conditioning and the dynamics of her gender (p. 106). I will discuss each of these, with a case example for each, and describe how a Gestalt therapist could use herself or himself as an agent of change in each case.

Lack of Support and Recognition of the Lesbian Relationship as a Valid Entity[1]

Society puts enormous pressure on the individual to be heterosexual. Markowitz (1991, p. 29) states that the themes of shame, secrecy, and fear of disclosure are inevitably part of the freight most gay and lesbian clients bring to therapy. Violence against lesbian, gay, and bisexual people continues to rise. Living as an open and proud lesbian in the world is still a risky stance to take.

Many lesbians live double lives, passing as heterosexual in a world that doesn't notice them unless they happen to fit society's stereotype of what a lesbian or a lesbian couple "should look like." Passing as a heterosexual is a healthy defense in a hostile heterosexist world when it is used with awareness and choice. The lesbian who knowingly passes as a heterosexual or acts as if she is heterosexual in an unsafe environment is protecting herself and acting in her own best interest. Lesbians pass as heterosexual in a number of ways. A lesbian couple may tell a potential landlord that they are roommates in order to get an apartment; a lesbian may change pronouns when talking about her partner with coworkers or relatives; she may take a male friend as her "date" to a required social event; or she may dress in a way that will help her blend in with other women at work.

Passing as heterosexual becomes problematic when the behavior becomes a rigid defense and when awareness and choice are no longer available to the individual. An example would be a lesbian who continues to act as if she is heterosexual with a reliable gay male colleague. Some lesbians live in so much fear of being exposed that they lose the ability to discriminate between a situation that is safe and one that is not.

Lesbians pay a price for passing as heterosexual even when it is a necessary decision made with awareness. Denial of one's essential self, even to survive, may result in feelings of shame and low self-esteem. Some studies have indicated, for example, that lesbians and gay men are more likely to have a problem with substance abuse than heterosexual women and men. Finnegan and McNally (1987, p. 31) point out that although there is some debate over the incidence of alcoholism among lesbians and gay men, research efforts generally suggest that alcoholism and/or alcohol abuse may affect about one-third of American gay men and lesbians. This incidence rate is quite high, given that alcoholism and/or alcohol abuse may currently affect about one-tenth of the general population.

Many addiction specialists believe that the high incidence of substance abuse problems in the lesbian and gay community is related to the oppression due to heterosexism. Some consider lesbians to be at an even greater risk than gay men because they live with the added oppression of sexism. In this view, lesbians of color are considered at the greatest risk of all for substance abuse problems, since they live under the combined oppressions of heterosexism, sexism, and racism.

Passing as heterosexual friends may cause boundary and relationship problems for the lesbian couple. One possibility is that the couple may find it difficult to establish the firm boundary around themselves that any couple needs to maintain itself as a separate entity. Rather, their boundary is overly permeable, leaving the couple vulnerable to unwanted intrusion that can stir feelings of powerlessness, anger, shame, and low self-esteem. Such feelings may be difficult for a couple to bear and process.

Recovery from heterosexism is possible, and it generally begins with coming out. It is the coming-out process that holds the promise of transforming the stigmatized identity into a positive affirming one. To come out as a lesbian is to engage oneself in an ongoing process of self-love and self-affirmation, and at the same time to seek and identify with an affirming community. The process begins by coming out to the self first and then to others. In Gestalt terms, this is the experience of making clear contact with the environment and changing as a result.

The lesbian couple go through a coming-out process just as the individual does. One woman in the couple may be more out in her life than the other, and this may create some conflict within the couple, especially if they have different beliefs about who to come out to and what makes a situation safe enough to come out.

As a lesbian or a lesbian couple come out, they need a community to support and encourage them. Community can provide a safe haven to couples who, regardless of how openly they live their lives, must monitor and curtail signs of affection in public to protect themselves from verbal and/or physical assault. Community can also be a source of role models, friends, and interests that validate the couple as well as each individual within the couple. Heterosexism, like any shame-based conditioning, is very difficult or impossible to recover from in isolation.

Recovery from shame can be stagnant in the therapy session if the couple are not fully out to the therapist and if the therapist is not informed and interested enough to pursue the issues and educate the couple coming out. This is another reason why it is important for the therapist to have a rich ground as she or he works with lesbian couples. She or he may need to share resources such as lesbian and gay newspapers, and a list of community groups to support the couples process. Also, the therapist may need to inform the couple of the legal steps they can take to protect themselves. Berzon (1988) highlights the need for lesbian couples to take careful legal steps to protect joint property, to ensure that they have the authority to act on one another's behalf, or for one to visit the other if she is ill in the hospital. It is not a goal of therapy to force a couple (or individual) to come out, but it is a goal to engage them (or her) in the process of making clear, conscious decisions about whether to be out or not.

Carol and Mirium are both secretaries. They met at work twenty years ago. They have lived together for eighteen years and they have raised Carol's two daughters, who are now twenty-three and twenty-seven. They have never considered themselves to be a lesbian couple even though they have maintained an active sex life. They have considered themselves to have a "special friendship." They have never acknowledged that they are romantically involved to anyone. They came to couples therapy at Mirium's insistence. She said she had pleaded with Carol to go to therapy with her for many months until she finally threatened to leave the "friendship," at which point Carol agreed to try "a few sessions." Mirium told me that she had recently met a coworker who is lesbian and out to her family and friends. Mirium described herself as being both fascinated with and frightened by this woman. She said that she has had several conversations with her about coming out. She now believes that she is a lesbian and she wants Carol to accept that too. She wants Carol and herself to begin to come out to some of their friends. Carol is very frightened by this change in Mirium, and they have had several explosive fights about this.

At the beginning of the first session Mirium and Carol do not look at each other. I tell them that I am aware that they aren't looking at each other. Mirium glances at me and says, "I don't want to look at her. I feel I have denied being gay all of my life and now that I want to be open and honest about who I am she doesn't want me to." She glares at Carol and then looks at her hands in her lap.

Carol looks directly at Mirium. Her face is red, and her fists are clenched. Her voice is raised and angry. She says, "I'm not a lesbian and neither are you." I have an image of her spitting in disgust.

I look at Carol and I lean my body in her direction. I tell her that I see that her fists are clenched and her face is red. Carol, looking past me and out the window says, "Lesbians are disgusting."

Mirium begins to cry. She covers her face with her hands for a moment. As she takes her hands down she rests her head against the back of the chair. She speaks in a quiet voice and says, "I'm not disgusting. I don't want to ever think that I'm disgusting again and I'm afraid that you are going to convince me that I am."

I notice several things as I observe Carol and Mirium's interactive process. For one thing, Carol and Mirium are not hearing each other, they do not ask each other questions about their feelings or their beliefs, and they rarely look at each other when they are speaking to each other. Their inability to listen and hear each other becomes the figure for me.

As I watch them I picture them meeting twenty years ago. They met in a time when homosexuals led secret lives, without the literature, community, and political savvy that exist today. Both the gay liberation movement and the women's movement were just beginning. Carol's daughters would probably have been taken away from them if anyone had known the true nature of their relationship. To me it is a miracle that they found each other, acknowledged desire for each other, and dared to be sexual given the fears they lived with. I speculate that they will need a lot of support to cope with the coming-out crisis they are in.

As I hold these thoughts and images in my mind, I am aware that I feel sad about the price they have paid to pass as heterosexual. Their self-esteem, their ability to be intimate with each other, their friendships, and their family life have all suffered. They have spent years in isolation without a community to support their growth. I feel angry at the oppression they have lived with. I am aware that I want them to appreciate each other's stories, including all that they have gained, all they have given up, and the fact that they have survived together. I also have a wish that they could listen to all the fears about being lesbian and empathically explore each other's ground. They would be figure and ground for each other, each providing the receptive field that the other needs.

Gestalt theory teaches that life is a matter of making contact with the environment in order to grow and change. It is at this point of contact, where the me meets the not-me, that change occurs. However, it is very challenging to stay open to the environment and make contact with it when one expects to feel rejected and abused.

Thus everyone develops resistances or interruptions to contact in order to protect herself or himself. The resistances are similar to defenses in psychodynamic theory, and like defenses, they may be viewed as blocks of good functioning, or as modulations of energy in the service of living and growing. In general, resistance becomes problematic in life when it is used without awareness.

The lesbian, like anyone else, reaches out to make contact with her environment. She is often rejected if she is identified as openly lesbian, or she may *project* a past rejection onto a new situation, which prevents her from taking in new data. She may be watchful for danger, and if there is a risk of being injured she will *retroflect* who she is (hold in and disguise her lesbian self), passing as heterosexual. She learns to *deflect* (change the figure) if someone's interest threatens exposure. Her self-esteem is damaged by the negative *introjects* (negative heterosexist messages) she has internalized, and she sometimes feels that she must be *confluent* with (make no objections to) heterosexist remarks made by people who might harm her in some way.

Carol passes as a heterosexual at all times, and she is not aware that she can develop situations where it is safe for her to acknowledge her lesbian relationship with Mirium. She projects a feeling of threat into every situation, and then she retroflects or holds back the part of her that loves Mirium. Because she projects and retroflects without *awareness*, she inhibits her own growth even when it is not necessary for her to do so. Mirium has recently become aware that she doesn't have to retroflect her lesbian self all the time. Her desire for more contact with her environment is shaking the foundation of the couple system that she and Carol have maintained for twenty years.

They have lived closeted lives under the control of heterosexist introjects. They have both accepted society's teachings about homosexuality with little question, and they have made those introjects their own with little awareness. Carol's statement that lesbians are disgusting is a negative introject that prevents her from listening to Mirium and opening herself to new experience.

In a couple system the resistances are shared, and they flow back and forth within the couple. The job of the couples therapist is to observe the couple's interactive process and note where it is inhibited by these resistances.

The Lesbian Couple as a System of Two Women

The dynamics that occur between two women in a couple may be quite different from the dynamics that occur between two men in a couple, or a man and a woman in a couple. Although the powerful influence of sex roles on a child's development may have lessened in recent years, boys and girls are still taught which specific behaviors are acceptable for someone of their sex. A male is still expected to be more dominating, independent, self-assured, aggressive, and knowledgeable about the world. A female is expected to be dependent and passive, to seek approval from other people, and to attend to and respond to the needs of others (Vargo, 1987, p. 63).

Vargo refers to the Brovermans' (1970) classic study of mental health workers' clinical judgments, which showed that the standards of mental health at that time were heavily influenced by stereotypes of masculinity and femininity. Male behaviors of competitiveness, assertiveness, and aggressiveness were considered the standard for normal adult behavior, but they were considered unhealthy when observed in women. This makes it impossible for a woman both to be "normal" and to meet the standard of "normal healthy behavior" (Vargo, 1987, pp. 161–162).

Beginning in the late 1970s with the publication of Jean Baker Miller's *Toward a New Psychology of Women*, a new women-centered literature on the psychology of women has evolved. Articles, books, and research published by Miller, Carol Gilligan, Janet Surrey, Julie Mencher, and others constitute a departure from the more traditional literature on the psychology of women because they are based on women's experience and how women perceive their experience rather than on whether their experience measures up to some imaginary standard of men's experience (a standard that may well not fit many actual men either).

Surrey (1991) notes that a major thesis of *Toward a New Psychology of Women* is the way in which "women's sense of self becomes very much organized around being able to make and then maintain affiliation and relationship" (p. 52). This thesis has been developed and expanded on by the relational theory group of the Stone Center at Wellesley College, Wellesley, MA. As Surrey (1991, p. 52) puts it: "Our conception of the self-in-relation involves the recognition that, for women, the primary experience is relational, that is, the self is organized and developed in the context of important relationships." In Gestalt terms, we would say that the development of the self is focused at the boundary of the other.

According to this relational theory, growth for a woman is achieved and maintained in the context of relationship, and her sense of self-esteem is tied to her ability to establish and maintain emotional attachments. This is in sharp contrast to all the traditional literature, which emphasizes separation and individuation as essential for growth. Carol Gilligan's (1982) work on women's development sheds a clear light on the misunderstandings that result from gauging women's development primarily in terms of autonomy and separation, which have traditionally been regarded as synonymous with maturity in much psychological literature.

This new body of literature is very exciting and useful, in spite of its having been written primarily from a heterosexual perspective. Just as women have been viewed through a male lens and have been perceived as having more pathology than men, so lesbian couples have been perceived as having more pathology than heterosexual couples.

In fact, lesbian couples present a different picture of relationship and intimacy than either gay male or heterosexual couples do. Falco (1991) notes that the studies show emotional attachment to be emphasized over sexual behavior in lesbian relationships (p. 81). Lesbians, Falco finds in her review of the literature, appear to prize a love relationship above all else in their lives. Love is frequently regarded as a prerequisite for sex for lesbians (pp. 9, 10). Likewise, Berzon (1990) describes men as programed by society toward being able to separate sex from love, at least at times, whereas women are programed by society to prefer a loving context for their sexual expression (p. 210).

In a gay male relationship the partners are two men who may primarily experience growth and self-csteem through separation and autonomy. In a heterosexual relationship the partners have different life experiences: the woman may tend to grow and enhance her self-esteem through relationship, while the man may tend to grow and enhance more of his self-esteem through separation and autonomy. And in a lesbian relationships both partners may well experience growth and self-esteem primarily through relationship.

Mencher (1990, p. 2) takes note of the fact that several researchers have measured patterns of intimacy in lesbian relationships by a male standard of separation and autonomy and have pathologized as "fusion" the intimacy they observe. She goes on to say that in the relatively small body of literature on lesbian couples at least fourteen articles have appeared in the last ten years that feature fusion as the prominent issue; she considers it rare to find an analysis of lesbian couples that does not address fusion (Burch, 1982, 1985, 1986, 1987; Decker, 1983–1984; Elise, 1984; Krestan & Bepko, 1981; Lindenbaum, 1985; Lowenstein, 1980; Pearlman, 1988; Roth, 1985, 1989; Schneider, 1986; Smalley, 1987). Mencher observes that several features are common to most definitions of fusion:

> Fusion is a state of "psychic unity" in which individual ego boundaries are crossed and two individuals experience a sense of oneness. . . . In the state of fusion the self is embedded within a relational context, and boundaries between self and other are unclear (Karpel, 1986). . . .
>
>   The literature notes that lesbians place a high premium on being intimately involved and experience difficulties when they are without an intimate relationship, frequently resulting in excessive tenacity to unsatisfying partnerships. The literature depicts the lesbian couple locked in an embrace of intimacy which values identification, mutual understanding and acceptance; and shared beliefs, behaviors, goals and wishes. Differences between partners are feared, often to the extent that the denial of differences is readily employed; conflict is either avoided or constantly remains unsolved. (Mencher, 1990, p. 2)

Mencher goes on to identify other indicators of fusion in lesbian relationships such as:

> The couple attempts to spend all or most of its leisure time together; social contacts are limited primarily to mutual friends, with few individual ones. They share professional services, e.g., doctors, lawyers, therapists, financial planners. Monies are pooled. Clothing and other possessions are shared, and the couple is in frequent telephone contact when apart, even if apart only during the work day. (Mencher, 1990, p. 3)

Some components of fusion are, of course, shared by hetero-sexual and gay male couples as well; however, Mencher (1990) explains that these characteristics of fusion, taken together, form the integral picture of a typical lesbian relationship as de-scribed in the literature.

In short, there is ample evidence in the literature of les-bian psychology to suggest that the patterns of intimacy of les-bian couples are different from those of heterosexual and gay male relationships. Moreover, many of these distinctive features have been pathologized by labeling them as fusion, which is agreed to be inherently pathological. Yet when fusion is recon-sidered in the light of the theory of the new psychology of women, which emphasizes a woman's capacity to nurture rela-tionships along with her desire for relationship to enhance her own growth and self-esteem, it may reflect the lesbian couple's capacity for intimacy rather than a pathological state.

In Gestalt theory fusion is termed *confluence*. Confluence may be regarded as a resistance to contact because the absence of clear boundary may deplete the contact experience. Yet the same confluence is also a form of contact, and one that is much devalued in the heterosexist model even among Gestalt writers (see Wheeler, 1991, for further discussion of this devaluing).

In a couple with confluent capacity, each partner identi-fies with the other's feelings, wishes, and desires as much as her own. Many lesbian couples report the experience of being con-fluent or fused as positive and pleasurable. Given that lesbian couples are denied legal status in this culture, confluence can serve also as a strategy to cope with heterosexism by providing a sense of relationship stability. On the other hand, difficulties do arise for some couples who join in confluence without aware-ness and conscious choice. Some couples report feeling torn be-tween their own needs and the needs of their partners, and can benefit from therapeutic help in this area.

Judy and Rose have been together for seven years. Rose, who initiated the couples therapy, feels disappointed in their relationship. She states that she loves Judy but she feels that she has lost herself somehow. Judy came to couples therapy because Rose pleaded with her to do so. She believes that

Rose has decided to leave the relationship even though Rose
denies it.

> Judy and Rose are sitting across the room from me
> in separate chairs. I have asked them to speak di-
> rectly to each other rather than to me.
>
> Rose shifts her position in the chair. She
> looks at the wall behind Judy. She says, "I'm afraid
> to say what is on my mind tonight." She quickly
> glances at Judy and then looks back at the wall. Judy
> puts her hand behind her neck and says, "I know
> what is going on with you but I want you to tell me."
> Roses crosses her legs and begins to play with her
> shoelaces. She is quiet for a few moments and then
> says, "I was very angry with you last night and I was
> afraid to tell you." Judy puts her hands in her lap
> and says, "I knew you were angry last night. I can
> read your feelings." She sounds angry herself. She
> folds her arms in front of herself and looks down.
> There is silence and I feel the tension between
> them. The silence continues and I let them know I
> am aware of the tension and the silence. Rose rocks
> in her chair and says, "If you knew I was angry why
> didn't you say something?" Judy keeps her arms
> folded, looks at Rose and then out the window. She
> raises her voice and says, "You know I can tell what
> you are feeling. You could have talked to me about
> it. You know I feel better if you talk to me about
> your feelings." Rose continues to rock in her chair.
> She runs her fingers through her hair and says, "I
> know you expect me to be more in tune with you,
> but sometimes I can't be. I'm sorry."

As I observe Rose and Judy a figure begins to form. I notice that Judy believes she knows what Rose is thinking and feeling and she expects Rose to be as perceptive about her. Rose is
apologetic when she doesn't know what Judy's inner experience
is. She feels she lets Judy down, but she also feels trapped. They

both seem to agree that they *should* know each other's thoughts and feelings at all times. They no longer live with the mystery of each other. They are confluent without awareness, not realizing that they are trying to erase all the differences between them. Then they use projection to try to put themselves in exactly the same spot they think their partner is in. This twisting pattern of confluence and projections is out of their awareness, leaving them in a state of anxiety and dissatisfaction.

This pattern of confluence and projection, which is figural for me, can serve as material for an experiment that will help them become aware of their differences and their individuality. As I consider experiments I recall what Rose and Judy have told me about their brief courtship. They dated only three times before moving in with each other. When they met they each had just broken up with another lesbian partner. They both felt abandoned by their former partners, and they both felt rejected and unlovable. Both experience this relationship as healing that pain. I appreciate that they desperately want to make their relationship work. They believe that they show their love for each other by experiencing each other's feelings, wishes, and desires as if they were their own.

I am aware too that as women their self-esteem is strongly tied to their ability to establish and maintain relationship. I know that confluence often lasts longer in lesbian relationships, and is often experienced as quite valuable and pleasurable. Thus the problem is not just that they are confluent per se, but that they are no longer making choices about being confluent, and as a result they cannot generate the excitement that is sparked by difference in a relationship. As I hold these thoughts, I notice that I am excited by the idea that they might rediscover their differences. I share what I have noticed so far about Rose and Judy's interactive process, emphasizing both the strength of their sensitivity as well as the possibility that this habit may weaken their ability to express difference, thus dampening their excitement for each other. Then I propose a simple experiment. In the experiment one partner is to speak of her feelings and experience while the other asks her numerous questions about them. Assumptions (projections) are not allowed. The partners are to switch roles back and forth. They are not enthusiastic but they are willing to give it a try.

What follows is not that first fumbling step, but rather a description of an interaction between Judy and Rose that took place after they had worked for several weeks on this ongoing experiment of expanding their awareness and appreciation for each other's feelings and experiences.

ROSE (*takes a deep breath and looks at Judy*): I feel trapped when you call me at work and tell me you have to speak to me right away.

JUDY (*crosses her legs and looks surprised*): I didn't know that! Why does it bother you?

ROSE (*leans toward Judy*): I feel like I don't have the option to say I'm too busy. I feel obligated to stop whatever I'm doing and speak with you or you'll feel hurt and rejected.

JUDY (*clears her throat*): You're right! I would feel rejected but it's about old family stuff and it's not your job to fix all that mess. You can't protect me from all those feelings even though I want you to. I have other people I can call but it's easier to call you.

ROSE (*crying*): I hate for you to feel rejected but it's better for me to know you'll call someone else if I'm not available.

JUDY (*shakes her head*): I don't want you to feel trapped anymore.

They smile at each other and hold hands. Rose looks at me and says, "I touched her hand out of choice that time. I didn't feel obligated to." Judy says, "Me too." I ask them what they are feeling and Rose responds first, saying that she feels relieved to tell Judy about her telephone calls, feels closer to Judy. Judy says that she felt scared at first because she always finds it grounding to speak to Rose, but she knows she can call some friends instead. She acknowledges that she too feels closer to Rose.

At this point in the couples therapy Rose and Judy were able to tolerate and appreciate having different needs, and to recognize that they cannot always respond to the other's needs. Not every moment was this clear and tender, and not every problem between them was solved. But the boundary between then was now clearer and less diffuse, and they began to move with some ease and sense of choice between clear contact and confluence.

Conclusion

While focusing on issues of heterosexism, women's development, and lesbian couple process, I have left a number of important issues related to the lesbian couple's life experience unaddressed. Any therapist—lesbian, heterosexual, bisexual, or gay—who wants to work with lesbian couples will do well to learn more about the following: lesbians and substance abuse, lesbians having and raising children, legal considerations, economic issues, sexual issues, and class and race issues within a couple. Each of these issues forms an important part of the *ground* of lesbian experience, and each enters into the emerging *figure* of lesbian couple process, in the present contexts of the therapy session and the couple's lives.

I consider therapy with lesbian couples a political act because I support growth and change in a system that some parts of this society would like to ignore or even destroy. Gestalt theory supports the use of the whole self, including my lesbian self, to help sustain a community of women who go on loving each other despite the odds. The power and excitement of Gestalt couples therapy lie in its ability to give the couple the opportunity to attend to this process as it is happening. This can be very validating and healing to the lesbian couple, whose attempts to communicate with each other and create an intimate system are rarely recognized and valued.

Note

1. Many of the issues mentioned in this section also apply to the gay male experience; however, because of the scope of this chapter, I will emphasize the lesbian experience.

References

Berzon, B. (1990). *Permanent partners: Building gay and lesbian relationships that last.* New York: Plume.

Dahlheimer, D., & Feigal, J. (1991). Bridging the gap. In *The family therapy networker* (pp. 44–53). Washington, DC: Family Network.

Falco, K. (1991). *Psychotherapy with lesbian clients: Theory into practice.* New York: Brunner/Mazel.

Finnegan, D., & McNally, E. (1987). *Dual identities: Counseling chemically dependent gay men and lesbians.* Center City, MN: Hazelden.

Gilligan, C. (1982). *In a different voice.* Cambridge: Harvard University Press.

Gilligan, C., & Brown, L. M. (1992). *Meeting at the crossroads: Women's psychology and girls' development.* Cambridge: Harvard University Press.

Heyward, C. (1989). *Touching our strength: The erotic as power and the love of God.* San Francisco: Harper & Row.

Karpel, M. (1986). *Family resources: The hidden partner in family therapy.* New York: Guilford Press.

Markowitz, L. (1991). "Gays and lesbians in therapy. Homosexuality: Are we still in the dark?" *The Family Therapy Networker,* Jan.–Feb.

McGoldrick, M., Anderson, C., & Walsh, F. (1991). *Women in families: A framework for family therapy.* New York: W.W. Norton.

Mencher, J. (1990). Intimacy in lesbian relationships: A reexamination of fusion. *Work in Progress, No. 42.* Wellesley, MA: Stone Center Working Paper Series.

Miller, J. (1976). *Toward a new psychology of women.* Boston: Beacon Press.

Nevis, E. (Ed.). (1992). *Gestalt therapy: Perspectives and applications.* New York: Gardner Press.

Rabin, C. (1992). The cultural context in treating a lesbian couple: An Israeli experience. *Journal of Strategic and Systemic Therapies, 11*(4), 42–58.

Roth, S. (1989). Psychotherapy with lesbian couples: Individual issues, female socialization, and the social context. In M. McGoldrick, C. Anderson, & F. Walsh. (Eds.), *Women in families: A framework for family therapy* (pp. 286–307). New York: W.W. Norton.

Sandmaier, M. (1992). *The invisible alcoholic: Women and alcohol.* Blue Ridge Summit, PA: TAB Books.

Surrey, J. (1991). The self-in-relation: A theory of women's development. In *Women's growth in connection: Writings from the Stone Center.* New York: Guilford Press.

Vargo, S. (1987). The effects of women's socialization on lesbian couples. In *Lesbian psychologies* (pp. 161–173). Chicago: University of Illinois Press.

Weinberg, G. (1972). *Society and the Homosexual.* New York: St. Martins.

Wheeler, G. (1991). *Gestalt reconsidered: A new approach to contact and resistance.* New York: Gardner Press.

Woolley, G. (1991). Beware the well-intentioned therapist. In *The Family Therapy Networker* (p. 30). Washington, DC: Family Therapy Network.

Zinker, J. (1977). *Creative process in Gestalt therapy.* New York: Brunner/Mazel.

8

Working with the Remarried Couple System

Isabel Fredericson and Joseph H. Handlon

Most people are committed to the institution of marriage. Nine out of ten people in this country marry, and many more than once. In fact, more than a third of all marriages are remarriages (Wright, 1987). These data are a testament to the hope for happiness that marriage symbolizes, a hope that can emerge even under the most dire circumstances. Witness the scene in the movie *Schindler's List*, where a young couple create a wedding and marry one another while barely surviving under the most depressing and horrifying circumstances of the concentration camp. Entering into a marriage, making a wedding, is both a step into the past, an acceptance of an ancient rite no matter how garbed in modern clothes it may be, as well as a belief in the future, a trust that the dream of happiness with another person can come true. This hope is even more apparent in remarriages, where previous experience has often belied that hope, when, despite the grief of widower and widowhood, or the agony of divorce, people try once again.

In addition to the reemergence of hope, there are many other factors that are unique to the couple in a remarriage. Given the frequency of remarriage, it is surprising that these characteristics, as well as their therapeutic implications, have received relatively little attention in the literature. Often the research on marriage does not discriminate between first-marrieds and remarried subjects, but has lumped all married people into one population for research purposes. Or, frequently, the major focus of interest has been on such issues as the effects of divorce on children, the problems involved in step-parenting, and the difficulties of blending two families (Wright, 1987). Even in the journal devoted specifically to this area, *The Journal of Divorce and Remarriage*, there is a noticeable paucity of articles relating exclusively to the remarried spousal relationship as compared to other topics. Yet both common sense and research (Crook, 1991; Martin, 1990) have shown that the quality of the couple relationship itself is the determining factor in the stability and well-being of the new family. The new couple's ability to develop a healthy and satisfying relationship is largely dependent upon how well they have resolved issues from their former marriages. The "unfinished business," the incomplete resolution of past experiences and the consequent displacement of emotions from one person or situation onto another, and the resulting misperceptions, projections, and misunderstandings that are the consequence, all lead to the lack of healthy contact between the couple at best, and to distance or estrangement at worst. Frequently, these are the reasons that bring a remarried couple into therapy. The therapists' tasks, then, are to help the clients differentiate between the issues of the past and those of the present, and to assist the remarried couples in resolving these past issues.

Because society as a whole has not fully institutionalized remarriage, family roles are both more ambiguous and flexible. Whereas family relations in first marriages are supported by custom, law, and language, those in remarriages are not (Grizzle, 1990). Our language itself contains negative connotations that the new family system has to work against. Associations to the word *stepmother* are connected to fairy tales in which they are always evil and wicked. A *stepchild* is one who is less than a full child. In many states, stepchildren have no legal rights related to stepparents, as in inheritance laws, even if these stepparents have brought them up from infancy. Because of this lack of societal norms, many remarried couples encounter difficulties when they tend to rely on inappropriate nuclear family ideology (Vanderheide, 1992). In these cases, the Gestalt therapist can assist the couple to expand their awareness of role options.

On the other hand, despite these inherent difficulties, the ambiguity and flexibility of roles also allow for less stereotyping of tasks, for example, in less gender-based segregation of household labor. It has been found that husbands in remarried families contribute significantly more to housework tasks of cooking, meal cleanup, shopping, laundry, and housecleaning (Ishii-Kuntz & Coltrani, 1992). They also tend to give in more often than husbands in first marriages (Hobart, 1991). Wives in second marriages tend to act more out of self-interest and less out of other-interest than first-married wives (Smith, Golsen, Byrd, & Reese, 1991).

Boundaries change enormously between first and later marriages, boundaries around each member of the couple as well as around the system as a whole. Usually, individuals in a remarried system have spent some years in independent living, have a clearer sense of their own identity and their own needs and expectations. Unlike with the younger couple in a first marriage, who often see bliss as fusion, the independence of the older couple in a remarriage often leads to difficulty in accepting dependency or interdependency. One's own money, one's own car, one's own property are seen as personal possessions and not joint assets. Paradoxically, whereas individuals' boundaries are more impermeable, those of the system are much looser, including, as they often do, children, stepchildren, former grandparents, new grandparents, aunts, uncles, and cousins, as well as a whole host of new relatives as a consequence of the new marriage. Ellen Goodman, in a nostalgic newspaper column a few years ago, described the difference between the guests who sat around her parents' Thanksgiving table in her childhood and those who currently sit at her holiday table. Whereas the guests of her childhood were all descendants of one couple—her grandparents—and included her siblings, parents, aunts, uncles, and cousins, the guests at her own table included her children, his children, current in-laws, former in-laws, cousins of stepchildren, cousins of her own children, and so on. The system surrounding the remarried couple has grown much larger and far more complex. It is to this increased complexity with all of its attendant dilemmas that the therapist working with remarried couples must bring awareness and to which she must attend.

The purpose of this paper is twofold. First, it will explore a number of features that are unique to remarried couple systems that are important for therapists to know about, and that may underlie the problems that such couples bring into therapy. Second, it will describe how a Gestalt therapist would approach and deal with some of these problems, and will express cautions about possible pitfalls.

Is It Different the Second Time Around?

In working with a remarried couple, one pitfall for the therapist, who may not have been part of a remarried system, is to be unaware of how it will differ from the traditional, first-time-married system. It is very easy for the unaware therapist to make the unwarranted assumption that "a marriage-is-a-marriage-is-a-marriage," and that all marital difficulties stem pretty much from the same interpersonal contextual ground. This can leave the unsophisticated therapist at a distinct disadvantage in dealing with the issues of a problematic remarriage.

Here are some critical differences between the first and subsequent marriages for the marital therapist to keep in mind:

1. Perhaps the most important difference is the very obvious one. It is the very fact that for one or both members of the remarried system, the current marriage is not the first one experienced. Thus the current marriage is invariably perceived by the spouses within the context of the previous marriage. Given this past experience, certain assumptions and expectations, both explicit and implicit, have been built up.

To begin with, for good or evil, comparisons with the first partner are inevitably made, with the current partner coming out ahead on some dimensions and behind on others. One fall-out of such comparisons with one's previous spouse is the impact that this often implicit process can have on the present partner, who may become obsessed with worry about whether he or she is measuring up. This can lead to an overcautious attitude about letting oneself go and becoming "my real self," a continuous walking on eggs for fear of not measuring up to the previous incumbent.

Another result of having gone through a previous marriage—especially one that ended in divorce—is the determination on the part of one or both members of the remarried system to "do better this time around." Despite this good intention, which according to common sense should "make things better this time," research shows that this is not always the case. Woods (1991) found no differences between first- and second-married persons in the amount and topics of marital conflict, marital conflict tactics, or communication styles in the course of marital conflict. However, there were some differences between persons whose *spouse* is in a first marriage and persons whose *spouse* is in a second marriage, with those with first-married spouses using closed styles of communication and also tending to experience greater amounts of marital conflict.

Because of a previous experience with marriage and subsequent divorce, it has been suggested (MacDonald, 1992) that the commitment to marital permanence might be less. For example, persons who have divorced once could be less inhibited about doing so again; thus it might be that there is now less willingness to tolerate a bad situation, and less inclination to stay together at all costs to "try to work it out."

2. The range of characteristics of the couple system is likely to be greater among the remarrieds than in first-marriage systems. The individuals in a first-marriage couple tend to be young, unencumbered, and with a limited history of being part of a stable couple. The disadvantage of this relative lack of marital experience is that it is easy to build up quite unrealistic expectations—often of a very romantic kind supported by our popular culture—about the unending joys of married bliss. Their inexperience with being a stable couple means that they

have not yet acquired the competencies of give-and-take compromise necessary for continued stability. At least the members of a remarried system have "been around the block" a few times, and are not naive about the hard work it takes to make a close relationship work. The remarried couple who come in for marital therapy are typically not surprised that "a marriage made in heaven" must "work like hell" to develop a stable satisfying relationship. Individuals in a remarriage may even have come to realize that some old interpersonal patterns from their past are being repeated, and that there might be some remote chance that they each could bear some individual responsibility for the mess in which they find themselves. Clearly, this is a potent source of therapeutic leverage for the clinician at the beginning of treatment.

3. Since the partners in a remarried system have typically lived longer, they have each developed a complex pattern of habits that constitute their individual life-styles. Coming together in a successful remarriage necessitates the blending of these two separate life-styles. This blending does not occur automatically without some stress in the system, especially since each has led a distinct life-style separately for a longer period of time than is typical for the partners in a first-time marriage. Negotiating the compromises necessary to blend the often-conflicting elements of unique life-styles requires particular skills that many couples do not possess. As in all compromises, something must be given up so that something can be gained, but individuals are often very reluctant to abandon precious elements of their life-styles that have been such a source of security for so long. Teaching the remarried couple to negotiate around the blending of life-styles can be a special challenge for the therapist.

4. In contrast to how they were in a first marriage, the individuals in a subsequent marriage are very likely to be less dependent upon and more autonomous of their partners. There is less tendency to view marriage as merely an extension of their nuclear family, where a certain degree of dependency was appropriate and often strongly encouraged by parents. Having been through a previous marriage, no matter how functional or

nonfunctional it was, the individual has learned to develop a certain degree of independence and freedom through a realization that total dependence upon the spouse is not going to work. The trick in the remarriage is how to maintain the degree of independence and autonomy that feels right for each of the members of the new system and still have an integrated system of interdependent, well-functioning parts.

A special challenge for the therapist dealing with a remarriage presents itself when one of the spouses has been married previously and the other has not. Here the degree of imbalance between relative needs for autonomy and dependence between the two members of the system can present particular difficulties. For example, let us take the case where the husband has been married before and has developed habits of considerable dependency upon his partner about household matters. Suppose he takes as his bride a woman who has not been married before, and who has for many years lived alone and been, out of necessity, quite autonomous when it comes to running a household. Her secret hope about her new married status is that she can unburden herself from "having to do just everything." Clearly, in the new married system, there is more than a little chance for considerable conflict about who has responsibility for what around the house and how each member of the system feels about the pressures around new role allocations.

5. Each partner in a remarried system brings to it a certain degree of "baggage" made up of extended parts of the previous first-marriage system. Such obvious "baggage" would include children, grandchildren, former in-laws, abiding friendships, long-term relationships with other couples, and so on. Each member of the new system must learn to deal, somehow, with the "baggage" that has been brought to the remarriage. This is not an easy task, since the other's "baggage" can be fertile soil for the development of competition, envy, jealousy, and other disturbing feelings on the part of a spouse. An added difficulty in the relationship is that such feelings are not admitted to readily, for who wants to be accused of harboring such negative thoughts when one is trying to make this remarriage "work"? Yet it is these seemingly untoward—yet very natural—feelings that

must be admitted to, looked at, and dealt with lest they have a detrimental effect on the remarried system, with the eventual possibility of destroying it.

6. Finally, in the area of finances, each member of the remarried system is likely to have accumulated over time personal assets that he or she may wish to keep separate rather than combine with the spouse's into "our income." This situation is very much in contrast to the typical first-marriage system, where there is a strong pull to pool resources right from the start as an indication of the couple's "togetherness." An example of a determined motivation to keep assets separate would be to ensure that one's own offspring from a previous marriage have a secure inheritance that they can count on in the future.

This desire for keeping assets separate on the part of only one of the partners can become the source of considerable tension, if not outright conflict, in the system, particularly where the expectations growing out of a previous experience are quite different for the two partners. Once again, this kind of issue in a remarriage stems from differing needs and expectations imbedded in contrasting life-styles built up over the years. Added to this dynamic are all the peculiar sensitivities we may have around the acquisition and spending of money, with its many symbolic meanings in our culture, that can make this an especially explosive area between the couple.

Not All Remarried Systems Are the Same

Just as the psychotherapist must become aware of the differences between the *general characteristics* of a remarried system as compared with a first-marriage system, so the therapist must become sensitive to the many important *differences between* remarried systems. In many ways, it should be obvious that each remarried system is a unique entity. Here are some potent differences between the constellations of such systems that the marital therapist must bear in mind:

1. The circumstances under which the previous marriage came to an end can make for significant differences in the kinds

of problematic issues with which the remarried spouses must deal. One major difference is between a marriage that ended in a divorce and a marriage that ended in the death of one of the partners. In the case of a death, the deceased previous spouse may be idealized. Such an idealization is bound to have its impact upon the self-assessment of the present partner. "How do I measure up compared to his or her previous mate?" If the previous marriage ended in a divorce, the previous spouse, by contrast, may be demonized. Again, this demonization can have an effect upon the present relationship when in moments of distressful anger the wife, say, accuses her spouse of being "just as bad as my first husband!"

In both these cases, the projected picture that each spouse carries around influenced by one or both previous marriages is bound to be a distortion that is influencing the expectations for the current marriage. If the remarriage occurs after a divorce, there will probably be a determination "to make this marriage different." In contrast, if the remarriage occurs after a death of a previous spouse, the survivor may well want the present marriage to be much the same. Thus, in both cases, there may be burdensome expectations laid upon the present system.

2. In the case of a previous divorce, the issue of which member of the previous couple took the initiative to dissolve the marriage, which can vary along the continuum from initiating a "friendly" separation all the way to sudden abandonment, can influence the assumptions and expectations brought to the remarriage system. If one initiated the divorce, one is more likely to have a sense of power and control over the destiny of the remarriage—at least to the extent that one knows how to take the initiative to end an untenable situation. On the other hand, if one sees oneself as the "victim" of the divorce, either by abandonment or by more gentle persuasion, one might be concerned about suffering a similar fate in the remarriage. These two contrasting expectations can influence how one views the remarriage and how one treats the partner.

3. It should be clear that the dynamics of a remarried system in which both partners have been married before will differ from those in a system in which only one of the partners has

been married previously. When only one has been married before, there can be important gender differences, particularly
when children are involved. A woman with children by a previous marriage brings to the new marriage very different assumptions and expectations than, say, a man who has never been
married.

4. Related to this is the whole matter of the dynamics of the
"blended family." Much has been written about this rather common phenomenon of the remarried system, which may well
contain "his," "her," and "our" children (Papernow, 1993), and
what the necessary ingredients are for successful versus unsuccessful family blendings. It is important to point out the obvious
fact that characteristics of remarried systems, including the degree of involvement, can vary enormously whether children
from a previous marriage are involved or not. For example, with
older remarried couples, where the offspring from one or both
partners are now adults living on their own, such "children" will
have a very different impact on the remarriage system than the
dependent children of a younger remarried couple.

5. In many remarried systems there are significant age differences between the couple. It is not unusual that the man is
considerably older than the woman. Here a conflict often arises
if the man, say, may be looking forward to retirement and a
more sedate life just at the time when the woman is getting settled into her long-delayed career, is feeling ambitious, and is
eager to move forward in her career path no matter where it
may take her.

The opposite pattern has also been increasingly noted (Peterson, 1983), in which the never-married husband in the remarriage is considerably younger than his wife, who has been
married before and has had several children. Here the issue can
arise about the couple having their own children, with the
younger man eager and the older woman somewhat reluctant
about repeating her motherhood role with a new set of children.

Avoiding the Pitfalls of Countertransference

The most basic tool that any therapist has is herself: not only her
theoretical knowledge and technical skills, but also her personal

history, talents and interests, and, even more importantly, her emotions, associations, fantasies, and feelings. It is these latter qualities that enable the therapist to guide the client toward increased awareness and more competent, fulfilling functioning.

However, the therapist's emotions, associations, fantasies, and feelings are also a double-edged sword. When the therapist's internal world is out of kilter, when her buttons get pushed by the client and when her emotional responses are inappropriate to the situation, there is potential for possible therapeutic pitfalls if not outright disaster. The psychological mechanisms leading to inappropriate responses on the therapist's part are commonly termed "countertransference."

It is particularly incumbent upon the Gestalt therapist to understand and become aware of when this happens, since the relationship between the Gestalt therapist and clients tends to be more personal and informal than in many other types of therapies. The Gestalt therapist often discloses more personal material than other therapists and relies to a great extent on her here-and-now perceptions and immediate reactions to determine the next therapeutic intervention.

Working with a remarried couple is bound to arouse potent countertransference issues by pushing old emotional "buttons" in the therapist. These "buttons" reactivate early feelings stemming from experiences in one's own family, both as a child and as an adult. The source of such feelings can be better understood if one considers answers to the following questions: Were the therapist's parents divorced? Should they have been if they weren't? Has the therapist been divorced? Is the therapist a child of a remarried couple? Is the therapist married now? Is this a remarriage? The strength of these countertransference issues stems from very early introjects and long-standing, unexamined projections that are based on the fact that our norms and values about family systems have their origin so early in life that they often lie beneath the surface of everyday awareness.

The therapist working with a remarried couple would do well to ask herself the following: What were my early unexamined introjects about the "sanctity" of marriage? about the appropriate basis for divorce? about the "correct" gender roles in a marriage? about committed relationships between same-sex partners? about multiple marriages? about living together without a legal marriage? Next, it is essential that the therapist ask herself: What is the current status of these old introjects? Have they been "chewed upon" so that what has been extracted now represents a well-thought-through set of values, or are there still some unexamined residuals left over from childhood?

If the past history of the remarried couple seeking help involves a divorce on one or both their parts, there is an especial potential for considerable countertransference interference that needs careful monitoring. Was the wife "justified" in walking out on her previous husband, leaving her children behind? Was the husband "correct" in abandoning his chronically alcoholic former wife even though she suffered from a long-term and eventually fatal physical illness? All of these thoughts and feelings can color the therapist's perceptions, behavior, and eventual effectiveness as she begins to help the remarried system deal with its problems.

Since there is really nothing that the therapist can do to make such countertransference processes disappear by magic, the best option is conscientiously to monitor such processes and continually ask oneself: How are my feelings, attitudes, beliefs, and values influencing what I am doing with this couple? The very act of answering these questions will help eliminate the untoward effect of countertransference on one's therapeutic work.

What Does the Therapist Do Now?

The Gestalt therapist works simultaneously with two different lenses. One is a wide-angled lens that includes the client's history, family background, previous marriage experience, current support system, present family structure, and so on—all the various factors that form the background and the context for the problem that precipitates the remarried couple embarking on therapy. The other is a close-up lens that focuses on what is visible and audible or otherwise learned by immediate experience—all the phenomenological data available to the therapist, including her own emotions, associations, and fantasies.

In working with a remarried couple the Gestalt therapist

is interested in how they look at each other, how they speak to one another as well as how they speak to her, who speaks first as well as who speaks the most, how close or far apart they choose to sit, whether or not they touch, and any other information that the close-up lens reveals. Whatever the so-called issue is that brings the remarried couple into therapy, it will become visible to the therapist through attention to their process in the therapy hour. Willy-nilly the couple cannot fail to act this issue out.

Whereas the theory and methodology of working with a remarried couple are not different from working with any other couple, the content of specific issues tend to be different. The experiences of the previous marriages are always present, either actively, as in dealing with current problems with children or former spouses, or in the background as a model for what should or should not happen in this marriage. More boundaries have to be managed because there is likely to be a larger, more complicated family system with stepchildren, biological children, former and present in-laws, and so on. All this increases the stress on the remarried couple in ways that they may not be aware of. Another challenge that a remarried couple faces is rebuilding trust. The losses experienced as the result of previous marriages may significantly influence their ability to do this, and yet it is vital to their development as a couple that they accomplish this task (Kvanli & Jennings, 1986).

The Addisons were a remarried couple who were dealing with many of the dilemmas peculiar to remarried couples. They had been together for over ten years and, through mutual agreement, had no children of their own but were actively involved with Mr. Addison's four daughters from his previous marriage, who were now all grown. Nora Addison was an unusually attractive, bright, and articulate well-to-do woman in her early forties who had been married once before, rather briefly, during her early twenties. Her face mirrored a wide range of emotions, but her body looked frail and her movements seemed constricted. John, on the other hand, seemed a specimen of good health. Although in his late fifties, he prided himself on his vigor and freedom from sickness. However, emotionally he was very constrained and revealed little about his interior world either verbally or expressively.

The Addisons' considerable wealth derived from John's inheritance from his mother. Despite their wealth, their ostensible problems were about money. John thought Nora was too frivolous in her spending habits, and Nora resented John's insistence on total control of the family's finances.

Upon entering the office the Addisons took seats at right angles to each other, not face to face or side by side. Their individual boundaries appeared to be stiff, and the boundary around them as a couple was barely visible. During the initial introductions and background history, Nora provided most of the information for both of them with few additions or corrections from John. Beginning the task of helping the couple to become more aware of themselves as a system, the therapist said, "This is probably not new to you, but I noticed that Nora answered most of my questions. Is that your usual pattern, that Nora speaks for both of you?"

For the first time since entering the room, John looked directly at Nora and said, with the slightest smile on his face, "She always has more to say. She's much better with words. It's one of her qualities that attracted me in the beginning." To this Nora responded, "You're so slow. If I wait for you to talk I go to sleep." Again John said nothing, but the smile left his face and his mouth drew a tiny bit tighter. The therapist noted the "complementarity" in the couple system, how Nora's energy fostered John's passivity and vice versa (Zinker, 1977).

She remarked, "You each seem to get some goodies from this pattern; I wonder why you both sound as if you are complaining about it."

Nora came back quickly: "I don't like it! I wish John would talk more. When we go out to eat in a restaurant, if I don't say anything we just look like an old unhappy married couple who have nothing to say to each other. What do you mean 'goodies,' what 'goodies'?"

"You get to put your spin on everything, you get listened to, noticed, while John gets to be able to play it safe in the corner," answered the therapist.

"That's true. Nobody pays attention to me, not even Nora," John said, emerging from his muteness.

"Well, nobody is stopping you from talking, are they?

Don't blame me for your feelings!" Nora snapped. The air in the room felt like sandpaper. What had obviously begun as an attraction in the relationship had become a powder keg.

The therapist found herself suddenly remembering the sickening sound of her own parents' quarrels, and how as a young child she would close her ears and hide under the covers, trying to escape from the sound of their voices and the queasy feeling in the pit of her stomach. If only her mother would hold her tongue everything would be all right, she used to think.

"Watch it! Don't project your life into this! Look at the system, think system," warned the therapist to herself. "They are both doing this; don't take sides whatever you do."

"Why," wondered the therapist to herself, "are they doing this? Where does the bitterness come from, and why is it being expressed this way?"

In the following weeks, as they continued the work, the reasons became clear. In John's previous marriage he had allowed his wife to make all the financial decisions, feeling that she had more expertise in this area than he did. In addition, he didn't want to make the effort to think about it and so he paid little attention to how his money was being handled. This turned out to not have been a wise decision. His wife did not have the expertise she had claimed and which John had allowed, nor did she do much thinking about it, which resulted in some serious losses. The trauma John experienced in discovering this was a major factor in the events that eventually led to the divorce. Lest that recur, this time John was determined to do exactly the opposite and keep control. Nora, however, had lived alone for several years between marriages and felt perfectly capable of managing their finances. John's lack of trust in her felt like a betrayal of their relationship. At the least, she wanted to feel like a full and trusted partner. Feeling impotent in this arena, Nora lashed out at John, using her skill with words to make him feel impotent in turn. But it only made John trust Nora less and feel more determined to retain control of what did give him power, the money. The trust that had existed between them was slowly being eroded. It was this lack of trust that led to the bitterness and danger that marked their interactions.

As the Addisons slowly became aware of how each of them was affecting the other in ways least likely to produce results they wanted, their individual boundaries became more permeable and the boundary around them as a couple became more solidified. John learned that Nora was very responsible financially when she had some control, that she was not like his first wife in this respect; and Nora learned that using overspending as a way of fighting back was not very useful.

Approaching the conclusion of their therapy, the therapist said, "Would you each be willing to tell one another how you see each other differently now?"

Nora, still the first, reached over to take John's hand, who was sitting on the couch beside her, and turning to face him fully, said, "I love it that you consult me now about our finances, that you are treating me like a partner and not an enemy. You tell me more about everything, and I feel more connected to you. You smile and laugh more and that makes me smile and laugh too." And she promptly proceeded to demonstrate her words with a broad smile.

John grinned back and, nodding his head in agreement, said, "I'm happy you see that, and I am happier in general so I smile and laugh. I see you looking healthier and more relaxed, not throwing darts at me with your words like you used to. I know now that there is no reason not to trust you."

Looking at them both, the therapist remarked, "I have been seeing what you describe happen and I feel really delighted about your work and the changes you have been able to make. You are working with each other now instead of against one another."

The Millers were a very different kind of remarried couple, young, poor, and each with a child from a previous marriage living with them. They had had a very romantic long-distance relationship for a year, during which time they saw each other every other weekend, alternating between their homes. Usually the children were with the other parent at those times, and the couple were able to devote their attention solely to one another. When they decided to marry, Howard chose to move to Pat's city, since her mother lived nearby, and they both agreed that it would be easier for Howard to find a job in a new city than it would be for Pat. As the months passed, after the marriage and the move, and it became clear that Howard was not finding the job that he had anticipated, and as Pat was bearing more of the financial burden, emotions erupted. By the time they came to see the therapist, Pat was ready to call it quits.

Although the Millers were in their late thirties, they both appeared much younger. The children, they assured the therapist, were getting along fine, each enjoying the company of another child in the family. In spite of what was happening between them, both the Millers were reluctant to disturb that relationship. The therapist remarked, "Well, you must be doing something right for that to be true. It wouldn't happen by itself." Pat and Howard looked at each other at that but said nothing. Pat's reluctance to tolerate a difficult situation stemmed directly from her feeling that she had stayed far too long in her previous marriage with a man who was an alcoholic and worked only intermittently. Howard's reaction to Pat's uncertainty about the future was fright, dismay, and partial paralysis.

"What's the use?" he said. "I gave up a lot to come here and now she doesn't trust me." He seemed more hurt than angry, and felt betrayed by Pat's impatience. Betrayal was a very sensitive spot in Howard's psyche, and easily touched. His first wife had had a series of affairs with other men and his sense of betrayal by her was profound.

The therapist worked at helping the Millers differentiate between what was happening between them and what had happened in their previous marriages, at helping them separate the intensity of their feelings from the reality of the situation.

"Three months of not working is not three years," pointed out the therapist. "Howard seems to be trying and is not escaping into alcohol." Howard began to acknowledge that Pat's anger had some justification and was not a betrayal. As a couple, they began to deal with the situation more realistically and with more energy, using resources they had not previously seen.

These two cases, briefly presented here, demonstrate only a very few of the many complicated dilemmas facing remarried couples as they work toward building new lives together, sometimes on the ashes of the old. In each case, the Gestalt model, with its emphasis on present awareness and the dynamic organization of the subjective field, supports a fuller contact between the couple members, a fresh encounter with more energy, bringing more of the self. When the contact is richer and more grounded, then the couple find their own solutions to the present problem—often things neither they nor the therapist could have thought of without that richer contacting ground.

We close with a paraphrase from another writer in the field (Messinger, 1984). One can make two kinds of mistakes in thinking about and counseling remarried couples: the first is to assume that they are just like any other couple; the second is to assume they are not. In our experience—as therapists who have worked with remarried couples, and as a remarried couple ourselves—both are true.

References

Crook, J. (1991). An exploratory investigation of stepfamily functioning (marital relationship). *Dissertation Abstracts International,* 53/02-B, 1057.

Grizzle, G. (1990). Remarriage as an incomplete institution: A critical examination of Cherlin's theory. *Dissertation Abstracts International,* 51/12-A, 4287.

Hobart, C. (1991). Conflict in remarriages. *Journal of Divorce and Remarriage, 15*(3–4), 69–86.

Ishii-Kuntz, M., & Coltrani, S. (1992). Remarriage, stepparenting, and household labor. *Journal of Family Issues, 13*(2), 215–233.

Kvanli, J., & Jennings, G. (1986). Recoupling: Development and establishment of the spousal subsystem in remarriage. *Journal of Divorce and Remarriage, 10*(1–2), 189–204.

MacDonald, W. (1992). The relative instability of first marriages and remarriages: The effects of incomplete institutionalization and commitment to marital permanence. *Dissertation Abstracts International,* 53/12-A, 4487.

Martin, R. (1990). Factors associated with marital adjustment in remarriage. *Dissertation Abstracts International*, 52/02, 1124.

Messinger, L. (1984). *Remarriage: A family affair.* New York: Plenum Press.

Papernow, P. (1993). *Becoming a stepfamily.* San Francisco: Jossey-Bass.

Peterson, S. (1983). The new dyad: Older women and younger men. *Dissertation Abstracts International*, 45/10-B, 3322.

Smith, R., Goslen, M., Byrd, A., & Reese, L. (1991). Self-other orientation and sex role orientation of men and women who remarry. *Journal of Divorce and Remarriage, 14*(3–4), 3–32.

Vanderheide, L. (1992). The reinstitutionalization of remarriage? *Masters Abstracts*, 31/03, 1096.

Woods, K. (1991). A comparison of conflict and conflict management behavior and their relation to marital satisfaction in first and second marriages. *Dissertation Abstracts International*, 52/10-B, 5553.

Wright, M. (1987). The quality of remarriage as related to perceived differences in spouses. *Dissertation Abstracts International*, 49/12-B, 5575.

Zinker, J. (1977). *Creative process in Gestalt therapy.* Cleveland: Gestalt Institute of Cleveland Press.

9

The Gestalt Couples Group[1]
Mikael Curman and
Barbro Curman

As human beings, we need love to survive. We need to be touched, to be confirmed, to feel that we can touch another emotionally, to have a receiver for our gifts. For the infant this is a matter of life and death: if the love of the parents is not enough, the child will likely blame himself or herself. Much later, when we meet another person who seems willing and able to give us the love we were longing for as children, and is ready to accept us as we are, our relief and joy are enormous. We were not crazy to long for this experience, which turns out to be possible in this world after all. At the same time, our pain, sorrow, and anger over all that we missed as children can start to wake up, and even overwhelm us. This reaction of rage and despair to the warmth we longed for for so long may be surprising and even devastating to both couple partners, and the relationship itself is threatened.

In love, everything is magnified and enlarged: needs and longings, both current and from the past; fears and negative feelings; and the old survival strategies we learned in order to defend our authentic self against an unreceptive or overwhelming environment, and to stay alive. In the reciprocal context of the intimate relationship, everything dysfunctional now about these old strategies and defenses is likewise magnified. By the same token, the greater visibility and accessibility of these problems and dynamics mean that the potential for successful and rewarding couples therapy and growth is equally enlarged.

The Special Context of Couples Work

The couples therapy setting is a unique environment for growth, in some ways more potentially powerful than even the individual setting. Individuals, after all, may choose, to some degree anyway, how much of themselves they show to the therapist; and then they may act and feel quite differently with a given therapist than they act and feel in other settings. When the couple come in, the members do not have the same options and choice: their strategies as well as their interferences in contact with each other will be obvious and available in the therapy. In the same way, the work of therapy transfers more directly to life outside the session than it may do in individual therapy. The couple, after all, go home together, so that their life in therapy and at home is more of an unbroken whole of process.

There are other potentials and advantages of the couples therapy modality. If human health and growth are the development and expression of more of the authentic self in exchange with the environment, as the Gestalt model maintains, then certainly the intimate couple relationship provides a unique setting for that growth. When individual issues come up, as they inevitably do in the couples setting, then the intimate partner is there in the crucial role of witness to the other's hopes, longings, fears, disappointments, and pain. At the same time each partner is directly involved in the other's new strategies and new organization of these problems and this pain, both old and new. This speaks to one of the most troublesome aspects of individual therapy, which is the way it can disequilibrate and disrupt an ongoing couple relationship, as one partner outgrows the mutual strategies and patterns that both have developed together to manage their contact and their lives.

Finally—and this returns in some ways to the theme of enlargement mentioned above—there is a sense in which couples therapy interrupts the kind of vicious circle of longing, expectation, and fear that the couple relationship itself may easily engender. The love relationship is very important to us, and the more we have felt painful experiences and unsatisfied longings from childhood, the more essential the current relationship will feel, for life and happiness. That importance heightens the fear that we may lose the relationship or remain injured or unsatisfied in the same way. That in turn activates and heightens the old survival and management strategies we learned in childhood. If we have children, the children may serve to remind us all the more of the painful experiences of our own growing up. Thus both our longing to heal those old wounds and our fear of being reinjured or of losing the relationship are magnified, which may make it all the harder for us to break a dysfunctional cycle in the relationship now, and risk trying anything new.

In therapy, the same sequence, with support, can turn into a self-reinforcing beneficent cycle, where new strategies and new behavior lead to new healing, which leads in turn to new confidence and higher expectations as each partner witnesses the other's struggle with painful issues from the past and learns to deal with her or his own past issues and current issues in the couple relationship. This in turn can reduce the fear and apprehension of new hurt and abandonment that were making new behaviors so hard to try out and use—and so on. The couple relationship functions here, with therapeutic support, as a safe and intimate *alternative reality* in which to test out a freer and more open way of being and contacting, and thereby to draw new and more hopeful conclusions about the world and each partner's relationships and possibilities in it—in Gestalt terms, to reorganize the experiential field so that more satisfying contact becomes supported and possible.

The Gestalt Model

In the Gestalt model, contact is both the goal and the means of the therapy. But what do we mean by genuine contact? We all live in and by an eternal ongoing exchange with our environment. In order to manage and accomplish this exchange we must take in percepts from the environment (which means organizing the sensory and thought data, external and internal, into coherent "gestalts" of awareness), react (first internally, then behaviorally), express these reactions in words or actions, stay in the interac-

tion to encounter the new emerging situation, incorporate or resolve what we need and what we can from the exchange, finish
the interaction ("closure," in Gestalt terms, at which point we re-
experience the personal boundary), and then integrate what we
have seen and done and learned. These are the necessary stages
of contact, and together constitute a complete contact cycle or
episode, with more or less satisfaction as the case may be.

In the couple exchange, this contact process takes the
form of an intimate dialogue—what Martin Buber called the
"I-Thou" mode of relationship. The aim of Gestalt couples therapy is to establish and support this ongoing "I-Thou" dialogic
process between the couple members, who can then proceed
with the process of exchange—agreement, disagreement, co-
operation, conflict, witnessing, self-expression, and so on—so
that individual and couple exchange and growth can take place.

Three Contact "Zones"

The work of Perls, Hefferline, and Goodman (1951) and other
authors speak of three modalities or "zones" of contact—three
sources of experiential data that go into the organization of
these contact cycles or episodes:

- The "outer zone"—what happens in the environment, outside the "me" boundary, and what can be perceived and organized through our senses directly (seeing, hearing, touching, smelling, feeling).
- The "inner zone"—what happens inside our personal
  boundary, including body sensations of different kinds, and
  the organized interpretations of body states we call emotions. (Notice, for instance, the difference between tears of
  rage, tears of joy, tears of sorrow, and so on, which is the different meaning we put on the same body state.)
- The "intermediate zone"—our thoughts, conclusions, memories, fantasies, dreams, plans, hopes, judgments, general-
  izations, and so on.

The "inner" and "outer" zones have more of the quality of "what
is," what is given, although here too the act of perception itself

is a construction, not just a passive reception of data. The "intermediate" zone, by contrast, is "about" things that are not necessarily immediately present or immediately grounded in sensory awareness. A full range of awareness and contact means access to all three awareness zones. A limited access to any zone, by contrast, means certain distortions in functioning:

1. "Outer-intermediate" access, with limited "inner" awareness, is a pattern shown by many men in Western culture. It is characterized by rationality and intellectual control, with relatively less awareness of body sensation and feeling and the "softer" wants and needs. In therapy it becomes important to stop and refocus on body states and immediate sensation to rebuild a full range of contact.
2. "Inner-intermediate" access, with limited "outer" awareness, is the "hysterical" pattern, characterized by intense awareness of body states and feelings, with less ability to orient to strong wants and move from feeling into coherent action. In therapy one immediate task is to focus on the world around: "What do you see right now? What are you hearing?" and so on.

By focusing in this way on the "contact boundary," we become aware of how the person is organizing and dealing with his or her life—how much his or her actions are oriented and energized by authentic wants and needs, and how much information from the "real world" here and now is going into his or her style and direction of contact. For example, when we see a person in an intense emotional reaction without an apparent outer cause, then we can assume "inner-intermediate" orientation, where sensations and feelings are organized with thoughts and fantasies without the correction of here-and-now input from the environment. The troubled couple often display a mismatch in awareness zone styles, so that they really are not talking the same "language." The group setting, which we will discuss below, is particularly powerful as a medium for reflecting and highlighting each person's "contact style" in this sense, and for the couple to be seen and to see where each misses the other, and misses a full experience of contact.

Strategies and Reasons for Avoiding Awareness and Contact

We speak as though awareness and contact were always desirable, but in fact there may be many reasons in life why we prefer to block awareness and diminish contact. Contact with our own real goals and feelings, for example, might bring us face to face with irresolvable conflict in the couple relationship. If, as we discussed above, we fear losing the relationship to the point of hanging on to it at any price, then we may prefer to avoid awareness of these troubling things and to limit fully differentiated contact (the exploration of a difference at the boundary) with our partner.

On the other hand, if we are not willing to give up a full range of contact, including differentiated or conflictual contact, then we have to be willing to risk the relationship, to stand up for what we are and feel and see, and to have the courage to encounter our partner as she or he is. This means risking our own beliefs and perceptions, since our partner will be encountering us as well, and some of our positions and assumptions and strategies may turn out to be "introjections"—stereotyped rights and wrongs about relationships, men, women, roles, marriage and family, and so on. Here too the group is useful as a mirror and context for this exploration, both for support and for challenge.

When our individual survival strategies conflict or collide in the couple relationship, the result is often a polarization in which each couple member becomes more extreme in his or her position, which is threatened by the other person. The polarity of pursuing/distancing is a common one; others include fighting/fleeing, blaming/feeling guilty, leading/following, caretaking/being taken care of, and personality "styles" like introvert/extravert. In each case each partner remains limited and incomplete in her or his own development because each resists the other's pole and each depends on the other to supply what is missing (while resisting it).

Likewise, two strategies may be problematic for the couple because they are too much alike. Both partners, for example, may move easily into hot combat, but nobody soothes, pulls back, or regulates the exchange. Or both partners may be extremely held in—"retroflected," in Gestalt terminology—so that the relationship is without energy, and nothing happens. In all these cases there is some good reason why the person avoids a fuller range of contact, with the couple partner and with the world—some risk or danger, as that person perceives it, in moving to new strategies and new contact possibilities. When these reasons and perceptions are explored in the couple, new ways of being and doing together start to open up.

Counterstrategies for Regaining a Fuller Contact Range

Gestalt couples therapy, like Gestalt individual therapy, is concerned with restoring or establishing a full range of contact strategies and skills in the interests of an expanded capacity to deal with life and its changing conditions and challenges. The difference in couples therapy, as we discussed above, is that both members are there, so there is little or no need for talking "about" the problem or working on it indirectly through fantasy or dialogue with absent figures, or even working on the problem as it comes up in the relationship between therapist and patient, as in individual therapy. The work proceeds along the lines of everything discussed up to this point: focusing on awareness, tracking each person's access to each of the three awareness zones discussed above, supporting the genuine dialogue between partners about the true thoughts and feelings they may have held back (even from themselves), exploring the strategies each brings with him or her for blocking or inhibiting certain kinds of contact between them, clarifying the issue of risking the relationship versus staying together at any price, surfacing the introjected ideals and images, identifying the polarities, the places where each is letting the other take over some important life function (and then resenting him or her for it), and so on.

All of this work involves confronting fear—fear of losing the relationship, fear of stirring up old issues, fear of not being able to deal with the new situation, fear of not being good enough, fear of being hurt or hurting the other person. Thus before setting out the couple need to have some sense of whether this enterprise is worth it. How solid is their common ground, the shared foundation of wants and desires that make the relationship worthwhile and that make up a large part of its meaning? In Gestalt, we maintain that all grounded action that leads to a satisfying result must be built on a foundation of clear awareness of wants, needs, and feelings as well as perceptions about the world. The formulation of a clear shared figure of desire is the crucial first step in identifying and establishing this common ground, both for the couple and for the therapist. In this process, a number of issues need to be heightened and explored:

1. Look for the fire! Our first assessment of the strength of the common ground of a particular couple begins with the way the couple relate to each other "here and now." We are interested in the amount and quality of energy between them now (whether well organized into satisfying contact or not), and also in the energy and spark that was between them at the outset, when they first met and found each other attractive. What are their memories of those times? What were their dreams and fantasies then, and how does the present compare and contrast? What happened to that original spark? What happens when they look at each other now? What do they see; what do they want to say?

2. Lay out the bottom line. If there is some question about whether the energy in the couple is enough to build on, then we ask each of them to say what he or she wants from a couple relationship. What are the essentials that are required for each of them to call it a love relationship? Are those the same, different, complementary, or contradictory? And then are they getting those things now, or do they think there is a realistic possibility of getting them? This hope is the basis for further work. Without it, we risk working in a situation where one or both partners have given up and are just hanging on, going through the motions.

3. Is there a match of childhood roles and experiences? Their survival strategies, whether colliding or not, are the outgrowth of childhood experiences for each person. These were

the ways they developed for managing and growing in a more or less difficult field. Do these strategies provoke and threaten each partner? Does each partner have a real sense of where the other's strategies and style of contact come from, why he is so sensitive about this, why she is so defensive about that? Can the partners experience something of each other's childhood with empathy and compassion? Or are they locked in defensiveness and threat?

4. Sensuality and sexuality: What is each partner's experience as a sexual being, in himself or herself and together with the other partner? What are the satisfactions and dissatisfactions? Are both partners open to talking about that, exploring and negotiating it? What is it to be a man, or a woman, to each of them—sexually, sensually, and otherwise? What do they find attractive, in each other or in others? Once again, a group is invaluable as a setting and resource for exploration of this kind. In the group, the multiplicity of perspective and experience serves to open up this very private area, where many of us do not question our own habitual ways of being and contacting.

5. Deal with the question of meaning. What is of greatest importance in my life? What would I do if I had five years left to live? Five months? Five days? How do I want to live the rest of my life? Very often, couples do not explore these ultimate ground questions of life and death and meaning, with a cost to contact and satisfaction for each partner and for the couple. Where do I want to be in ten years? twenty? thirty? Again, if the two partners are not going in the same direction in life, and if those different directions are not compatible, then the work is compromised before we start. And again, the fear of digging up all these difficult issues may be a reason for the couple to avoid deeper and broader contact in the first place. If this is their choice, then it is better to make it openly, and with awareness, before the work of therapy begins.

Why a Couples Group?

We have already begun to touch on some of the reasons why we value the group as a setting for exploring couples' issues. Our own original learning of contact strategies and when and how to use them came after all from a group—the original group of the family. In that earlier setting in one way or another we were not free to risk all of our authentic selves, and instead learned certain masks and strategies for avoiding a full range of contact, in the sense developed above. Now in the new group we live that style and those strategies out—as we do in the couple, but without the intensity of the stakes that we feel in our love relationship. Thus our style can be seen and experimented with, by us, by others, and with the witnessing presence, at least, of our couple partner. The group then, like the couple itself, is another "alternative reality" in which we can test out our assumptions and strategies for achieving or avoiding contact of various kinds. As I employ one strategy or another, the diversity of the group means that there will likely be somebody there to challenge me, somebody to support me (perhaps my partner, coming to my defense!), somebody who has been where I have been and understands, perhaps somebody else who is alarmed or threatened by my behavior. One person will be inspired by the risks I am taking; another person will see himself or herself (or her or his partner) in my position, and gain a new perspective. All of us learn something in the exchange, while the person's partner, who may or may not have been directly involved in a particular exchange, has a chance to see me with more support, and possibly less at stake for him or her at the moment than when the two of us are in the same battle together.

Our work as therapists is to provide a climate where it is safe and supportive to live out more of the "authentic self"—all those feelings and thoughts and voices that were suppressed in childhood, and that we long to have heard and honored in our couple relationship and elsewhere now. We support norms of a less guarded expression of strong feeling, with rules of safety and the promise that no one will be abandoned or condemned for risking a new behavior. Making use of our own authentic presence in the group, we model the sharing of feeling reactions, not to "work our own issues," which would be inappropriate, but to support the growth of a language in which all of us can get to know more of ourselves, our partners, and each other.

The presence of a witness transforms the interaction of a couple, who become more aware of themselves and each other in the reflection of the witness's awareness. This is true in therapy and couples therapy generally, and it is even more powerfully true in the group. Most couples are isolated in their private lives; the witnesses let them know that we are part of a community.

At the same time, the witnesses serve as a reality check. Am I making magical assumptions about my partner's telepathic powers? Am I being clear? Am I hearing what is said to me? Most of all, is my way the right way, the only way to see and map the situation? Every genuine feeling reaction on the part of the group members is ultimately reality orienting and nourishing. Not every attack, every character assassination, in the distance-maintaining contact style of many couples, but rather every statement that is a genuine statement from and about the person making it, is useful. This is the strength and the paradox of the Gestalt group: that sharing where you are, as authentically as you can, is actually more orienting and nourishing to the other person than sharing your "intermediate zone" thoughts and interpretations about the other person himself or herself. And once group members can learn to do that with each other, they can transfer it more easily to the more difficult challenge of doing the same thing within the couple relationship.

How Do We Work with Groups?

Again, we have already begun to discuss this issue, which is not a matter of particular techniques but of the general stance, our assumption that the genuine encounter with "what is" in the other person is inherently healing and promotive of growth. This is the "I-Thou" dialogue, subject to subject, which is the full, uninhibited contact we work to establish for each couple. To achieve this, again, we begin with the issue of the clarity of awareness. Out of what "zone" is the person speaking at the moment, and is that the kind of awareness that is needed now to get where the person or the couple are trying to go (as when we need to know how our partner feels but can only get her or his opinions and judgments)? How sharp and clear is the figure of attention at each moment? Does the figure build, through the stages we outlined above, of perception, reaction, expression, staying with, resolving, finishing, and integrating? Or are certain stages always missing or arrested? What does the person want, really? Is his or her awareness and communication built around that? If not, then the chances of a satisfying outcome for the couple are slight.

The material of the group is much of the material discussed above. What does each person want, in life, for now and for the future, and in the couple relationship? Are the partners satisfied or dissatisfied? What do they want to change? Do they hope for and believe in change? Is their sexual and sensual exchange nourishing? If not, do they want to hear each other about that, and try to do something about it? What are their images and expectations, of themselves and their partner? Are these their own, or are they "introjected" without examination? What were their worlds in childhood, and how do they enter into their strategies for achieving or avoiding certain kinds of contact today? What matters most to them in life, and how do they want to spend the rest of their lives, together or otherwise?

At the beginning of the couples group, the issue is very much trust or distrust, as in any group. Who are these people? What am I doing here? Will they accept me? reject me? hurt me? be hurt by me? How open can I be here without feeling shame myself or making my partner feel betrayed? At this stage we always need clear structures in the form of goals and norms and guidelines to orient ourselves and reassure everyone that the new environment is at least safe enough to try out, for a start.

And then, as with any group, the couples group moves beyond this stage of establishing connections toward something more differentiated. How are we different? What does that mean for us here? Will certain people be heard and not others? How will my partner fare? Do I need to protect or restrain him or her? This is the period, again as in any group, of authority struggles and power issues, with the difference here that there is always a double focus: on the person's issue with one or another group member and on how that same issue comes to life within the couple. This is also a period of subgroupings. In the heterosexual couples group, one natural subgrouping is the men and the women, but there are many others: the talkers and the quieter members, the "feeling" types and the "rational" types, the caretakers and those who may feel more entitled. In the couples group, a particular feature of subgrouping is that the members of one couple often belong to different subgroups and alliances in the group. This makes for a texture of support for everyone's experience and everyone's point of view.

With more differentiation of the group comes richer contact and more possibility for (and fear of) intimacy. Attractions and alliances in the group may cause jealousy for couple partners, not just on a sexual dimension, but also around the issue of closeness, intimacy, and greater understanding. Again, this provides a live opportunity for the couple to explore what is missing in their relationship now, and what each longs for from the other. The mature, intimate couples group then becomes the context in which each individual can grow and develop as a person, as the ground for the growth and strength of the couple.

Is the Group for Everybody?

The contact possibilities and demands of the couples group, with its crosscurrents of different boundaries and loyalties, can be intense and for some people overwhelming. People who are in crisis may have difficulty working as a couple and even more difficulty with the couples group, where air time is always an issue. Likewise, people who are not appropriate for groups for other reasons—for example, hyperdefensiveness, which may cover a fear of losing self-cohesion—may have great difficulty in the couples group. And for some the warmth and contact of the group may be too rich a diet, again provoking a regression that the group is not equipped to handle. For most of the rest of us the couples group is a rich and rewarding setting, like couples therapy in general, for the exploration and growth of the relationship and of the self.

Note

1. This chapter was translated from the Swedish by Mikael Curman and Gordon Wheeler.

Reference

Perls, F., Hefferline, R., & Goodman, P. (1951). *Gestalt therapy.* New York: Julian Press.

10

Trauma Survivors and Their Partners: A Gestalt View

Pamela Geib and Stuart Simon

Jim and Eileen, married for ten years with two children, entered couples therapy two years after Eileen began to recover memories of childhood sexual abuse. Eileen's memories were triggered when her daughter turned six years old, the age at which Eileen's father began to abuse her.

The precipitant for treatment had been an episode of unusual behavior for Jim. Feeling depressed and overwrought, Eileen had greeted Jim as he returned from work by expressing the need for emotional support. Jim, who prided himself on his ability to be a steady presence and a source of support for Eileen, became enraged. He angrily attacked Eileen for being so needy and demanding. He complained bitterly that none of his needs seem to matter anymore, and he told Eileen that he wasn't sure he could give her the continuous support she seemed to need. This explosion left Eileen feeling hurt, frightened, and mistrustful of Jim. Jim felt ashamed and confused. However, he also acknowledged still being angry at Eileen. Both Jim and Eileen realized how much the marriage had suffered since Eileen began psychotherapy.

When a new couple enter our office, we all struggle to observe the process that unfolds with a clear and unbiased perspective. In Gestalt psychotherapy we attend to phenomenological data, and we observe the couple's ability to make contact with each other. By contact we mean the couple's capacity to develop genuinely shared interest. For example, we look to see if each member can attend to and become interested in the feelings and ideas of the other, or at least understand how the other is looking at the world. We may also watch to see if the couple can develop common goals. Our interest is in the process of how the couple join together to find and achieve some shared purpose. In Gestalt theory we call this coming together "the formation of joint figures." These shared figures emerge from the background of the present moment.

It is the thesis of this chapter that when a couple present with one member in the *crisis of trauma recovery*, the couple's ability to make contact will be compromised in some very specific ways. The abuse history from which the survivor is trying to recover represents an "unfinished gestalt." By this we mean that the traumatic events have not been assimilated enough to become part of the survivor's background. Consequently, this past trauma becomes an active and distorting presence in the couple's relationship, inhibiting contact by confusing past and present realities. Because the couple's inability to make contact is engendered by the survivor's crisis of recovery from *trauma*, the therapist must use an understanding of trauma, and in particular post-traumatic stress disorder, to actively structure the process from the beginning. This chapter will explicate and demonstrate this process.

To create a frame for our discussion of treatment, the first section of this chapter will describe the effects of trauma recovery on the survivor, the partner, and the survivor/partner system. We will also talk about how the therapist is affected by entering this system. In the second section we will discuss interventions. To focus the discussion, we will follow Jim and Eileen in the course of their treatment. First, we will describe how the therapist needs to support the partner and help him or her understand the impact of trauma. Second, we will discuss the importance of attending to the couples' contact boundary when one partner is a survivor.

We will then identify what we believe to be the essential work with survivor/partner dyads: how the abuse has become an unfinished gestalt. We will provide specific techniques for helping the couple separate past from present. As we go along we will give specific examples of how a Gestalt perspective informs our work. We will continue by noting that this kind of system can often be out of balance, with the survivor in the role of the identified patient. Here our interventions will be aimed at rebalancing the dyad by helping the partner explore his or her own role in the system. Finally, we will attend to the work of forging a new relationship based on the changes each member has undergone.

In this chapter we have made certain word choices regarding gender, sexual orientation, and marital status. Clearly, sexual abuse and childhood trauma are not limited to either sex. Similarly, couples seeking therapy include gay, lesbian, and straight, married and unmarried pairs. Because the case we have chosen to discuss involves a married, heterosexual couple, we have made the following choices, which we will use for the remainder of the chapter.

- In describing the survivor member of the couple we will use the pronoun *she.*
- To describe the other member we will use the word *partner* and the pronoun *he.*
- When referring to therapists in general, we will use *he* or *she,* alternately.
- Because the therapeutic work was done jointly, case discussions and scenarios will use the pronoun *we.*

In addition, a brief description of trauma and abuse from a Gestalt perspective may be helpful. For our purposes here, we will define *trauma* as the experience of being so overwhelmed by an event that in the moment one cannot organize the sensations into constructive meaning or action. For example, when a child is sexually violated or a woman is raped, she is both physically and psychologically overwhelmed. She will most likely cope initially by dissociating, and later construct meanings imbued with shame, self-blame, and self-hatred. Without immediate therapeutic help, the sensations may rigidify, so that all future events run the risk of being interpreted in the light of the trauma. *Abuse* occurs when someone in a position of power uses his or her power to physically, sexually, or emotionally traumatize another.

The Effects of Trauma Recovery

The Survivor

As therapists, we have learned that the abuse survivor almost always feels worse before she feels better. The process of recovery in therapy is the process of reexperiencing and gradually coming to terms with the abuse. It involves exploring the territory created when repressed or minimized abuse begins to be felt with its full weight and horror. As a result, "recovery" can temporarily transform a life of low-grade depression, attenuated ability to connect, and vague fears into a chaos of conflicting feelings. In Gestalt terms, we could say that the survivor's habitual self-organization, characterized by repression and low energy, has been deconstructed but not yet reorganized into a stable and reliable structure.

This process is manifested in many ways. Flashbacks that temporarily obliterate the present reality are common. As the survivor comes to terms with the betrayal inherent in being abused as a child, she may feel distrustful and hypervigilant. Her moods may be volatile, as she swings through cycles of belief and disbelief in the fact of the abuse, as she moves from reexperienced helplessness to rage and back again. She may begin to dissociate, or dissociate more frequently, in response to memories of abuse that are brought into greater awareness through the process of therapy. In these moments of dissociation, she will not be fully present in the here and now. Because of the past violation she may feel that sexual contact and in some cases touch of any kind are unbearable. Because of her absorption in this process, she may experience lowered levels of functioning at home and/or at work.

The Partner

Of course, if the survivor has a partner, the partner will also be experiencing the effects of these changes. As the survivor has become less available both emotionally and physically, the partner may have become lonely, sad, and depressed at the loss of his companion. This loss of companionship can occur on various levels. It can include the lack of an ongoing sexual relationship, or even a complete absence of physical contact.

More generally, the partner may no longer be able to rely on the survivor for the usual types of companionship that relationships provide. The survivor may be too preoccupied to join in shared recreational activities, support the partner in times of distress, or even listen to how the partner's workday went. To make matters worse, the partner may feel that the survivor does have energy for others. Specifically, the partner may feel outside the dyad of survivor/therapist, or excluded from a circle of survivor friends or support group members. In Gestalt terms as well as traditional family therapy terms, we could say that the boundary of the couple has been expanded and relocated.

The partner may also be feeling angry and exhausted from absorbing some of the day-to-day tasks of managing a home and family that previously felt more evenly shared. Further complicating the partner's experience is his own response to the survivor's memories. Like the survivor, the partner's response may range from denial to impotent rage at the perpetrator. However, without adequate support, the partner may feel compelled to keep these feelings to himself, thereby leaving him even more isolated.

What makes this loss of companionship and partnership especially devastating is that the partner typically has little understanding of post-traumatic stress disorder (PTSD) (see American Psychiatric Association, 1987), and consequently no way of genuinely making sense of the survivor's behavior. Without adequate knowledge of PTSD, the partner is almost bound to experience the survivor's withdrawal as personal rejection. As he becomes overwhelmed from taking on the extra daily tasks, he may begin to see the survivor as self-indulgent. The survivor's erratic and moody behavior, especially expressions of suicidal thought, may frighten and confuse him. All of these behaviors, and his responses to them, can leave the partner worried about the health and well-being of the survivor and greatly concerned about the future of the couple.

The System

As couples therapists, it is necessary to look not only at the experience of each individual in the system, as described above, but also at the system dynamics. A number of system variables come into play in this recovery-engendered crisis.

One dimension common to systems thinking is that of power. In survivor/partner dyads, power is often both imbalanced and complex. On the one hand, the survivor is in the one-down, patient position because of her symptoms, lowered level of functioning, and periods of regression. The "nonpathological" partner is often seen as more powerful and "in control." In our discussion of interventions we will discuss how we work to depathologize the survivor and invite the partner to look into himself, thus equalizing the power imbalance.

Paradoxically, the *partner* is in a completely powerless position regarding the unwanted changes in his spouse and his relationship. He cannot control or even influence his wife's progress or pace of recovery. Part of our work is acknowledging this powerlessness and then helping him determine what *is* in his power to ask from his spouse, or to deal with in himself.

Another relevant dimension in couples dynamics is that of distance regulation or interaction at the contact boundary. For example, any couple system may become polarized and rigid, with one member becoming stuck in a distancing position while the other becomes a stuck pursuer. However, in the survivor/partner dyad, there are particular difficulties in this area. In these couples, boundaries can more easily become battlegrounds. The survivor may experience the partner as violating her boundaries just at the point when her awareness of the past

violation is most raw. The partner may feel the survivor's difficulties encroaching into every area of his life, as when he receives numerous daily phone calls at work. Or one or both people may feel isolated on the other side of a boundary too high
and too impermeable for satisfactory contact. These couples
often present such issues with a mixture of anger, sadness, and
confusion at the unexpected changes they are experiencing
that keep them from being in satisfying contact. In other words,
the stable ground of the relationship is so disturbed that shared
figure formation is beyond reach.

The Therapist

From the moment a couple enter treatment, the therapist has in
some way joined the system. With a survivor/partner dyad, the
therapist must be particularly aware of the degree to which this
joining is affecting her. Like the partner, the therapist must bear
the knowledge of the horrible things that have happened to the
survivor. And like the partner, the therapist must accept the limits of what she can "do" in the way of healing the trauma. Because of the powerful affects the couple bring, the therapist can
easily feel drawn into strong countertransference experiences.
The therapist may need to work especially hard to hold all parts
of the system. This will mean understanding the intensity of the
experience of recovery with the survivor, as well as understanding the meaning of the dramatic changes in the partner's life.

Interventions

Psychoeducation and Support

> As Jim and Eileen began therapy it quickly became
> clear that Jim's anger was a result of festering re-
> sentment. At first Jim talked about his impatience
> with Eileen's mood swings, erratic behavior, and
> constant dependency. However, after several inter-
> views, Jim realized that his frustration and anger
> were due in large part to how long the recovery was

taking. Although he tried to be sympathetic to what Eileen was going through, he believed that two years of therapy should have been enough to see substantial results. At times, when Eileen seemed better, he had become hopeful. However, when Eileen's treatment once again stirred up feelings and symptoms, he became increasingly confused and frustrated. In fact, he began to wonder whether Eileen would ever get better, and whether their life would ever return to normal.

Though Jim had not talked directly with Eileen about his frustrations, she reported that she was aware of his increasing unhappiness. This frightened her. In response, she sometimes became even more dependent. At other times she withdrew from Jim and relied more on her friends and support group members. As Eileen was reporting this, Jim interrupted. He said that he was totally confused by Eileen's healing process, that he could see no cause and effect, and that he couldn't understand why there weren't more concrete results.

As this vignette illustrates, a significant part of the couple's conflict can be due to the partner's confusion and lack of knowledge of PTSD and the recovery process. As a couple begin treatment, clinicians need to be especially aware of the partner's understanding of trauma and healing. It is critical that the therapist first validate the partner's experience of how difficult the relationship has become. Then the therapist should be prepared to actively expand the partner's understanding through education.

In addition to lacking knowledge about the symptoms of trauma (flashbacks, hypervigilance, dissociation, sensitivity to touch), the partner can be confused about the vicissitudes of the recovery process itself. In Jim's case he did not understand the cyclical nature of recovery. Nor was he aware of why recovery would be so long and time consuming.

Realizing that Jim truly didn't understand the process of recovery from trauma, we began to teach

Jim about its spiraling and uneven nature. We explained that recovery often appears chaotic and can even seem to proceed without results. Jim was relieved to hear that survivors usually went through times when current adult reality gave way to the horror of the past. He also learned that cycles of adult functioning followed by feeling more trapped in the past abuse were common—that the movement was not linear. We explained how these periods in which the past held sway might always occur, but their occurrence would become gradually less frequent. We helped Jim understand that the problem-solving approach that he found helpful at work was only one part of what was useful to a survivor. We also made sure Jim understood that the patience required to see Eileen through these ups and downs was enormous. We made sure Jim knew that he too was being understood and supported, even as he heard the hard news of recovery.

This education process is helpful in several ways. It can calm the partner by helping make sense of the survivor's behavior, and it can empower him by bringing him into the circle of "experts" who have entered his mate's life. In addition, it can begin to right the imbalance created by the survivor's "patienthood" by helping the partner understand that PTSD is not a mental illness, but rather a set of normal responses to extreme and horrifying events.

Intervention at the Boundary

Couples therapists are trained to observe how each member of the dyad establishes and respects boundaries. Typically we use our observations to raise clients' awareness, and therefore effect change. However, in working with survivor/partner dyads, the therapist may have to become active in helping the couple establish and maintain boundaries.

At its core the act of sexual abuse violates a child's boundaries. The sexually traumatized child grows and develops with

an attenuated sense of autonomy. The ability to identify needs
or wants and to state them without ambivalence is compromised
dramatically. Consequently, survivors typically have a variety of
difficulties in making contact. Overwhelmed by fear of violation, they can become hypervigilant and fiercely protective of
their boundaries. Overwhelmed by fear of abandonment, they
can too easily give in to the needs of others. Additionally, when
a survivor does feel intruded upon, the event can trigger a flash-
back, an experience neither the survivor nor the partner expects. Thus a simple touch can be experienced as an invasion,
and an overture for sexual contact can be experienced as force.

In our work with Jim and Eileen, we soon discovered how
Eileen's difficulties in maintaining her boundaries and Jim's responses were affecting the couple.

> Eileen and Jim's sexual relationship had signifi-
> cantly diminished over the past two years. For the
> most part Jim had been patient, since Eileen's dis-
> tress had been so evident. However, recently Jim
> and Eileen had attempted to resume their sexual
> relationship. The results were disastrous. In the
> therapy we discovered that in fact Eileen had
> agreed to have sex to please Jim, because she had
> become worried about disappointing him. Conse-
> quently she had ignored her own signals and found
> herself angry afterward. The next time Jim ap-
> proached Eileen sexually, she exploded, accusing
> Jim of completely ignoring her pain.
>
> In response, Jim became both confused and
> hurt. Speaking of their last sexual encounter, he ac-
> knowledged some awareness that Eileen might be
> simply trying to please him. However, he was
> crushed and angry at the accusations that followed
> his second overture.

Clearly Eileen was having difficulty identifying her needs,
maintaining her boundaries, and consequently making genuine contact. Because this extreme reaction was a departure

from their prerecovery life, Jim was also having difficulty. In addition, without the knowledge of trauma described above, Jim, like many partners, easily personalized Eileen's responses.

If the couple are indeed in crisis around this issue of boundaries, raising awareness may not be an adequate intervention. The therapist may need to become more active in helping them structure their interaction, temporarily taking over boundary- and limit-setting functions. For example, he may come to believe that, even with raised awareness of the issues involved, the survivor and partner cannot work together to protect the survivor's boundaries. In this case he may suggest that they temporarily refrain from any sexual activity.

Although we have been talking about therapist activity on behalf of the survivor's boundaries, it is important to remember that the partner may also need help. Partners often bring their own difficulties with boundaries to the relationship. A good example is Jim's uncharacteristic outburst that had precipitated couples therapy. Upon reflection, Jim had discovered that he had been missing his own signals about how drained he had become with the level of caretaking he felt was required of him. This failure to maintain his own boundaries, particularly in terms of his own needs for nourishment, had resulted in the unexpected expression of anger.

Raising Awareness of the Unfinished Gestalt: Retriangulating the Abuse

Although all couples struggle with ways that past and present can get confused through transference, projection, and projective identification, the past can invade the present in a particularly powerful way in a survivor/partner dyad. This became clear in a piece of work with Jim and Eileen.

> Although Jim presented with the problem of having become increasingly frustrated and sometimes quite angry, he was certain of his commitment to the marriage. In fact, he prided himself on his steadfastness and his integrity. He was wounded be-

cause, despite his reassurances and protestations, he could not convince Eileen that he was there to stay. Eileen had become so frightened of his expressions of frustration that she was often convinced he would abandon her. In addition to being hurt by what he understood as a "vote of no confidence," Jim felt guilty that he had expressed anger in the first place. The messages concerning anger that he'd received in his family of origin had taught him that any expression of discomfort could have serious consequences. Although it wasn't grounded in present reality, Eileen's terror of abandonment seemed to bear out this parental message. The couple went around and around on this issue, but Jim's insistence on his commitment never served to reassure Eileen, and Jim continued to feel both unacknowledged and wrong.

Obviously, this couple needed help in disentangling the past and present realities. A powerful past intrusion requires a powerful response. We have conceptualized this response as "retriangulating the abuse."[1] First we try to discover how the distorted beliefs were engendered by the traumatic experience. This means going back and paying close attention to the survivor's story. Next, we name the abuse as a third presence in the couple's system, bringing it into the room so that the source of the negativity can be clearly seen to be this past trauma. Often we do this dramatically, by the use of an empty chair to represent the abuse experience. In this intervention, the therapist clearly states that not all the trouble the couple are experiencing originates with them, either individually or as a relationship. The "badness" they are experiencing, either internalized or projected onto the other, resides in this presently experienced *past* abuse, which is making mischief and misery. If the abuse is made concrete and has its own seat in the room, it can be called to account for its role in creating the confusion and pain the couple are experiencing. In this way, the notion that the partner is a secondary victim of this abuse is reinforced. And it's now apparent that there is indeed a common enemy.

In this work, the survivor is asked to check whether a negative experience of herself or of the partner is accurate, or whether the abuse is persuading her of something that isn't currently true. The chair can be used as a point of reference or it can be used psychodramatically. This intervention has roots in both Gestalt theory and the work of Michael White (see, for example, White, 1989). Though empty chair work in Gestalt therapy is typically a process of identifying and reintegrating projections, in this case it serves to frame a boundary for the abuse as distinct from the couple's present reality. White's work on externalizing the problem provides a model for how *symptoms* can be externalized. In this case it is the *abuse* that is to be externalized.

The therapist must be extraordinarily careful here to attend to the real possibility that the survivor's perception of her partner is accurate, and to attend to such a complaint in the way any such upset in couples work is addressed. The partner needs to be helped to avoid using this concept as a weapon, minimizing or invalidating everything the survivor has to say. The continuing job is to disentangle current reality from fears and distortions that spring from abuse.

> This intervention was helpful in addressing Jim and Eileen's stuck system. In listening carefully to Eileen's story, we found that she had an initially warm relationship with her father, whom she had counted upon in the face of her mother's distance and coldness. When her father began sexually molesting her, she had felt abruptly abandoned, her sense of trust and security betrayed. The feeling that she was doomed to betrayal and abandonment was the voice of abuse, and it was blocking out Jim's clear statement of commitment. As we listened to Eileen's story, the message of the abuse became clear: a seemingly caring man will betray you. We

invited the abuse into the room by using an empty
chair. This was helpful to Eileen, who was able to
see Jim as more clearly differentiated from her father. It was an enormous relief to Jim to see that his
inability to convince Eileen of his loyalty hadn't
been "his fault." Additionally, the couple felt more
united facing the abuse that was affecting and hurting them both.

Balancing the Dyad

Although it may have been the extremity of the survivor's symptoms that led the couple to seek therapy, each interaction remains a systems event. Although the survivor's process of recovery often takes center stage, it is important that the therapist
not overlook the partner's role in the system. Conversations
that include his history, the strengths and painful trigger points
he brings from his own family of origin, are crucial in de-
pathologizing the survivor and keeping the systemic nature of
the interaction in the foreground. These partner-focused conversations need to start with the therapist's clear statement that
the partner is a secondary victim of the abuse. Both he and his
spouse are coping with a situation they didn't ask for and
did not create. If the partner can be assured that he is not
being blamed for being the problem, an investigation of how
his history intersects with this current crisis can be extremely
helpful.

> We began talking to Jim about his history when it
> became clear to us that he was deeply frightened by
> and ashamed of the amount of anger he'd been
> experiencing during this difficult time. Inquiry
> into his family of origin yielded the following pic-
> ture: Jim was the oldest of two sons. He had grown
> up identified with his father, whom he experienced
> as quiet, strong, stoic, and emotionally distant. He
> described his mother as being quietly depressed,
> and sometimes unable to fully function as a home-

maker. His father had silently filled in the gaps. He had neither complained about his own burdens nor commented about his wife's obvious unhappiness. In making a genogram, we found that Jim's paternal grandfather had been an alcoholic, given to unpredictable rages. With some help, Jim was able to guess that his father's stoic, emotionally distant style was a way of promising never to be the fearsome father he himself had known. We were able to understand the unspoken rules Jim had learned. (1) Anger is dangerous. Just do what is needed and be quiet. (2) It is a man's job to take care of women, but don't notice out loud that there is any trouble.

Understanding his history in this way was both interesting and relieving to Jim. We noticed that the caretaking ability he had learned from his father was a strength in this situation, as long as it did not cancel out his ability to notice his own needs and limits. Jim saw that his reaction to anger was learned behavior and that anger did not necessarily have to be destructive. Eileen listened attentively. She came to have an increased appreciation of the strengths and difficulties Jim brought to what she had framed as "her problem." As a couple, they became more aware of his role in their current system.

This conversation with the partner has several therapeutic aims. One is the balancing of the dyad, as described above. Another is that it enables the partner to discover that, although there is much that is out of his control (he cannot undo the abuse, nor can he set the course or the pace of his wife's recovery), he can achieve mastery of and learn from his own individual responses. Although he is a victim of the abuse, he does not have to be a passive victim. This crisis can be seen as an opportunity for him to consider his past and present in order to heal.

The New Marriage and Contact in the Present

If the couple are able to weather the extended crisis of the survivor's recovery, there will come a time when the abuse is no longer center stage, and the current, everyday realities of the relationship can become foreground. In Gestalt terms we can say that the abuse has become less figural, thus becoming part of the ground for the couple. At this point, the couple may begin to feel the work is finished. However, preceding termination, the therapist needs to help the couple become aware that they cannot return to the former state of affairs. The people who made the original commitment have changed. They are each different, renewed, with new needs and expectations. At this point, therapy can help them articulate and practice living in this new situation.

In this stage there is often a difference between the survivor and partner's recollection of the "old days." The partner may remember the prerecovery past with nostalgia. The survivor, who was always struggling to keep the memories, self-hatred, and fear at bay, may remember the old days as flat and mechanical, part of a kind of false self in an existence predicated on repressing the abuse.

Both realities need to be validated. Grieving for what will not be again, as well as for what never was, must be done to make room for the new. Then there are new selves to be recognized, new role expectations to be negotiated.

Jim and Eileen were surprised that both of them had changed during this process. Because they had originally held the belief that the "problem" was Eileen's, they had expected that she would change, "get over it," and life would return to normal. Our first therapeutic conversation concerning the new marriage occurred when Eileen expressed surprise and some dismay at the changes in Jim. He was putting into practice *his* new belief that he had the right to speak about frustrations and upsets as they came up. Although Eileen appreciated the fact that Jim was more emotionally present in the relationship, she was not entirely prepared for the new ability to assert himself that came with it. Also, she feared losing him as a source of continuous support, since he was trying not to fall into the dutiful-but-secretly-resentful role he'd learned from his father.

Discussions of these changes helped Eileen notice that, although Jim might indeed be less compliant as a caretaker, he would be more present as a husband.

Jim had to face the fact that, as Eileen became more aware of her own boundaries, she was more able to say "no" in matters of sex and touch. He found that when they did have sex she was actually more present with him, but that she was careful to monitor her own signals and not go ahead with love-making merely to please or pacify him. As Eileen's recovery progressed, she began to volunteer time to publicize the problem of child abuse and do fund-raising for this cause. This new sense of competence and independence was just what Jim had imagined he wanted. However, he did have to come to terms with a feeling of dislocation, some degree of "unemployment" from his past role of being her main source of comfort and self-esteem.

As couples therapy drew to a close, Jim and Eileen were able to appreciate the ways in which they were in more genuine contact than ever before. They became less fearful of the changes in each that made them differentiated, and were willing to live with the fact that increased awareness and presence meant that they would sometimes have more overt conflicts.

Summary

Couples such as Eileen and Jim enter therapy because the surfacing of the past trauma has created an active and distorting presence in their relationship. Because of the crisis and turmoil that accompany recovery from trauma, the therapist will often work in both active and specific ways. This may include educating the partner about the effects of trauma; attending to, and at times structuring, interaction at the contact boundary; identifying the unfinished gestalt and retriangulating the abuse; and finally, rebalancing the dyad by working to include the partner.

Ultimately, for this work to be successful, the couple must come to terms with change. The survivor is different as a result of her own recovery work. The partner will also be changed; the system will have shifted. For the relationship to survive and thrive, the therapist must help the couple accommodate to new roles and expectations. New skills for making contact may be needed.

Like any treatment that involves trauma, we have found this work to be difficult and emotionally draining. It requires us to sit with powerful affects and terrible stories—affects and stories that we must help to organize into a manageable framework for the couple. To do this, we have needed to expand our breadth of knowledge to include the devastating effects of trauma, the process of trauma recovery, and the intricacies of a couple's system struggling with these issues. We have had to be flexible and use many different clinical skills—empathic listening, raising awareness, supporting, educating, and at times actively structuring the couple's interaction.

Despite the difficulties, we have found this work to be extremely rewarding. Because these couples are in crisis, they present with enormous pain yet also enormous potential for healing. Because trauma affects people at such profound levels, couples therapy with a survivor/partner dyad holds the possibilities for significant growth for the couple, and deep satisfaction for the therapist.

Note

1. The term *abuse* is used instead of reference to the actual perpetrator. This is because survivors have various experiences of the abuser during the process of recovery. Some are trying to come to terms with parts of the abuser that

were or are positive; some are trying to forge a new relationship. It is respectful of this possibility to extract the abuse, which is completely and clearly negative, from the person of the perpetrator.

References

American Psychiatric Association. (1987). *Diagnostic and statistical manual of mental disorders* (3rd ed., rev.). Washington, DC: American Psychiatric Association.

White, M. (Summer 1989). The externalizing of the problem and the re-authoring of lives and relationships, *Dulwich Centre Newsletter.*

11

Couples' Shame: The Unaddressed Issue

Robert Lee

T om, sitting straight in his chair, his face drawn, says beratingly to Claire at the beginning of their second couple therapy session, "I'm angry that you were late getting here. Can't you ever be reliable?" Claire, not looking at him, replies disdainfully, "Why are you so finicky about time? It was only ten minutes. Can't you loosen up?"

I intervened in their process at this point, but we can imagine the way this conversation might have gone if I had not. Tom might have replied something like "That's typical, you're unreliable and you blame it on me." And perhaps Claire would have responded, "You are just like your father, stiff as a board." Then possibly Tom would have said, "Well, at least I'm not irresponsible like your family. I live up to my obligations and I'm not a spendthrift either." And Claire might have followed with "And I am? I suppose you are referring to the other night when you were too tight to go out to dinner and a movie," to which Tom might have replied, "You just want to spend money; you'd think you were royalty or something." And Claire could have returned with "You're just not man enough to quit being Casper Milktoast and ask your boss for a raise so we can live the way we should." Perhaps at this point one of them would start yelling or stomp out of the session.

This is, of course, just one possible direction that Tom

and Claire's interaction could have taken that would have been problematic for them. Other directions could include one of them withdrawing or becoming controlling, punitive, symptomatic, obsessive, and so on. Interactions such as these are common among troubled couples. In working with such couples, we might try structural or strategic interventions, or we might use systemic or historical interpretations. But as we know all too well, with escalating couples our best-thought-out approaches are all too often unsuccessful. What is going on here? What is it that makes these interactions speed out of control in such a destructive manner?

With Tom and Claire, as with many other couples caught in this kind of sudden and explosive escalation, when we slow down and take their interaction apart with them, we find that the underlying, unspoken dynamic is shame. It is shame that makes Tom and Claire talk always at each other, never about themselves. And it is shame that makes each accusation carry the sting of an increasing level of attempted humiliation of the other. In other similar situations between couple partners, it is shame that causes people to flee inwards in withdrawal or to issue ironclad rules in attempted control or to become physically aggressive, dominating, and/or violent.

The trouble with working with shame is that shame often can't be seen directly. Rather, what stands out are the defensive behaviors that people use to camouflage and to attempt to escape their experience of shame, such as the desperate measures (including violence) that people may use in attempting to shift unbearable shame off themselves and onto their partners. Understanding the dynamics of shame in these as well as less dramatic instances often untangles what otherwise seem like mysterious knottings in couple interactions.

Shame in Individuals

What is shame, and why is it so powerful in our lives? The ubiquitousness of shame in human experience is reflected in the many labels given to all the variants of shame: shyness, embarrassment, chagrin, humiliation, low self-esteem, feeling ridiculous, sheepishness, discomfort, disconcertedness, abasement, disgrace, ignominy, dishonor, mortification, degradation, self-consciousness, discouragement, guilt—and the list goes on (Kaufman, 1989; Lewis, 1971; Retzinger, 1987). Although shame has been discussed from a variety of theoretical perspectives (for example, Jordan, 1989; Lewis, 1971; Lynd, 1958; Nathanson, 1992; Nichols, 1991), the Kaufman/Tomkins theory (Kaufman, 1989; Tomkins, 1963), because of its theoretical clarity and its phenomenological base, meshes best with the organismic, con-textualistic (I/Thou) worldview of Gestalt theory.

Tomkins postulates that shame is one of nine innate af-fects, part of the survival kit with which everyone is endowed at birth. Shame's function, according to Tomkins (1987), is to regulate the affects which he calls interest-excitement and enjoyment-joy. "The experience of shame is inevitable for any human being insofar as desire outruns fulfillment sufficiently to attenuate interest without destroying it" (1963, p. 185). Thus shame in its simplest forms, such as shyness and embarrassment, is a natural process of retroflection, or holding back, that serves a protective function through life. It guards our privacies around such areas as friendship, love, spirituality, sex, birth, and death and provides a protective screen for the ongoing process of self-integration (Schneider, 1987). In the Gestalt model we might describe this normal, protective function of shame some-what differently. In Gestalt, the person is seen as negotiating, co-constructing, and exploring at the boundary of the inner and outer worlds. Shame in this view can serve as a signal that the *state of the connection* at the boundary between me and my world is threatened or needs attention. Thus shame can make me hold back, as in the Tomkins model, or it can make me attend to the other person and his or her need of me—possibly at the tem-porary cost of my own self-expressiveness. (Thus Gestalt helps us see the creative connection between shame and "codepen-dence." As a "codependent" my attention is forced almost en-tirely on the other person, shoring him or her up to receive me, with a consistent, habitual cost to my self-expressiveness.)

For the most part, this is the healthy, functional side of shame. Shame becomes dysfunctional, even toxic, as it becomes internalized in the form of *shame-binds* (Kaufman, 1989). Although this can happen anytime throughout one's life, it most often starts in childhood. When the primary nurturers in a child's life are unable to notice, accept, and respond adequately to a particular need, affect, or sense of purpose of the child, normal shame helps the child pull back from making contact around that need, feeling, or desire. If this process is repeated often enough or is traumatic enough, an internalized linkage or bind is created between shame and the particular need, affect, or sense of purpose (Kaufman, 1989). The nurturer's inability to respond or to respond appropriately to the child may stem from the nurturer's reaction to his or her own internalized shame or even perhaps from misunderstandings of basic differences in temperament or abilities between child and nurturer. However, whenever the child thereafter experiences the particular feeling or urge, he or she will automatically also experience shame. In time, with continued shaming sequences, the child loses awareness of the original feeling or desire and simply experiences the shame (Kaufman, 1989). Thus the child loses a "voice" for that part of his or her being—part of the self is split off or shut down. The loss of voice develops in response to the real fact, or "environmental condition," that there is *no one to receive the voice.* With the loss of voice comes a sense of alienation and inferiority, a sense of disconnection and worthlessness. This sense of alienation and inferiority is due not only to the child experiencing the voice as shameful and not worthy of being heard, but also from the fact that without the voice the child is now less able to inform the world about who he or she is, in the event an empathic listener does come along. This is all part of the experience of *internalized shame.*

From a Gestalt perspective, this loss of voice, this shame-bind, is a negative introject—a given belief or internalized message about the self, the world, and the possibilities of contact. The converse is also true. Negative introjects are shame-binds. Understanding shame allows us to understand more of the nature of negative introjects.

It is impossible to go through life without developing some shame-binds. For example, cultural support for child-

266 On Intimate Ground

rearing in our culture is heavily shame based. Girls are often shamed around their developing sense of competence in the world—"nice girls aren't forward" (Gilligan, 1982). And boys are often shamed around their feelings of distress, sadness, and, most excruciatingly, shame itself—"big boys don't cry" (Balcom, 1991). In fact, gender and shame are so intimately intertwined in the culture that *almost any gender-dystonic feeling or behavior is likely to be seen or experienced as shameful.*

Any situation in which a person's feelings, desires, or ways of being in the world are consistently not noticed, validated, or responded to respectfully has the potential for engendering shame-binds. This happens especially in hierarchical relationships in which one person is dependent on another for caretaking, protection, or power itself, such as in parent-child, child care person-child, teacher-student, coach-player, supervisor-supervisee, employer-employee, therapist-client, and doctor-patient relationships. In these relationships, power may be abused or may fail to be used empathetically and constructively when needed. Also included here are situations of severe loss. The most severe clusters of shame-binds originate from instances of trauma, such as sexual or physical abuses, severe neglect or loss, combat, and so on; shame goes hand in hand with PTSD.

We all have at least an unawares knowledge of this process, as shown, for example, by the common retort to hearing of someone's ill treatment or loss: "What a shame!" Once we become attuned to this knowledge that exists in our culture, we find it used frequently, associated with a vast array of loss and hardship ranging from the trivial to the tragic, from missing the bus to the atrocities of war and persecution. I'm reminded of a client who sadly was discovering that a new man in her life, whom she was enjoying in many ways, could not let go of attempting to control her as a way of dealing with the differences between them. She attributed his behavior to the wrenching adjustments that he was forced to make early in life in response to the sudden death of his father and the subsequent helplessness and distraught, chaotic demands of his mother. My client ended with a sigh, saying, "That's really a shame!" How true.

With multiple shame-binds, the imagery, language, and feelings associated with the various shame-binds can merge to form linkages of shame with more global aspects of one's personality such as body image, relationship, competence, and overall character (Kaufman, 1989). Thus with higher internalized shame, shame resides as part of the ground that reinterprets new experience in the light of prior experience and *inevitably reproduces shame.* Common indications that internalized shame is engaged in its pernicious work are utterances of self-blame, self-contempt, or comparison-making in which the person always comes out on the short end (Kaufman, 1989). But remember that shame is not usually observed directly; rather, it may be the more or less desperate countershaming or other defensive and coping behaviors that we observe—putdowns, blaming, superiority, emotional withdrawal, numbing, or "acting out" in all its various forms, from substance abuse to sexual addiction to violence itself.

Once shame becomes internalized, a shame spiral or "shame attack" can be set off by an otherwise benign external or internal event. The event may be purely internal (such as a person experiencing a feeling or desire that has been shame bound) or it can be more external, such as a communication from another in which the person notices some nonverbal or verbal cue that he or she interprets as rejection or devaluation— or both. As another example, a person's internal shame might be triggered by something as simple as comparing himself or herself with the experiences, skills, abilities, or status of a friend with whom he or she is talking.

At this point in a shame attack, the person may be flooded with shame and self-hate—or might be frantically trying to fend off this flooding. He or she may want to "sink through the earth." The person may then experience "shame-rage," which leads to a further sense of shame because he or she is partially aware that the rage is inappropriate. Thus the shame becomes "locked in" in a self-escalating spiral of misery, self-abuse, and perhaps abuse of others (Kaufman, 1989; Lewis, 1981).

Once into a full-scale shame attack, people have difficulty reasoning or noticing anyone else's needs or intentions. All systems are on "red alert." In Gestalt terms, the self-process—the process of "integration at the boundary of the person/environment field"—is now in a state of breakdown. People are consumed with their shame until the shame attack passes. That can take a long time—hours, days, months—or a lifetime.

It is shameful to have shame, particularly in this culture. Thus, although people experience shame and often rage in a shame attack, they most likely won't show their shame and often not their rage either. What is seen from the outside, again, are the defenses and strategies that people use in attempting to hide and escape from their own distress: withdrawal, rage, contempt, attempts to control, subtle or more blatant criticism, perfectionism, addictive behavior, obsessive behavior, violence and other abuse, and so on (Bradshaw, 1988; Fossum & Mason, 1986; Kaufman, 1980, 1989; Lansky, 1991; Nichols, 1991; Retzinger, 1987). Because the experience of internalized shame is so devastating, people who are shame prone in this way usually learn to deny their shame and to incorporate some blend of the above-mentioned defenses and strategies into *scripts for living life,* rigid behavioral sequences or "fixed gestalts," in attempts to avoid or manage shame in the future (Tomkins, 1979).

Unfortunately, as Kaufman points out, these scripts and strategies only serve to generate additional shame in the long run. For example, withdrawal leads to a greater sense of isolation; rage often begets embarrassment and/or retaliation, which can be degrading and isolating; addiction frequently leads to failures of various kinds; and so on. Not only do these strategies lead to the possibility of more shame from the outside, but they also further camouflage and isolate the person's underlying desires and feelings (his or her elements of potential connection) that are shamed, thus leaving the person less able to make contact with the world around these important parts of self. This can lead to an existence that is centered around shame and its avoidance (Kaufman, 1989).

In summary, internalized shame is distinguished from shame as affect in that shame as affect functions only to inhibit the affects of interest and enjoyment and can serve to protect people's privacy. Or, as we say in Gestalt, it serves to draw the person's attention to problems in connection with another person or with the world. On the other hand, internalized shame can be a major shaper of identity. This more pernicious *internalization* process starts when shame becomes linked with various affects, needs, or goals (the formation of negative introjects). The imagery, language, and affects associated with various shame-binds can then merge to form linkages of shame with more global aspects of one's personality such as body image, relationship, competence, and overall character. Shame then resides as part of the ground that reinterprets new experience in the light of prior experience and *inevitably reproduces shame.* People with high internalized shame are subject to shame attacks that may be all too easily triggered by internal or external events. Because the experience of shame in this form is so devastating, people with internalized shame develop defenses and strategies as attempts to cope with and avoid their shame. The higher the degree of internalized shame, the more people's lives come to revolve around the attempted control and avoidance of shame.

Shame in Couple Systems

When two people couple, they each bring with them their own histories of living in the world—their own joys, hopes, and fears and their own histories of feeling shame, toxic or otherwise. Depending on the fit that has existed between them and their environment, the empathic reception they have received for their own self-expression, they will each have developed more or less internalized shame. The degree of internalized shame that they each carry (which may be similar or different; Lee, 1993) might have had something to do with their mutual selection. For example, each might have mastered ways of being in the world that were taboo but still necessary for the other (Prosky, 1979; Zinker, 1983), or they both might have common problems that emanate from the shame they carry, or they might have had significant figures in their lives that had a similar level of shame as their partner, and so on.

Each partner will have developed what Kaufman (1989) refers to as *governing scenes* around the clusters of shame they have accumulated. These governing scenes are examples of what is known in traditional Gestalt language as "fixed gestalts," part of the associated dynamic of "unfinished business." In Gestalt self-organizational theory (Kaplan & Kaplan, 1991), these scenes have been termed "experiential steady states"—a kind of blueprint that the self system will organize back toward *autopoietically*, to use the current term from self-organizational literature (Maturana & Varela, 1980). But note how in Gestalt theory—unlike in some readings of self-organizational theory and unlike in psychoanalysis, with its "repetition compulsion"— we recognize the person's inherent drive to find a new "creative adjustment," a new solution to the repeated scene. Likewise, to Tomkins and Kaufman the scene always contains the possibility of a new creative resolution.

In essence, in governing shame scenes, shame has become connected in a dynamic fashion with images, affects, language, kinesthetic movements, and so on that represent the event or events in which the shame-bind or set of shame-binds were originally formed. These governing shame scenes then act to screen new experiences for possible recurrences of the scenes. The word *scene* is useful in naming this phenomenon because it describes people's experiences of literally being thrown back into an old situation when the governing scene is triggered and they experience a sickeningly familiar, full-scale shame attack.

Depending on the degree of internalized shame that each partner carries, he or she will have more-or-less powerful governing shame scenes with more-or-less sensitive "trigger points"—or "trip wires"—for reconstructing a scene and setting off a full shame attack. In addition, the partners may or may not vary in whether their governing shame scenes are centered around similar needs, feelings, or urges associated with one or more shame-binds, or to what extent their governing shame scenes cover more global aspects of personality such as body image, intimacy, competence, or overall character.

The experience of shame that mushrooms into a shame attack is problematic in couple systems in a number of ways. The partner in a shame attack is thrown back into an old shame scene and loses his or her ability to notice what is actually occurring in the couple interaction, in what might be referred to as a loss of ego function or a borderline split within the self. In Gestalt language, we might speak of an inhibited self process or diminished contact functions. That is, of course, problematic for the couple in terms of developing couple identity—maintaining continuity, building shared couple awarenesses of basic underlying needs, and so on, and translating these awarenesses into common goals and plans. However, shame can affect couple systems in a much more complex and dynamic manner.

In many instances, depending on the level of internalized shame that each partner carries, it is not simply the linear effect of one partner's shame attack and resultant behavior on the couple's interaction that is troublesome for the couple, though certainly this can be destructive enough in extreme cases. Even more complexly problematic and potentially destructive are the agonizing and vicious spirals of shame that can emanate from the *systematic interaction* of the two partners' respective shame issues. In other words, shame becomes systemic in a couple system when the verbal or nonverbal response to an experience of shame (triggered by either an internal or external event) by *one partner* intentionally or unintentionally induces shame in the *other partner* (Balcom, Lee, & Tager, in press). The resulting impairment or rupture in the basic bond or connection between the partners (Kaufman's "interpersonal bridge," 1980) can quickly worsen if the receiving partner is thrown into a full shame attack in his or her turn and then retaliates, and on and on.

Couples with low internalized shame are often—not always—able to repair such occurrences relatively easily. The shame they experience may be of a milder form such as shyness, hurt feelings, or embarrassment. Moreover, they are better able to tolerate these mild shame states than people with high internalized shame. They have less need than people with high internalized shame to resort to defenses and strategies to escape and avoid shame, such as rage, contempt, withdrawal, blaming, control, and/or addiction. Since they both have low-internalized-shame partners, they each have a partner that is less likely to employ such defenses, in turn, to cope with or avoid shame. Thus they are each confronted with less that might potentially throw them off balance and into a shame attack when their partner experiences shame. In addition, each has more resources to initiate and continue a beneficent cycle of empathy and repair that can restore their mutual sense of emotional safety.

In these low-internalized-shame systems, shame enables members of a couple to determine what are appropriate risks at various points in the development of their relationship—risks in exposing and sharing themselves or in reaching out to their partners—and thus to modulate contact. (Note that, by *appropriate*, in the Gestalt model, we always mean *supported*—Wheeler, 1991.) Again, the innate, healthy function of shame, from Tomkin's (1963) theory, is to modulate interest or enjoyment whenever the intensity of either exceeds the self-perceived chance of attainment, that is, when such interest or enjoyment threatens a disconnection in the relationship. Thus, with low-internalized-shame couples, shame as affect, perhaps in the form of shyness or embarrassment, helps members of a couple to delay exposing themselves and to be aware when the other is not available for the desired contact, for example, in seeking comfort, affection, companionship, or sex, or in addressing some other particular personal or couple issue.

At the other end of the internalized shame continuum, in the case of high-internalized-shame people, the same experiences can mushroom into severe shame attacks. Any disappointment now carries the potential for the high-internalized-shame person to be flooded by shame. In addition, the activities required in common couple interactions are themselves now landmines of potential exploding shame attacks.

A look at the Gestalt Interactive Cycle (Papernow, 1993; Zinker & Nevis, 1981), which describes the stages of a typical couple interaction, adds clarity to this situation. In the Gestalt Interactive Cycle (which is supported by research—Wyman, 1981), the first phase of a couple interaction is usually an *awareness* phase in which couple partners check in with themselves and each other and explore their joint needs, wants, or desires. In the *energy/action* phase, a common area of interest emerges and the couple move into an activity that has the potential to satisfy the shared need. Satisfaction of the shared desire occurs in the *contact* phase. This is followed by the *resolution/closure* phase of the cycle, in which the couple take care of any leftover energy and turn to reviewing the experience they have just been through. The cycle ends with the *withdrawal* phase, with members of the couple turning their energy from each other to themselves, thus separating until they are ready to start a new cycle.

For high-shame people, in the awareness phase, being noticed can be experienced as being exposed and humiliated, and noticing can be experienced as intruding or shaming one's partner. In the energy/action phase, proposals can be taken as criticism or inferiority, and shame is a likely companion of feelings experienced in the contact phase. Talking about what happened afterward can seem like humiliation in the resolution/conclusion phase; in the withdrawal phase, separation can be experienced as abandonment. With high internalized shame, people are vulnerable to experiencing shame attacks in even normal, essential phases of common interactions with their partners.

Remember that, in the attempt to cope with and avoid shame attacks, high-internalized-shame people will resort to defenses and strategies (usually without awareness) that deflect and camouflage their experience of shame. And as we have seen, these defenses and strategies (rage, blame, contempt, control, withdrawal, and so on) are often potentially shaming to the partner.

If the other partner has low internalized shame, he or she may be able to deal with the high-internalized-shame partner's defenses without escalating the situation. However, the basic trust and emotional safety of the low-internalized-shame partner will be adversely affected. Moreover, the ability of the couple to form shared awarenesses of their individual needs, desires, and goals is hampered. Shame attacks or the fear of shame attacks limits the capacity of the high-internalized-shame partner to expose himself or herself or to notice his or her partner. And the low-internalized-shame person may become reticent to bring up or discuss certain issues because of the threat of disconnection that can result when the high-internalized-shame partner is thrown into a shame attack. Thus their problem-solving capacity is diminished, and the actions in which they engage lead less to satisfaction for one or both couple members.

(See Zinker & Nevis, 1981, for a fuller description of a couple's mutual goal-seeking process from a Gestalt perspective.)

In these "high-low shame" couple situations, the extent to which such couples can develop realistic shared awarenesses at all of their needs, feelings, desires, goals and so on, and engage in actions that bring satisfaction to both is then largely dependent on the interpersonal skills of the low–internalized-shame partner: skill in tolerating the defenses of the high-internalized-shame partner, skill in reading the *code* of what lies under the defenses, and skill in creating forms in which the high-internalized-shame partner feels safe enough to participate. Indeed, the low-shame partner has a unique set of problems to solve: what to do when the high-shame partner experiences a shame attack, how to read the code of what might really be happening, how to set needed limits for self-protection without shaming, how to deal with the loss of the high-shame partner at such times, and how to attend to his or her own needs.

When *both* partners have high internalized shame, the defenses and strategies (e.g. rage, contempt, blame, control, withdrawal, etc.) employed by each in attempting to cope with and avoid shame are more than likely to trigger a parallel or simultaneous shame attack in the other. Thus any experience of shame in one partner has the potential of emotionally escalating into ever-increasing levels of shame and defensive maneuvering that lead to consequences such as vicious attempts to humiliate the other, domestic violence, and severe emotional ruptures in the bond between the partners. And as we have seen, viewed in this perspective, much of what couples in trouble do, even on less pathological levels, can be seen as attempts to deshame and countershame. We had a glimpse of this starting to happen with Tom and Claire at the outset of this chapter, as each moved to shift the shame or blame off the self and onto the other partner. For the therapist, the sign of this starting to happen is whenever a *feeling, need,* or *wish* is couched as a *reproach,* as Tom and Claire's were starting to do.

Unfortunately, as we know, these strategies are doomed, because they only produce more shame. Under these conditions, the couple learn to fear intimacy and collude to maintain an emotional distance from each other sufficient to avoid these dangerous and painful interludes. However, this leaves them isolated and without a partner to help them adjust to the problems they encounter in life, which are exacerbated by the limitations imposed by their internalized shame.

This profile of how shame affects couple systems is supported by research. In a study I conducted in 1993, couples in which both partners scored low in internalized shame had a equality to their relationship that was characterized by a *sense of emotional safety*. They reported feeling safe enough most of the time to bring up their deepest concerns, feelings, desires, or problems; they had clear expectations of each other; and in general they thought of each other as best friends. They also reported good problem-solving capacity and high interest in each other. These couples scored high in marital intimacy and in marital satisfaction.

Conversely, the relationships of couples in which *both* partners scored high in internalized shame were best characterized by unsafety and poor communication. They felt significantly less safe, most of the time, to share their deepest concerns, feelings, desires, or problems. They reported having less clear expectations of each other, and did not consider the level of their friendship to be as close. These couples reported having lower problem-solving capacity and, not surprisingly, lower interest in each other. They reported that their communication with each other was much more frequently marked by characteristics and behavior such as insults, broken agreements, stomping out of the room, disagreements that go on too long, and not knowing when to stop on certain issues. Not surprisingly, couples with high internalized shame scored low in both marital intimacy and marital satisfaction.

As this study confirmed, internalized shame is indeed a major limiter of marital intimacy. From my own experience as a couples therapist, internalized shame cuts at the heart of intimate relationships, both because it acts as a prohibition against knowing oneself, limiting the extent to which the self can be known to the self, and because it impedes developing interest in and acquiring knowledge of the other. The presence of internalized shame hinders people's ability to engage in intimate interactions. People with internalized shame find it difficult to do such things as reveal their feelings, determine when self-disclosures are appropriate, respond to the feelings of their partner, express desires and preferences, notice the desires and preferences of their partner, face and resolve conflicts, manage couple differences, and tolerate their own and each other's limitations. The higher the level of internalized shame, the more difficulty people tend to have in all these regards.

Working with Shame in Couple Systems: A Gestalt Approach

This study helps us focus on important issues encountered in working with couples in therapy. First, internalized shame arises and thrives developmentally in the context of a past relationship in which there was little sense of emotional safety. Healing internalized shame and restoring shame to its normal function depend on developing emotional safety in *current* relationships. This starts with the emotional safety that the therapist helps provide in his or her relationship with the couple.

Thus it is crucial for therapists to learn about and address their own shame, and to know the subtleties of how *their own personal therapeutic style may shame clients*. In addition, a therapeutic relationship that promotes emotional safety for the couple is based, among other things, on empathy and on setting clear boundaries around areas of therapist-client contact such as length of session, fee setting, method of payment, phone availability, cancellation policy, emergency support for suicidal or special needs clients, and so on. The absence of clarity and carefulness about any of these implies a *"down-weighting"* that recreates the experience of shame for the couple, lowering the emotional safety they experience in therapy.

However, there must be more than vigilance about not "down-weighting" the clients. Therapist-client contact around all these procedural contact issues must be carefully constructed so that it offers a positive message that the clients are important, valid, and worthy of careful treatment and consideration (since the absence of these is what the development of shame is all about). Also, issues of physical and emotional safety need to be addressed from the start of therapy. If situations arise or continue during the process of therapy that endanger the physical or emotional safety of either member of a couple, not only will the couple be unable to deal with their shame, but in addition, the therapy will be supporting shaming behavior (Balcom, Lee, & Trager, in press).

Again, working with shame goes hand in hand with helping couples establish emotional safety. Underneath the couple's defensive style is deep, perhaps lifelong shame that hides an equally deep *longing for emotional safety*. Helping couples acquire an experience of emotional safety in the first sessions is essential for enabling them to acquire the courage and motivation they need to face their shame in larger ways through the course of therapy. But to reach even a temporary place of emotional safety, couple members must face and possibly expose some aspect of their sense of vulnerability and isolation, as well as their need to be cared about and to care about the other. This is part of the content of their shame and, in Gestalt language, is the impasse of their lives together. By *impasse* (a favorite word of Perls), we mean that *past creative solution* to unsafe conditions that enabled each person to manage and go on, and even grow (since in the Gestalt model, it is the creative solution that is growth), but that now serves to block or distort further growth. The power of the impasse lies in the fact that the person knows well that the very behavior that is so problematic now was important, even necessary, for the establishment of enough emotional and personal safety in the past. In other words, to help establish an atmosphere of emotional safety for clients, the therapist must help them face shame to some degree from the start of therapy.

The Gestalt work of Zinker and Nevis offers a model for noticing and dealing creatively with this paradox. In this model, the couple are given support to talk to each other. The therapist breaks into the couple's interaction from time to time, but then the couple are encouraged to continue their interaction. A strength of this format is that both the yearnings, tentative or strong, between couple members (the interest and enjoyment) and the methods they use to achieve and to resist these goals and yearnings (including indications of underlying shame) can be seen when the partners talk to each other, while the therapist hangs out and observes the contact, watching what habitually happens to that *figure of desire* for closeness, safety, and self-expression and the reception of the other. For example, tentative yearnings may be seen through glances out of the corner of one's eye, intonation of voice that is inquisitive, probing, or searching, body posture that leans forward or is engaging, if only for an instant, and then disappears, or an occasional word or phrase that seems to want something from the partner that is not quite spoken. The Kaplans (e.g., Kaplan & Kaplan, 1987) have long advocated that therapists follow these possible *yearnings for contact* with the other. They refer to them as signs of seeking "support for modification of experimental organization"—the clues that the couple does long for a different way of doing and being. From the perspective of shame, these hints and signs are instances where interest or enjoyment is strong enough to counter the anticipation of shame that occurs if the person's desires are not well received by the other, thus enabling the person very cautiously to explore the possibility that the other might be receptive. In the low-shame person this is simply a matter of shyness or embarrassment. But for the higher-shame individual, staying with such a desire is a highly fragile enterprise; shame is ever ready to pull the person back from his or her desire if he or she gets the slightest hint, real or imagined or too severely feared, that he or she won't be received. One way through the experience of shame is for the individual to develop more longing or enjoyment. And finding support from the other for tentative interest or enjoyment allows that interest or enjoyment to grow. But what often happens in higher-shame couples is that not only is the desire itself camouflaged, but the other partner is too involved with his or her own shame to notice the signs. In addition, since shame is a phenomenon centered around being seen or seeing, the activity of noticing the other might be itself shaming to the receiving partner. Thus these small cues of possible connection all too easily get lost by both partners. Gestalt therapy offers a number of methods and techniques that are well adapted to dealing with these sensitive shame issues, even though in many cases shame itself may not have been mentioned explicitly. This follows from the fact that the Gestalt model focuses on the *conditions of contact* and the state of the boundary (Wheeler, 1991), and these are what shame is all about.

Putting the focus on shame helps one appreciate even more what fine Gestalt therapists have been doing all along. The Kaplans' attention to couple members' fragile yearnings is an example of this. In another example, Sonia Nevis teaches that the first intervention with a new couple should be to focus on a strength of a couple, something that the therapist appreciates about the couple's skills, style, interest in each other, and so on. In explaining the rationale for this, Nevis might say simply that no one likes to hear something bad. *Bad* is of course a word for shame. New couples have a fear that when they expose themselves in front of a therapist (and talking to each other is much more exposing than talking to the therapist and telling him or her stories about what is wrong with the relationship), they will be seen as inadequate, inferior, inappropriate, or wrong, and thus be shamed. The therapist establishes emotional safety for the couple partly by showing that he or she can see and appreciate what is good in their relationship. On an unawares level, the couple can then imagine the possibility of the therapist receiving the lost voices that they carry somewhere within themselves, and thus the possibility of the couple exposing hints of these voices and eventually the voices themselves.

The Gestalt perspective on "resistances" or "defenses" likewise emphasizes the couple's health and creativity. Going back to their original shame scenes and helping them identify how their experience and actions made sense in that context is itself deshaming. Gestalt offers a number of techniques that are helpful in that regard, including giving voice to parts of the self, developing and exploring metaphors, body and movement awareness, and experiment itself. Gradually the couple partners become familiar with their own shame scenes and can interact with their partner's shame scenes. As they are able to disengage from their shame scenes and become nurturant observers of their shame dynamics, their sense of emotional safety increases. This is not a linear path. Couples must be helped to expect that they will have shame attacks and that each time through is an

opportunity to learn more about the nature of their shame—
the triggers and the urges, feelings, and desires that lie under
that shame. In the meantime it is important to problem-solve
with the couple around strategies and resources they can use in
protecting themselves and each other and in containing shame
cycles when they occur—letting each other know when things
get too hot, agreeing to stop the argument and bring it into
therapy, separating (taking a walk around the block), calling a
friend, exercising, calling the therapist, and so on. It is important that these strategies become honed so that what each does
to contain the individual and couple shame cycles has the least
possible shaming effect on the other. For example, in one couple, one partner's leaving the house, even in a very respectful
manner, further touched off the other partner's fears of abandonment and threw her deeper into her own shame attack. On
the other hand, her leaving the house was manageable and even
somewhat nurturant for both of them.

What happens if the therapist does not address shame issues? For change to occur, people must face their shame. Shame
is what holds "fixed gestalts" in place and keeps lost voices si-
lenced. People deny their shame and will not face it until they
experience enough emotional safety. If shame is not addressed,
people have little hope that they can live through experiencing
their shame and are left with the necessity of maintaining the
defenses and strategies they use in attempting to cope with and
avoid their shame. Thus the pressure for entrenched positions
and blaming, the attempt to control or dominate, the exclusive
focusing on the behavior of the other, sudden withdrawals, escape into addiction, and so on will continue. And, of course,
their lost voices will remain out of awareness and silent.

Returning to Tom and Claire

Both Tom and Claire were primed for their own individual
shame attacks when they entered my office that morning. Tom
had come from work and Claire from home. The time was ripe
for shame attacks because they were that week moving into a
house they had built, and both had seen this event as providing

the possibility for a fresh start with each other. Thus each had allowed himself or herself to have yearnings that could be easily shamed if not received by the other (or possibly even if they were). I intervened when I did because I saw Claire glance out of the corner of her eye at Tom. I imagined that the glance might mean that she wanted something different from Tom than was then happening in the session. When I asked her about the glance, she confirmed that she had hoped that Tom would not be this way. Focusing on this yearning, I asked her just how she hoped Tom would be. She said that she would have liked Tom to be more like he was the previous night when they were talking about their new house. She said also that she knew the effect her being late had on Tom, and so she had started a half-hour earlier than normal from home but had run into unexpected traffic. She had felt guilty all the way in and had worried whether what Tom usually said about her lateness was something innately bad within her. I asked her to say all that to Tom. Tom was silent in reply. When I asked him what his reaction was, he said that he didn't believe her! It was some kind of a trick. But there was a look of something else in his eye, and still following and imagining the true longing, I said quietly, "She's really important to you." At this he nodded and started to cry softly. He said that he didn't think that she really meant what she had said the night before, that it would all evaporate like it had in the past after such talks. I asked him to say this to her, which he did. After several minutes of gentle talking they were holding hands and looking filled with nourishment and feeling.

When I subsequently suggested to Tom that he had been experiencing a shame attack, and explained the nature of shame attacks, his reaction was relief. He said he hated himself when he found himself feeling and acting the way he had (angry and attacking).

Throughout the course of therapy, Tom and Claire returned to the place of emotional safety that they experienced that day. At first they could do it with certainty only in my office. The question became, What was shamed in them (what were the negative introjects) that blocked their return to this place of safety? The more difficult pieces to work on were undoing the *ground* introjects (the underlying beliefs about the possibilities for contact). For example, neither one of them carried in their governing scenes a picture of the possibility that someone would be interested when he or she had a need. They didn't know that their basic assumption was that the only way to get someone else's attention when they had a need was to get angry. They felt shameful and inappropriate at the thought of approaching their mate with warmth when they had a need. In fact, they had come to me saying that they wanted to "deal better" with their anger—not to have to take care of the other when they got angry. Underneath this, both longed deeply for interest and caring from the other, and they welcomed the therapist's *recognition* and support for this longing.

John and Susan

A common shame pattern for couples, only slightly different from Claire and Tom's, is for one partner to complain about or attack the behavior of the other while the other withdraws and/or defends against being the "bad" person in the relationship. Couples who assume this structure often come from families of origin where a scapegoat was used in an attempt to deal with the collective internalized shame of the family.

There are two keys to unlocking this type of couple shame cycle. In solely complaining about the other the complainer (even when right) does not give information about himself or herself. Usually this person is shamed around exposing his or her needs, feelings (except anger and disapproval), or problems in the shared couple—awarenesses that are constructed by both partners. And thus the complainer cannot really get the quality of attention he or she really wants or get help with his or her actual problems. At the same time, the receiver of complaints is too busy defending to notice that something is going on with the complainer. Usually the defender has been shamed around the activity of noticing the other and as such is relegated to just improving or defending against improving his or her behavior. Together, this couple do not pay attention to the complainer.

John and Susan were an example of a couple with this pattern. Susan would lead off a session with how angry she was at John (or talk about how she was blocked by her anger at John). She said that he didn't follow through on what he promised, he spoke too harshly to her daughter, he wasted his time playing golf, and so on. John, on the other hand, was set to expect and to notice criticism and spent his time explaining his behavior. He said that he was sorry that he didn't keep his promises at times; he was overwhelmed and didn't know how to handle all that he needed to in his life; he needed to handle his relationship with his stepdaughter in his own way; he spent a lot of time trying to get the energy he needed to face the problems in his life and golf helped him do that; and so on.

I pointed out to John and Susan that in listening to them I learned much more about his experience and problems in his life than I did about hers—they were both talking about him. I asked them if they could converse in the other direction: if he could become interested in her and she could reply solely with her own experience and problems. They tried, but it was extremely difficult for them. He could not let down his guard, because he could not help thinking that she was going to criticize him. Essentially, he felt unsafe focusing on her rather than on himself. When he was able to ask her questions about herself and she attempted to speak about herself, she felt overwhelmingly vulnerable and embarrassed, which she related to a common feeling that she had encountered in other situations since childhood. At the same time they both reported that there was something they liked about relating in this manner. It took therapist support over a number of sessions for the couple to feel at all comfortable in this position. Support for this new organization of contact between them came from tracing shame back to its origins, exploring shame in other areas of their current life, and continually attending to the reemergence of shame in the interactions between them.

Listening for and Recovering Lost Voices

Once a couple have been helped to establish a growing sense of emotional safety, which means that they have acquired some knowledge of their individual and couple shame cycles and have been able to disengage from much of the behavior that shames the other, then it becomes more and more possible to identify and recover access to feelings, needs, and urges—ways of being in the world—that have been shamed. At this point the emphasis shifts from safety and healing per se to a new sense of individual and couple *growth*. Couples can now use the emotional safety they have developed to explore deeper issues.

Joyce and Glen entered therapy just before they planned to marry. They had had a stormy two-year courtship that was marked by Joyce breaking off the relationship several times. They said they deeply loved each other and wanted a format in which they could work on how they "got into trouble with each other." Joyce, who was somewhat older than Glen, presented herself as confident, warm, and the person in control. She was an incest and physical abuse survivor whose father had been manic-depressive. Her family-of-origin experiences were extremely chaotic. Joyce's younger sister was also diagnosed as manic-depressive by the time she was a teenager. As a child, Joyce was the family "troublemaker." She recalled being frequently angry, constantly picking fights, and never letting anyone in her family close to her.

Glen was in the middle of a job transition in which he felt lost and tentative. He came from a family in which his father had been constantly critical of him. But apart from his dad's yelling at him and at his brothers, there was little talk about problems, and less about feelings. When he was age three, with the birth of his younger brother, his bedroom was moved to a converted basement. For years after that he remembers crying himself to sleep.

A typical shame cycle between them is one that was reported and worked on about a year into therapy. They reported that they had terrible fights on Saturday nights. The arguments erupted because Joyce wanted Glen to come to bed and he wanted to stay up. When Glen wouldn't come to bed, Joyce would verbally attack him in a manner described by both as vicious and relentless; he would either retaliate verbally or withdraw. On exploring their reports, it became clear that during these incidents she was experiencing shame attacks and was using rage and blame to try to defend against the sense of shame and worthlessness she experienced when he wouldn't join her in bed. Her rage and blame then triggered Glen's shame. He felt like a "bad boy" and would then use blame, rage, or more withdrawal to attempt to defend his shame. This—especially the withdrawal—would then reinforce her shame, and the couple shame spiral would escalate.

In addressing this couple's shame spiral, I started by focusing on Joyce. With help in exploring what she experienced when Glen did not come to bed, Joyce discovered that she felt afraid and abandoned. This was not the first time that fear emerged from under Joyce's anger. It appeared that Joyce had a shame-fear bind, covering (as always) a lost *voice*. She avoided the *experience* of fear at all costs. (And note that *voice* and *experience* are very close: we experience, in a full sense, what we have a voice for, which in turn implies a *nonshaming listener*.) When she could acknowledge that she was afraid, she felt silly, foolish, or even disgusting.

To help Joyce recover her lost voice around fear, I proposed an experiment that she and Glen could carry out at home. What I had in mind was how you help little children deal with the fear of being alone at bedtime. Joyce would go to bed at the time she wanted and Glen would stay up. At preassigned intervals—say, every twenty minutes—Glen would go into their bedroom and be with Joyce for five minutes. In addition, Glen would come to bed at a preassigned time. They carried out this experiment every Saturday night for a period of two months. Each week the details of what happened the previous Saturday night would be reviewed and the details of what would happen the next Saturday night would be adjusted through a process of consensual agreement. For example, at one point Joyce reported that from the time Glen left the room on one visit she was constantly aware of exactly when Glen would be coming into the room next and anxiously looked forward to seeing him. But when he came in she would find herself pretending that it didn't matter to her that he was there. To help deshame Joyce's longing for Glen when he was out of the room, I suggested to them that during the next weekend's experiment, when Glen came into the bedroom, he might say to her that he knew she was happy to see him even though she wouldn't be able to say so. Joyce thought that might help.

In Gestalt, the experiment is not just a new "trial behavior," though it is also that. The experiment is intended to be an *undoing of the old creative adjustment* so that a new constellation of experience, one with more room for the fuller self in the new, more nurturing field, may emerge. In this case, the old creative adjustment was denying the need to have comfort and to be seen when afraid. Take it away, and you expect an access, often a flooding, of all the old feelings and signals that the old creative adjustment was designed to manage and contain. The therapy must then support and deal with all this difficult "new" material, or the behavioral change remains merely an exercise.

In the week following the adjustment in Glen's behavior when he entered the bedroom, Joyce experienced dreams centered around abandonment in which her mother, her father, and her husband were present. In the dreams something awful had happened in the house. Joyce was scared, her parents were screaming, and Glen was knocking at the front door. Although she knew it was Glen at the front door, she could not let him in. In succeeding weeks she recovered childhood memories of being afraid to the point of terror at night and of hiding under her bed.

During the course of this experiment, Joyce wrote her dreams and memories in a journal and shared them during the couple sessions. Glen was taught by her, with my assistance, what she wanted from him in his listening to her. Mostly that turned out to be, not surprisingly, his empathic understanding of her feelings and of what had happened according to her memories, and for him not to try to "fix it."

When they terminated, about a year later, Joyce said that those experiments were what stood out to her the most from the therapy. She said that she felt substantially less shame when she was afraid, most of the time she could tolerate her fear, and when she wanted Glen's support she could tell him about her fear and other feelings.

This was an example of a couple shame cycle that was predominantly initiated and sustained by one of the partners (Joyce's shame-bind around fear). Glen's "piece" in the process was enough to keep the cycle going but was not issue specific or as intensely felt. Glen's more general process of feeling like a "bad boy" was worked on throughout the therapy by keeping him in touch with how he was uniquely important to Joyce and by helping him in his struggle to attain a career that was satisfying to him (as well as by exploring the source of these feelings in the past). In the course of the therapy, the techniques that were used to address shame included active listening, identifying shame sequences, exploring the roots of shame in the family of origin, use of journals, modeling the survival of one's own shame, and helping them find more respectful and nurturant ways of being with themselves and each other.

This is just one example of the use of the Gestalt experiment, much developed and written about by Zinker (1977), Wheeler (1991), and others, in a couple setting. Remember that the basic couple experiment, the underlying "undoing" of an old, habitual structure dynamically held in place by fears, doubts, and the threat of shame, *is the new behavior of coming to therapy* in the first place. This gesture itself contains all the hope and longing that the old creative adjustment, which has become a "fixed gestalt" with its inherent shame-binds, was designed to bind and manage. Now, with new support, this old dynamic pattern can be released and the process of constructing new creative adjustments can be restored.

Concluding Comments

Paradoxically, shame can be either an enabling or a limiting factor in couple interactions. Whereas *shame as affect* helps couple members monitor and regulate their interpersonal boundaries, pulling them back when the other is not available for a desired contact or when the other needs attention in another direction, *internalized shame* can lead to shame attacks, desperate attempts at camouflaging and deshaming, severe ruptures in the couple bond, and spiraling cycles of damage to both partners.

Once we start to understand the nuances of the dynamics of shame in couple systems, we understand the driving force behind many otherwise unexplained occurrences in couples' interactions in and out of the therapy setting—occurrences that might include missed appointments, broken promises, entrenched positions, sudden changes of topic, one-way flow of information, inability to apologize, raging, blaming, preoccupation with outside interests, affairs, illness, perfectionism, violence, and so on.

Underneath the camouflage lies a protected (and perhaps out of awareness) longing for connection. Internalized shame is about inferiority and alienation. It's about wanting (or the denial of that wanting) to belong and to grow and being afraid that an "inappropriate" action, thought, or feeling will mean rejection and loss of support. Helping couples over time simultaneously to face their shame and to build an atmosphere of emotional safety destructures the creative adjustments of the past, which are now dysfunctional, and builds and restores their ability to respond to each other in the present.

References

Balcom, D. (1991). Shame and violence: Considerations in couple's treatment. In K. Lewis (Ed.), *Family therapy applications to social work: Teaching and clinical practice* (pp. 165–181). New York: Haworth.

Balcom, D., Lee, R. G., & Tager, J. (in press). The systemic treatment of shame in couples. *Journal of Marriage and Family Therapy*, 1995.

Bradshaw, J. (1988). *Healing the shame that binds you.* Deerfield Beach, FL: Health Communications.

Fossum, M. A., & Mason, M. J. (1986). *Facing shame: Families in recovery.* New York: W.W. Norton.

Gilligan, G. (1982). *In a different voice.* Cambridge, MA: Harvard University Press.

Jordan, J. (1989). *Relational development: Therapeutic implications of empathy and shame.* Wellesley, MA: The Stone Center.

Kaplan, M. L., & Kaplan, N. R. (1991). The self-organization of human psychological functioning. *Behavioral Science, 36,* 161–178.

Kaplan, N. R., & Kaplan, M. L. (1987). Processes of experimental organization in individual and family systems. *Psychotherapy, 24*(3s), 561–569.

Kaufman, G. (1980). *Shame: The power of caring.* Cambridge: Shenkman.

Kaufman, G. (1989). *The psychology of shame.* New York: Springer.

Lansky, M. R. (1991). Shame and fragmentation in the marital dyad. *Contemporary Family Therapy, 13*(1), 17–31.

Lee, R. G. (1993). *The effect of internalized shame on marital intimacy.* Doctoral dissertation, Fielding Institute, Santa Barbara, CA.

Lewis, H. B. (1971). *Shame and guilt in neurosis.* New York: International Universities Press.

Lewis, H. B. (1981). Shame and guilt in human nature. In S. Tuttman, C. Kaye, & M. Zimerman (Eds.), *Object and self: A developmental approach.* New York: International Universities Press.

Lynd, H. (1958). *On shame and the search for identity.* New York: Harcourt, Brace.

Maturana, H. R., & Varela, F. J. (1980). *Autopoiesis and cognition.* Dordrecht, Holland: Reidel.

Nathanson, D. L. (1992). *Shame and pride: Affect, sex, and the birth of the self.* New York: W.W. Norton.

Nichols, M. P. (1991). *No place to hide: Facing shame so we can find self-respect.* New York: Simon & Schuster.

Papernow, P. L. (1993). *Becoming a stepfamily.* San Francisco: Jossey-Bass.

Prosky, P. (1979). *Some thoughts on family life from the field of family therapy.* Unpublished manuscript.

Retzinger, S. M. (1987). Resentment and laughter: Video studies of the shame-rage spiral. In H. B. Lewis (Ed.), *The role of shame in symptom formation* (pp. 151–181). Hillsdale, NJ: Lawrence Erlbaum.

Schneider, C. D. (1987). A mature sense of shame. In D. L. Nathanson (Ed.), *The many faces of shame* (pp. 194–213). New York: Guilford Press.

Tomkins, S. S. (1963). *Affect, imagery, and consciousness: The negative affects* (Vol. 2). New York: Springer.

Tomkins, S. S. (1979). Script theory differential magnification of affects. In H. E. Howe and R. A. Dienstbrier (Eds.), *Nebraska symposium on motivation* (Vol. 26, pp. 201–236). Lincoln: University of Nebraska Press.

Tomkins, S. S. (1987). Shame. In D. L. Nathanson (Ed.), *The many faces of shame* (pp. 133–161). New York: Guilford Press.

Wheeler, G. (1991). *Gestalt reconsidered: A new approach to contact and resistance.* New York: Gardner Press.

Wurmser, L. (1981). *The mask of shame.* Baltimore: The Johns Hopkins University Press.

Wyman, L. P. (1981). *The intimate systems research project: Report number 1.* Cleveland: The Gestalt Institute of Cleveland Press.

Zinker, J. C. (1977). *Creative process in Gestalt therapy.* New York: Brunner/Mazel.

Zinker, J. C. (1983). Complementarity and the middle ground: Two forces for couples' binding. *The Gestalt Journal, 6*(2).

Zinker, J. C., & Nevis, S. M. (1981). *The gestalt theory of couple and family interactions.* Cleveland: Gestalt Institute of Cleveland Press.

12

Intimacy and Power in Long-Term Relationships: A Gestalt Therapy-Systems Perspective

Joseph Melnick and Sonia March Nevis

In our society today, many view the ability to create, manage, and nurture long-term intimate relationships as the primary prerequisite for happiness and well-being (Schaefer & Olson, 1981). Furthermore, an increasing number of psychotherapists and developmental theorists also perceive the capacity to relate to an other on equal terms as the essence of maturity. At the same time, our high interpersonal anxiety and catastrophic divorce rates reflect the difficulty of creating and sustaining intimate relationships.

Although the topic of intimacy has received much attention by the popular press (Lerner, 1989; Rabin, 1983), little has been written in the family therapy field (Weingarten, 1991). Even more surprisingly, we have found virtually no written discussion of intimacy by Gestalt therapists.

Our purpose is to begin to correct this omission. We will use a Gestalt therapy perspective to focus theoretically on long-term intimacy, a concept that implies a substantive relationship between two or more individuals over an extended period of time. First we will analyze the concept of intimacy from a process perspective and list our working assumptions. Then we will describe four common relationship patterns that are sometimes mistakenly viewed as intimate. After listing the essential ingredients for the development of intimacy, we will introduce the Gestalt Cycle of Experience. We will conclude by focusing on the concept of power, first describing the connection between power and responsibility, and then outlining how power is managed in relationships.

One final note before starting. Unless otherwise noted, the term *long-term intimacy* will refer to Western, middle-class, heterosexual relationships. This focus is for clarity of presentation, and is not intended to place a higher value on this than on other forms of coupling.

The Problem of Defining Intimacy

Intimacy is a difficult concept to define. Some experts describe it as a closeness and depth between two individuals, an awareness of the innermost qualities of another (Sexton & Sexton, 1982). Other authorities emphasize reciprocity and an attitude of mutual permeability: "intimacy is an intentional action between like creatures whose will is to bridge the echoless silence of the universe" (Denes, 1982, p. 136). Still others take a more existential intellectual approach, defining intimacy as "a cognitive state that relates to knowledge of one's psychic reality" (Mendelsohn, 1982, p. 39). For some the emphasis is on the sense of wholeness in the moment that can occur even between antagonists in a boxing match, for example (Wilner, 1982). Lastly, some view intimacy as a capacity or a characteristic that varies more or less among individuals (Mahrer, 1978; Weingarten, 1991); and more recently the question of difference in capacities between men and women has been emphasized (Luepnitz, 1988).

Part of the difficulty in arriving at a consensus regarding the meaning of intimacy lies embedded in the powerful feelings, images, and archetypes that it evokes. Although we may disagree regarding a precise definition, we somehow seem to know it when we experience or see it. For example, one can easily envision a mother nursing her newborn child, two lovers walking hand in hand along a deserted stretch of beach, or two elderly companions gently rocking side by side.

In our attempt at definition we will try a different tack. Our approach will be one of *process*, a perspective that is deeply imbedded in the Gestalt approach. By "process" we mean to describe the phenomenology of an encounter, emphasizing *how* experience is organized by looking at specific habitual patterns of energy exchange in two-person systems. Thus a Gestalt therapist might be interested in specific characteristics or patterns such as complexity, robustness, liveliness, creativity, and balance, to name a few. Because of its purely descriptive nature, a process approach allows us to avoid pejorative or judgmental constructs and language. For terms such as *dependency* or *autonomy* are ultimately contextual and refer to a certain aspect within a two-person system.

We have chosen to use the concept of *power* as our main way of organizing and describing the encounter between two individuals. For we believe that a long-term balance of power is the necessary condition for intimacy to flourish. Before proceeding we would like to list some assumptions.

Basic Assumptions

A. The terms *intimacy, power,* and *abuse* describe aspects of relationships that exist between two or more people.
B. All people have deep-seated yearnings to experience intimacy, power, and nurturance.
C. Intimacy in adult two-person systems is based on an equal balance of experienced power within the context of a long-term relationship.
D. Nurturance is a quality found in intimate relationships. Nurturance occurs when positive energy (in the form of food, words, touch, and so on) is absorbed from the environment by an individual or larger system. In a vibrant, balanced, intimate relationship both individuals receive as well as give nurturance.

E. Abuse, the psychological, emotional, or physical rupturing
    of a boundary, also unfortunately occurs in all intimate
    relationships.
F. As one's power in relation to another diminishes, one
    1. is more open to receive nurturance.
    2. is more open to being abused.
    3. has a diminished capacity to abuse the other.
G. As one's relative power to another increases,
    1. the power to abuse or nurture the other increases.
    2. the opportunity to be abused diminishes.
H. Intimacy can be adequately described through the use of
    the interactive cycle of experience (Zinker & Nevis, 1981).

Experiences That Resemble Intimacy

Many relationships when viewed from afar appear to be intimate in nature. However, when inspected more closely, we find
them lacking in one essential ingredient or another. In this section we will describe four common forms: intimate moments,
pseudo intimacy, isolation-a-deux, and certain forms of contact.

Intimate Moments

An intimate moment can occur when two or more people have
the same degree of energy or interest in the same thing at the
same time. In that instant, they experience an equal openness
to know and be known. (A mild and benign example is when
two strangers find that they have a friend in common.) Unlike
long-term intimacy, intimate moments do not require a balance
of power, but can be experienced in a long-term but unequal
power relationship or in a short-term relationship with uncertain power equality (a soft glance during a blind date).

    Although these moments do take place at any point in
time, they often occur around events of significance such as
birth, marriage, sickness, and death. These occasions, the great
equalizers and levelers of society, serve to create a powerful and
compelling figure that temporarily suspends the traditional
boundaries and power differentials that usually exist between

people. Examples might include a father and a son hugging joyfully upon witnessing the birth of the son's child, or a therapist and patient crying together at the patient's announcement that she or he has cancer.

Intimate moments are usually experienced as something that "just happens" and is out of one's control. Although one can work toward achieving the conditions for these transitory experiences (in psychotherapy, for example, one of the goals is to create the potential for such intimate interactions), they do not require direct effort. In fact, they are characterized by the element of surprise and a sense of boundarylessness or confluence, accompanied by feelings of connectedness and mutuality. For in an intimate moment, one does not experience the other as separate and differentiated from the self. Rather, self and other, figure and ground, temporarily become one.

These transient interactions are best savored and completed. However, it is not uncommon to attribute a meaning and significance to them that can ultimately lead to sorrow and hardship. For example, many of us have mistakenly assumed at one time or another that the experiences of infatuation or love at first sight carry with them the necessary ingredients for building a long-term relationship. Similarly, too many psychotherapy patients have fallen victim to a therapist who at the height of an intimate moment has ignored the inherent power differential (Melnick, Nevis, & Melnick, in press). This abdication of therapist responsibility, unfortunately, has at times resulted in the emotional and sometimes sexual abuse of patients.

Pseudo Intimacy

A second form of interaction, sometimes confused with long-term intimacy, is *pseudo intimacy*. Pseudo intimacy exists when one incorrectly experiences oneself in an intimate relationship because she or he has failed to notice the absence of mutuality. Since the other person does not experience an equal sense of connectedness or relatedness, the interaction is one-sided. Thus the power of perceived intimacy exists for one and not the other. Unrequited love is an obvious example.

Pseudo intimacy requires an incorrect projection of a figure of intimacy onto another. It is often accompanied by an inability to turn away. Certain forms of positive transference fall within this domain, as do the imaginary relationships that ordinary people have with famous and powerful people. Such relationships may serve various purposes, but they are certainly not intimate.

A most powerful form of pseudo intimacy involves the one-sided ending of a long-term relationship. This can occur when one person's energy wanes while the other still experiences feelings of deep caring. The one who is still "in love" experiences an inability to move away, to turn to another figure. This fixed focus on a no longer nurturing relationship can result in much longing and pain.

Isolation-a-deux

A third form of engagement that may be mistaken for intimacy is an *isolation-a-deux* (McMahon, 1982). When viewed casually, it appears to resemble a long-term intimate relationship. However, upon closer examination one discovers that the interaction has a cardboardlike quality, never getting beyond surface depth. According to McMahon, the transferential distortion in this type of interaction is so great for both individuals that the other hardly exists in his or her own right. The interaction takes on a compulsive, unsatisfying quality with both individuals making only narrow contact with each other or with their own selves.

Contact

Before turning toward a more detailed description of long-term intimacy, it is necessary to discuss one other form of interaction, *contact*. Contact involves the meeting of the self and the environment (often in the form of an other) at a boundary. Although all moments of intimacy involve contact, contact does not necessarily imply intimacy. Intimacy involves a syntonic experience between two or more people, whereas contact can occur between a person and an inanimate object or the environment as a whole. Examples include being deeply touched while reading a book or feeling a sense of tranquillity while walking through the woods.

Long-Term Intimacy

It is our belief that the most important requirement for the development of long-term intimacy is that it occur among equals. This means that there exists between intimate individuals a system of mutual and balanced caring and concern. Ultimately, the survival and growth of any long-term relationship rests on a genuine relinquishing of one's need to be more (or less) powerful than the other (Hatfield, 1982) and a deep understanding that individual resources equally belong to the system.

For long-term intimacy to develop, both parties must share a willingness to be neither strategic nor political. Thus each agrees to be open to the truth as she or he knows it. At its worst, this openness to the flow of experience can be terrifying, for it lessens the predictability and safety (or the illusion of safety) that many seek in long-term contact. At its best, it can create a lively, vibrant, self-correcting system capable of integrating new data and responding to a wide range of environmental shifts.

As stated previously, time is an essential component for the development of long-term intimacy. One needs to spend many hours with another for intimacy to start to develop. Not only must there be moments of connectedness, but the moments must be numerous. Furthermore, these periods need to occur in a wide variety of contexts. Thus long-term intimacy develops as the variety of content areas in which intimate moments are experienced increases.

Because the capacity to function in a long-term relationship involves learning, the couple can become more practiced in moving in and out of these experiences. Ideally, a trust in the self and the other evolves, so that a seemingly effortless rhythm emerges.

To reiterate, long-term intimacy is the result of individuals experiencing a wide range of intimate moments over a significant period of time. Furthermore, these moments have a cyclical character. There is a definite structure that includes a beginning, middle, and end. Paradoxically, however, these time periods also have endless variety. Each event carries with it a special uniqueness. As one completes short, deep, long, shallow, fast, and slow cycles of experience with another over time, long-term intimacy increases. It is to this cycle of experience that we turn.

Interactive Cycle of Experience and Long-Term Intimacy

Varieties of experiences created through the interaction of two individuals in relationship can be articulated and analyzed through the use of the Interactive Cycle of Experience (Zinker & Nevis, 1981). The interactive cycle is an outgrowth of the Cycle of Experience model developed at the Gestalt Institute of Cleveland (Zinker, 1977; Melnick & Nevis, 1987). The cycle describes an experiential continuum beginning with *sensation* and moving through the *awareness, mobilization, contact, resolution,* and *withdrawal* phases.

Because each individual's movement through the cycle is unique, much like a fingerprint, the cycles of any two individuals are often different. These differences are a function of a number of variables, including the time spent and the energy invested at each phase. As one moves through many cycles with another person, habitual forms, much like a dance, develop. Ideally each learns to respectfully modify his or her rhythm to create a mutual synchronicity that is satisfying to both.

A simple example might involve the eating of a meal that begins with a couple deciding to eat dinner at a restaurant. Assuming that the couple are able to reach a mutually satisfying decision, a whole new series of cycles begin as they enter the restaurant, choose a table, and determine seating arrangements. Upon receiving menus, they might find their selection styles to be discordant. He might prefer building a broad awareness before deciding. This can involve a complete reading of the menu, a look back at the foods most recently consumed, a caloric check of food items, and a list of questions to ask the waiter. On the other hand, she might be a person who knows what she likes and so has no need for devoting energy here to this sensation-awareness stage. She quickly makes her choice and is waiting to order, while he is only beginning his deliberations. If the waiter appears at this moment, her mobilized energy might be transformed into impatience and his incomplete awareness might turn into anxiety. In a well-practiced system, he might learn to speed up his process by eliminating irrelevant possibilities more quickly, and she might learn to slow down. Furthermore, they might both learn to create a boundary around the external stimulation of the waiter by asking him to return later. And so it goes throughout the remainder of the meal. At the end, his preference for sipping a slow cup of tea while critiquing the quality of service will have to be considered by the couple in light of her need to "eat and run."

Thus an intimate experience can occur when one is either in rhythm with another in terms of placement within the cycle, *or* aware of the differences that exist between them in the moment. This mutual awareness and connectedness provide the ground that supports the experiences of intimacy. In addition, there are typically other elements present, such as an individual awareness of the synchronicity of the moment as well as a shared (usually verbal, but sometimes visual or tactile) acknowledgement of the experience. This mutual acknowledgement supports the development of this "middle ground" of shared cycles successfully achieved (Zinker & Nevis, 1981).

Ultimately, intimacy has less to do with the quantity of energy expended than with the equality of energy focused around a shared figure. As previously discussed, if two individuals consistently display discordant amounts of energy within their system, a power differential has been created, and the potential for intimacy is diminished. It is to this issue of power that we now turn.

Power and Intimacy

The concept of power has been popularized as well as oversimplified by contemporary American society. The media speak of power as almost a concrete substance, as reflected in *power break-*

fasts, power suits, and even *power desks.* This indiscriminate use of the word ignores its process meaning. For *power* is a process concept describing the relative influence of two or more individuals in the creation of shared interests. In a two-person system, the one exhibiting greater influence in the moment is said to have more power; the one exhibiting less is consequently less powerful.

One may influence a relationship in many ways—sexually, intellectually, politically, and emotionally, to name a few. One of the most important uses of power is in the creation of a vision. A process perspective implies that a system involves more than its transactions. It involves a projected sense of what the system wishes to become, a prediction of what a healthy relationship will be in the future. How the vision is created, and how influence is utilized, provide a blueprint of the values, norms, and health of the relationship.

Power differentials exist in any system, intentionally or otherwise, because individuals bring different competencies to the relationship (for example, one is a better cook than the other). In an intimate system focus is constantly in flux, and so are power differentials. At any moment one individual is more aware, one knows more, is more grounded, than the other.

However, inequalities are not only the result of real and tangible differences. Often they are also the result of a shared myth created from the histories (both shared and separate) of the individuals involved. Typically, these myths are maintained by a projective contract in which one party amplifies or diminishes his or her power and the other supports this distortion.

As relative power in a relationship increases, be it a function of competence or projection, so does the capacity to nurture or abuse. The most common form of abuse occurs with the physical or emotional rupturing of a boundary, for example, a slap or a sadistic comment. However, more subtle forms of mistreatment also occur. For example, mistreatment might involve the silent inattention to the power differential by the one who is more powerful. For along with increased power comes the responsibility to be aware that a power differential (whether situational and temporary, or permanent and fixed) exists, and to commit to increased responsibilities for the maintenance of both the relationship and the other individual. This issue of responsibility in relation to power is of great importance.

Power and Responsibility

The responsibilities of the more powerful in relationships are many. Primary is the necessity to know the effects of one's actions on the less powerful, for by definition the less powerful are less able to protect themselves from hurt. Furthermore, responsibility exists, even without awareness. Although the degree of culpability for one's actions is mitigated by degree of awareness, there are certain aspects of engagement that the more powerful must be held accountable for—conscious or not!

There are many examples in the legal arena concerning this long "hook of responsibility." For example, one is responsible for following tax laws whether aware of them or not. A series of recent legal decisions mandates the psychotherapist to break the confidential contract and act on incomplete knowledge if she or he suspects that the patient might seriously injure self or others. In this case, the therapist must choose between two potential negative outcomes: hospitalization of the patient versus possible homicide or suicide.

With power comes the responsibility to stretch one's awareness far beyond one's self-interest. This creates a dilemma exemplified by a male therapy patient enamored with a naive, married woman. Because he (the patient) has had previous extramarital experiences (power born of experience), he has (or should have) the wisdom to know the potential consequences of an affair, both to the woman's marriage and to other individuals involved. Does he have no obligation other than to act in his own self-interest? Or does his responsibility stretch a little further? Is his "conscience clear" if he explicitly warns the woman of the potential consequences of the affair? Or must he go even further? Is he responsible for suspending the relationship until the woman can regain her balance and realistically weigh the possible outcomes? Is he ethically bound to deprive himself for the good of the other? And lastly, what is the responsibility of the therapist in his or her unequal relationship with the patient? Is the therapist to sit nonjudgmentally, empathizing with the patient's plight? Or is it the clinician's job to confront the patient with the power differential implicit in his infatuation, and the ethical and moral implications involved?

The ethical implications of remaining silent in the face of potential abuse are great. For abuse once committed is rarely confined within the limits of a dyadic relationship. In the above example, the ripple of abuse could affect the woman's husband, children, parents, in-laws, work environment, and so on. Much like a virus spreading from person to person, abuse is hard to contain within immediate parameters encompassing the initial act.

Power in Unbalanced Long-Term Relationships

Be that as it may, power differentials of a consistent and relatively fixed manner do exist in many intimate systems. Furthermore, as an individual matures through living, the pendulum of power will fall more and more on his or her side of the boundary. In the previous section both the heightened responsibility and potential misapplications of power were articulated. In the following the positive aspects of power in an unbalanced relationship are discussed.

Well-used power generates a rich and protected interactive culture in which the less able can learn and grow. Effective parents are thus able to provide the protection, consistency, and safety necessary for the child to develop unencumbered by adultlike concerns and issues. Similarly, strong teachers take responsibility for the tutelage of the student, creating a milieu in which modeling and introjection of ideas and values can occur. Lastly, the able therapist creates a setting and atmosphere in which the patient can ultimately integrate more "negative" aspects of self that had previously been disowned and rejected.

Throughout this article, the heightened accountability that goes hand in hand with increased power has been highlighted. Unfortunately, as one's power increases, one has to give up the possibility of receiving ongoing maintenance within that relationship. Thus, as one matures in more and more relationships, nurturance and substance are to be given rather than received.

Morris (1982) discusses this difference between what he terms a balanced versus a caregiving relationship. He points out that love, mutual regulation, and emotional safety characterize both. However, in a caregiving relationship the child is only expected to give cues as to its needs, whereas it is the caregiver's role to meet her or his needs elsewhere. Erickson (1950) in his theory of psychosexual development points out this aspect of generativity in which the adult is able to place the other first. Batson (1990), in a recent review of altruism (the ability to value and pursue another person's well-being as an ultimate goal), cites experimental research to support this characteristic in caring relationships.

If individuals are doomed to live in a world in which maturity means that they progressively give more and receive less sustenance, at least in their caretaking relationships, then pleasure within those relationships must be generated through other means. A cluster of values consisting of pride, artistry, philanthropy, universal connectedness, and humility serve as vehicles for satisfaction for the more powerful. The experience of pride in contributing to the development of another is one such value. For example, teaching a child to ride a bicycle and enjoying the child's excitement at his or her first solo excursion is an experience never to be forgotten.

A second form of pleasure is the artistic satisfaction connected to nurturing that is aesthetically correct within the context of the relationship. This includes the satisfaction of contributing to the growing autonomy of the other person. To be appropriately "caught," confronted and encountered, by a maturing patient is one of the bittersweet fruits of good therapy.

There is also a philanthropic aspect to support that is freely given. It involves the bestowal of a gift with no strings attached and with no need for acknowledgment. Thus the primary concern is the continuous well-being of the other.

Also, for many, along with the philanthropic aspect of nurturing, there emerges a far-reaching perspective concerning relationships that transcends the immediate dyad. It takes the form of connectedness with "a higher power," whether family, society, world, or God. Further, it includes an understanding that the impact of any moment reaches forward into the future and backward into the past. To give of oneself for the betterment of others beyond one's immediate influence is the height of benevolent power well used.

Above all, if one is lucky, an increased sense of humility and ordinariness comes with increased personal power. Thus we come to accept the fact that, for better or worse, we are all fragile, imperfect creatures. To paraphrase Becker (1973), our minds can soar to the heavens, but at the end we are food for worms. Ironically, increased awareness provides a burden as well as a blessing, for the more one is capable, the more one has to carry not only his or her own weight, but the weight of others.

Power in Balanced Long-Term Relationships[1]

In long-term intimate relationships where the power equilibrium ebbs and flows, individuals have the difficult task of interacting within a shifting flow of contexts. Both partners share in the creation and management of a system that supports the positive use of power in the service of intimate contact.

Power can be used positively within a balanced system in a variety of ways. When the long-term balance of power is endangered, one must have the awareness and capacity to empower the other. Foremost, the liveliness of the relationship must be valued over domination or manipulation for individual gain. The environmental texture must be constantly manipulated so as to protect and enhance the couple system.

To use power wisely one must be wary of winning or of "being right," yet still be willing to stand behind beliefs and convictions. Using power positively implies a willingness to put one's pride on the line in the service of the relationship. Further, when conflict occurs, the individual must have the ability to favor contact over withdrawal in dealing with interactional injuries. Thus hurt must be viewed as a by-product of intimacy—painful yes, but completely avoidable, never.

Powerful individuals in a mature system know how to move between provocative and evocative stances. They are able to make power shifts gracefully and with awareness. They know when to move toward the other with intention and focused energy and when to give ground. To be willing to be dependent, to surrender, allows the other to serve as a model, guide, consultant, nurturer, and resource. On the other hand, in a mature system individuals know when to support their own autonomy by using energy to nourish their own creative process.

In a balanced long-term relationship both individuals carry within them the experience of the other as a choosing person separate from themselves. They each can stand alone, and each respects the capacity of choice in the other (McMahon, 1982).

Further, both are willing to risk revealing their innermost styles and characteristics. Also, individuals are capable of regressing and of welcoming regression of the other. These slips into unintegrated primitive structures of the past are viewed by both as spontaneous opportunities for deep-seated learning and connectedness.

The powerful individual displays an ability to lend energy to potential transactions. This commitment to the enhancement of common pleasure is not limited to contact but to each phase of the entire interactive cycle of experience. Thus in a system with shared power it is not just figures but ultimately the ground that becomes available to the other. Each has the capacity to create and supply a supportive structure in which the other might grow. Competency is used not to cancel but to inspire vision and create meaning.

In a balanced relationship individuals know how to live within the life space of an impasse. They have the capacity to temporarily move away from another and turn toward themselves graciously, even when not satisfied. Upon turning back toward the other the interaction incorporates playfulness, humor, and philosophical humility. It is these qualities that soften resistances and foster reconnection and reconciliation.

The art of reconciliation is practiced in well-functioning long-term relationships. One needs to know not only when to move forward and when to move backward, but when to give up autonomy, experience dependency, and stretch one's sense of responsibility to include far-removed others. To risk interacting with someone who has injured you requires not only courage but a wide range of skills. Well-schooled intimate systems have developed interactive structures designed to support reconciliation.

Lastly, members of long-term intimate relationships have learned to manage hurt well. Hurt, the experience of having one's boundaries stretched or broken, is a necessary component of relationship. An extreme avoidance of hurt leads to confluence and stagnation. A lack of respect for the short- and long-term consequences of hurt can result in sadism and ruptured relationship. When hurtful words or actions must occur, the initiator must be committed to remaining in contact and to not turning away. For the hallmark of a long-term intimate relationship is the willingness to bear fully the impact of one's behavior on the other.

Closing Comments

Our discussion of intimacy suggests a radical change in how we view the mature individual. For our society was built on the autonomy of the individual, and on the belief that self-support is the hallmark of maturity and high-level functioning in the world. We instead believe that the responsibility for one's actions in the world does not stop at the contact boundary between the self and the immediate other. Instead, the concept of the boundary must be extended not only to other individuals, family, community, and the world, but forward and backward in time. We must honor not only our grandchildren but also our grandparents.

We also differ with the traditional American perspective that values independence as the highest ideal. Instead, we advocate embracing dependence as a value to be acknowledged and moved toward. Intimacy includes the willingness to give up autonomy, experience neediness, and stretch one's sense of responsibility to include far-removed others.

What of maturity as self-support? Independence and self-support are necessary when no "intimate other" exists for dependence and support. However, dependence and awareness of the other are necessary for relatedness when an "intimate other" is available. For in a true intimate relationship, both individuals have the capacity to aesthetically blend the poles of the autonomy-dependency continuum.

Note

1. We would like to thank Joseph Zinker for his contribution to this section.

References

Batson, C. D. (1990). How social an animal? The human capacity for caring. *American Psychologist, 45,* 336–346.

Becker, E. (1973). *The denial of death.* New York: Free Press.

Denes, M. (1982). Existential approaches to intimacy. In M. Fisher & G. Stricker (Eds.), *Intimacy.* New York: Plenum.

Erickson, E. (1950). *Childhood and society.* New York: W.W. Norton.

Hatfield, E. (1982). Passionate love, compassionate love and intimacy. In M. Fisher & G. Stricker (Eds.), *Intimacy.* New York: Plenum.

Lerner, H. G. (1989). *The dance of intimacy: A woman's guide to courageous acts of change in key relationships.* New York: Harper & Row.

Luepnitz, D. (1988). *The family interpreted: Feminist theory in clinical practice.* New York: Basic Books.

Mahrer, A. R. (1978). *Experiencing: A humanistic theory of psychology and psychiatry.* New York: Brunner/Mazel.

McMahon, J. (1982). Intimacy among friends. In M. Fisher & G. Stricker (Eds.), *Intimacy.* New York: Plenum.

Melnick, J., & Nevis, S. (1987). Power, choice and surprise. *Gestalt Journal, 9,* 43–51.

Melnick, J., Nevis, S. M., & Melnick, G. N. (in press). Therapeutic ethics: A Gestalt perspective. *The British Gestalt Journal.*

Mendelsohn, R. (1982). Intimacy in psychoanalysis. In M. Fisher & G. Stricker (Eds.), *Intimacy*. New York: Plenum.

Morris, D. (1982). Attachment and intimacy. In M. Fisher & G. Stricker (Eds.), *Intimacy*. New York: Plenum.

Rabin, L. B. (1983). *Intimate strangers: Men and women together*. New York: Harper & Row.

Schaefer, M. T., & Olson, D. H. (1981). Assessing intimacy: The PAIR inventory. *Journal of Marital and Family Therapy, 7*, 47–60.

Schlipp, P. (1957). *The philosophy of Karl Jaspers*. New York: Tudor.

Sexton, R., & Sexton, V. (1982). Intimacy: A historical perspective. In M. Fisher & G. Stricker (Eds.), *Intimacy*. New York: Plenum.

Weingarten, K. (1991). The discourses of intimacy: Adding a social constructionist and feminist view. *Family Process, 30*, 285–306.

Wilner, W. (1982). Philosophical approaches to interpersonal intimacy. In M. Fisher & G. Stricker (Eds.), *Intimacy*. New York: Plenum.

Zinker, J. (1977). *Creative process in Gestalt therapy*. New York: Brunner/Mazel.

Zinker, J., & Nevis, S. M. (1981). *The Gestalt theory of couple and family interactions*. Cleveland: Gestalt Institute of Cleveland Press.

13

The Grammar
of Relationship:
Gestalt Couples Therapy
Cynthia Oudejans Harris

A century ago, when Freud developed psychoanalysis, his famous patient Bertha Pappenheim ("Anna O.") called it "the talking cure." In fact, psychotherapy will always remain an intensely verbal undertaking. Thus it is appropriate, in a book about Gestalt couples therapy, to look closely at the basic themes surrounding grammar and language in Gestalt couples practice. We will pay particular attention to how normal language development is related to emotional development, attending especially to the linguistic characteristics of present-focused work (the "here and now") and to the role of pronouns. Both choice of tense (present versus past or future, or even conditional) and choice of pronoun (*I*? *we*? *one*? *it*?) have very much to do with revealing and shaping our self-identification in our own lives, our existential stance with regard to our own actions and experience. We will then go on to discuss the way "Cartesian" language—the language of "objectivity" or disidentification—has permeated our unconscious minds, and how this emphasis on "thinking about" as opposed to "speaking to" can confuse couples' relationships and inhibit the healthy flow of process.

In this chapter I will be distinguishing between the grammar of relationship, which is usually spoken language, immediate and personal, and the language of objectivity, which may be spoken but is most appropriately used (as in most of the page you are reading now) as written language or the language of thinking.

When we use the grammar of relationship, we speak to another person or group using the corresponding pronouns and the present tense. Gestalt couples therapy consists essentially in helping the two members of the couple speak to each other with appropriate awareness and feeling. This necessitates helping the two persons become comfortable with the intimacy and immediacy inherent in relational grammar.

Among those thinkers who have explored interpersonal, as opposed to objective, speech, Mikhail Bakhtin is particularly helpful, stressing (as does Gestalt theory) how growth and learning take place most clearly at our boundary with another person. As Bakhtin wrote beautifully in 1929, "I am conscious of myself and become myself only while revealing myself for another, through another, and with the help of another. The most important acts constituting self-consciousness are determined by a relationship toward another consciousness (toward a thou)" (1984, p. 287).

Grammar and Emotion

In therapy, as in marriage and life, the truly moving words are those that are spoken and heard, words that penetrate the person who hears them and that also move the speaker as she or he perceives their impact. Often when we speak we know that although our words have been perceived, we have not been heard. Only the words that we hear may help to heal us, whether they are words of our therapist or of our spouse or partner.

It seems that the language through which we express and experience emotion is learned before we have learned to speak. Indeed, we hear spoken language while we are still in the womb, many months before our eyes glimpse the world. And it is through learning our own names and the pronouns that we grasp that "I" am "me," that "I" am "Cynthia" and "you" are "you," that "you" are a particular name, that "we" are "us"—and, in many societies most important of all, that "they" are "them" and not "us."

This pronominal learning takes children practice and time to construct. I have a young friend, two-year-old Maxie, who with his creation of the word *my* expresses either "I," "mine," or "me" as the situation may call for. This is an imaginative solution for Maxie, who is discriminating first between the "me" and the "not me" in general—what Goodman would call the ego function of identification—before going on to articulate further boundaries and distinctions within each of these two great realms (Perls, Hefferline, & Goodman, 1951).

One of the earliest sounds we hear repetitively postnatally is the sound of our own name, and it may be universally true that the earliest, and possibly most important, meaningful sound we learn is our name. (As Sonia March Nevis put it, "Find me a culture where the people do not go by names, and I will admit that human cultures can be more different than alike."—personal communication.) Yet our name is so very different from any other word in the way it governs our emotions and behavior that it is an error to call it simply a word. It has a particular significance for us. By means of our name we have a handle on the world, and the world has a "handle" on us. We can all identify with the humiliation of the Jews in the Holocaust, and other groups, when they were stripped of their names and given only numbers instead.

Before we can say our own name, others call us by it. Before I knew much else verbally, I knew that I was "Cynthia." When we are called or ordered or commanded to do something, generally it is by name. My ear picks my name out of a blur of sounds over a loudspeaker, or my head turns to see who is saying "Cynthia" in a crowd. This beginning tone of our sense of identity takes on life before we can address others, at a time when we can only be addressed ourselves, at least in words. From there on, the link between name and action is often almost unmediated. If someone says, "Cynthia, get out of the road!" or even just "Cynthia, please pass the salt," my body mobilizes automatically for responsive action. And likewise in intimate situations such as couples therapy, when one partner uses the other's name—tenderly, beseechingly, angrily, coldly, humorously—the resultant mobilization of energy supports contact.

Language Development

At birth we already possess a repertory of smiles and wails, to which laughter and tears are soon added. By the time we are two, our emotional repertory has been enlarged by our first excursions into language. People have called us by our names, have given us nicknames (which may have particular power for couples later on), have given us imperative commands and evocative calls, asked us simple questions, addressed us with angry shouts as well as reassuring statements—all of this before we master speaking at all, even before our first stumbling attempts at words and names. This is the time when we learn about the dialogic nature of emotional life. I hear my parent's words; my parent hears my frightened call. Or possibly I scream in terror, and there is no response. The parts of ourselves that learn to relate to these expressive sounds and the vocative voice of our grammar gradually build our emotional clarity of awareness, our emotional and relational selves. Much of this is already well established before we ourselves can speak.

This development makes the first part of linguistic learning the grammar of relationship. Patterns of repeated failure to experience being heard at this early, prespeaking phase of our lives determine many of our characterological patterns later on—indeed, are our character, our stance in the world. This means that in couples therapy we have the character and relational history or grammar of each partner live in the room with us, in the way each speaks or does not speak, listens or does not listen to the other. When one partner says, speaking of his or her irrational traits or fears, "I'm just made that way," she or he is referring to some failed preverbal dialogic experience, not just deflecting from the present encounter. Perhaps the fears reflect terrors he or she experienced as a two-year-old when no one came, or later when no one listened—or worse.

The final phase of learning the grammar of relationship,

from about age three to age seven, encompasses the years we need to master this grammar fully. By age three we have learned fairly well how to use words to express ourselves, and now we are beginning really to talk. We are refining the skill of using words and are experimenting with talking with other people, not just to them. We are refining our use of syntax. We talk a lot to adults, ask a lot of questions, talk some with other children. We master quite a sizable vocabulary, a couple of thousand words. We talk almost exclusively to other people now (or to imagined people such as dolls or action figures, in games), not just to ourselves. We use all parts of speech appropriately.

When we are about seven, and have mastered the grammar and syntax of relationship, we lose our baby teeth, our first molars come in, and our brains reach their final size. At this same time our relationship to our linguistic capacity changes as well. This has long been recognized: in the old days, it was the age at which the children were sent off to school. Once they knew the basic syntax of language, they could go to school and begin to read.

When our adult teeth come in we can chew better, possibly mentally as well as physically. (Perls, 1947, made much of the analogy between how freely and aggressively we are or are not able to "attack" our food and how we approach ideas and interpersonal contact.) At the same time we begin to master a new aspect of language: the language of objectivity. We master this language fully by our late teens. This is the language with which we can speak "the truth," "objectively." The language of objectivity is the language we use to talk about things, a linguistic mode characterized by speaking in the third person and in the indicative. It is language that is not addressed to any particular other person but that takes a stance of being true for all potential listeners. Inherently it tends toward and intends coolness and distance, dispassionateness or "objectivity."

We begin to master the language of objectivity roughly between the ages of seven and ten, when we discover that if we want to converse, nobody has to be there—we can talk to ourselves silently, or we can write it down. A little later we realize that in talking to ourselves we are thinking. As Einstein reported of himself, we can turn our "clear muscular and visual images" into words after we have felt or seen them (1955).

We learn that we can figure things out in our minds—some things other people have already figured out, and some things we may be the first to know. We learn that we can actually imagine things that we simultaneously know aren't real. We learn that we can dream dreams. When Descartes wrote, "I think, therefore I am," he had this stage of development in mind, this separation of self from mental object, which gives life a new dimension. And as we know, it is this "objective" or scientific stance, which is developmentally adolescent or preadolescent, that has dominated our mental approach to the world at least since Descartes's time.

Our ability to think is then elaborated into our ability to write and to read objective language, which in turn gradually fans out into oceans of specialized thought and information and knowledge. This immense fanning out of our mental life, which dwarfs us all, has blurred for many in our time the simple existence of the grammar of relationship that we learned in our early years, and that we continue to need in our affective, relational, and intimate life. When we were small children, emotional learning far outweighed "objective" learning in importance. Only later on, when we grew older (and perhaps in many cases more resigned about emotional connectedness), did that more distant kind of learning expressed in the *he-she-it* indicative language of objectivity begin to dominate our attention. Often much of the work of couples therapy is recapturing or reenlivening a more direct, less "objectively" judgmental language of *I, you, we, us,* our feelings, and our personal names.

Language and Change in Couples Therapy

In terms of growth and change in psychotherapy, the grammar of relationship is immensely more important than the language of objectivity. Only when we are moved do we change or grow emotionally. The grammar of relationship has direct emotional power, whereas the language of objectivity has (only) logical, mental power. When we are children, before the age of six or so, we live in the here and now and in you-I-we language: we haven't yet learned to think "about ideas" and the "past" and "future." Gestalt therapy, with its here-and-now focus as a starting point and its insistence on personal speech and personal pronouns, helps us recapture that childhood immediacy of experience. Emotional growth occurs most easily and most profoundly in such immediacy: that is the way we grew in the beginning of our lives, and that is the way we always grow, in experience and meaning making. Only insofar as insight moves us can it help us change.

In work with couples, work in the here and now using the personal pronouns (*I* and *you* and *we* rather than *it* and *one*) and present-tense language is important, because it is the inability to negotiate this relational speech and work out their difficulties in the emotional immediacy of this mode that brought the couple into therapy in the first place. The energy carried and organized by these simple changes in language, which recreate or release the closeness and impact of early experience is what enables the couple to grow and change now. Their new awareness of the difference this different grammar makes is then a tool they can use in future interactions.

Phenomenologically speaking, *awareness* refers to an intrapersonal process. Properly speaking, a couple cannot "be aware." Only one of us at a time can express our awareness. But what is crucial for couples therapy (and couples' lives) is that that awareness becomes created and real to us in the sharing of it with another person. It is this sharing of awareness in the here and now that is integral to Gestalt therapy. At the simplest level, a wife may be asked by the therapist to say what she is aware of when she looks at her husband. She may look at him and say, "When I look at you I'm aware that I can't hate you as much as when I look away." And the husband might be supported to share his awareness in response, saying, "When I hear you say that I'm aware that I feel a little scared, I feel my heart speeding up." The sharing of awareness in this way is both the vehicle for enhancing the couple's (and the therapist's) understanding about problem areas and the construction of the awareness itself (in the sharing), and the means of working the problem through. By the same token, it is a significant source of the energy for the couple's work, and for their life. Such sharing is also risky work that may need considerable support from the therapist and honest commitment from the clients, who must be responsible for their own willing participation.

The Here and Now

A central aspect of Gestalt couples therapy is this here-and-now focus, again using the grammar that speaks accurately of what is felt and meant. Psychological work in the here and now is achieved, in the way discussed above, by the use of the first and second personal pronouns when that is what is actually felt, not slipping into the easier and safer substitution of *it* or *her* or *him*, with the resultant lessening of risk and loss of energy. This shift of pronoun use brings us into the "here." The third-personal and impersonal pronouns are "not here," by definition; they are physically and/or psychologically distant from us.

The present, the "now," is evoked in the therapy session by emphasizing the present tense—not exclusively, of course, which is merely gimmicky, but selectively, so that it will heighten and support the energy for the work. This can be done even in the recounting of a memory, whether of a childhood trauma or a current marital dilemma. This shift in tense makes the emotions fully available and present to both couple members (and the therapist) in the consulting room.

The problem may have started in the past; change is assuredly possible only in the present. The language of this fluid present, personal and here and now, renders us more alive—and thus more vulnerable. When someone gets right to us as a "thou," or when we sense our own power and agency directly, as in "Yes, I will," or "No, not me, not now, not that," then we sense our own being, which at other times is background to our outward focus. At these times, in relationship with energized engagement, we truly know "ourselves" (and "become ourselves"). Afterwards, in the recalling, we may tell about our experience in the narrative mode (the past tense). But if our own pronouns of engagement and agency, and our own sense of present experience in present tense, have not preceded the narration in a felt way, then the story itself is "ungrounded," bland, without focus or energy.

The remarkable part of this process is that telling someone else about our own awareness, using the *we-you-I* mode and the present tense, actually can speed our physical heart rate and respiration, bring sweat to our palms and brow, even tapping to our feet. It can bring past into present, and bring us moments of great emotional clarity. When, on the other hand, we talk "about" our problems, our feelings, in the indicative third person, past tense (even, for more distance, the conditional "it would have," "he might," "one could"), we may talk on for hours, even years, unmoved by our own lives—and failing to move the other person.

The fact that talk in the first and second person, present tense about important matters has such profound physical and emotional impact is as surprising a discovery as Chomsky's investigation of "deep structure" in our neurological makeup, underlying language itself. Chomsky (1988) posits a "deep structure," an innate neurological pattern of organization that, when first triggered by hearing language, "operates quickly, in a deterministic fashion, unconsciously and beyond the limits of awareness and in a manner that is common to the species," and "yields a rich and complex system of knowledge, a particular language" (p. 157).

Chomsky's structural hypothesis argues convincingly that our knowledge of syntax, our capacity to organize the linguistic experience, is inherent to the species. Likewise, the full implication of Gestalt work in the here and now is to show that the emotion and energy that directly relational discourse and grammar generate in us is also a neurologically inherent, preexistent pattern of reaction and self-organization. Couples generally come into therapy, as I said above, because they are more or less unable to manage this kind of clear talking with each other. Rather, their discourse remains flat and unenergized, or else frustrated and angry in mutual isolation, with nowhere for the energy to go. They may not know how to go about this kind of talking; they may need first to be given the experience of doing it, from which they can then analyze out the component parts, such as the shift of grammar and tense. Or it may be that they have dynamic reasons for avoiding this immediacy and engagement—and again, these reasons will surface in the course of the experiment, which is the experience of doing it. Then those reasons themselves become the new awareness, the new figure to be brought into the here and now and worked on together.

Alexandrinian Grammar

So far I have spoken extensively only of the pronouns *you* and *I* and *we*. These are the pronouns of our grammar of relationship. These are the words that locate and define community and the relationships that make up community. This is the language of public order as well, to the extent that command and rules are invoked ("Thou shalt not . . . " and so on), as well as the language of intimate relationship. We now turn to a brief consideration of the language of objectivity, the *he-she-it* indicative mode of scientific and intellectual language in which we speak about (not to) absent persons or things.

First, in order to understand this pronominal use in some depth, we need to investigate its history. Wheeler (1991) refers to all that is in the back of our minds when we are focused on a figure of attention as the "structured ground." In emphasizing the therapeutic relevance of background and history, Wheeler writes, "This [emphasis on the here and now] does not mean that Gestalt therapy is anti-historical, ahistorical, or just plain uninterested in history. On the contrary, in the terminology of the argument developed throughout this critique, the personal subjective past is part of the structured ground, which conditions the dynamic creation of the present figure" (p. 106).

In the same way, just as we need to know our full individual past to more fully experience our personal present and to move ahead with our own lives, so we also need to understand our common historical and intellectual past to move ahead with our communal and sociopolitical lives. In Jung's metaphor, we all possess a "collective unconscious." This unconscious is made up, among other things, of historical creations and conventions that we continue to use without being aware of them. One such historical convention of relevance to our discussion here is Alexandrinian Grammar and the way it uses—and we use—the various personal pronouns. Alexandrinian Grammar is now about 2200 years old (Encyclopaedia Britannica, 18th ed., Vol. 8, p. 266). Through this grammar, and in contrast to the *we-I-you* sequence suggested here, we have unconsciously accepted the following sequence, as the way language simply is: *I—you— he/she/it; we—you—they.* And as we use language, so we think, so we accept life as being organized. Freud, for example, placed ego first. Even Martin Buber wrote of "I-Thou," whereas, as we have seen, "we-thou-I" or "thou-I-we" would be more in accord with our actual development and experience. Likewise Paul Goodman, acutely aware as he was of language and community issues in life, nevertheless used this sequence when he wrote, "Speech is good contact when it draws energy from and makes a structure of the three grammatical persons, I, Thou, and It; the speaker, the one spoken to, and the matter spoken about; when there is need to communicate—something" (Perls, Hefferline & Goodman, 1951, p. 321).

Let us look more closely for a moment at this sequencing:

I love	we love
you love	you (plural) love
he/she/it loves	they love

Now that looks quite harmless and self-evident, because we are so used to it. However, two things have happened here: first, the left column contains the singular, the right column the plural. That is to say, the individual is located prior to the community. This is a developmental and existential impossibility, since each of us requires an other, preferably an ongoing duo, ideally a duo embedded in a community, to come into existence. Moreover, the pronoun *I* has been labeled the "first" person, *you* the "second" person, and *he/she/it* the "third" person. Confusion is caused by our thus imagining that "I" am indeed the "first person," and that in fact "you" are the "second person." This is the shaping of experience itself by language usage. These patterns lead us to imagine that "I" then precede "you," that "I" am more real than "you" (since "you" are only "second," or after "me"), and so on. These usages probably led Buber to give "I" the lead in the title of his famous book—clearly an unconscious choice, and one that flies in the face of the overall thrust of his work.

This *I-you-he/she/it* sequence of pronouns also tells us something about how people thought in classical days—and perhaps still think today. The fact that the "third person singular" includes *it* as well as *he* and *she* suggests on a deep level that there is no intrinsic difference between people and things—or for that matter between the sexes. "He" and "she" and "it" are all the same, though of course "he" comes first. And then in the "third person plural," *they* can refer to any nonpresent collection, whether persons or objects or abstractions. Here our language itself, as well as the Alexandrinian grammatical categories, makes no distinction between the personal and the impersonal. Such a distinction is not treated as necessary. Any group referred to as "they," whether people or objects, is in any case not emotionally present to us.

When we recall that slavery existed everywhere at the time the Alexandrinian grammar was developed in the third century B.C.E., we realize that in those days we *were* treated as objects, and not as persons. We were bought and sold, we *were* auctioned at the block, and we were spoken of as "he" or "she" in our presence as if we were personally absent. More recently, this occurred on our own shores, when African natives were the chattel of white North Americans. (And notice how, in this paragraph, the use of the word *we* moves you more than a *they* possibly could, regardless of your color or identification with a slave heritage.)

Thus pronouns define and orient us in important ways. Just as the so-called "first" and "second" persons can give us life and energy, so the "third" person can turn us into objects and deprive us of real personhood and agency. Of course, it is important for us to possess great skill in speaking and writing this language of "objectivity:" It is our bastion of perspective and distance where distance is appropriate and needed. When we need to know what "the facts are," in a consensual sense, we use this mode of speech. But there are obvious dangers here, as when the language of "objectivity" and authority combine to inhibit questioning and independent thought. Moreover, for more than three hundred years, since the time of Descartes, we in the West have been intellectually under the spell of a sense of language that has ignored interpersonal modes of speech and attended primarily to the *he/she/it* indicative language used in "objective" scientific matters. This linguistic habit has contributed to the difficulties of the couple relationship, since the language of "objectivity" is also the language of right and wrong, one-up and one-down, and shame. Thus our language easily supports our sense of being "right" and thus separate from our partner, who is correspondingly "wrong" when a difference arises. This mode of interaction is frequently encountered in dysfunctional couples. Couples therapy is thus often in large measure a process of helping two people shift away from trying to make do with the "third-person" indicative language of "objectivity" in intimate relational matters, and learn to talk together in the grammar of relation.

The Couple and the Language of Objectivity

In the words of the French psychoanalyst Jacques Lacan (1978), "the Freudian field was possible only a certain time after the emergence of the Cartesian subject, insofar as modern science began only after Descartes made his inaugural step" (p. 47). By this Lacan meant that we could only become true individuals (and thus candidates for analysis) sometime after Descartes declared that sharp distinction—with his "Cogito ergo sum"—between subject and object, the thinker and the "thought about." And we have been hard at work on it ever since, as both Freud and Perls exemplify. Individualism, however, with its "I" emphasis, is an inadequate basis for living as a member of a couple, although it is certainly an essential precondition for it. Paradoxically, *individualism as one energized pole of self* may enhance the vibrancy of relationship in a couple; but it may also vastly increase marital strife or lead to stalemate as two ironclad individualists meet to joust with one another.

When Descartes tied his ability to think to his being alive at all, he asserted the intellectual primacy of objective speech over the *we-you-I* mode of relational language, which I have been contrasting to it. At the same time, with his "I think, therefore I am," he asserted the primacy of solitary reflection over the experiential reality of dialogue and relationship as the defining characteristic of human beings. And as Lacan noted, Descartes's "ergo sum," the "I am" of the individual (usually understood as the individual male, to be sure), was the individualistic thrust that made it possible to "analyze" the individual person apart from her or his social context, whether in psychoanalysis or in Gestalt therapy, and that made it possible for us to search for our individual essence distinct from all other people, and to believe in its centrality. Fritz Perls, one of the founders of the existentialist psychotherapy called Gestalt therapy, crusaded against the language of objectivity (which he called "aboutism") and against the third person and the past tense to such an extent that he called his own autobiography *In and Out of the Garbage Pail* (1969), meaning the discarded detritus of the past as opposed to the glistening colors of immediate life. At the same time, he tended to glorify the individual over the relationship, sharing with Freud a deep distrust of the oppressive potential of the community. It is time now for Gestalt therapy to move beyond this imbalance by returning to its roots in Gestalt perceptual holism in the field model of Kurt Lewin and in the communitarianism of Paul Goodman. In this way both the individual pole and the relational pole of experience can be honored, in the couple and in other therapy settings, while the creative tension between them can be developed and lived with in our language and therapeutic work, to the benefit of our patients in their individual and couple lives alike.

Conclusion: The Language of Health

We need to be limber and flexible in our language use to be healthy as patients, as couples, and as therapists. We need to experience ourselves easily as "you," for example, when we are listening to another person. Many clients find that quite hard to do, seeking rather to seize the word themselves before really experiencing themselves as the addressee of another. Similarly, we need to shift fluidly into experiencing ourselves as an "I" when we take up the word ourselves. And we need equally easily to be able to experience ourselves as parts of a "we" and to speak from and for the couple or group of which we are a part. Each voice must be held availably in the "structured ground" when another voice is "foreground" for the moment. For this we need new therapeutic models. In the words of my own mentor, Eugen Rosenstock-Huessy, to whose influence I owe many of the reflections in this chapter, "Freud has no place in his theory for himself as 'you.'" Clearly being part of a vibrant and healthy couple includes a profound experience of being a "you" in this sense (Morgan, 1987).

Similarly, we need to be free in our appropriate use of tenses: speaking in the present tense when that is called for, calling up the past when necessary, and beckoning to the future as we need to. Clients generally have the greatest difficulty learning to stay in the present, slipping easily into a tense of "timelessness" ("you always . . . " "You never do . . . ") or the present "objective" masquerading as the relational ("I know why you always do that . . . " "You aren't able to [whatever] because . . . "), a way of speaking about the other person while seeming to speak to her or him. But as therapists we also need to help our clients to talk about the past when the past is relevant (and to be sure it has been relegated to the past), and to learn to call up the future life they hope and dream for, which orients their decisions and choices as a couple today.

Gestalt couples therapy, with its foundation in phenomenological reality and the construction of experience, is well adapted to support the flexible use of all these modes: the syntax of relationship as well as the language of objectivity, the clear movement among the "I," the "you," and the "we" voices of relationship, and the time boundaries of experience as reflected in the tenses of spoken language. A rich, ripe, and mature language based on this clarity and this flexibility means a complex and mature therapeutic process, and a rich and more promising couple life.

References

Bakhtin, M. (1984). *Problems of Dostoyevsky's poetics.* (Caryl Emerson, Ed. & Trans.). Minneapolis: University of Minnesota Press. (Original work published 1929).

Chomsky, N. (1988). *Language and problems of knowledge.* Cambridge: MIT Press.

Einstein, A. (1955). Letter to Jacques Hadamard. In *The Creative Process.* New York: Mentor.

Lacan, J. (1978). Four Fundamental Concepts of Psycho-Analysis. New York: Norton.

Morgan, G. (1987). *Speech and society.* Gainesville: University of Florida Press.

Perls, F. (1947). *Ego, hunger and aggression.* London: Routledge.

Perls, F. (1969). *In and out of the garbage pail.* Utah: Real People Press.

Perls, F., Hefferline, R., & Goodman, P. (1951). *Gestalt therapy.* New York. Julian Press.

Wheeler, G. (1991). *Gestalt reconsidered.* New York: Gardner Press.

14

Giving and Receiving

Richard Borofsky and Antra Kalnins Borofsky

We would like to begin this chapter by telling you a story. It's a story about a famous rabbi by the name of Rabbi Nachman.

One day, a student of Rabbi Nachman asked him, "Rabbi, what is hell?" After a few moments reflection, the rabbi answered, "Hell is an enormous hall. In the center of this hall there's a big table which is completely filled with food. The people in hell can come up to the table just close enough to reach the food and pick it up. However, they are not able to eat the food because they cannot bend their elbows. They can only hold the food in their hands and look at it and want it. This is hell—a place of perpetual hunger and wanting in the midst of abundance."

Then the student asked the rabbi, "What is heaven?" The rabbi answered: "Heaven is almost the same as hell. There is the same large hall with the same people, and the same table with the same food. In heaven, as in hell, the people are also not able to bend their elbows. Only one thing is different. In heaven the people have learned how to feed each other." (Buber, 1973)

As a couple who have been together twenty-four years, we are familiar with both the heaven and hell of being in relationship. Also, as conjoint couples therapists, we know the suffering of couples coming for help, who feel acute relational hunger because they cannot give to and receive from each other.

In this chapter, we will describe and demonstrate our approach to couples therapy. In essence, our approach involves helping couples learn how to feed each other and their relationship by giving and receiving whatever is actually, authentically available in the present moment. In what follows, we will elaborate on what we mean by this and offer a transcript of portions of an initial couples therapy session with some commentary to clarify how our approach works in action.

Relationship as Giving and Receiving

> The motto of life is "Give and Take." Everyone must be both a giver and a receiver. Who is not both is as a barren tree.
>
> —Hasidic saying

A basic assumption that underlies our work is the belief that life is the activity of exchange, or the activity of giving and receiving. As the Gestalt model insists, all forms of life exist in an environment and create an exchange with their environment in which something is given and something is received. For example, as animals we give carbon dioxide to plants and receive their oxygen. As economic creatures we exchange goods, services, currency, and credits with others. And in intimate relationships we exchange attentions, feelings, favors, meanings, intentions, dreams, and eventually, perhaps, vows. We see intimate relationships as an elaborate economy of experience that is given and received between two partners. This process of exchange is the means by which bonding occurs. Relationships are not, we believe, made in heaven—or in hell. Rather, the bond between two people is cocreated moment by moment, year after year by the process of giving to and receiving from each other. As Wendell Berry writes in *The Country of Marriage*, "Our bond is no little economy based on the exchange of my love and work for yours. . . . We don't know what its limits are. . . ."

The health of a relationship, like the health of an economy, depends on the ease and frequency of exchange. When this exchange goes well, relationships thrive. Both partners become increasingly present, alive, and aware. They become deeply connected with each other yet are respectful of their separateness. Partners are able to freely share with each other the unique truth of their experience and both are able to value, receive, and learn from the contact with each other's otherness. There is a reciprocity or balance of giving and receiving so that both partners are equally givers and receivers. The exchange is fair and mutually empowering. There is also an acknowledgment of both partners' interdependence. Both partners recognize that each has a limited range of experience and limited capacities, and that they need each other's differentness. Through giving and receiving each has access to new possibilities, and, through the exchange of these possibilities, both partners become more flexible, compassionate, and whole human beings.

That is to say, they change. An important corollary of this view of relationship is that change occurs through the process of exchange. We do not see change as something effected by one person on another. Rather, we see it as the result of an exchange between them that changes them both. This may be an exchange of each person's subjective truth—feelings (positive, negative, neutral, or mixed), needs, meanings, values, or dreams. It may be the exchange of attention, nurturance, or support for each other's goals. Or it may be a contractual quid pro quo in which each agrees to perform concrete actions requested by the other (for further discussion, see Lederer and Jackson, 1968).

When the process of exchange between partners is not working, the relationship and both partners suffer. There is a weakening of the bond that connects them. There is also a sense that nothing is changing, that they are stuck with each other's limitations, and that neither is teaming or growing in the relationship. Often there is also a power struggle between partners in which they try to control, devalue, and even hurt each other. This is the relational hell allegorized in the story at the beginning of this chapter.

Learning to Give and Receive

We assume that giving and receiving are skills that are gradually learned through experience with significant others in one's life. Inevitably, these habits of giving and receiving are transferred to present relationships. In the best case, both partners become aware of these habits and together as a couple learn how to progressively refine their skill at giving and receiving. When there are breakdowns or disconnections in the process of exchange, the couple focus on learning from them rather than on blaming each other, generalizing about the relationship, or resorting to psychological interpretations. In the worst case, couples endlessly repeat the same failed exchanges without learning from their failures. They do not see giving and receiving as a skill that they must learn through conscious practice; they see their relationship as something that just happens—or doesn't happen—without knowing how.

Knowing how to relate successfully involves learning how to give and receive with precision and grace. This requires four things: being present, being aware, sharing responsibility, and practice.

Being Present

Being present is essential for any successful and satisfying exchange to occur in an intimate relationship simply because one can't have an exchange in the past or in the future. Exchanges can only occur in the present. And they can only make use of what is actually, authentically available in the present. Unlike economic or intellectual exchanges, the content of the exchange in an intimate relationship is present experience itself—the personal, palpable, always-changing flow of moment-to-moment aliveness. This is the essence of intimacy.

Awareness

As opposed to thinking about a relationship, awareness is the simple act of noticing how one is actually relating in the present.

To relate successfully one must notice what both partners are doing and the effects of what they do. In relationships, as in driving a car, there are fewer collisions and injuries when one stays attentive to what is happening at each moment. In relationship, one has to be aware not only of oneself or the other, but also of the process of giving and receiving between self and other.

Shared Responsibility

To have successful and satisfying exchanges in a relationship, obviously both partners must do their part. When there is a sense of shared responsibility, one holds oneself and one's partner equally responsible for the successes and failures of relating. This greatly reduces the power struggles that occur so frequently in intimate relationships, as well as the blaming and recrimination that result from these struggles. Shared responsibility makes it possible to learn from each other.

Practice

We learn how to relate through experimentation and practice. If we fail in our efforts to create mutually satisfying exchanges with others, we must be willing to try again, to observe carefully, noticing what works and what doesn't work. In this way each failure becomes the starting place for new learning. This is the spirit of practice, which is absolutely essential for developing skill in giving and receiving. Intimate relationships require that the level of skill keep improving, and this can only be accomplished through continual practice and refinement.

The Gestalt Cycle of Giving and Receiving

What, then, are the skills of giving and receiving? To help us answer this question and to refine our awareness of this process, we have developed a model that we call the "Gestalt Cycle of Giving and Receiving," growing out of the Gestalt "cycle of experience" model described and elaborated on by Zinker (1977), Zinker and Nevis (1981), and other writers. Our model defines eight phases in the process of exchange—four phases of giving and four phases of receiving. We assume that in order to have satisfying exchanges, all phases of this cycle are necessary and must be present. When any of these phases are missing, the quality of a relationship—and the people in it—are likely to suffer.

Although we will describe the phases of giving and receiving separately, in actual experience giving and receiving always go together. They are both happening simultaneously. This giving–receiving is one process, very much like a couple who takes turns leading and following each other as they dance. We will discuss how the phases of giving and receiving go together after we have briefly described each phase.

Giving

Gathering. A prerequisite for all giving is having something to give. This must be something that is actually, presently available as opposed to something one used to have or would like to have in the future. In our view, the most precious thing that one can give is something that is always available—the truth of one's present experience. But one must notice what it is and, in Rilke's phrase "gather [the] sense and sweetness" of one's experience—one's sensations, feelings, thoughts, needs, impulses, hopes, intentions, and so on—in order to discover what one genuinely has to offer. Doing this creates a feeling of authenticity and integrity.

Offering. To relate to another, one must offer something—something of oneself—and extend it toward the other. This might be a statement, a feeling (positive, negative, neutral, or mixed), a need, a movement toward the other, or simply an offering of one's attention. When one does this successfully, a feeling of generosity arises.

Aiming. To be sure an offering reaches the intended other, one must precisely aim what is being given. One must focus one's attention exactly where the giving is going. Aiming gives one a sense of direction and intentionality.

Releasing. In order for an exchange to be complete, one must release whatever is being given to the other. This involves letting go of control and ownership. Whatever has been given is now in the hands of one's partner. If the letting go is complete, there is a surge of energy and excitement. One feels joy and a sense of freedom and ease.

Receiving

Reaching. To receive is not merely a passive process. One must actively need or want something and reach out to find, select, and take from what is available. This reaching is the first step in the process of receiving. Reaching evokes desire and longing.

Readying. When feeding a small child, one has to get the child to open its mouth to be ready to take in another mouthful. This readiness is the second step in the process of receiving. It involves opening one's self so that one can be given to. This phase evokes feelings of hope and anticipation.

Accepting. Obviously, to receive one must accept what is given. Acceptance involves bringing something that is not-self inside the self-boundary, thereby expanding one's self. This creates the experience of compassion.

Assimilating. For one to feel nourished and satisfied, it is essential to fully digest or assimilate what has been taken in. One makes whatever has been received one's own. This is only possible if one completely lets go of the connection with the other and takes the time to withdraw into oneself. When this happens, feelings of gratitude and satisfaction arise.

To represent graphically how the cycle of giving and receiving works, we can arrange the eight phases in a circle like this:

OTHER

Release   Reach

Aim   Ready

GIVING   RECEIVING

Offer   Accept

Gather   Assimilate

SELF

From the diagram one can see that giving is a process of moving from self toward other, and that receiving moves from other toward self. The diagram also helps us to see exactly how giving and receiving go together. The four phases of giving can be paired up with the four phases of receiving that are opposite them on the circle in the diagram:

Gather — Reach

Offer — Ready

Aim — Accept

Release — Assimilate

These pairs are completely interdependent. For example, one can't offer something unless there is someone ready to receive it. And one can't be ready to receive unless something is being offered. Similarly, one can't really accept or take in something that is aimed at someone else. And one can't properly aim something at another unless the other is willing to accept it. This circularity makes it impossible to separate giving and receiving. They are mutually determined.

Likewise, all phases of the cycle are interdependent with each other. When functioning well, the cycle of giving and receiving begins with "gathering–reaching." One partner gathers what is available to give in response to the other partner reaching out, wanting to receive something. When done sensitively and skillfully, this reaching also evokes in the other the impulse to offer what is wanted. This offering, in turn, evokes the readiness to receive. The readiness focuses the other's attention, making it possible to aim what is being given. The clarity of aiming makes it easier to accept or take in what is wanted. Acceptance facilitates the full release of what has been given. And finally, this release allows the full possession and assimilation of what was given.

Couples Therapy

In our work with couples we find it useful to see most difficulties in terms of a failure in the process of giving and receiving.

Our approach is practical and operational. We don't ask why there is a failure, but rather look at how the giving and receiving are not working and try to help both partners learn how to improve it. This requires being able to precisely diagnose and describe the difficulties that are occurring and knowing how to intervene.

We use the above model to guide us in our diagnosis and intervention. This model helps us locate where the process of giving and receiving is breaking down. We can see, for example, which phases of the cycle are missing or poorly developed and which ones are stuck. We can also see and describe how partners are "out of phase" with each other. It enables us to identify which exchanges are most important, which partner is best able to give and which best able to receive at a given moment. Further, the model helps us decide where, when, and how to intervene. It helps us find our next step. To illustrate how we do this, we will present some episodes from an initial couples therapy session with a brief commentary to help clarify our approach.

A Couples Therapy Session

Thomas and Joan are a white, middle-class, middle-aged couple who have never been in therapy before. He is tall, somewhat formal in his manner, self-contained, and clearly ill at ease at the start of this session. She looks about ten years younger than he and appears frustrated and annoyed when they come in.

Episode 1

Antra: We'd like to begin by asking you both to take a few moments to think about what you are wanting from each other, what's bringing you here, and what you would most like to have come out of our first meeting together.

(One–half minute silence.)

Joan: Well, it's not an easy question. The first thing that came to me when you said that was that I want you (looking at Thomas) to let go of me. (Pause.) And I just would like for us to see some hope.

Thomas: I'm struck with the irony of it. What I want from you is not to be so distant. Also, I guess I'd like to just have a sense of direction. I think we've lost our way.

Antra: Could you tell us a little bit of history about what's happened that's brought you here to this point?

Rich: Whatever you think is most important for us to know right at the beginning.

Joan: Well, we had this big blowup. We had a huge fight about three weeks ago. I've been feeling like things have been going downhill for quite some time, but this fight really crystallized things.

Thomas: Joan was upset about what our son said to her.

Joan: He called me "a selfish pig."

Thomas: So she came into my study and—

Joan (interrupting angrily):   No, I wasn't upset with what he said to me. I was upset with the way you handled it! Or didn't handle it.

Thomas: So she came in and wanted to talk about that. It's the end of the school year, I'm a principal at a high school and there's a lot to do, and I said, "Can it wait until the weekend?"— because it sounded like it was a serious discussion. Then one thing led to another, and Joan flew off the handle. I stormed out of the house. I came back in the house and then I stormed off again. And it's been tense ever since.

Because the goal of therapy in our approach is to create a successful and satisfying exchange between Thomas and Joan, we start with the first step of an exchange—reaching and gathering. Antra asks them what they want from each other and from this meeting, so that we know what they are trying to exchange. We also ask them to take some time to reflect on this so they can really "gather" or collect themselves and sense what they have to offer each other. We hear that Joan wants Thomas to "let go" of her, and that he wants her "not to be so distant." Since these wants do not seem well formed, we decided not to start working with them right away. We will come back to them later.

We see a more likely starting place for an exchange in their present feelings about each other. As they talk about the fight they had three weeks ago, we pay close attention to the process of giving and receiving between them. We notice that Joan is angry at Thomas, and that she's stuck aiming her anger at him. She talks pointedly to him, aims angry glances at him, and abruptly interrupts him once. But we can see that she is not able to release her anger. This helps keep their fight unresolved. On Thomas's side, it seems that he is frightened and hurt by Joan's anger. He is not able to accept her anger or assimilate it and learn something from it. Nor is he offering to share with her how frightened and hurt he feels, which could create the closeness he craves. Thomas and Joan are caught in a kind of emotional gridlock. She can't release her anger at him unless he takes it in. He can't offer her his fear and hurt unless she becomes more receptive.

This impasse is what we choose to work with first. We will try to help her give this anger to him and then help him share his fear and hurt with her. Our first step is to have them both become more present so that they can have an exchange with each other.

Antra: Right this moment, how much of that feeling of being in a fight is there between the two of you? How connected or distant are you feeling from each other right now?

Thomas: It feels pretty distant. *Fight* may not be the right word. It just feels like she's on one side of the field and I'm on the other side of the field.

Our second step is to get them to look directly at and talk to each other. This, too, increases the chances of an exchange happening between them, since Thomas has been talking mostly to us, and both have been avoiding eye contact with each other.

Antra: And how would you like it to be?

Thomas: I think I wish we were closer, but what I get from Joan is that my wanting closeness is too much sometimes. It's what I want, but it doesn't feel right in some way.

Rich: Would you be willing to try an experiment? Could you tell her directly that this is what you would like?

Thomas (in a resigned tone):   I'll say the stuff I've said before. (Turning to Joan.) I just wish we were closer, and I feel like when I reach out to you sometimes it's not like you just pull back. You get angry. I'm afraid to ask because if I ask you to be closer then you're going to get angry. It feels like I can't win.

Antra: Joan, what is happening for you? Can you share with Thomas what it's like hearing him?

Joan: On one hand I can see that you're in a bind, but on the other hand I don't care. I feel like I'm still really mad at you, and I almost can't get past that to hear you when you say you want to be close to me. I'm still really angry with you because I feel like you have shut me out in a lot of ways that you're not even aware of. And so part of me just wants to reject everything you say.

Thomas: What do you mean, "shut you out"? I feel like I want you to be the central part of my life.

Joan: You say that, but I feel like a lot of times you're not really there.

Thomas: I know, especially this past year I've pulled back a little, but that has to do with work and all. And you've pulled back, too. (Pause.) But I don't want it to be like this.

Joan: I don't want it to be like this either!

When Thomas looks like he wants to get away from the intensity of this encounter, Rich urges him to stay with it.

Rich: Stay with it, Thomas, please. Just look at her. Just stay looking at each other and feel the frustration and difficulty between you. Both of you are saying, "I don't want it to be like this." And you both feel there's something in the way. Try to feel what's in the way as you look at each other.... Something painful, something difficult.

Thomas: I feel like you hate me.

Joan: I feel like that sometimes.

Thomas: I don't get it. I know I can be a pain sometimes, but hate feels so final.

Joan: I don't know if *hate* is the right word. I get pissed at you!

Joan's anger is still somewhat generalized. It is not clearly focused. We try to make it more precise, more personal, and more present.

Antra: Right this moment are you pissed at him?

Joan: Yes, right now even, looking at you I just . . .

Thomas: What is it I'm doing?

Joan: You're just, you're just . . .

Joan interrupts her anger just as she is about to release it. Rich supports her, hoping this will help her focus it and let it go.

Rich: Try to put it into words. There is something he is doing that's annoying you.

Joan: The way you're kind of sitting and sighing. And, I don't know, there's something kind of pitiful about you. It bugs me.

Rich: I see that too.

And with this support, Joan is able to aim and release her anger for the first time in this session. (This releasing is an energetic phenomenon that is difficult to sense in a written transcript, but is quite obvious when one sees it happening.)

Joan (raising her voice):   It's like in the fight we just had about Robbie. You didn't stand up to him, and I feel like you don't stand up to me! I get mad at you, and you just float away. You just vanish!

Episode 2

The previous episode completes the first half of an exchange. Joan has given some of her anger, but Thomas has not yet received it. Almost certainly, as he becomes more receptive she will give him more of it. However, to preserve a balance between them, it is important that now Thomas be able to give something to her. We also hope, now that she has released some of her anger, that Joan may become a little more receptive to Thomas. Our next step, then, is to help Thomas share with Joan what he is feeling. To do this Antra asks him to turn his attention inside himself so that he can start to gather a sense of what he's presently experiencing.

Antra: What do you feel right this moment?

Thomas: I don't know. There's something.

Antra (slowly):   Can you take a moment to look inside your body and notice the sensations that are inside? How does your breathing and your chest feel? What's happening inside your face and eyes and hands? What do you notice?

Thomas: My stomach is all knots. (Pause.) Maybe it's not knots. It's like snakes, all these snakes.

Thomas now is beginning to have some sense of how he's feeling, but he is unable to offer this to Joan. He becomes frightened that she will criticize him again for being "pitiful" and so he interrupts himself just as he starts to show her how he feels. This interruption is the hallmark of transference—the recreation of old patterns of giving and receiving. He expects to be criticized, and this expectation becomes self-fulfilling when he interrupts himself.

Thomas: But I feel like I'm not supposed to feel that way, because if I feel sad or upset or what you call "pitiful," then it's not good enough. I'm supposed to be some other way. (Pause and a sigh of resignation.) It's like there's no way out.

Thomas seems to be giving up moving toward Joan. To keep him mobilized and involved, Rich confronts him while Antra takes him in compassionately. This exerts both a strong push and pull on him to keep offering himself and his experience.

Rich: Now that sounds pitiful to me. That does sound self-pitying.

Antra (to Rich): I'm feeling something different. I'm feeling compassion.

Rich (to Antra): He sounds like he's giving up. He's saying, "I can't do anything about this. I'm helpless." (Pause.) How do you experience him?

Antra: What I sense is that there's a lot of fear inside him and that he's stuck inside that fear. I feel caring coming up in me.

Rich: I see.

This open disagreement between us has a powerful effect on Joan. Antra notices this.

Antra: Joan, I'm curious about what's happening inside of you right now. If you look inside your body right this moment, what do you notice?

Joan: My throat feels incredibly tight. It almost feels like there's a noose around me or some kind of bandage around my throat. And my hands feel kind of clutchy, like I'm clutching at this chair.

To help Joan start to become more receptive, Rich asks her to focus on what she needs.

Rich: Do you have a sense of what you're needing right now?

Joan: I just saw this image of somebody in those movies where they tie someone up to a chair. I want to get to a knife and get untied. That's what I feel like.

Antra: And then what would that be like? Once you were untied what would you do?

Joan: I think I would just run, just run for a long time.

Antra: So this is the freedom, this being free that you're wanting?

Joan: Yeah, yeah, yeah.

We want to relate her need to Thomas in order to create some exchange between them.

Rich: And do you feel he's tying you up at this moment?

Joan: I just have this feeling that I need to ask his permission to get untied, like I need to check with him to see if it is OK.

Rich: Do you want to do that?

Joan (to Thomas): But then I get so mad that I have to ask you!

Joan wants to be released by Thomas, but doesn't want to ask him. She resents the dependency that asking implies. Antra encourages her to ask anyway.

Antra (playfully): Well, you don't have to ask him. You could just decide to ask him.

Joan: Oh. (After a brief pause she turns to Thomas.) Can I be released?

Thomas: I'm not tying you down.

Indeed, it is true that Thomas is not tying her down. (As we point out later, she feels tied up because she is stuck attending to him.) However, it is also true that he is clinging to her, and this makes her feel engulfed. We see both as equally responsible for creating this impasse, and both will have to do their part to get out of it. Antra asks Thomas to go first because he is more able to give something at this moment.

Antra (to Thomas):   What would it be like to say "yes"?

Thomas: Scary. (Turning to Joan.) But I can see you're really unhappy if you stay tied up. I really don't want you to be unhappy. So, yeah . . . yes.

Antra (to Joan):   And how is that "yes" for you?

Joan (to Thomas):   It's really hard for me because, even though you just said "yes," now I'm starting to infuse it with "no."

Here Joan describes her own transference. She so strongly expects him to deny her what she needs that she's not ready to hear it, let alone believe it. But Thomas really takes aim and insists that she accept what he's saying.

Thomas: Listen, this feels like the bind we keep getting into. It's like what happened when you wanted to go back to work. (Raising his voice.) I'm saying yes! OK? Yes!

Joan: Yes, but you'll resent me the whole time.

Thomas (Poignantly, looking at her):   No . . . I'll be scared.

Thomas gives Joan his fear. But because her negative expectancy or transference is so strong, it is quite possible that she could not see and receive it. To be sure that her response is based on the present happening rather than on the past, we ask her to look at him.

Rich: Could you look at him right now, Joan, and see how he's scared? Can you see his scaredness?

Joan: Yes.

Rich: Can you tell him what you see?

Joan: I see that you're scared, and I could really see how hard it was for you to say that. (Pause.) I know this is really hard for you. (Pause.) I'm sorry I don't acknowledge it more.

Thomas has given Joan what is most authentically true at this moment—his vulnerability, his need to be close, and his fear of losing her. His gift is beautifully aimed and released. This in turn releases Joan. She can now assimilate Thomas's fear and empathically feel it inside herself. This completes the first full cycle of giving and receiving.

Episode 3

This last exchange between Joan and Thomas brings the session to a new level of authenticity and presentness. And as often happens in therapy, when both partners become more present with each other, past experiences emerge that are blocking their ability to give and receive. These are usually experiences that they have not yet been able to share with each other because they are too painful. The beauty of the Gestalt approach is that we do not have to go on an archaeological exploration to unearth these important past experiences. Rather, they emerge on their own when they are needed to resolve the present impasse.

What emerges at this point is the memory of Thomas's first wife, Theresa, who was killed, along with their daughter, in a tragic car accident eighteen years ago. As Thomas talks, it becomes clear that this event has had a major impact on his relationship with Joan. He is afraid of losing Joan the way he lost Theresa. He describes the panic and grief he felt when he heard of Theresa's accident and how it was reactivated recently when Joan had a minor car accident.

Thomas: I'm thinking about Theresa.

Antra (to Thomas):   Who is Theresa?

Thomas: My first wife.

Antra: What happened to Theresa, and how is she part of this?

Thomas: She died in 1975. She was killed in an auto accident with my daughter.

Antra (compassionately): Is there still a lot of pain in you from this?

Thomas: Sometimes I feel like I'm over it, that it's not there, and then something just happens.

Antra: What happens?

Thomas: Some old memory comes up. I think what happened this last time with Joan and me ... her wanting to go away. (Pause.) Joan was involved in an auto accident a couple of months ago. She was away. She was in Albany. She called me and told me that she had been in an accident. She said that she was OK, but she wouldn't be able to drive the car until the next day, so she had to stay another night. (Pause.) I don't know what my reaction was. I just ... until she came home, I just felt like everything was happening all over again. I mean, I knew it wasn't ...

Thomas is struggling to collect or gather himself and the intensity of his feelings. We gently try to help him take the next step of offering this to Joan to make this a present exchange.

Rich: Thomas, did you say this to Joan, that you were afraid it was happening all over again?

Thomas: No, I didn't say that.

Rich: Could you say it now, please?

Antra: Please look at her. And Joan, please look at him.

Thomas (to Joan): I know I haven't really talked to you much about Theresa, and I know this thing about the accident really irritates you now. You don't want to hear about it anymore. But from the time you called me until you came home, I just felt like it was happening all over again. (Crying silently.) It's like when her father called me on the phone. I didn't know what to do. I knew I couldn't show you when you came home.

Here is a very important exchange that is incomplete. Thomas has not been able to share with Joan his grief about Theresa's death or his fear of losing Joan because it is too painful for him. And she is not yet able to accept all this as part of their marriage. He offers her a deeply moving glimpse of his suffering, but the intensity is too much for both of them. Thomas interrupts his story and starts to apologize for being so upset. In turn, this precipitates Joan's rage.

Thomas: I know it's not fair to you. I know it's not right.

Rich: Could I ask you to stop here for a moment, please? What you said is very moving. But your saying "It's not right" or "It's not fair" takes away something.(To Joan.) How was it for you, Joan, to hear this?

Joan: At first I really felt your pain, and then I just got pissed at you all over again.

Rich: At what point?

Joan: Well, somewhere in the middle. (Becoming really enraged.) I feel like you just are always hurting!

Rich: Is it too much for you, too much hurt? Does it feel like it's engulfing you or overwhelming you? Is this some of what you feel is tying you in your chair? His grief, his . . .

Joan: Yeah! I just . . . I had the urge when he was talking, I had the urge to jump up and down and just scream and . . .

Rich (encouraging Joan): Yes, what would you say?

Joan (screaming): I would say, "Fuck you! I'm sick of hearing about fucking Theresa! She's dead!"

For the second time in this session, Joan has been able to release her anger. Rich receives the truth and intensity of her feeling since Thomas is not yet able to take it in and assimilate it.

Rich (long pause): Yes. She's dead. That was in 1975.

Joan (to Thomas): I know you're still hurting, but I'm just . . .

Thomas: I'm not hurting about Theresa.

Joan: You're hurting about me, but it's like I'm her! I'm not her! I'm me!

Rich: Do you feel he heard that? That's an important statement. Do you feel like he got that?

Joan: I feel like you're hurting about me, but I'm not just me, I'm me and her and the kids, too. I'm sort of everything.

Thomas: Well, sometimes you do feel like everything. It's like when we met. I felt like I could live again.

Because they are starting to lose their focus, we try to bring them back to the present and to focus on their exchange with each other.

Antra: What's happening right now?

Thomas (looks frustrated): I don't want to do this.

Rich: You were just saying to Joan, "When we met, I could live again. I feel sometimes you are everything. I love you that much."

Thomas (turning to Joan and getting really angry): But I don't want to say this to you. Because if I say this it's my self-pitying bull-shit, it's my pain, it's Theresa, it's all of that stuff! All you want me to do is be angry! Just as you say I'm hurt all the time, that I carry all this fucking hurt, it feels like you have all this anger!

Thomas has just let her have it. For the first time in this session, he matches the intensity of Joan's anger and gives it back to her. We can see from her reaction that this is what Joan has really been wanting from Thomas—to be met as an equally powerful partner. She is immediately released from her anger and, to his surprise, is delighted by his getting angry.

Antra (to Joan): How are you now? How is this for you?

Joan: I feel like he's . . . he's kind of getting mad! I mean . . .

Antra: Can you tell him what it's like?

Joan: Well, I feel sort of delighted that you're getting mad!

But Thomas is not delighted. He is genuinely confused by the change in Joan's demeanor. He doesn't understand that anger (or any other negative feeling) becomes a gift when it is given and released. (It is withholding one's experience that makes it negative.) But even with Antra's insistent urging to look at Joan he is not really ready to receive her excitement.

Antra: Thomas, can you look at Joan . . . look in her eyes. Her eyes are wide open, and they're smiling . . . But you're not looking. Can you take a look?

Thomas: This is crazy!

Antra: It may not make sense, but just take a look at her. Take a look.

Thomas: Is this what you want? You want me to be angry?

Joan: It's just like I saw this sign of life. I can't explain, it was just kind of like . . . I feel delighted, like a little kid or something.

Antra: Take a look at her. Take a look. Keep looking.

Rich: Joan, right now how is it having him look at you?

Joan (to Thomas): For a moment it's like you really saw me. And I had a little bit of a sense of when we first met, a little bit of that feeling.

Antra (to Thomas): Can you tell her what it's like looking at her at this moment?

Thomas: This whole thing feels a little crazy.

Antra: You mean it doesn't make sense? Is that what you mean by "crazy"?

Thomas: Yeah.

Antra: What are you feeling?

Thomas: Well, I like it more like this than the other way.

Eventually, Joan acts frustrated at Thomas's inability to understand and receive her excitement and starts to withdraw.

Rich: Now, what's happening with you, Joan?

Joan (discouraged): I don't know, it just changed after he started to talk. I just started to feel like, "Oh no, we're back where we were . . . we're back . . . nothing's changed."

Episode 4

Working with couples sometimes feels like trying to get a car out of a snowbank. One tries to rock the car back and forth in order to get unstuck. In the previous episode, after some very intense exchanges back and forth, Thomas and Joan have settled back into their rut. In this next episode, however, they are able to get unstuck and move on to something genuinely new. This episode begins with Rich asking Joan to withdraw inside herself. He does this because Joan's inability to attend to herself limits her ability to receive, which in turn limits Thomas's ability to fully give to her.

Rich: Joan, I'd like to ask you to try an experiment. (Slowly.) Could you put more of your attention inside yourself, inside your body? For example, right now as I'm talking to you, be aware of your breathing, and let go of attending to us. (More slowly.) Be with yourself. Give yourself permission to ignore us, to not have to listen.

Antra: To really feel that you're free . . .

Rich: . . . to put your attention wherever you want. (Long pause.) Do you understand what I'm asking you to do?

Joan: I do, but I'm just having a little bit of a hard time. Once I start to notice what I'm feeling, I have a hard time even remembering what happened before.

Rich: Is that all right?

Joan: Yes, it's just new. I've never done this before, so. . . . It's just so interesting (turning to Thomas) because that's sort of how I've been feeling every time I look at you. I just am totally in the past.

Joan has had a little glimpse of being present. Yet even this glimpse enables her to let go of her anger at Thomas and to allow things to change. To deepen this experience of being present, Antra asks them both to take turns exchanging sentences beginning with the words "Right now. . . " And for the rest of this episode they continue this, gradually becoming more and more present with each other. As they allow positive and negative feelings to come and go, giving and receiving the truth as it changes, there is an intimacy that starts to develop between them.

Antra: I'd like you both to try something. Could you exchange some sentences beginning with the words "Right now"?

Thomas: "Right now?"

Antra: Yes. For example, "Right now, I . . . "

(Pause.)

Joan: Right now, I'm feeling very confused.

Thomas: Right now, I'm exhausted.

Joan: Right now, I wish I could lie down.

(Pause.)

Thomas: Right now, I was just thinking of how much I love you.

Joan: Right now, it's still a little hard for me to hear that.

Thomas: Right now, I know that. Still, that's what I feel.

(Pause.)

Joan: Right now, I feel a little scared.

Thomas: Right now, I'm confused again. It's weird.

Rich: Please stay with this, with all these changes: "I love you," "I'm confused," "I'm afraid," "I can't hear this. . . . " See if you can just stay with these changes and not make any of them a problem. Just allow them to keep changing.

Thomas: Right now, I'm remembering our first date.

Joan: Right now, I feel embarrassed!

Thomas: Right now, I feel edgy.

Joan: Right now, I'm edgy too. I'm aware of you two watching me.

Thomas: Right now, I don't know where all of this is going.

Joan: Right now, I just feel proud that you're trying.

Thomas: Right now, that makes me happy.

Joan: I feel happy too!

As Joan becomes more and more receptive, Thomas is more and more able to offer his love to her. She is just beginning to be ready to receive the closeness that he feels. He decides to take the plunge.

Thomas (hesitantly): Right now, I want you to know it's like . . . it's a little bit . . . it's like a paragraph. Right now, I have a paragraph to say.

Rich (encouragingly to Thomas): Go ahead. Do you want to say it?

Thomas (turning to Joan): Please bear with me. Some of this may touch on stuff that I know irritates you. (Pause.) When your accident happened, and I went through all that . . . part of it was remembering Theresa and what happened then and how scared I got. But there was something else I realized. As much as I loved Theresa and as important as she was to me, you've brought something very special to my life that I can't imagine

anybody else could bring me. And I think that's why I hold on
so tight sometimes. I'm trying to say this in a way that doesn't tie
you down. (Pause.) You're my best friend. I've never had a
friend like you, and I don't want you to feel unhappy or tied
down. (Pause.) So, if you want me to learn how to get pissed at
you, I'll do it. It isn't easy for me. But I'm willing to work on it.
That's all.

Thomas's gift of love and friendship is deeply felt and freely
given. However, she is not quite ready to receive it. She is so
identified with the role of giver that she has a hard time receiving Thomas's love without feeling that she's supposed to say or
give something back to him. But just openly acknowledging her
difficulty helps her soften a little.

Joan: I feel overwhelmed by your love for me, and I feel scared
that I can't live up to it. I'm afraid I'm not good enough.
(Pause.) And now I feel a little sad. I don't know why. But it's not
a bad kind of sad, just kind of a little bit sad.

Antra: How are you feeling right now, Thomas?

Thomas: I feel like I've been running scared for so long. It feels
like, just for this moment, I don't know how long it will last, but
at least for this moment I feel like I don't have to run.

Joan: I don't feel like I want to run either right now. I said I
did before, but I kind of feel like staying put right now.

Right now, Joan and Thomas are quite present with each other.
There is nowhere to go to, and nothing to get away from.
There is just one more thing that Thomas wants—to hold
Joan's hand. However, his way of telling her this doesn't quite
work. So Rich intervenes to help him make this a gift for her
rather than something he is asking from her.

Thomas (tentatively to Joan):   Right now, I'd like to hold your
hand.

Rich: Thomas, the way you said that made it sound like there was less than a 50 percent chance that Joan would want to hold your hand. It sounded like something she probably wouldn't want to do.

Thomas (laughing):   Oh, god!

Rich: I can feel you really want to give her something. So, see if you can make it something that you're giving her, rather than something you're asking for that she won't want to give you.

Thomas (laughing and groaning):   This is going to take forever! (Pause.)

Thomas: Well, to quote the inimitable John Lennon . . . (Both laughing.) One of our all-time favorites, right?

Joan: Yeah.

Thomas (looking directly into her eyes):   I want to hold your hand.

Thomas is giving Joan what he treasures most—the feeling of closeness. His sincerity and directness touch Joan deeply. She completely takes in the closeness he is giving her.

Joan: I feel like I want to cry.

Thomas (holding and looking lovingly at Joan's hand):   Amanda's got hands just like you. (Amanda is their eight-year-old daughter.)

Then it's her turn to give him what she loves best, the energy and excitement of their differentness colliding. Thomas gladly joins her when she raises her hand in the "high five" position and says, "Slap me five!" They both slap hands and laugh.

Through this deep sharing and exchange, both Thomas and Joan have been able to fully give themselves and deeply receive each other. They have accepted and assimilated each other's experience and so have a new experience of themselves. Thomas is more able to get angry, and Joan is more able to feel vulnerable and close. Thomas is more able to give, and Joan is more able to receive. They have both been changed by their exchange. And like the couple in D.H. Lawrence's poem, "History," they have created a new union (Lawrence, in Bly, Hillerman, & Meade, 1992, p. 354)

> Your life, and mine, my love
> Passing on and on, the hate
> Fusing closer and closer with love
> Till at length they mate.

Episode 5

In this final episode our aim is to create a sense of completion. Among the four of us, we have had a richness and variety of exchanges. To help them begin to assimilate some of this experience, we ask them to take a moment of silence.

Rich: There are a couple of things that I'd like to ask you to do before we stop. One is to take a moment of silence to help you digest what we've been doing here. (Long pause.) Please see if there's anything that you want to say to each other before we stop.

Having gone through this process of becoming more present and exchanging with each other, both of them feel that they have rediscovered their connection with each other.

Joan: I have some hope for us. I know it won't be easy.

Thomas (looking lovingly at Joan):   I just want to say, "thank you."

Joan (very tenderly):   You're welcome.

This last exchange is the completion of all the work they have done in this session. Although they exchange only a few words, the quality of how they say them is deeply loving. The bond between them is palpable.

Before we stop, we also want to help them conceptualize what we have been doing and to encourage them to practice being present together by giving and receiving whatever appears in their experience.

Rich: I think what we've done here is to ask you to say what is true and to be with the truth as much as you can, with as much courage and compassion as you have available, and to not turn away too quickly if it gets scary or uncomfortable, but just try to stay with the changes that are happening ...

Antra: ... noticing and sharing the changes in your feelings about each other, as they're happening each moment, and offering that to each other.

Finally, we need to receive something from them.

Rich: Before we end, could you please say a little about how this experience was for you?

Joan: At first, I just couldn't fathom it. I came in, and I couldn't figure out how I was going to talk to you both. But there seemed to be kind of a flow that happened. (Pause.) Also, it was hard for me to be in the present versus the past. That was very hard for me. (Pause.) But I feel like this is the most honest we've been able to be with each other for a long, long, long time.

Thomas: I felt like somehow, something happened so that there was no time for a while. It felt like time stopped. This hasn't happened for a long time. That's what it used to feel like in our first few years together. There'd be these moments when time would stop. It's very nice to feel it again. It's nice to think we could have this again.

The sense of truthfulness, of things flowing, and of time stopping are part of the experience of being present with each other. It is an experience of the intimacy that they had lost—and now have recreated through their giving and receiving.

Conclusion

Reflected in every intervention we make is the assumption that the principal task of intimate relationships is the exchange of self and other through an ever-deeper giving and receiving. As we learn how to do this more fully and more fairly with each other, we are able to be together intimately, authentically, in true mutuality.

We believe that to see and accept the truth of this present moment, no matter what it is, is an act of great courage. To wholeheartedly offer this truth to our partner is an act of great generosity. And to wholeheartedly receive this truth from our partner is an act of deep compassion. This process of giving and receiving is how we create and sustain our bond with each other. It is the operational definition of love from the poem "Married Love," by a 13th century Chinese woman poet (in Hass & Mitchell, 1993).

> You and I
> Have so much love
> That it
> Burns like a fire,
> In which we bake a lump of clay
> Molded into a figure of
> you and a figure of me.
> Then we take both of them,
> And break them into pieces,
> And mix the pieces with water,
> And mold again a figure of you,
> And a figure of me.
> I am in your clay.
> You are in my clay.
> In life we share a single quilt.
> In death we will share one bed.
>
> —Kuan Tao Sheng

Note

This chapter is based on a presentation of a videotaped couples therapy interview by the authors to the Harvard Medical School Conference on Couples Therapy, October 16, 1993. A copy of the videotape is available from the authors at The Center for the Study of Relationship, Boston Gestalt Institute, 86 Washington Avenue, Cambridge, MA. 02140.

References

Berry, W. (1975). *The country of marriage.* New York: Harvest/HBJ Books.

Bly, R., Hillerman, J., & Meade, M. (1992). New York: Harper-Collins.

Buber, M. (1973). *Ten rungs: Hasidic sayings.* New York: Schocken Books.

Hass, R. & Mitchell, S. (Eds.), (1993). *Into the garden.* New York: HarperCollins.

Lederer, W. & Jackson, D. (1968). *The mirages of marriage.* New York: W.W. Norton.

Zinker, J. C. (1977). *Creative process in Gestalt therapy.* New York: Brunner/Mazel.

Zinker, J. C. & Nevis, S. M. (1981). *The Gestalt theory of couple and family interactions.* Cleveland: Gestalt Institute of Cleveland Press.

15

The Aesthetics of Gestalt Couples Therapy[1]
Joseph Zinker and Sonia March Nevis

> The basic concepts of Gestalt therapy are philosophical and aesthetic rather than technical.
>
> —Laura Perls

The essential dimension of Gestalt therapy with couples that we both try to exemplify and teach is the value and efficacy of an *aesthetic viewpoint,* a way of looking and experiencing interpersonal interaction as it unfolds between two persons (Zinker, 1994). The term *aesthetic* comes from the Greek word *aisthanesthai,* meaning "to perceive." We perceive by watching, listening, feeling, and thinking. We sit with couples and change our focus so that we can behold them in their many forms: as an organism, a living being, a metaphor, a lovely or awkward dance. In witnessing a couple's interchange, we are a combination of audience member, director, and critic of an ongoing drama. A dysfunctional couple are poor actors: watching them is poor theater. They cannot rise above their habitual patterns into the excitement of dramatic authenticity; they cannot let go into the joy of their own comedy; nor can they reach down into the depths of their own souls for the real tragedies of life. Gestalt couple therapy is about teaching a pair of human beings, joined by many bonds, some weak and some strong, how to live authentically with one another—from their hearts and bodies, from their longings and laughter. In return, we are rewarded with their revealed beauty.

As Gestalt couples therapists, we aim to teach people how to live more beautifully. We "therapize" for an aesthetic mode of authentic existence and base our aesthetic vision—gazing now through the eyes of an artist and at other times through those of an artisan—on the here-and-now awareness of the gestalt process.

The Good Form of Interpersonal Contact in Couples Therapy

The phenomenon of gestalt formation—originally discovered by Gestalt perceptual psychology, to which Gestalt therapy is so indebted—begins with the awareness of an organized stimulus-entity standing forth against, and from, an amorphously structured ground of all potential stimuli. The formation and destruction of gestalten is an aesthetic process, not simply a utilitarian one. Figures emerge and become real and, depending on the strength of their inherent urgency, grow, brighten, unify, and energize, demanding attention, action, and completion. This is the essential modus operandi of the intrapsychic awareness-action-contact process of organismic homeostasis. As emerging gestalten—needs, wants, expressions, and so on—are attended to and completed, they submerge back into the structured personal ground and a new figure appears in its place and the rhythm continues on.

As within the intrapsychic process of the individual, so within multiperson systems. When a couple struggle successfully through a dilemma, the experience feels whole, complete, right, good, and beautiful. Completed gestalten, fully ripened experiences that we take into awareness, experience, assimilate, and eventually let go, are graceful, flowing, aesthetically pleasing, and personally affirming of our worth as human beings. They have a "good form." Incomplete gestalten, unsolved problems constantly gnawing at a couple, feel sad, faceless, ugly, and frustrating. These incomplete rhythms, like broken records, are aesthetically unpleasant to experience and to witness.

Gestalt couple therapy envisions "pathology" as interruptions in the natural process of gestalt formation and resolution that lead to repeated, vain though often brave efforts to solve a problem. Pathology in this regard is an interruption of process—an adamant "stuckness," an existential cul-de-sac.

Every "symptom," every "illness," every "conflict," is then seen as an effort to make life more satisfying, more pleasing, more aesthetically rich. When a couple get stuck in their problem solving, failing again and again, it interrupts their rhythm of moving apart and coming together. The moment we look at the couple as a single figure caught in a unified attempt to become "unstuck," we have an opportunity to see how the system works, the *goodness* of its behavior, and to observe it trying to solve a problem as a total organism. When it is successful, its actions are in synchrony, balanced, and complementary. A couple system stuck in an incomplete interactive cycle is not in "bad form," but *is manifesting the best form it is capable of at this point in its life cycle.* Laying blame at the feet of one or another member misses the point. Blaming only heightens resistance, which magnifies the problem.

We base our concept of good form on the smooth flow of gestalten structuring and destructuring through the process of awareness, energy mobilization, action, contact at the interpersonal boundary, closure (new learning), and withdrawal (reestablishment of boundary separation). From this simple, organismic process we are proposing an aesthetics of human interaction in working with couples.

Relational Space

Certain schools of psychology believe there is no such thing as a "relationship," that it is an illusion, a mental construct. These schools believe that in a field of two people there is no such thing as a "third entity," the relationship between them. To them we reply that their position is the result of overintellectualizing the problem: a failure to make use of direct sensory and phenomenological data. There is a special kind of energy when two persons are together that is experienced not only by them but by others as well. Granted, human consciousness is a solitary thing, but it is relational. This is because the relational space between two persons is cocreated by their mutually establishing a boundary of their specialness together and what that means to them in relation to each other and to the rest of the world.

Circumstances and events do not stack up like numbers or figures or straight lines flowing from origin A to goal B. We recognize patterns of events, and by studying whole patterns—gestalten—in their entirety, we slowly begin to make sense of the complex structures of small and large systems, from couples to families to corporations. Given this, there is little meaning in such clinically righteous expressions as the "schizophrenogenic mother" or the "criminal family."

In problematic or dysfunctional marriages, it is naive to conclude that one or the other of the partners is the culprit, the troublemaker. To see him or her alone in therapy does not help the therapist understand the dysfunction because another part of the problematical relationship is not there. So we study one partner, then the other, and then the relational "space" between them. Then we discover the influence of their respective parents, families, and children. To manage all of this in our office, we say to ourselves, "At this time I will draw a boundary for this situation around the couple, or around the parents and their children, and this will be the system I study and influence today."

The quality and configuration of the couple's boundary determine how they are in the world. For example, a couple with a thin or overly permeable boundary allow others and outside events to intrude upon their togetherness. Other couples with "dense" boundaries appear to lead secret lives, since they have overly isolated themselves from the outside world.

Gestalt and other therapists accustomed to working with individuals have to make a cognitive and perceptual leap from looking at the boundary of one person to experiencing the couple's boundaries. The "relational organism" becomes much larger, and in order not to drown in it, the therapist moves his or her chair back to see the couple as a whole configuration. The reductionist language so typically used in our culture fails

us because we are dealing with complex, multidetermined phenomena; we must think in terms of metaphor, analogy, and images when seeing whole configurations rather than discrete
parts. The therapist's sense of metaphor and creative imagery
will help him or her find the patterns of the larger organism.
The therapist must switch from analysis to synthesis, choosing to
create wholes rather than taking things apart into smaller units.

Being able to see the couple as a "third entity" is essential
for doing Gestalt couple therapy. After all, a couple is a system,
a gestalt in its own right. To begin experiencing a couple in this
way, the therapist must first "move away" from them, both intellectually and experientially. The therapist begins by seeing both
partners in his or her visual field and watching their physical
movements—their swaying and tilting—in relation to one another. He or she listens to the ebb and flow of their voices, their
tonal qualities, as they speak to one another. How much and
what kind of energy do they create when together, how much
movement, how much shared awareness, how much mutual
contact? Using the couple system itself as a source of data, the
therapist can then make phenomenological observations of its
process:

- "You both are sitting so tensely upright and staring at each
  other so intently you remind me of two duelists each waiting
  for the other to fire the first shot."
- "You appear so light and happy together, it's like you're sitting in a summer field having a picnic."
- "You're like two secret agents, each one trying to get information out of the other without giving any yourselves."

These simple yet direct (and phenomenologically validated) observations lead the couple to increasing levels of awareness about
themselves as individuals and their "being together" as a couple.
In the Gestalt model, awareness of process leads to change.

A Philosophy of Awareness-Process-Change

Every therapeutic approach to couples work possesses a philosophy, explicit or implicit, about how people change both as in-

dividuals and as a two-person relationship. The fundamental premise of how change occurs in Gestalt therapy, regardless of the size of the system, is based on *awareness of process*. Awareness and individual and systemic change are conceptualized as being directly proportionate to one another: the greater the awareness, the greater the opportunity for change. By the same token, greater change makes greater awareness possible.

Awareness

What is awareness? How is it generated? How does it grow in power and clarity? We define *awareness* as the intentionality of consciousness operating at the contact boundary with the actual. Awareness is the pure subjectivity of the conscious "I." As consciousness it is always *consciousness of some thing*; its continual focus (at least in normal everyday states of consciousness) is always in a sequentially forward movement from one "object of awareness" to the next.

Primarily we are aware because we are physically incarnate in the space-time location-moment of the here and now. Being embodied, we have a point of view from which we look out into the world (and into ourselves) that is uniquely our own and makes our experience a private, subjective one. Since to be aware is always to be aware of something, our awareness is fed primarily through our own neurological sensorium, our senses and cognitive functions, both "seeing" and "thinking about" (though in Gestalt therapy we may emphasize the former as more fundamental and more neglected).

The point that distinguishes the Gestalt position from others is its insistence that to be aware of something (or someone) necessarily means to be in *relationship*. Sentience means to be consciously related to some thing. Philosophies of existence have always tended to emphasize the solitude of consciousness: that is, each human being is separate and alone in the prison of her or his own positional awareness, and thus there can be no true union, no fusion of being with the Other. I cannot become one with you at the experiential level. We may share the same ideas and emotions and opinions and states of being, even the same bed, but we will never be fully able to experience the interiority of one another. You cannot coexist with me in my body. You will not accompany me when I die. As such, we are isolated, little islands of consciousness and experience.

And yet, even in our forlorn exile from one another, we are related. We are always, barring states of pathological removal or unconsciousness, in contact with some other thing. Thus awareness is positional, intentional, negational, and relational. We would also add that given these factors conscious awareness is paradoxical, in that it exists by including the "not-I" while excluding it simultaneously. In Gestalt theory, this point of inclusion-exclusion where differentiation occurs is called the "contact boundary." And it is at the contact boundary, the boundary where two different things meet, that *meaning* arises. Awareness, then, is always meaningful, or at least holds the possibility for meaning to be created or cocreated. Thus from the Gestalt point of view, awareness is relational, paradoxical, meaningful, and creative.

Process

Awareness is a linear process moving from one thing to another with varying degrees of intensity, speed, and contact. This process is founded on the intrapsychic structure of human experiencing and is further elaborated below in what we call the "awareness-excitement-contact" cycle of experience (Zinker, 1977). This intrapsychic process, when experienced by two or more persons in relationship, now grows to encompass simultaneously shared, multiple experiences and is termed the interactive cycle of experience (Zinker, 1994). This will be further described below as well.

In Gestalt theory, human nature is *process*, as opposed to historical conceptions and fixed notions like "Man is a rational animal." We as individuals and in relationship with others are in a constant state of becoming. Our nature is potentiality; and our essence is not predetermined; indeed, *process is our essence*. We are a process in constant motion; our boundaries are ever changing. Process is action that continues and progresses. Process implies a living, organic, spontaneous movement.

Process is curvilinear, patterned, in constant flux, uncontrived, unplanned, pure—propelled by the energy of two or more persons. Process thinking is devoid of obsession with, or preoccupation about, content and the push to create particular outcomes. *To be one with one's own process is to be fully alive.* Attending to the process of the therapy session—*how* two persons are being together with one another—almost always supersedes the content of *what* the couple are talking about.

Paradoxical Change

Gestalt couples therapy asserts that change occurs paradoxically in the heightened awareness of "what is." This is known as the "paradoxical theory of change," which states that "change occurs when one becomes what he/she is, not when one tries to become what he/she is not" (Beisser, 1970, p. 77). In regard to applying the paradoxical nature of change therapeutically, Edwin Nevis (1987) has described the therapist's role in change this way: "Change does not take place through a coercive attempt by the individual or by another person to change him/her, but it does take place if one takes the time and effort to be what one is—to be fully invested in one's current positions. By rejecting the role of change agent, we make meaningful and orderly change possible" (p. 305).

What does it mean when we say we look at "what is" in a couple? We give the couple an opportunity to examine what is experienced, what is done, what actions occur, what feelings and sentiments are available and expressed, as well as what may be held back. We encourage the couple to see and to experience the goodness, the usefulness, the creativity of what they discover when they examine themselves. Our basic position is that couples and families are generally unable to see the goodness and competence of their present positions. They receive little if any affirmation of what they do well in their relationship; foreground for them is the discomfort of their predicament.

When couple members begin to experience their competence and creativity even in their troubles, they experience affirmation and dignity that were not previously available to their awareness. This in turn gives them the courage to look at what is missing in their system, what is on the other side of their strengths—the "underbelly." They can then say, "We do this well, but we pay a lot for it. Perhaps we could try doing things another way that may not leave us feeling as lonely and as isolated as we have been." Going more fully into "what is" allows the journey to continue moving toward what is optimal and more fully adaptive in the life of the couple.

The paradox is that the more the couple experience what their relationship is and how it operates (rather than how it "should be"), the greater the chance that they can move on to a better life, a more fulfilled way of being together. On the other hand, the more a couple are pushed to change their ways of thinking and doing, the more they will resist change. Accepting "what is" is the cornerstone of our therapeutic position, and thus we insert ourselves into the couple's life at this basic level of curiosity and awareness. We try to pique their curiosity about how they are, how they function, and what is important to them. The moment they can look at each other and begin to examine what they are, at that very moment they are involved in the process of change. The level of their combined awareness begins to change. Greater, richer awareness gives them more choices, and therefore a better chance for a good life.

This is accomplished by the therapist's supporting the awareness of "what is," by making phenomenologically based observations about the couple's process in the immediate encounter of their being together. That is, we support what is, not what should be or what we would like to be, or what we or they would prefer, but simply *how* they are being together as a couple in the moment. In this way, awareness begins to grow within them as individuals and as a couple system, and they are given opportunity for change to emerge. See Figure 15.1 for a schematic picture of how this kind of intervention for change is focused.

Essential Aspects of an Aesthetic Approach to Couples

This chapter describes a fundamental vision through which we can encounter two individuals in relationship to one another. A

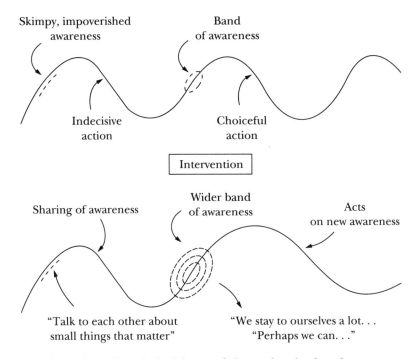

Skimpy, impoverished awareness

Band of awareness

Indecisive action

Choiceful action

Intervention

Wider band of awareness

Sharing of awareness

Acts on new awareness

"Talk to each other about small things that matter"

"We stay to ourselves a lot. . . "Perhaps we can. . ."

Figure 15.1. Paradoxical theory of change: how it takes place.

"vision," much like a gestalt, is a unified whole, and since it possesses a cohesive structure that creates its own unity, it is difficult to break apart for presentation and assimilation. Be that as it may, we can take our vision of the aesthetic validity of interpersonal action and, without "breaking it down," can still define a number of distinct aspects. Our vision of the good form of a couple's interaction is inextricably interwoven with our technical approach: they are synonymous. To our way of thinking, to "do" Gestalt couples therapy without a vision may be possible, but the work fails to reach the level of a coherent whole.

Increased awareness promises change at every level of our lives. In Gestalt couples therapy, again, *awareness of process* is the foundation for meaningful change. As a rule, couples are not aware of their own process—its flow, its cognitive solidity, its energy, its potential contactfulness. They attend to the content of what they do, and it is to that that they are most passionately attached. When their process goes well, they need not be aware of it. A couple's process goes smoothly when each can start at a different place, draw together, do something, then feel finished and satisfied. Any interruption in that process will result in leftover energy, which is experienced as dissatisfaction or malfunction, a something "not right." When their process is poor, they experience pain, and that is when they seek therapy for relief.

As long as the process works well, it remains background. When the process malfunctions and becomes foreground, then you are forced to examine it. When a couple go to therapy, they stop just living and shift their attention from the content of living to the process of living. Then when life is smooth again and leads to satisfaction, the process once more becomes background.

What must a couple do to correct their process? They need to talk about what is going on with them, their thoughts, feelings, and experiences. They must stay with that process until they tap into something that has interest, caring, or energy attached to it. They need to arrive at a "figure" that each of them is attached to and cares about. Then they live it through, digest it, finish it, and pull apart once more.

As therapists we go through the same process as our clients. We watch the couple, not yet knowing what we care about, what interests us, or what matters to us. We allow something to become figural in that process, then tell the couple about it. We call this sharing an "intervention." The intervention widens the couple's awareness, drawing something from the background to make it figural. If the couple can chew over the awareness, get something out of it, and choose to change their behavior, we are satisfied.

If the couple cannot do this, we create experiments that provide a structure for playing with this new awareness in a concrete framework. The experiment exposes the couple to a new behavior, experience, or insight. Then they can choose whether or not to incorporate the new experience into their repertoire of living. Having introduced the couple to a novel way of seeing themselves, we close the "unit of work," and perhaps the session, by discussing and integrating what has been learned.

But then what does stand out for us, as therapists? What

do we choose to invest energy and attention in, with and for the couple? Let us imagine that you are sitting with a couple, and the number of things "going on," as always, is beyond count. Without a theory of human behavior, a lens for selecting out certain features of the field, you are simply not going to see anything. It will all be too confusing. Only with a "cognitive map" will information be organized, stand out, and lead to an intervention. (See Figure 15.2.) All the tools and perspectives we talk about in Gestalt therapy are the "lenses," the "eyes" through which we see the world. There are four major such tools or lenses that you can use to organize what you see and hear: sensation, awareness, energy and action, and contact.

Sensation

At the initial stage of sensation, couples usually look at each other, often with great intensity, but tend not to really see or

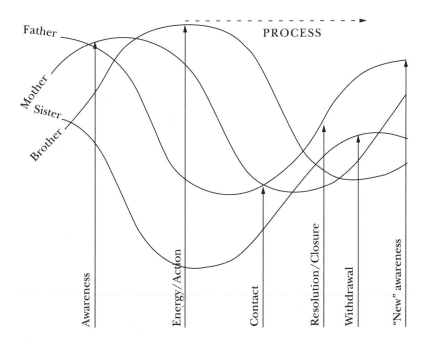

Figure 15.2. Gestalt interactive cycle.

hear one another. They may sit like this for a while, silently rehearsing in their heads what would be a "good opening" or a potential rebuttal or what topics they'd like to avoid. Even though in this physical position they are receiving a great deal of experiential information from one another, they are not in contact with their senses but with their own cognitive planning and fantasizing.

They are, for whatever reason, desensitized to one another. This is the most obvious "what is" about how the couple are being together at this moment, and so this is the starting point for the therapist. The therapist, at this point, encourages the couple by directing their awareness to what they are doing and how they are doing it—just looking at one another in silence—and asks what each of them sees. This intervention breaks the internal self-dialogue of fantasy encounter and puts them squarely into their immediate experience of one another—the existential here and now—the "what is" of the moment. As they begin to focus more on one another, making observations, sharing feelings, wants, and needs, the therapist assists as a supportive presence grounding them further in the immediacy of their "we-ness" with observations of how they are together. Helping a couple to see clearly their own process of being with one another teaches them most of what they need to learn about their strengths and weaknesses individually and together.

Awareness

Fuzzy, muddled, or indistinct sensing leads to poor awareness (or, at the extreme, even dissociation), whereas strong, definite contact with sensations supports, creates, and enhances strong awareness. Partners, usually through a variety of resistances (Perls, Hefferline, & Goodman, 1951; Polster & Polster, 1973; Zinker, 1994, 1977) or habitual "contact styles" (Harris, 1981; Wheeler, 1991), tend to internalize a variety of feelings, thoughts, wants, and needs rather than to express them directly to the other. When resentments are withheld and feelings left unspoken, boundaries become blurred, contact is anemic, and assumptions, uncertainty, confusion, and anger build up in the system; emotional vitality atrophies and the system experiences a kind of interpersonal "arterial sclerosis."

Awareness begins with being clear about what is experienced in the present. The couple are encouraged to state to one another what each is aware of in the moment, what each person wants and needs, what is being felt, and so on. This leads to expressions of what is wanted and needed from one another and what is experienced as a consequence of that want and/or need being left unspoken, unnoticed, or unfulfilled. It is during this early stage that the couple begin to negotiate a shared "figure" of what they as a unity need to work on—what is going wrong between them. The therapist stands at the ready watching for any habitual interruptions in this process and supporting fuller awareness, expression, and clarity.

Typically, most couples are stuck in awareness of hurt and blame while righteously talking one another to death. They keep a kind of interpersonal scorecard tallying every "You-did-this-to-me" item in their awareness. These are what we call "the stamp collectors," because they catalogue each slight or hurt and carry it around with them to use against their partner. These couples seek our help because they cannot move beyond this immobilized state of righteousness and blaming into actions that will help them satisfy their needs or wants. The intervention in this case would be to call their attention to their blaming process—how they righteously attack one another and how they repeatedly fail to get what they really want and need from each other. The therapist would seek to raise their awareness of this experience as a starting point and explore what emerges from their experience of their stalemated encounter.

Energy and Action

Once awareness has been raised to the point at which a "figure" emerges, that is, a mutually shared item of interest about the dilemma of their process, the couple should begin to experience a growing energy to do something about it, to explore it further. The Gestalt couple's therapist will then take their figural interest and energy about it into a structured encounter called "an experiment." For example, once our couple fully realize the futility of their locked process of blaming and want to do something about it, they could be invited to take turns blaming each other. Then each one could share how he or she felt in the moment when blamed by the other. This, of course, would raise awareness about how they hurt one another and so would build mutual empathy. Or, instead of blaming one another they could take turns telling the other what they did and how they feel about those experiences in the moment. The exact kind of experiment that is done is not the primary issue (since its design comes from their figural material, and much depends on the stage of therapy with the couple). The primary concern is that their shared energy, awareness, and needs are "made real" by actions in the present moment with one another.

At this stage of the intervention, the therapist supports an even exchange of energy in the system so that one partner does not overwhelm or dominate the other (with the other allowing the domination). We seek to establish equality in power because if power is predominantly held by one partner the possibility of intimacy diminishes; an example would be a sadomasochistic relationship. In politics and love, power corrupts, and two people cannot realize a true adult relationship with an imbalance of power; they may have a relationship like a parent-child one or a sadomasochistic type, but these are not *adult* relationships.

It is also during this stage that the therapist needs to watch for two major resistances: confluence and retroflection. In terms of the power differential, one partner is able to dominate because the other goes along with being dominated. Retroflection, the holding back of energetic expression, occurs because there is a fear of the possible (fantasized) consequences within the system; both partners cooperate, consciously or unconsciously, to preserve the known safety of the status quo.

The key in dealing with either situation is twofold. First, the therapist must teach (usually by modeling the behavior) how to express the physical and emotional energy—including anger—in a responsible and constructive way. "Retroflected couples," because they are so isolated from others outside of their boundary, need to be taught how to ask for help, how to reach out to others for support.

Second, it must be remembered that all individual behaviors and resistances are mutually created and maintained. There is no such thing as a "projector" without a "projectee"; one cannot be confluent without someone to be confluent with, every masochist needs his or her sadist, and so on. Therefore, anything you witness in watching a couple interact should be held as a *system* phenomenon and not the independent behavior of one or the other partner. To do otherwise would be to disrupt the boundary of their "couple-ness" by drawing out an "identified patient," a most destructive intervention and label.

Contact

Contact, like *awareness,* is often difficult to define because its meaning has been trivialized into jargon by overuse and misuse by the Gestalt psychotherapeutic community. What is "contact"? What does it mean to be in "contact" with another? What does it feel like? What does it look like? How do you know?

Contact, as stated earlier, occurs at the boundary of what is different from the self, and has been aptly described elsewhere (Latner, 1992; Perls et al., 1951). Contact is the experience of encountering the difference of the other and is known by the excitement or energy generated by this meeting. Growth occurs at the point and moment of contact—the contact boundary. It is the event-moment when we organize ourselves to meet the environment and change it and ourselves in the process. When the contact moment is over, the boundary disappears and a new one forms with something else; again, we see this aspect of the sequentiality of consciousness.

The creative use of the couple's energy through experimentation heightens awareness and contact and renews their feeling good about being together. Here we are talking about contact as a qualitative experience whose quantity and frequency are not usually the important thing. A small moment of pure intimacy is more meaningful than hours of noncontactful being together. On the other hand, even an intensely provocative display of anger, as long as it is experientially authentic and responsibly performed, heightens contact and often leads to intense intimacy afterward.

After the contact moment passes or the experiment is completed, the therapist must stop the couple and ask them to report to one another what they experienced. This self-report prevents any premature disconnection; validates their experience; gives them time to "chew things over," even those experiences considered unpleasant, shameful, or embarrassing; supports the practice of being truthful and open; and highlights the value of what contact offers them as a couple. Finally, the therapist should always take a moment to positively acknowledge the quality of their contact and their description of what they learned from it.

It has long been a notion in Gestalt therapy that contact is somehow of greater value than the other steps of the experience cycle. In our style of Gestalt couples work, we are not attached to any one stage of the cycle more than another but prefer to look at the whole process, the couple's "dancing" together through this rhythm of rising awareness, energized union, experience of fulfillment, and gentle parting. Dance is the best metaphor for thinking about a couple's being together; they are partners moving together and apart to the beat of their own special music.

Resolution, Closure, and Withdrawal

Some couples can become locked in what we term "pseudo contact," which may appear to be actual contact but is actually itself a kind of resistance; it's what used to be called in the early days of Gestalt therapy, with its particular interest in the oral resistances, "the hanging-on bite." It's an inability to let go, separate, and move away from one another. Although the interaction appears contactful, it lacks energy, and even watching it begins to feel heavy, tiresome, or just plain boring. This reluctance to close is seen in the everyday world with persons who just can't seem to hang up the phone or end a personal conversation or continually make more work out of what started as relatively manageable projects. In couples, it appears as a preoccupation with processing their own experience, and then processing their processing, and then processing the processing of their processing, *ad infinitum* (and *ad nauseum*). This is typical of "new age" couples, therapists, or those with issues of insecurity or abandonment.

The therapist must draw to the attention of these couples that this is part of their process and that there is a stopping point, a resting place. They must be encouraged to experience letting go and to find satisfaction in meeting and parting along with all that those experiences bring up for them. Life is a rhythm of ebb and flow, give and take, hellos and goodbyes. After the closure is made and the experience is shared and as-similated, the couple reach the time of withdrawal. The thera-pist, at this time, teaches the couple that silence and private ru-mination in this context constitute a form of groundedness. There is a time of quiet in which the next thing can be heard and come forth. This meditative separateness is the culmination of the Interactive Cycle of Experience and marks the end of a piece of work. It also marks the value and validity of each part-ner's independence and self-support when apart and when to-gether. When we use the Interactive Cycle of Experience to ob-serve, "critique" in a balanced manner, and intervene in a couple's process, we are taking an aesthetic view, in that we are watching them as they transact a simple piece of "interpersonal business." They talk about something, and, as they do so, we watch for where and how their process becomes "stuck" in order to help them through a piece of work with a definite beginning, middle, and end in the course of the therapy hour.

Content Issues

Our job in Gestalt couple therapy is to see the process—how clients say what they say and not what they say. This is quite a challenge because it is easier to float along with content. *Content is seductive.* Think of all the potential content issues in your daily practice that could entangle you without being helpful to the couple in the least. We cease "working" the moment we become

entangled in the content. Our *work* is to see the couple's process
and to help them change it. Their work is to get on with their
content. If we simply join the couple in their content, we are no
longer adequate consultants to the process but become part of
their problem.

Our assumption is that malfunctioning of the system occurs over and over again, independent of what the couple is talking about. They could be dealing with sex, money, or moving to
another city, but the areas of interruption will tend to be the
same. And that is process. It is not the content they get stuck on.
This is not to say that some content will not stick them more
than others, but it is in the process where trouble most often
occurs.

A couple might be stuck with processing too much
through their awareness and not being aroused enough to
make a strong contact. For example, when wrestling with a financial problem, they can talk about money for a long time, but
as long as they do not invest their energy in making something
happen, their efforts will fall flat. Or they can talk about moving
to another city, but if they don't generate enough aroused excitement, their conversation won't carry them to resolution.
Getting stuck in awareness without excitement flattens our experience of things, no matter what the content. In awareness,
the energy investment is relatively low. The figure is not exciting yet. We are not attempting to hook anybody with it. We are
just laying things out. Awareness itself is a low-energy modality.
We need very little electricity in the brain to make awareness.
We don't need muscles for it. And it is important that it remain
low because it is experimental. We want to be able to throw away
half of our ideas because, if we don't, everything becomes important and we will be stuck in place forever.

What if the couple achieve a smooth cycle and then ask
for information from us? How do we handle this? Because our
opinion is more informed than the general population, people
who come to us have a right to expect advice about certain issues. These are tricky moments, because no matter what we
know as a result of our expertise, no matter what we believe, we
really do not know what is best for someone else. It is our job,

however, to take the risk of saying what we believe would be best. What makes this a potentially frustrating and volatile area is that it is usually in the more retroflective systems, the systems with tighter boundaries, the systems that do not ask us anything, to whom we want to give our opinion because there are so many obvious things they don't know. It is hard to counsel a couple that ask nothing yet have content information that seems wildly incorrect to you. For example, you may believe that children do very well in situations where both parents work, yet your clients say that it would be bad because the child will feel unloved or become delinquent. You may feel an enormous temptation at such moments because you so dearly want to correct their opinion.

We urge therapists not to intervene and always wait to be asked before doing so. If you are not asked, the chance of your being heard is minimal. It will not be useful to jump over working on the process by giving them content information. However, as professionals, when we are asked (even though we know we do not know what is best), we can give an informed opinion, and it should be presented as such.

The contract we lay out at the beginning is that we will watch the couple's process and tell them about that rather than give them content information. We wait to be asked more often than we do with process information. The reason for this is that we feel much freer with process information and more certain that our values are clear. We believe it will be good for them to learn these things and that it will be useful, so we are more willing to intervene with process issues than with those of content. Also, in the process intervention, we are much more clearly anchored to the data that emerge during the therapy hour.

Polarities Askew

The Gestalt theory of the self includes the idea of polarities. The most notable examples in psychology of this phenomenon are Freud's "reaction formation" resistance and Jung's "shadow" side, meaning that each personal quality carries with it an equal and opposite quality often hidden out of awareness but still exerting real or potential force in everyday behavior. Gestalt

theory envisions the human personality as an organized con-
glomeration of polar forces. It is a simplification to think about
polarities in terms of dichotomous being-states such as good versus evil, peaceful versus violent, strong versus weak, and loving
versus hateful because each one of us possesses not just one opposite but several related opposites, what we call "multilarities"
(Zinker, 1977, p. 197). Polarized states of being and doing are
intricate structures with complex dynamics related to each person's history, self-image, survival patterns, wants, needs, and perceptions of reality—their "facticity" and "historicity," as the existential thinkers would say. Ideally, the "healthy" person would
experience a balanced flow of the many thousands of polarities,
from one to another, with no one polar force dominating or operating out of conscious awareness. Such is the ideal, but the reality is that certain polarities tend to be stronger than others and
so lead to intrapsychic conflict within the individual and, when
played out in partnership, to interpersonal conflict.

Any polarity that is askew, that is out of balance, can be a
potential intervention. If the couple system is healthy, each part
develops many potentials. If one person is too heavily invested
in a function while the other is not, they encourage skewed
polarities and run into internal and interactive difficulties. If
this lopsided condition persists, it will result in psychological
stasis and deadening or psychological agitation, anger, and
irritability.

How does polarization occur in our development? What
happens when we get together with another? There will be parts
of the self that remain undeveloped for a long time simply because, for whatever reason, we are developing other parts in ourselves. The result is that all of us develop certain psychological
traits while leaving other traits "in the shadow." For example,
taking care of others may be very well developed, but taking care
of oneself may be in shadow. Or perhaps seriousness is well developed but humor is underdeveloped.

Seeing in someone else a quality that is underdeveloped
in oneself looks delicious. It is easy to obtain that undeveloped
part simply by joining the other person; suddenly you have
humor or self-caring, a sense of being lively or well organized.

It is an instant self-realization and a wonderful sensation. We call it "falling in love." The person feels "complete" and, indeed, is complete in that moment. And the other person, who has different things to develop, will also find the beloved attractive. So they join together and become a unit. Together they, as a couple, make a whole, new person.

Very often, however, things start going wrong in a couple after several years, ironically, because of their underdeveloped sides. One reason is that the partners do not value the characteristic compensated by the other in the same way they each value what they each did develop. At the same time, however, they know it is important and in some way essential and so are ambivalent toward it. So they stay with their partner and enjoy the rewards of that particular characteristic. However, it is not long until the shadow side of that pleasure becomes evident. And the very thing one partner liked before, the very thing that drew him or her to the other, he or she now finds repulsive.

This is the most difficult time that every relationship must transcend: the partners must detach their eyes from what the other does well and poorly and reown what they do well and poorly. They must acknowledge what they have learned from the other about a particular characteristic. They also need to take responsibility for those characteristics they may have projected onto the partner. Each must stop the process of keeping his or her eyes glued to the partner. The result will be freedom of choice and experience. Once a shadow quality is brought to light and developed, once its complexities are known, one is freed from being positively or negatively attached to the other person.

What can you, as a therapist, do when seeing skewed polarities? For example, you see that he keeps making jokes while she looks like she is in a lot of pain and wants to tell the story of their difficulties. The answer is quite simple: you make a clear and precise statement about what they are doing in the moment. Here is a potential intervention: "Okay, I want to stop for a minute. I'd like to tell you something I notice. I notice that there is both seriousness and humor in your interaction. For whatever reason, one of you is the serious one and one of you is the funny one, and you seem to keep it that way. Have you ever noticed that? Do you do that at home as well as here?" After they answer, you could ask something like the following: "Why don't you tell each other how you feel about this? Would you like to do that? Or would you like to see if you can make some changes in it?" If they are interested and want some changes, you could suggest experiments, such as reversing roles, that would help them become aware of their polarities.

Complementarity and the Middle Ground

Fusion versus Differentiation

The experience of fusion with another person, especially the first time, is a powerful, almost overwhelmingly ecstatic event. Fusion with the other is the primal experience, the original dream of union with the mother. In the beginning of life this fusion was not what we call "love" in the usual sense. Fusion as we know it is a "need," a primordial image, a kind of undifferentiated longing. It's a psychological sensation with only the vaguest of awareness and is first felt long before one's first words are uttered, long before one can say, "I love you" or "I long for something." It comes into awareness at the time of physiological sensations. And when the need for union is not met in some way, the infant or child is damaged.

It is only later in life that this enormous longing acquires the words with which to make itself known. These words differ from culture to culture as different societies have developed their own ways of meeting this unmet need. Therefore, love has different meanings at different times in one's life, at different stages of development, but the experience of "falling in love" and the need for fusion remain an essential mystery and, regardless of the words, constitute a form of "psychological alchemy."

This "alchemy," like the magical chemistry that it is, is bewitching. There is the overpowering feeling that one is somehow less whole without the other. By the same token, one forgets that the other is a whole, unique person in his or her own right. The fantasy overpowers one's sense of curiosity of who the other actually is in reality. In alchemy, the ancient mystics tried melding opposing metals in an attempt to make "gold." This is, in a sense, analogous to the golden ring of engagement and marriage. As there is a "psychological alchemy," so there is an alchemy of sexuality. The other is different, mysterious, and in the heart of this mystery is something that makes the moment of contact so compelling, so exhilaratingly delightful.

But, sad to say (and as if you haven't ever wondered about it), fusion eventually fails. Sooner or later it fades and yields to a new and stronger need. The fetus dies if it stays in the womb. If a young person stays at home with mother, he or she dies not only spiritually but in other ways as well. What must follow fusion is separation, and separation always involves differentiation. Differentiation means that the couple move away from fusion and begin developing their own selves.

In Jungian terms this is "individuation," while we in Gestalt therapy call it "boundary formation." In Gestalt therapy we believe the only way you can have adequate contact is with adequate boundaries. You can't have contact with mush. You can't have conflict with mush either. You must evolve from a psychologically homogenized blob into a differentiated, bound organism with a special identity and sense of integrity. Then, when making contact with another at the point of your special boundedness, you experience the delightful friction leading to interpersonal fire. Fire, in this case, not only consumes joyfully, but warms and illuminates as well.

We conceive what happens in a two-person system as a two-beat rhythm of fusion and separation. We touch each other at different places in our lives. We also touch each other with different intensities; sometimes with ecstasy, sometimes in rage, but mostly with just a nice bit of magnetism. After this touching, we move away and then come together again. This process of flowing back and forth is the dynamic juice of being in relationship.

The theme of fusion and separation is a lifelong experience appearing in different forms that match different times.

Couples experience fusion when they first fall in love. They are inseparable. They sit and stare into each other's eyes while professing their undying love. Later, as they proceed with their everyday jobs and become more familiar with each other, there begins the slow and subtle process of separation. This is a time of increasing recognition of differences and a return to the task of self-actualization. Fusion becomes more difficult when children are born, although it may be sublimated into the system including children and the family. Separation is again experienced as the children grow up and leave. Once again the couple are alone, hopefully as more mature and separate adults who choose once again to become deeply intimate with one another. Later, illness and death confront the couple with separation from one another and the expectation of fusion with some eternal power in a final experience of transcendence.

One is brought into this world only to give oneself away again and again. The need for asserting the "I" as between mother and child follows fusion. After the falling-in-love experience, each stands separately and is once again confronted by the self—its internal needs, conflicts, and special talents. Each partner tailors his or her mode of functioning in the relationship, the partnership, to make it work. Each person needs to gain an awareness of self as a separate entity different from awareness of the other. Each person must learn to differentiate his or her internal experience from the appearance, awareness, and experiences of the other. Before the couple can experience the "we" of the contact between them, they need to articulate the "me" of self-boundaries. The therapist supports individual boundaries and so might ask each person to say sentences like the following:

"You look . . . "
"I sense . . . "
"I feel . . . "
"I want . . . "
"I don't want . . . "

Each person says these things in turn and not reactively to the other. Introjection, projection, and confluence are favorite resistances to contact at this level: "I feel like you look hungry" or "I feel tense and you look tense" or "You look angry with me." It is only much later after their internal vision becomes illuminated that each can truly validate and care about the experience of the other. Before this can happen, however, confluence-contact must be replaced by conflict-contact. One cannot have differentiation without conflict. Karl Jaspers, in a similar vein, refers to "the struggle of love" in that two souls need to engage in a "creative combat" in order to form themselves (Schlipp, 1957). But many couples have been hoodwinked by Hollywood into feeling that conflict means "we are no longer in love" or that "we are not really suited to each other." This is because many couples have never witnessed the healthy expression and resolution of conflict—followed by expression of caring—in their own families of origin. The couple may be scared by their fantasized image of conflict and fear of subsequent failure of their relationship.

The Gestalt therapist at this point teaches the couple how to fight cleanly and how to resolve and integrate differences in a way that enhances both and does not cause loss of esteem for either one. The therapist validates the experience of each while encouraging both to respect the other's way of seeing a situation. Having supported both partners, the therapist moves on to support the "we" by encouraging them to find a creative integration of their divergent qualities. The heat of resolved conflict leaves the couple drawn to each other with renewed interest and often even passion. Differentiation is followed by fusion. And so this rhythm goes on and Nature follows her course.

Some differences, on the other hand, are not reconcilable and must be accepted as such. One can love and respect one's partner and learn to accept the existential reality that not all problems are solvable. Just as Hollywood and Madison Avenue sell us the myth about love as fusion, the personal growth movement sold us a bill of goods that all interpersonal problems are resolvable. This introjected ethic forces some couples to fanatically heighten and negotiate all differences until they part feeling exhausted, shamed for failing, and disappointed in the relationship.

Differences are essential in a mature relationship. Differ-

ences keep the relationship alive. Differences taken to an extreme lead beyond healthy separation to an irreparable rupture
in relationship.

The Complementary Function

Complementarity is the functional aspect of differentiation. It is
how differentiation is lived out. From a developmental point of
view, one partner chooses another to complement the parts of
himself or herself that are not in awareness, are not accepted,
or are aesthetically repugnant. The qualities are seen in the
other in a romanticized form. Two half-persons come together
to make one whole being to more effectively cope with the
world.

As discussed earlier, the complementary function is accepted
and appreciated in the other as long as it is not experienced in
oneself. Later, when that disowned quality begins to move to the
surface of oneself, the partner's complementary behavior may
be experienced with annoyance, anger, irritation, and embarrassment. What was romanticized is now seen in its utmost cru-
dity—the sociable extrovert is seen as a "loudmouth" and the in-
trospective one is seen as "depressed." At this point, the Gestalt
couple's therapist can help each partner experiment with his or
her disowned polarity as discussed in the previous section. Some
complementary modes, both characterological and stylistic, will
remain as stable characteristics in a particular partner no matter how much individual growth takes place. It is here that true
(nonneurotic, nonprojected) complementarity can work to
lend variety and excitement to the couple's life. The more fully
each partner develops individually, the more his or her own polarities are filled out and stretched and the more he or she can
appreciate the "crazy" or idiosyncratic behavior of the other.
    Whereas complementarity stresses differences, the mid-
dle ground attracts similarities. Life takes place in the middle,
not at the extremes. Mostly, life is just ordinary. So it is with the
life of couples. There are chores, work, paying bills, errands,
phone calls, morning showers, meals, resting in one another's

arms at the end of a long day. It is only when we take the time to stop, look, and reflect that the extraordinary aspects of life emerge.

Whereas complementarity raises the voltage, the excitement of the couple's life, the middle ground provides a place to rest, a place where energy is even rather than peaked—where energy levels synchronize. Whereas complementarity stimulates conflict, the middle ground is the repository of quiet confluence.

The couple's survival and growth are determined by a balance between complementarity and confluence. The figure of differences is only meaningful against a background of agreements, understandings, compromises, and ordinary pleasures. The figure of confluence is viable only against a ground of color, difference, lively discussion, arguments, and emotional explosions. One could say that the survival index of a couple is some ratio between confluence and contact, or between middle ground and complementarity.

To determine the middle ground and to balance the work, as well as the couple's perception of themselves, the therapist may wish to explore their middle ground: How did you meet? What did you like about each other? What are your common beliefs? What do you enjoy together when things are all right? Answers to these questions remind the couple of their common ground: their loyalty, devotion, friendship, and hard work. Or the therapist may readily discover that this couple's middle ground is not ground at all, but a sheet of thin ice. The therapist may find, in fact, that they didn't use their best judgment in moving toward each other. Each may have denied feelings in himself or herself and lied to the other, making for an impoverished friendship. Finally, the therapist may discover that feelings of loyalty and devotion are strangely foreign to this couple.

The therapist can judge in the here and now how much conflict this particular system can tolerate without breaking up. The couple may need to be confronted with these questions, be asked if they are willing to start building a basic ground of trust between them in order to sustain the kind of conflict in which they are engaged.

Validating Experience by Supporting Resistance

Resistances are what happen at the boundary between any two subsystems and so are a form of contact. Resistance can occur within the couple at their contact boundary, or the couple may form a subsystem in resisting the therapist's interventions. People generally have "favorite" resistances. They are ego-syntonic and characterologically true; that is, a couple will use the same resistance in their interactions with their therapist as in their relationship with each other. For example, people who retroflect with each other will hold together as a system and avoid contact with the therapist by retroflecting. Their relationship as a couple with their therapist will mirror their relationship with each other.

We often talk about resistance as if it were an exclusively intrapsychic phenomenon: "I am a retroflector" or "I am a projector" or "I am confluent." Resistances, however, originate in interactions. It takes two people to produce a resistance. Resistances become intrapsychic when they become habitual as the same interactions are repeated again and again. The person responds to each new situation as if it were an old situation, not noticing other things that are happening and therefore carrying intrapsychically into new situations what he or she learned interactively.

Presence

Forming boundaries gives meaning to a set of events or experiences and differentiates the couple from their environment, just as the boundaries within the system give meaning to and differentiate subsystems. Boundaries are not just concepts; they exist. Although our sensory equipment doesn't directly see them, they are real. They are actually energy fields. We experience a boundary when people stand too close while talking to us: they seem to impinge on our personal space. We want to send our thoughts at our own pace and rhythm. If the other person is too close when we send out a thought, it touches the other's boundary before we are ready.

At all times, when the therapist is looking at a couple, one task is to see the boundaries. Therapists ought to be able to pull back at any time and identify the boundaries. Gestalt theory states that the boundary is where you experience the difference—where there is a "me" and a "you" or a "we" and a "they"—and that growth takes place when there is contact at the boundary. Differences must be heightened before you can make contact: I have to know that you and I are different before we can be together.

When a therapist sits down with a couple, there is a moment when he or she switches from being a bystander to being a presence for the others. The therapist's establishment of his or her presence creates an aura and reinforces a clear boundary around the couple. It is at that moment that you know you are doing couples therapy. Without presence, the therapist is merely a witness who's making comments.

The dictionary mentions "spirit" or "ghost" under *presence*. Although this is far from an adequate definition of presence, it hints at that special state of being fully here with *all* of oneself, one's body *and* soul. It is a way of *being with*, without *doing to*. Presence implies being here fully—open to all possibilities. The therapist's intrinsic being-here stimulates stirrings in the deeper parts of my own self. The therapist's presence is ground against which the figure of another self or selves can flourish, brighten, and stand out fully and clearly.

When I experience another's presence, I feel free to express myself, to *be* myself, to reveal any tender, vulnerable parts, to trust that I will be received without judgment or evaluation. My therapist's presence allows me to struggle with my own inner conflicts, contradictions, problematic questions, and paradoxes without feeling distracted by leading statements or overly determined questioning. My therapist's presence allows me to confront myself, knowing that I have a wise witness. Perhaps the term *presence* can be better described by what it is not.

- Presence is not a way of posturing or self-conscious posing or strutting before another; there's nothing flamboyant, dramatic, or theatrical about it.

- Presence is not style.
- Presence is not charisma. Charisma asks for attention, admiration. Charisma calls to itself, whereas presence "calls to the other." Charisma is a figure competing with another figure, whereas presence is ground "asking to be written on."
- Presence is not posed religious humility (which is really a form of secret pridefulness).
- Presence is not polemic. It does not take sides. It sees wholes.

Most people acquire presence through the continual pounding of time, time that reminds them again and again how much there is to learn and how little they know. Presence is the acquired state of awe in the face of an infinitely complex and wondrous universe. To acquire presence, one must learn many things and then cast them away. To learn presence, one must give oneself fully away, much like a rich person who, after working for many years to acquire great wealth, one day discovers that the greatest pleasure is in giving riches away.

When we speak of a therapist's presence, we mean that the therapist communicates another dimension of self beyond verbal interventions. When the therapist is truly present, his or her vision is peripheral and diffuse. In a silent and subtle way, the therapist is grounded and slow rather than lightheaded and rushed. In this state, one's breathing is deep, full, even. One's sense of time is slow and measured. One's body-self is supported and aware. One does not "care" in the sense that one is not overly attached to the content of the client's stories. In a moment when the couple are stuck, for example, the therapist rides the silence until the tension in the room is ripened for a strong, clear entry. The couple are relieved and do not feel abandoned. In the beginning these well-timed, cognitively clear, well-crafted entries enhance the couple's confidence in the therapist's role and personal power.

As the therapist steps forward at the right moment to articulate an idea and connect with everyone in the room, so he or she also leaves plenty of psychological space for dyadic interaction. The couple feel validated and supported as a whole, with each member feeling fully heard and seen. The therapist's silence as he or she listens and attends is as important to the total configuration of a given session's impact as the words he or she speaks. The silence of presence evokes liveliness in the system.

This means operationally that we do not make small talk or otherwise distract the couple from their main task of becoming more fully aware of their own process. Whereas each intervention is strong and bold, the space between interventions belongs fully to the couple, and the therapist neither hangs nor lingers to draw further attention to him or herself. Presence and timing frame the power of each intervention while supporting the person of the therapist as an important figure in the room. At the same time, the couple feel respected (seen) and cradled (encircled) by that important person.

Like the couple, therapists also have a field of energy that must be managed. We must establish the rhythm of awareness. At first, we lean forward and enter the system to begin the session or make an intervention. Then we pull back, sitting quietly and free-associating. To withdraw from the system and make a clean boundary, we must be able to manage our own energy to create a state of creative indifference: an alert, open, nonmobilized state.

When we are working with a couple, we must be aware of when we are breaking into their boundary to make ourselves a part of their awareness. We must know when we want to be part of the couple's field in order to influence, and when we just want to watch. In watching, we don't want to pull energy toward ourselves, whether it be concern, interest, or simply looking. We do this only when we want their full attention . . . and then we move away again.

A "Dialectical" Strategy of Intervention

A Three-Step Plan of Intervention

As therapists, we must watch long enough, listen long enough, and experience what is occurring with the couple so that we can get enough data about their process to create interventions appropriate to their dilemma. To do this we must establish our presence in the system and elicit the couple's participation in an examination of their process.

The first thing we do is to engage in a certain amount of small talk. This establishes our presence as therapists and initiates contact with the couple. This is the ordinary social talk of welcoming. We make sure we make contact with both persons and provide the warmth that enables talk about intimate matters.

Next, we discuss the therapeutic ground rules. We tell the participants that the best way we can help them is to watch them, that we are going to ask them to talk to each other about anything that is important to them, and that we will act as witnesses who will interrupt when anything stands out for us that we believe will be of interest or use to them. We have never given these instructions without meeting with resistance. These are the comments that we hear time and time again:

> "But we've already talked about it at home, so it won't be of any use for us here."
> "There's no point in talking about it because he (she) won't listen anyway, and that's why we're here."
> "I didn't expect this."
> "I want to tell you . . . don't you want to know anything about us? Don't you want to know our history or how we got to this place?"
> "What we came for is some advice from you, not to talk to each other about the same old thing."
> "That would be too embarrassing to do. I don't know if I could just talk in front of you while you just sit and listen."
> "That feels contrived and theatrical. It's a faked situation and I don't see what good it would do if we just fake it."

At this point, we highlight the resistance (as we do in all good therapeutic work) by staying with it until we get each person to express all of his or her resistance to the situation. For example, if the clients say it feels very contrived and phony and they feel uncomfortable "acting" for you, our response might be: "I appreciate that you can tell me that you're uncomfortable. You're right, it is contrived. The therapeutic situation is not natural. However, it is very important to me to be able to watch you so I can see how you communicate. I know it's contrived and uncomfortable, but I hope you'll be able to do it anyway because I believe that's the best way I can be useful to you."

We also explain that, just as we can interrupt them when we see something that we want to tell them, they can turn to us at any time they need help or get stuck, or when they want to inform or question us. As soon as our instructions are clear, we back out of the system and draw a boundary. As they talk to each other, we watch their process and wait for something to become figural.

First Step.   The therapist begins by encouraging the couple to talk to one another about something that matters to all of them. This gives the therapist an opportunity to observe the couple's level of awareness within their own boundaries. After obtaining enough phenomenological data, the therapist makes a statement of observation. *This is the first intervention.* The observation is based on real data. Its purpose is to support the couple's competence, goodness, and sense of creativity; it brings what exists to the couple's awareness.

The therapist allows time for the couple to respond, find exceptions, change meanings, and enrich their awareness of how they are as they are. The therapist "glides" on the system's generated energy, rather than pushing against that energy. As the couple feel supported, they become hooked on the therapeutic process. When there is something that stands out for us, we interrupt them to make a second intervention.

Second Step.   The therapist then focuses on the other side of the couple's competence, namely, what they pay for their goodness. This can be termed the "dark side" of the system's operation; it is the uncovering of their incompetence. *This is the second intervention.* Often this is a major area of difficulty, and the therapist should expect resistance in the form of denial, shame, guilt, anger, or just plain unawareness. This is a subtle turning point where the system's awareness of itself is potentially stretched; the therapist encounters much questioning and discussion.

Resistance, as it arises, is always supported. The couple are encouraged to fully chew on the generated data rather than to swallow it whole. The experienced practitioner is aware that if the couple accept his or her views too readily, learning and change do not take place. Both members of the couple are supported equally. Interventions are balanced. This approach also minimizes polarization between the persons within the system as well as between the system and the therapist. Only when both of their needs are legitimized will they let go and open up to the world.

Third Step.   The therapist can then move on to raising questions about what can be done (operationalizing what is learned) to change the implicit rules of enmeshment into explicit behaviors that support loosening of boundaries between the couple and the environment. The Gestalt therapist uses experiment for this purpose; *this is the third intervention.* As it is set up, the therapeutic situation with the couple is in itself an experiment. We build on that by introducing another experiment. All experiments are contrived, dramatic, or artificial situations. Nevertheless, they are a slice of life where we can see what is happening and lay it bare. Once we have a good handle on the couple's process—what is figural about their being together—we work from there. The couple can move with it, or we can create an experiment in which to chew it over and learn something from it.

We end the session by reverting to small ta" We change from an artificial, structured situation back to a more social, easy, and natural human contact. We wish them well and say good-bye. The session is like an airplane ride: we take off, reach a certain altitude, travel for a while, and then we land.

How to Intervene

To intervene is to make something figural for the couple by telling them something you as therapist see or experience about their behavior of which they are unaware. There are several useful guidelines.

Intervene Boldly.   Your own sense of arousal about your observation must stand out if your statement is to be received. Examine your objections to being bold. You may ask yourself,

"Suppose they don't find it relevant?" Then you may ask them, "What doesn't fit for you about what I said?" This will give you more information about the couple's thoughts and feelings. Never argue your point when meeting with objections to your observation, since you will simply meet with increased resistance. Instead, be curious about the couple's way of experiencing themselves.

Provide Phenomenological Data.   In order to be heard, always give phenomenological data as support when you hear or see something you want to use as an intervention. Tell the couple what you observed, and describe the role each person plays in creating the loss of clarity. The intervention is more likely to be well received because it is not judgmental. Thus, a "good" intervention

- Describes what is actually there.
- States how all parties contribute to a phenomenon.
- Implies a potential action that each participant can take to improve the system.

Report What Is Evoked.   Reporting what is evoked in you, the therapist, can be a powerful intervention. This is especially true after you have seen the couple for several sessions and have earned their trust.

- As I sit here with you, I feel invisible, unseen by anybody.
- I want to tell you how you move me with the care you take responding to each other so gently.
- I feel like a translator at the United Nations.
- Sitting here with you, I feel so helpless. If I only had a magic wand!
- After twenty minutes with you, I started getting so lethargic and sleepy.
- It's only been a few minutes into our session and already I feel as if someone is spinning me around. I feel dizzy and disoriented.
- You are doing so well that I can feel comfortable enough to make myself a cup of tea.

When you feel something deeply and share it clearly and strongly, people often respond at the same level within themselves from which your message came. This is not a trick. It is a heartfelt message that you develop out of your emotional generosity as a witness to a drama you care about.

If, for one reason or another, you cannot bring yourself to care, don't bother sharing your feelings, unless "not caring" is evoked by the couple's way of being with you. Then telling them how you "turn cold" in their presence is yet another powerful way of letting them see themselves.

Teach. Teaching is another way of intervening. It is a pleasure to teach when a couple directly ask for help. Remember, in the very beginning you offered them the option of turning to you and asking for help. Too often, a couple are so retroflected that their energy is turned inward toward each other and they do not have the impetus to turn toward you. They may not be fully aware of your presence as a significant resource for them. After all, they had been behaving in the same rigidly bounded way with the rest of the world before they came to you.

If they do choose to ask for help, you have the opportunity to teach. Teaching is an art. It is not always giving information, although information often offers great help *and* relief. You can also talk about books you have read or experiences you have had, or draw them out about the things they already know that will apply to their present problem or situation.

Aesthetic Values of Gestalt Couple Therapy

To appreciate a couple aesthetically means making evaluative judgments about their form. By "form" we are primarily talking about process, although to a much lesser degree we include content, qualities, characteristics, quantities, and so on. Making judgments implies the presence of values; something is good or beautiful because it is perceived as such. Values, in turn, imply that something is preferable or more important than something else. To have an aesthetic vision of healthy interpersonal contact necessarily means having a system of values upon which this aesthetic is grounded.

Historically, our values arose and developed from the collective labors of the founders of Gestalt therapy: Fritz and Laura Perls, Paul Goodman, Isidore From, and many others. After having worked with their principles and refined our thinking over the years, we are now in a better position to articulate our own views more clearly and fully.

As we began to work more with couples, groups, families, and corporations, we were forced to enlarge the arena of the explicit and implicit meanings of interactions at the boundary. First, we began to develop a more coherent process model out of Perls's individual concepts of sensation, awareness, excitement, movement, and contact. We created a cycle in which one phenomenon follows another in a kind of chain, moving from vague sensory experience to the formation of a gestalt, to the excitement that asks for satisfaction, then to the movement that reaches out, and finally to the contact that satisfies. As our work progressed, we adapted a series of values and principles from systems theory and incorporated them into our Gestalt approach. This notion of moving from sensation to awareness to completion and satisfaction became our first and fundamental aesthetic value.

Gestalt couples therapy values what is—the actual, the immediate, and the tangible. We are not interested in speculation, interpretation, or categorization. This does not necessarily mean that we eschew the basic tools of our business, such as personality tests, genograms, the DSM-IV, and other diagnostic instruments. For example, in the Gestalt approach we tend to "diagnose and classify" system phenomena in terms of contact-resistance and boundary patterns. Such tools are important for clinical determinations and provide good background information, but they remain just that: background and only secondary in purpose. Every therapy session is a new meeting, and so what remains figural for us at all times are the phenomenological aspects of the immediate interactive encounter of the couple. These aspects include time, space, change, awareness, sensation, polarized specialization, energy, choreography of movement and location, beauty, balance, harmony, complementarity, rhythm, contrast, quality of contact, nature of withdrawal, capacity to "let go" and start over again, humor, and "a sense of the philosophical."

Our "cardinal" values, developed over time and through trial and error, have grown to twenty-two. These values, along with corresponding intervention principles, are presented below. The categories of our Gestalt value system are Balance, Change, Development, Self-Awareness, Holism, and Form.

Values of Balance

1. Value   Balanced relationships.
   Principle   It is our life work as human beings to become both dependent and autonomous. We teach self-support and also model mutual support: the balanced rhythm of fusion in the couple and individual differentiation from it.
2. Value   The importance of the sharing of power in the couple.
   Principle   We try to understand and observe the differential of power in small systems. Strong discrepancies in power can result in abusive behavior.
3. Value   Clear boundaries in both the couple and the therapist.
   Principle   We never take sides or lose our boundary. We balance one intervention with another; we model and work for good boundary definition and management.

Values of Change

4. Value   Self-actualization through organismic self-regulation.
   Principle   A vision of the couple as striving for a wholeness, integration, fluidity, and spontaneity of functioning. The system strives for balance between stasis and forward movement.
5. Value   Learning through doing.
   Principle   Learning through doing works better than ra-

tional discussion alone. We teach, encourage, and support experimentation with novel, fresh behavior to move the couple beyond their present stagnant, limited functioning.

6. Value   Change through awareness.

   Principle   Change that takes place through awareness and active choice making is more fully integrated and longer lasting than change that bypasses awareness and choice.

7. Value   Paradoxical change.

   Principle   We support resistance while *joining* the couple. The more support there is for what is, the more change will occur.

8. Value   Process over content.

   Principle   It is almost always more important *how* a couple express themselves than what is being discussed.

Values of Development

9. Value   The rule that there are exceptions to every rule.

   Principle   We need to understand and appreciate *development* and what is developmentally appropriate in our interventions. Although they can be most useful, all rules are potentially stupid and dangerous (including this one).

10. Value   Equality in experiential development (or "What's good for the goose is good for the gander").

   Principle   We believe that therapists, like clients, are in a state of constant change and development and that they need the nourishment of exposure to their own therapy as well as a full life in a world much larger than their own craft.

Values of Self-Awareness

11. Value   The therapist "colors" the couple.

   Principle   As therapists, we constantly "track" our own

moods, desires, conflicts, needs, and changing ideologies because the couple sitting in our presence will be affected by them in one way or another, consciously or unconsciously.

12. Value   Professional humility.
    Principle   We respect the systemic integrity of the couple. No matter how dysfunctional they appear, they do have the capacity to change *on their own.*

Values of Holism

13. Value   Systems theory—the whole colors all individual parts and is larger than their sum.

    Principle   We conceive of the couple as related to a larger system context of the extended family, the neighborhood, and the community at large.

14. Value   "No person is an island."
    Principle   Every intervention must carry as ground the pattern of the couple's "outside" world. We seek to understand the "soup" in which they float in their daily life (as if all the characters of the patient's life are standing behind him or her like an ever-present "Greek chorus").

15. Value   The "third-person" entity of the relationship.
    Principle   In couples work, interventions must be both systemic and complementary. Interventions to one and not the other—positive or negative— will not be beneficial to the system.

16. Value   The collective voice of the couple.
    Principle   We attend to both the unique "voice" (in the psyche and system) as well as to the pattern of voices.

Values of Form

17. Value   Completed gestalten.
    Principle   We focus on how the couple's very strength creates disowned parts that need to be uncovered and reintegrated into their inner life. We

		always start from their strengths, not their weaknesses.
18.	Value	Good form.
	Principle	We let the couple *be*, and we let them *go*. (And, regardless of how they are being and where they are going, we support the good form that is "just good enough.")
19.	Value	The importance of the whole therapeutic relationship as an integrated entity and aesthetic event.
	Principle	We stress the process of therapy (and intervention) and its quality of movement. We value seeing beauty, as well as ugliness, and the aesthetic validity of the client-system's struggle with its symptoms and pathology.
20.	Value	The developmental integrity of Gestalt therapy.
	Principle	We seek the simple beauty found in therapeutic interventions that have themes, developments, and resolutions. Every therapy encounter is potentially a work of art.
21.	Value	The integrity of the couple as they are right now.
	Principle	We accept the couple where they are, join them and encounter them with a sense of appreciation for their existing competence.
22.	Value	The phenomenology of the here and now.
	Principle	We look for patterns in both the psyche and the larger system. The most useful observations are based on actual, here-and-now, phenomenological/process observations. (See discussion in Farber, 1943.)

We view not only the couple's process but the entire system of therapy, including the aesthetic form of the therapist's presence and interventions, as an aesthetic event. The couple, as individuals and as a whole, struggle with their problems, and the therapist is there working at their boundary as a benevolent, supportive, and involved witness. Much of what we do as "artists" is based on framing phenomenological data about the system's process in terms of a metaphor or a theme. This gives the couple a greater perspective on how they are with one another and their problems.

As in the earliest days of our personal Gestalt therapy experience, we help our clients leave the consultation room feeling "friendlier" with the very source of their bothersome, painful experiences. We help couples recognize that their symptoms and behaviors, even their resistances, are creative efforts that have goodness, aesthetic validity, and purpose. We strive to help them leave each therapy session with the sense that they as persons are affirmed as "good."

Note

1. All rights reserved by Joseph C. Zinker, Cleveland Heights, Ohio, and Sonia M. Nevis, Brookline, Massachusetts. This chapter was made possible with the editorial assistance of Paul Shane, one of our associates in graduate school at Saybrook Institute, San Francisco, California. Portions of the material were adapted with permission from *In Search of Good Form: Gestalt Couple and Family Therapy* (1994) by Joseph Zinker, Jossey-Bass, San Francisco, California, and "The Gestalt Approach to Couple Therapy" (1992) by Joseph Zinker, from *Gestalt Therapy: Perspectives and Applications*, edited by Edwin C. Nevis, Gardner Press, Inc., New York, New York.

References

Beisser, A.R. (1970). The paradoxical theory of change. In J. Fagan & E.L. Shepherd (Eds.), *Gestalt therapy now*. New York: Harper/Colophon Books.

Farber, M. (1943). *The foundation of phenomenology: Edmund Husserl and the quest for a rigorous science of philosophy*. Albany: State University of New York Press.

Harris, E.S. (1981). *A new revised Gestalt theory of resistance*. Unpublished manuscript and personal communication with the authors.

Latner, J. (1992). The theory of Gestalt therapy. In *Gestalt theory: Perspectives and applications.* New York: Gardner Press.

Nevis, E. (1987). *Organizational consulting: A Gestalt approach.* New York: Gardner Press.

Perls, F., Hefferline, R., & Goodman, P. (1951). *Gestalt therapy.* New York: Julian Press.

Polster, E., & Polster, M. (1973). *Gestalt therapy integrated.* New York: Brunner/Mazel.

Schlipp, P. (1957). The philosophy of Karl Jaspers. New York: Tudor.

Wheeler, G. (1991). *Gestalt reconsidered.* New York: Gardner Press.

Zinker, J. (1977). *Creative process in Gestalt therapy.* New York: Brunner/Mazel.

Zinker, J. (1994). *In search of good form.* San Francisco: Jossey-Bass, Inc.

Epilogue:
The Aesthetic Lens
Stephanie Backman

Maturana tells of research on a certain species of African bird, a close relative of the parrot that lives in a dense forest, with little or no visual contact with others of its species. Under these conditions, mating couples form through means of a common song. Researchers took a spectrogram of some of the songs. It seems each bird builds a phrase, and then the other picks it up and continues. This makes a duet, which can properly be called a conversation since the two birds do not sing simultaneously. The melody they develop is established during their mating and then remains constant for that couple's lifetime. Offspring produce different melodies. The particular melody of each couple is peculiar to that couple and is limited to their lifespan (Maturana & Varela, 1987, p. 194).

Throughout the course of this book you have heard a range of voices on the subject of working with couples under the Gestalt model. Though richly diverse, they all use the Gestalt perspective to move beyond a merely "objective" point of view, which may well miss the client and the couple as persons entirely. In Gestalt we seek to understand the client's

400

own experience, the couple's own construction, individually and together, of their own experiential world.

In this final section I want to talk about the therapist's experience and experiential stance in work that is informed by a Gestalt perspective. The therapist uses what I call the "aesthetic lens." This is not a particular technique or method per se, but an attitude of mind, an experiential state that the therapist can take up and that has direct practical consequences for the work.

In Maturana's story, the researchers were surprised by their own perception of unity in the song of the coupled birds. In fact, so great was the sense of continuity and wholeness that they first thought they were hearing one bird. That wholeness and that surprise are what the Gestalt psychological model calls an "emergent property." An emergent property is one of the characteristics of the couple as a couple. It cannot be perceived by the examination of each member or the analysis of their behavior separately: it belongs to the whole, not the parts. It is peculiar to that couple and distinguishes one couple from another.

Two individual people in a dyadic unit make up a conversation, a "song" with two voices, with facial expressions and bodily gestures in the same rhythm (Brown, 1991). The work of the couple is on the rhythm of this song, this whole of form and meaning. This whole, this "song" may be in full and satisfying co-rhythm—that sense of seamlessness and individuality the researchers first saw in the song of Maturana's birds—or it may break down or fall short of development and articulation. The work of the therapist, along with all the more specific tasks and interventions that come up, is to perceive this whole, this aesthetic form, and then mirror it for the couple so that they too can have a sense of their own form, their life together as a creative shape with its own Gestalt qualities of coherence, boundary, context, meaning, and that particular quality of form the early Gestalt psychologists called "pragnanz," the way a form holds energy to go somewhere, to lead on to the next thing in a coherent and organic way.

The therapist sees this emergent property of the couple by using the aesthetic lens. By this I mean the capacity to step back, to let all the parts become background—not just the content, but the roles, the "dynamics," all the behaviors of the couple members as separate acts—so that the whole becomes the figure, and the therapist's own experience becomes what it is like to be with that particular song, that particular whole. This stance, which is a disciplined act of the therapist, does not replace the analysis of the "parts," of the behavior and dynamics, but rather precedes and underlies it. Perls (1947) wrote of this attitude as a state of "creative indifference": not in the sense of not caring, but in the sense of not prejudging, not categorizing, not yet analyzing the gestalt into its endlessly possible component parts. In this way the figure emerges from the scene rather than being imposed on it by the therapist's own preconception; and the first evaluation is the therapist's own experience, as she or he is "taken by" that figure.

How do we take up the aesthetic lens, and how does it become useful to the couple? An example may serve to clarify:

> John and Maria are discussing trial separation. John describes his worries: this may mean the end of the relationship, and Maria may find someone new. Maria, in anxiously reassuring tones, says that they have separated before, and goes on to speak of the great respect she has for John. The conversation stops at this point, and each turns to the therapist for help, saying that this is where they routinely come to a dead end.

In the therapist's experience, the conversation never forms into a shape. It ends (again, for the therapist) abruptly, before the figure is ever fleshed out, articulated, or energized, able to stand out from the general background of anxiety and concern. There is no information, no novelty in it, no shared figure of concern: little to arrest and hold the therapist's attention. Actually, it is not a conversation at all, in the sense of the song of Maturana's parrots, where each phrase took up organically from the one before, connected with it, and then took it someplace new. Rather, this is two monologues in resigned imitation of a conversation. Each is lost in his or her own worries, without really joining with what the other has said.

In other words, the perspective of the therapist at this point, her or his aesthetic perception of the conversation as a whole, is evaluative without being judgmental. To describe is also to evaluate; there is no nonevaluative description, no selection of features and figural qualities not colored and codetermined by the perceiver's own experience, as the Gestalt perceptual model makes clear. Indeed, it is that evaluation of the experience of being with their conversation, as the therapist experiences it as a whole form, that we are after here. But this is not the same thing as judging or grading their creation according to some "objective" standard outside the therapist's own experience in the present moment. Maintaining this distinction, which is a different state of mind, a true paradigm shift, is again a disciplined act on the part of the therapist.

To be sure, Maria and John's conversation has the beginnings of a pattern to it, a behavioral sequence that both agree is a familiar one to them. He says something; she provides fast reassurance, more or less talking him out of his experience; and it ends there, with both lapsing into hopeless silence and isolation. But the habitual pattern never reaches the level of form in the full sense, any more than patterned marks on a page are necessarily meaningful writing, much less a visual design with interest, energy, coherence, boundary, and balance.

Much of the power of taking up this lens and then feeding the experience back to the couple lies in the powerful effect of being seen, both as a couple and as individuals trying so hard to come into co-rhythm together. The painter and critic Roger Fry says that only when an "object exists in our lives for no other purpose than to be seen [do] we really look at it." (Edwards, 1992, p. 84) When we say that the aesthetic lens is nonjudgmental, we mean it in this sense. At this moment we are interested in looking at Maria and John's interaction purely for the experience of seeing, of appreciating what that experience is like—not for correcting, improving, judging, or even yet analyzing how their pattern lacks form and their song is still without music. At this point we are interested more purely in what is, how the parts before us fit or do not fit into a whole. We lose this focus on the whole the minute we begin to track content, motivation, dynamics, and the like. With it, the couple experience our seeing them, and their experience of themselves can begin to be transformed.

The aesthetic perception is to approach the phenomenology of the couple, the essence of the Gestalt stance from the point of view of the therapist's own experience. Here is another example: Bill and Bettina are discussing a relationship issue with a strong push of words. Each takes a turn at a brief, clear, highly energized personal statement, which is followed by a statement by the other. They seem to be "in contact," coconstructing a rhythmic if staccato dialogue of interest and importance to each of them. Yet with each successive exchange their language becomes less and less personal, their voices grow softer and flatter. Although both stay on the topic, somehow the energy of the conversation seems to disappear in each person at the same time.

Like Maria and John's conversation, this conversation goes nowhere, for a similar reason. The parts never cohere, in the therapist's eye, into any greater whole. Here it is not a matter of an abrupt stop with no fleshing out of details, but of something else missing that would have given their exchange unity, energy, and development, that sense of enoughness that is not too little and not too much. Since each is putting out a great deal of energy yet not really connecting with what the other says in any nourishing way, the conversation becomes exhausting. Bettina states that she feels enormously tired, almost ill; her husband shakes his head and says bitterly, "Only when you talk to me." Once again, the familiar habit does not rise above the level of sequencing: the couple "fall apart" into two individuals, each alone with her or his hopelessness and pain. Once again, one thing follows another in a familiar, predictable way, but no whole configuration adds up to anything more than the sequence of parts.

Here is one more example of a pattern that fails to reach the level of form:

> Molly and her partner Angie are talking about something that matters intensely to Molly, her coming out as a lesbian to a colleague at work. The news has somehow fallen flat, in Molly's experience, and she feels upset. Angie gives a few examples of the same kind of experience in her own life, and be-

gins to cry. Soon both are focused on Angie. This is the third time in that hour that Angie and Angie's experience have become the focus and are more fully attended to and described than Molly's, with Molly avidly drawing out more information about Angie and Angie readily providing it.

Without awareness, Angie and Molly are avoiding achieving real form in their conversation by having no balance. One partner, Angie, seems to weigh more, take up all the space in the picture, become more articulated and filled out. The experience of the aesthetic observer (i.e., the therapist) at that point is of leaning too far over to one side, as if waiting for a seesaw to swing down and it never does. Once again, the forming of the couple breaks down into the two separate individuals. In the experience of the observer, one of these two is emerging in living color while the other is fading from the screen.

Properties of the aesthetic whole that contribute to unity and a higher level of organization—and avoid confusion, monotony, and chaos—include development, "just enoughness," and balance. Others might be theme, variation, restraint, contrast, connectedness, harmony, ratio, and proportion, as well as the qualities of cohesion, energy, and others mentioned above. When a couple present for therapy, they usually lack the ability to hold form or pattern in this full sense. They have certain habits, certain linear sequences, but these sequences interrupt rather than support the formation and completion of a real pattern, as when the parts of a picture or the notes of a melody are all transformed and given meaning by their location and role in the larger whole. Unlike the recursive redundancy of real music, their redundancy is mere monotony, a repetition without enrichment and growing satisfaction. This dissatisfaction and monotonous redundancy are noticed and felt by the couple in some way, and this is what brings them to therapy: not the content or problems of their lives only, but the sense that their music isn't rich enough to hold the notes they need to play.

Crucial to the therapist with an aesthetic lens is the idea that a fuller and more complete pattern will hold new information, new possibilities about the self and the other and about the couple as a whole. We are "wired" to perceive in patterns and to make use of information when (and only when) it belongs organically or aesthetically to a larger whole of meaning. Pattern completion or better form in a couple's interaction makes possible the integration of enough new information for self-development and evolution. In place of the redundancy that is mere repetition, we have the recursive rhythm that supports something new. The novelty or new information, which is the development, needs to fit organically and meaningfully with the many other similar and dissimilar pieces of knowledge. The conversation with organization, pattern, and consummation is the beginning and the vehicle of that fit.

Oliver Sachs (1987) gives a striking example of the way aesthetic form holds new information, shaping experience and action. He describes the case of a young woman, Rebecca, who was so clumsy and disoriented that she could not find her own way back home from a short distance away, or open a door with a key. She was physically awkward and unable to dress herself alone. Yet when music was playing she could dance spontaneously and gracefully. She could not read to herself, yet she loved to hear stories and epic poetry, which she understood exceptionally well. Special classes and training were of little help to her, but music and narrative organized her experience. In Rebecca's own words, "I'm sort of like a living carpet. I need a pattern, a design, like you have on that carpet. I come apart, I unravel, unless there's a design" (Sachs, 1987, p. 184).

For Rebecca the way the key turns in the door is always a new piece of information, never integrated into her nerves and muscles. Then when she hears music and can hold the novel information long enough to move coherently and purposefully, everyone is amazed. Left to itself, her nervous system holds not the recursive and organized whole but only the perpetual novelty, which is to say chaos and perceptual confusion.

Underneath our outward competencies and our catalogue of information, all of us require pattern, whether from inside ourselves or from outside, in order to hold new information, a new and better-organized design for living. As therapists too we need a pattern or template for taking in the unmanageable array of data in the couple before us. This is what a theory is—a pattern or lens for organizing experience. And this is what the aesthetic lens is: a particular stance or state that enables us to lift that organization up to the level of the whole, and to perceive and then intervene differently than we might at the level of the parts.

In the words of Mikhael Bakhtin, a relationship "involves the construction of ratios; it is aesthetic in much the same way that a statue or a building may be judged in terms of how its parts have been constructed with respect to each other." The relationship is never static, always "in process of being made and unmade" in the present interaction. Thus "the relation of self to the other [is] a problem in aesthetics" (Holquist, 1990, p. 29). This problem is an asset and a potential new dimension in the work of the therapist who uses the aesthetic lens. It allows the therapist to experience wholes before analyzing parts, and to connect his or her own felt experience with the felt experience of the couple.

References

Brown, P. (1991). *The hypnotic brain: Hypnotherapy and social communication.* New Haven, CT: Yale University Press.

Edwards, P. (Ed.). (1992). *The encyclopedia of philosophy* (Vol. 1). New York: Macmillan.

Holquist, M. (1990). *Dialogism: Bakhtin and his world.* London: Routledge.

Maturana, V., & F. Varela (1987). *Tree of knowledge: The biological roots of human understanding.* Boston: Shambala Publications.

Perls, F. (1947). *Ego, hunger and aggression.* London: Routledge.

Sachs, O. (1987). *The man who mistook his wife for a hat.* New York: HarperCollins.

Index